Balancing Freedom, Autonomy and Accountability in Education

Volume 3

Balancing Freedom, Autonomy and Accountability in Education

Volume 3

Charles L. Glenn
Jan De Groof
editors

Balancing Freedom, Autonomy and Accountability in Education
Volume 3

Charles L. Glenn, Jan De Groof (eds.)

ISBN hardcover: 978-90-5850-911-6
ISBN softcover: 978-90-5850-909-3

Publisher: Willem-Jan van der Wolf
Publishing assistant: Simone Fennell
Design: Ditty Vos

Published by:

Wolf Legal Publishers (WLP)
P.O. Box 31051
6503 CB Nijmegen
The Netherlands
Tel: +31 24 355 19 04
Fax: +31 84 837 67 00
E-Mail: info@wolfpublishers.nl
www.wolfpublishers.com

Table of Contents

Detailed Table of Contents

Introduction

Background

A decade ago, we published a two-volume study of how more than two dozen national systems of education balance *freedom of parental choice, autonomy of school management*, and *accountability to common standards* of educational quality and equity (*Finding the Right Balance* volumes 1 and 2, Utrecht: Lemma 2002). This overview grew out of the meetings and publications of the European Association for Education Law and Policy, of which De Groof was founding President in 1993 and Glenn was also an original member.

Why did we focus on these three aspects of education law and policy for our study? While each is an important element of current education reform efforts, we were concerned that policy-makers do not always pay sufficient attention to the tensions among them. Thus freedom or school autonomy may be sacrificed to accountability, or accountability may be weakened in an effort to provide a wider range of choices for parents, or to give more decision-making authority to individual schools.

We were convinced that wise design and implementation can produce a successful balance among freedom, autonomy, and accountability, and that considering the approaches adopted by different educational systems could help policy-makers and others to think more resourcefully about both design and implementation. None of the countries described had achieved the perfect system, but something could be learned from each of them.

Educational freedom is important because parents have a fundamental right, recognized in national and international law, to guide the development of their own children and therefore to choose a school in which they have full confidence. For many parents, this will mean a school that shares their own views about what is most important in life, their religious or philosophical worldview. To deny that choice, or to make it impossibly difficult for parents of modest means, is unjust and unworthy of a free society.

School autonomy is important because it is the essential precondition for the creation of schools with a clearly-focused mission, schools in which staff and parents and the controlling board or other authority share the same understanding of how best to educate. We are long past the days when educators could promise that they had a single formula for providing the best possible education to every child or youth. We know that different schools work best for different pupils, and that teachers find professional satisfaction (and enhanced professional status) in schools where they share a common vision with their colleagues.

Accountability for common standards is important because today's pupils will be the parents, adult citizens, and productive workers of tomorrow. Society has a strong interest in ensuring that they are well prepared for those roles, and that they share an understanding of the virtues required by a free society. Society also has an obligation to ensure that no child or youth is harmed by neglectful or abusive parents or schools. It would be unjust to simply let the choices of parents and the enthusiasms of educators result in some pupils (typically those most disadvantaged by economic circumstances if not also by ethnic minority status) receiving an ineffective education.

Our conviction about the importance of balancing these three aspects of educational policy has been reinforced in recent years by much significant research that was not available to us a decade ago. To cite just one study, Woessmann, Luedemann, Schuetz, and West (2009) used the PISA 2003 international student achievement test that encompasses more than a quarter of a million students from 37 countries to consider the relation between our three factors and national achievement levels, holding constant a host of background variables. They found that "rather than harming disadvantaged students, accountability, autonomy and choice appear to be tides that lift all boats. .. In particular, the additional choice created by public funding for private schools is associated with a strong reduction in the dependence of student achievement on SES" (xi).

In the first edition of our study, we included 25 country profiles, most of which we wrote on the basis of a variety of sources, and a second volume of essays on the legal and historical dimensions of these issues, in the writing of which De Groof contributed the legal and Glenn the historical part. An abbreviated Italian version was prepared by Daniele Vidoni (*Un difficile equilibrio: Europa continentale e mediterranea*, Milan: Armando Editore, 2003) and another abbreviated version was published and widely distributed in Eastern Europe (*Education Freedom*, The Hague: Foundation for International Solidarity Eduardo Frei, 2004).

Several years later, we prepared a new and expanded edition in three volumes with a different publisher, and with some of the country profiles written by experts from the various countries, although the majority remained our work based on available sources and thus inevitably missed many nuances of the situations "on the ground" (*Balancing Freedom, Autonomy, and Accountability in Education* volumes 1-3. Nijmegen: Wolf Legal Publishing, 2004.

In the second and third volumes of the 2004 edition, we (and several co-authors) reviewed educational laws and policies in forty countries, seeking to understand how each (and, in some cases, its policy-making regions) has chosen to strike a balance among three dimensions or vectors of educational management:

> the freedom of parents to make fundamental decisions about the education of their children, choosing among schools (or home education) which offer real alternatives;
>
> the autonomy of those who are engaged with individual schools B their boards and their teachers and administrators B to shape and implement a distinctive educational mission; and
>
> the responsibility of government, on behalf of society and of the interests of children, to ensure that every child and youth has the effective opportunity to receive an adequate education.

Our profile of each country placed present laws and policies in brief historical context and sought to assess how those laws and policies had affected the realities of freedom, autonomy, and accountability.

In the introductory volume, we provided a more in-depth discussion of the legal and the policy principles which undergird and are expressed in the commonalities and differences observed among the countries in our study. We began with a discussion of the sources and nature of controversies over educational freedom, asking why it is often challenged by those who in other respects are strong supporters of human rights. This was followed by an historical overview of the state role in regulating and providing instruction at the elementary and secondary levels, with special emphasis upon France.

The next sections discussed the primary characteristics of educational freedom as a human right, the policy framework within which this right is exercised or frustrated, and the legal framework created by national and international law. We then reviewed two of the primary dimensions along which educational freedom is sought: some parents and some educators are concerned especially with the religious character of schools, others with the cultural character, and we showed how each has both policy and practical implications. The following chapter discussed – primarily but not exclusively with reference to the United States – the then-recent phenomenon of 'vouchers' for school tuition. We went on to discuss the two crucial dimensions of the practical implementation of educational freedom: public funding for non-state schools and the extent to which schools – state and non-state alike – enjoy the freedom to shape a distinctive educational provision.

We concluded our discussion with a review of the principal issues, showing briefly how the various countries included in our study had chosen to address them. This was followed by a series of summary presentations of the situation in each country and an effort to compare the various countries with some methodological rigor; Gracienne Lauwers coordinated this aspect of the study with indispensable and intelligent diligence.

Realizing that the 2004 edition lacked, in most cases, the perspective of experts from the various countries and that the situation in some of those countries may have changed significantly, we decided that a new edition was called for.

The 2012 Edition

For the new edition, we sought authors from countries around the world, and were delighted to be able to attract almost one hundred collaborators, all completely uncompensated as are the editors. Some are the authors of the standard works on education law for their countries, others are graduate students in law or educational policy. The country profiles that they prepared cover sixty-five national systems of education. In addition, we have included in a few cases the country profile from the 2004 edition for half a dozen countries for which, sometimes because of last-minute difficulties, we were not able to obtain updated texts; these are noted in each case. In the present volume, the chapters on Argentina, Cuba, and the Philippines are in this category.

We are keenly aware of the omissions from the roster of countries covered in these volumes, notably from Africa and the Middle East as well as Latin America. Repeated efforts to recruit an author for Turkey, for example, proved unsuccessful for one reason or another. We trust that readers will understand that a project carried out without budget or staff and in competition with many other obligations cannot hope to be encyclopedic.

Volume 1 includes integrative and overview essays by a number of authors focusing on particular dimensions of the country reports or on regions of the world which may share some commonalities.

Volume 2 includes twenty-nine profiles of national systems in Europe (though note that Flanders and Wallonia in Belgium are treated separately, as are England, Scotland, and Northern Ireland in the United Kingdom; a profile of Wales appears in Volume 4).

The present volume includes profiles of twenty countries scattered around the world. It is our pleasant duty to thank the authors, Nikoleta Mita and Juliana Latifi on Albania, Cara Stillings Candal (updating the 2004 version by Hugo Carranza and Rodrigo Agrelo) on Argentina, Brian Caldwell on Australia, Iryna Ulasiuk on Belarus, Nina Ranieri on Brazil, Derek J. Allison and Deani A. Neven Van Pelt on Canada, Francisco J. Leturia I. and Francisca Vallejo on Chile, Jorge Alberto

Mahecha Rodríguez and Luis Enrique García De Brigard on Colombia, Daniele Vidoni on El Salvador, Margrét Hardardóttir on Iceland, Amos Zehavi (updating the 2004 version by Moshe Cohen-Eliya) on Israel, Mahasen M. Aljaghoub on Jordan, Rosa Elena Terán Morales on Mexico, Carol Mutch on New Zealand, Louay Constant, Charles A. Goldman, and Gail L. Zellman on Qatar, Rika Joubert, Willem van Vollenhoven, Johan Beckmann, and Justus Prinsloo on South Africa, Charles Russo on the United States, and Pablo Landoni on Uruguay. We have also included two chapters as published in the 2004 edition, by Daniele Vidoni on Cuba and Vivian Talisayon and others on the Philippines (though Professor Talisayon reviewed the text for the 2012 edition).

The longest profile (as was the case also in the 2004 edition) is of Canada, in which each province requires separate treatment and the accommodation of language and of religion adds further complications to a truly magisterial account. The profile of the United States makes no attempt to be as thorough, and indeed to do so for the fifty states and other jurisdictions, in the present context of constant policy innovation, would require the whole volume; it has therefore been supplemented with an essay by Cara Stillings Candal, a young researcher who has collaborated with us from the start, and by an overview of recent school choice initiatives by Paul DiPerna, who monitors them for the Friedman Foundation for Educational Choice.

The other country profiles in this volume speak effectively for themselves, and for their authors. It may be important to mention that those authors were in no case selected because they held particular positions on the hotly-debated issues of educational policy with which these volumes engage; they were simply asked to be objective. In some cases it would be instructive to compare what I wrote about a country in the 2004 edition and how the same country is represented in the 2012 edition, as an illustration of the significance of the points of view that we inevitably bring. We believe that this diversity of viewpoints is not the least of the merits of this collection.

The Overall Theme

If there is a unifying concern in the questions to which we have asked our authors to respond, it is the extent to which their countries promote and protect educational freedom.

"Educational freedom" is a phrase with several different meanings. It can refer, for example, to the style through which instruction is provided. Those who support education which allows children to decide for themselves what and how they will learn (often referred to as "progressive" often claim that it is more "free" than traditional teacher-controlled forms of instruction; whether it produces adults who are more intellectually independent is, of course, another question.
Educational freedom can also refer to the freedom of individual teachers to express

their views in the classroom. Of course, the manner in which a teacher chooses to express personal opinions may have the effect of limiting the freedom of pupils to develop their own independent opinions, which should warn us against using "educational freedom" in this sense as though it were an unambiguous and obvious Good Thing. In addition, the freedom of teachers to work in a school whose mission is consistent with their own views of education, and thus to be part of a team of mutual support, depends to some extent on a restriction on the freedom of teachers in that school to undermine that mission by promoting divergent approaches; there is thus a "duty of loyalty" in schools with a distinctive character.

Our concern in this study is primarily with a third application of the concept, the freedom to operate schools according to a distinctive understanding of education and with a fourth, the freedom on the part of parents to choose such schools. Our working definition of educational freedom, then, contrasts it with educational monopoly, whether on the part of the state or by another party, such as a religious organization. We are concerned with laws, policies and practices which support or limit freedom as exercised by parents and by those operating schools.
The *Universal Declaration of Human Rights* (1948) states that "parents have a prior right to choose the kind of education that shall be given to their children" (article 26, 3). According to the *International Covenant on Economic, Social and Cultural Rights* (1966),

> the States Parties to the present Covenant undertake to have respect for the liberty of parents . . . to choose for their children schools, other than those established by public authorities, which conform to such minimum educational standards as may be laid down or approved by the State and to ensure the religious and moral education of their children in conformity with their own convictions (article 13,3).

Similarly, the First Protocol to the *European Convention for the Protection of Human Rights and Fundamental Freedoms* provides that "in the exercise of any functions which it assumes in relation to education and teaching, the State shall respect the right of parents to ensure such education and teaching in conformity with their own religious and philosophical convictions" (article 2).

This freedom of parents requires, in a pluralistic society, that distinctive forms of schooling be available, which goes to the question of school autonomy, and that choosing an alternative to a government-operated school not pose an inhibiting financial burden on the family.

It is relevant, for example, whether the board or the director/principal of an individual school can select a team of teachers who share the same vision for education, or whether teachers are assigned by government on the basis of criteria of formal qualifications and seniority.

The reader will find much more extensive discussion of such questions in the essays collected in Volume 1.

We believe that there is ample material for reflection in these country profiles, and we trust that they will serve to inform and stimulate the discussions of educational policy that increasingly are occurring on a global scale.

Finally, our deep gratitude toward the many authors who contributed to these volumes.

Charles L. Glenn and Jan De Groof

References

Ludger Woessmann, Elke Luedemann, Gabriela Schuetz, and Martin R. West. 2009. *School Accountability, Autonomy and Choice around the World.* Cheltenham, UK and Northampton, MA, USA: Edward Elgar.

Albania

by Nikoleta Mita[1] and Juliana Latifi[2]

Overview

Education in the Republic of Albania is a national priority. During the past 20 years, Albania has experienced large political, institutional and socio-economic changes. From a deeply isolated country of constitutionally denied freedoms and rights and imposed atheism, it has been transformed into a country of political pluralism, a country where the freedoms and rights of individuals and minorities are respected and guaranteed, a country of free initiatives.

The democratic changes that occurred in Albania were also reflected in education. In an effort to create a modern system of education, in compliance with the European integration processes and the Millennium Development Goals, the Government has undertaken education reform. The National Strategy on Pre-university Education (2009-2013)[1] is the main policy document that foresees the short term and middle term development objectives and states the strategic priorities.

The vision of education in Albania is to guarantee a national modern education system that promotes sustainable economic development, increases competitiveness in the region and beyond, and consolidates democracy.

The educational reform, which aims to reform the whole pre-university education system in Albania, is focused on three main areas:

Legislative and administrative areas. The educational leadership and its administration are executed on three levels: the central level includes the Parliament, the Permanent Parliamentary Commission for Education and Media, Council of Ministers, Ministry of Education and Science (MoES), and its subordinate institutions. The upper local level includes the council of districts and regional directories; the lower local level includes the councils of municipalities or communes, regional educational directories and educational offices. The institutional level includes principals, school boards, teachers' councils, students'

1 Faculty of Social Sciences, University of Tirana
2 Faculty of Law, Justicia University

governments, and parents' councils. The new legal framework and policy aims to shape and develop a democratic school, to support the process of decentralization and increase local initiative, to strengthen the links with the community, to increase the level of teachers, students, parents and community participation in education decision making process.

Curriculum. In terms of curriculum reform, significant progress has been made to bring the national curriculum of basic and secondary education to contemporary standards. The main aim and achievement of the new curriculum reforms have been shifting to a student-centred philosophy.

Human resources. Improving the quality of human resources in general and teachers in particular in implementing the new curriculum and the democratization of the educational process.

Five strategic priorities of the educational reform are: reforming and enriching the policy making, increasing management and decision making capacities; improving education quality, improving the efficiency of education financing; developing human resources; and developing vocational education and preschool education.

Education in Albania is both public and private. Public education is funded by the state. The share of expenditures for education in the state budget in 2009 was 10.4 percent, or 3.4 percent of GDP. Figures show that the public expenditure on education had decreased compared to 2008 (10.8 and 3.5 percent)2 and it is still low compared to other fast-growing economies and to the government's target of 5 percent.

The country is highly dependent on foreign grants or loans when it comes to initiatives such as building or refurbishing basic infrastructure, introducing curricular innovations, and equipping schools with computers, textbooks, materials and other equipment.3 The foreign donors, such as World Bank, Commission of the European Union, UNICEF, Soros Foundation, Swiss AlbVET, German GTZ and others have contributed to public education.

The number of pupils per 1000 inhabitants decreased from 192 in 2007-2008 to 186 in 2008-2009.4 The average of schooling years (ISCED 0-6) was 11.9, which is lower compared to the EU and Balkan countries. Gross enrolment rates in 2008 amounted to 50 percent in pre-primary education, 92 percent in basic education, 57 percent in upper secondary education, and 19 percent in vocational education.5

The main challenge of education is to improve the quantitative and qualitative indicators of education to average EU standards.[6]

The Structure of Schooling

The pre-university educational system in Albania is composed by: pre-primary education, basic compulsory education, secondary education, and special education. Pre-university education is offered by the public and private educational institutions. The following kinds of institutions function within the pre-university education system: kindergartens, schools, and complementary education institutions. The educational institutions offer full time, part time and distance learning programs.

Pre-primary education

Pre-primary education in Albania consists of nursery schools and kindergartens. Nursery schools are institutions subordinated to the local government, for children between the ages of 0 and 3. Kindergartens are institutions subordinated to MoES for children between the ages of 3 and 6. The MoES aims to involve all 5 years old children in preschool institutions.

Pre-primary education is not compulsory, and it can be offered full or part time. Nursery schools run throughout the year.

Teaching in the pre-primary education system is conducted on the basis of educational programs approved by MoES. The mission of pre-primary education is to provide early education and contribute to the development of children's personality, so as to prepare them for school. The teaching process in nursery schools and kindergartens of ethnic minority regions is conducted in their mother tongue.

From the total number of 1,774 pre-primary institution registered in 2009, just 89 were private. The total number of preschool children that attended kindergartens in 2009 was 75,445, while 3,464 children were registered in the private institutions.[7]

Basic education

The basic education in the Republic of Albania is compulsory. This kind of education stars at the age of 6; lasts 9 years (from September 2009) and attendance is mandatory until the age of 16. Basic education consists of two cycles: primary education (grades I-V) and the lower secondary education (grades VI-IX). It terminates with the School Leaving Exam.

The goal of the compulsory basic education is to provide pupils with intellectual, creative, practical and physical abilities and skills, as well to develop their personality and offer fundamental principles of general culture and civic education.

Institutions of basic education are established all across Albania.

Curricula and textbooks for basic compulsory education are approved by the Ministry of Education and Science.

In 2009, of 1,605 institutions of basic compulsory education, 128 were private. Of 457,886 pupils who attended this level of education, only 20,452 attended private schools.[8]

Secondary education

Secondary education is not compulsory. Secondary education in Albania is provided through Gymnasia and Secondary Vocational Schools.

Gymnasia provide general education. Studies last three years and upon completion; students take the State Matura Exams. Gymnasiua also offer part-time programs available for adults that last four years.

Article 30 of the Law "On Pre-university Education System" states that "Public general secondary schools provide pupils with comprehensive knowledge; they further expand and deepen the knowledge and skills acquired in basic compulsory education".[9]

The new secondary school structure and the new teaching curricula were implemented for the first time during the academic year 2009-2010. The curricula consist of nine key fields of knowledge: Albanian Language and Literature, Foreign Languages; Mathematics; Technology, IT & Computers; Natural Sciences; Social Sciences; Arts; Physical Education and Sports; Career Promotion and Personal Growth. Secondary school curriculum consists of the core curriculum and the elective curriculum. Curricula and textbooks must be approved by the Ministry of Education and Science.

Vocational Education

Vocational Education is one of the options of secondary education after basic education. It lasts 2, 3 or 4 years. Its goals are to enable students to develop their vocational skills and practical knowledge. This type of education yields craftsmen with the necessary skills for a specific job, but also allows pupils to carry on with higher education.

Starting with the academic year 2009-2010, pursuant to the Law "On the Vocational Education and Training in the Republic of Albania," Vocational Education is organized around a new structure, comprising levels and timelines compliant with the educational structure in the Republic of Albania. The new Vocational Education structure is based on the vocational qualifications platform, as recommended by the Albanian Qualifications Framework (AQF); it is in conformity to the International Standard Classification of Education (ISCED), and with the European Qualifications Framework (EQF).

- Basic Vocational Education, Level I (ISCED 3C, allows access to the labor market), is oriented towards a wide-range of vocational profiles (22 profiles) and it lasts two years. It is equivalent to Level II of AQF and EQF. It awards a certificate of basic vocational training (partly-qualified employee/assistant) and allows for transition to Level II of VET or to join the labor market.
- Vocational Education, Level II (ISCED 3C) is oriented towards vocational profiles and it lasts one year. It is equivalent to Level III of AQF and EQF. Upon completing this level, a certificate of vocational competency for a qualified employee is awarded. At this point, transition to Level III of VET or access to the labor market is possible. A 1-year bridge-course focusing on general education is offered to pupils that opt to complete the general State Matura and pursue university studies.
- Technical/Managerial Education, Level III (ISCED 3A) is also oriented towards general vocational profiles; this level lasts 1 year and it is equivalent to Level IV of AQF and EQF. Upon completion of this vocational education level, pupils take the Vocational State Matura Exam and the Integrated Vocational Exam. At graduation of level III, a certificate of technician/manager in the relevant profile and the Vocational State Diploma are awarded. Graduates may join the labour market or pursue university or post/secondary studies.
- Technical or Managerial Education, Level III (ISCED 3A), as a specific training-track, is oriented towards specialized vocations (it is only applicable to particular vocations). It lasts four (4) years and can be pursued after the completion of compulsory basic education. It is equivalent to Level IV of AQF and EQF. Upon completion of this level, pupils take the Vocational State Matura Exam and the Integrated Vocational Exam. At this point, a certificate of technician in the specialized field / profile is awarded, as well as the Vocational State Diploma. Similar to general vocations track, graduates may opt to join the labor market or attend university or pursue post/secondary studies.
- Vocational post-secondary education, Level IV, (ISCED 4B), is an upgraded level oriented towards specialized vocations. It lasts (1-2) years, following the completion of secondary education (either general or vocational). It is equivalent to Level V of AQF and EQF. At the end of level IV, graduates are awarded the vocational competency certificate (in the specialized vocation) and are qualified to enter the labor market.

We would agree with the comment: “The Albanian system lacks a number of elements that would help to strengthen the links between VET and the labor market and increase the relevance of VET provision.”

Special Education

Public Special Education is a part of the public education system in Albania. Public Special Education aims to ensure the fullest possible development opportunities for persons who present physical, mental, learning disabilities in accordance with their needs and requirements for a more dignified life.
Education of children who present special needs is offered for free at public educational institutions. The state is seeking to ensure necessary conditions for the realization of integration of the children with special needs in the regular schools. There are functioning special schools and agencies, where specialized treatment is offered free of charge for children who present special needs that cannot be met within the regular school system. The criteria for determining which children receive special education are approved by the Council of Ministers.

The Legal Framework

Education is regulated in accordance with the Constitution, legislation, international agreements and treaties ratified by the Republic of Albania, and the traditions of national education.

The legal framework of pre-university education is composed by:

- The Constitution of the Republic of Albania approved by the Popular Assembly on 21.10.1998 and decreed by the President of the Republic on 28.11. 1998.
- Law No. 7952 "On Pre-university Education System" approved on 21.06.1995 and changed on 30.07.1998 by the Law No 8387, "On Some Amendments and Changes in the Law No. 7952 on Pre-university Educational System".
- Law No. 8652, date 31.7.2000 "On the Organization and Functioning of Local Governance".
- Law No. 8872, dated 29.03.2002 'On Vocational Education and Training in the Republic of Albania'".
- Law No.10 171, date 22.10.2009 "On Regulated Professions in the Republic of Albania" changed by the Law No. 10357, date 16.12.2010.
- Law No.10247, date 2010 "On Albanian Qualifications Framework".
- Normative Provisions for the Pre-university Education approved by the Ministry of Education and Science in 2002.
- Bylaw acts on pre-university education, issued by the Council of Ministers and the Ministry of Education and Sciences.

The Republic of Albania has ratified the following international documents that contain rules on education:
In the framework of UN

- International Covenant on Economic, Social and Cultural Rights, New York.
- Convention on the Rights of the Child.
- Convention on Elimination of all Forms of Discrimination against Women.

In the Framework of UNESCO
- Convention against Discrimination in Education.

In the framework of Council of Europe
- European Convention on Human Rights.
- European Social Charter (revised).

All these international documents are directly applicable in the domestic legal order and they have been invoked in the domestic courts. The Constitution of the Republic of Albania gives a special status to the international instruments. According to the Constitution, every ratified act becomes part of the domestic law and is implemented directly with the exception of the acts that are not self-implemented and require the approval of special legislation. The Constitution recognizes that the conventions have a dependant status but super juridical power. This status of the international conventions constitutes another warranty that secures their implementation even in regard to linguistic rights.
The Constitution of Republic of Albania[10] introduces the right to education as a fundamental right of all the citizens.

Article 57 states
1. Everyone has the right to education.
2. Mandatory school education is determined by law.
3. General high school public education is open for all.
4. Professional high school education and higher education can be conditioned only on criteria of abilities.
5. Mandatory education and general high school education in public schools are free.
6. Pupils and students may also be educated in private schools of all levels, which are created and operated on the basis of law.

The legislation that regulates the pre-university educational system secures equal rights for all and guarantees the right of the individuals belonging to national minorities "to have the opportunity for instruction in their mother tongue, and study their history and culture in the curriculum. The state also creates all conditions for the minorities to learn the Albanian language, study Albanian history and culture."[11] The curricula as well as the proportion of the use of the mother tongue in regards to the official language in instruction are determined by special acts of the MoES. Education for members of minorities is conducted in special educational units and institutions. Their opening as well as their functioning is regulated by the procedures determined by the Council of Ministers.

The following are the fundamental criteria that regulate education in the mother tongue for national minorities: *First, education in the mother tongue is non-obligatory.* The decision does not foresee or guarantee the mandatory bilingual education.

However, it defines as a general criterion a minimum number of 20 students necessary to start a class in the mother tongue. *Second, opening a bilingual class or school depends on the will of the community of the minorities and it is initiated as a response to its request.* The request is written by the students' parents or wards and it is addressed to the respective Regional Education Department. The request must include the students' enrolment list. Upon verification of the list and the satisfaction of all regulations of the request, the Director of the Regional Education Department submits the latter to the Prefect, attaching his opinion.
Although the acts of the Council of Ministers charge the Ministry of Education and Science with responsibility for overseeing the education of bilingual students and the curricula of their educational units, the bylaws do not clarify the procedures for starting or terminating these educational units. Including the institution of the prefect in decision-making and coordination of local and central government only complicates matters unnecessarily. The local government should be given the right to make decisions in regard to opening of the bilingual educational units, based on Law No 8652, date 31.7.2000 "On the Organization and Functioning of Local Governance".

As an implementation Act of the Constitution of Albania, the Law "On the Integration and Family Reunification of Individuals Who Have Been Granted Asylum in the Republic of Albania" regulates all the procedures that guarantee the right to education of foreigners that have acquired asylum or have applied for it. In addition to recognizing the right to education of this population, this law guarantees its implementation through positive actions of the Albanian state. The Refugee Office organizes courses for Albanian language, civic education and vocational education.

The secularity of public education is determined by the law. There are some legal documents that regulate the relationship between education and religion.
The legislation regulates the right to religion and religious education; the relationship between the state and the non-public schools that offer religious subjects as well; relationship between the state and the religion communities; the requirements for establishing and controlling the activity of non-public schools that offer religious subjects; rules for the teachers and parents in exercising the right to religion.

The Constitution of the Republic of Albania states that "The state and religious communities ... cooperate to the good of each and all."[12] This means that the position of the Albanian state in the field of religious education must be not only a neutral and unbiased one, but must also include positive interventions to ensure freedom of education in the religious field. The legal formula of the solution is given by the Constitution and is realized through agreements between the state and four main religious communities in Albania.

The sixth paragraph of Article 57 of the Constitution of Republic of Albania, which recognizes the right of students to education in non-public schools at all levels, must be seen as closely linked to Article no 24 of the Constitution, which permits the exercise of religion through education. This establishes the freedom of religious education both through religious schools and by permitting information of religion to be treated in public schools.

Article No. 5 of the Law "On Pre-university Education System"[13] states that the MoES is responsible for the enforcement of the state policy on secular education, approved by the Council of Ministers. So, MoES is not taking responsibility for the religious part of the private schools that offer religious subjects as well nor for the religious schools.

Article No. 14 of the Law "On Pre-university Education System"[14] prohibits teachers from influencing students' social, political and religious beliefs.

In Albania there are no legal provisions related to the right to refuse pupils from other religious beliefs.

Freedom to establish non-state schools

There are some articles of the Law "On Pre-university Education System"[15] that set the rules for the establishment of private schools.

Article 4 states: "Education in the Republic of Albania is conducted in public and private educational institutions, in accordance with the provisions of this law".

Article 46 presents two main requirements for opening a private educational institution: a) to prove that institution has relevant teaching personnel with appropriate qualifications and b) to have the required infrastructure equipped with teaching aids to implement the requirements of the curriculum.

Article 48 clarifies two different issues related to the activity of private schools.

48.1 For private schools compulsory license shall be granted only when they undertake to implement the requirements of the required curriculum for public schools established by the Ministry of Education and Science.

48.2 In cases of removal of the license given to private schools of compulsory education, the Ministry of Education and Science and its district authorities take the necessary measures to accommodate students at another school.

The procedure for establishing a private educational institution has two steps: at first the application must be presented to the National Licensing Center, which then asks approval from the MoES. MoES evaluates the application based on the criteria set in the Decision of the Council of Ministers No 538, date 26.05.2009 "On licenses and permits from or through the National Licensing Center and several other rules of the common bylaws".

The procedure for establishing a secular private school, according to the Pre-university Education Law and the Decision of Council of Ministers No. 248, date 28.05.1999, is different from establishing a religious school or a non-public school where classes are taught in a foreign language. While a secular private school, where classes are taught in Albanian, receives its license from the Ministry of Education, the approval of the Council of Ministers is needed for a non-public school that offer religious subjects and for a non-public school where classes are taught in a foreign language.
Non-public education institutions and complementary non-public education institutions that offer religious subjects or that offer instruction in a foreign language are required to provide information about various extracurricular activities that they organize.
Private schools are free to select the teaching methodology of their choice, but they have to get approval from the MoES to use a curriculum different from the national curriculum.

According to the data published by the Institute of Statistics, in 2009 private kindergartens represented 5 percent of pre-primary educational institutions, private schools of basic education represented 7.9 percent of basic education institutions and private secondary schools represented 24.1 percent of secondary education institutions.[16]

To date the government does not give financial support to private educational institutions. The new draft law on pre-university education that is in the process of approval has foreseen two articles related to the financial support for the private institutions.

- Ministry can support financially the local private educational institutions, which are nonprofit and have at least five years operating as private institutions. According to criteria established by the Council of Ministers, the financial support for private schools can be differentiated according to their ranking in national education examinations as well as in international testing and competitions.
- Private schools use only financial support for excellent students in the national and international activities.

Home schooling

According to the Article 49 of the Law "On Pre-university Education System"[17], MoES determines the special cases when compulsory education can be offered privately at home. The level of learning quality can be measured and evaluated through the exams given in the public schools of compulsory education. Currently in Albania, home schooling is implemented in the cases of the children isolated at home because of the feuding phenomenon.

School choice not limited by family income

Access to public institutions of pre-university education is free. The state covers expenses for the learning environments, the teaching materials, and the teaching staff in the public educational institutions of the pre-university education system.[18] However, other costs of schooling such as cost of text books, uniforms, cost of extra-curricular activities, accommodation and food when pupils stay in dormitories and other educational supplies are covered by the parents or in rare cases by different associations. In the framework of the social policy, the government through the initiative against poverty helps children belonging to economically poor families. MoES offers financial assistance to students from poor family background and scholarships to all vocational school students from the north-east and south-east areas of the country.
Private schools charge tuition to their students, and the amount of the tuition varies with private schools' policies. There exist no regulations in relation to school fees at private schools. There exists no policy on government subsidies for the private pre-university institutions.

School distinctiveness protected by law and policy

From 1995 the legislation has sanctioned the right for private education. This is a possibility for a different alternative in education. As the educational system is centralized, legislation does not assign school policy in terms of a specific model. The current legislation gives a controlled limited freedom.

In terms of general education, most private educational institutions of the pre-university system differ slightly from the public educational institutions.

The Ministry of Education and Science has prepared a policy document on decentralization[19] on the education sector. The decentralization is foreseen as a possibility for more autonomy to schools. In the framework of this policy, discussions and consultations among all interested parties have been focused on the following components.

- The need for clearly defined roles for a broader autonomy at the district, municipality, and school level.
- Allocation of responsibilities associated with the transfer of competences at the local level, determining the modalities of accountability.
- Decentralization of decision making in education.
- Strengthening capacities at all levels of education.
- Reshaping of financial scheme through gradual decentralization.
- Establishing a system of indicators that allow measuring and evaluating performance.

While this sounds progressive, the implementation in practice is not an easy issue.

Distinctive character

Curriculum policy is centralized. Curriculum, content and learning standards are determined by the Ministry of Education and Science, while the Council of Ministers determines the standards for the development of curricula of vocational education based on the recommendations of the National Council on Vocational Education and Training. According to the Law on Vocational Education, the Council of Ministers, in cooperation with the social partners, reviews curricula of vocational education and training continuously and in line with economical developments.[20]

Regional Educational Departments are responsible for approval of the educational program that will be implemented in kindergartens.

Curricula of all categories and types of schools of pre-university education are approved by the MoES.

MoES orders the specialized agencies to develop educational curricula for kindergarten and subject matter curricula for primary and secondary education. MoES organizes textbook competitions, establishes evaluation procedures, and approves the textbooks that can be used in schools.

Public schools have the right to choose textbooks among those approved by the MoES.

Private educational institutions are required to follow the national curriculum. A private educational institution can use a curriculum different from the national one if it is a foreign school that operates in Albania, or it can use the national curriculum with small changes with approval from the MoES.

All types of educational institutions are free to select teaching methods and extracurricular programs.

According to the new MoES guidelines, teachers have the right to adapt the 20 percent of the curriculum according to the school context, but it is not implemented yet in the practice since teachers are not prepared to exercise this "window of autonomy". Each school is required to develop an educational plan describing how it will apply the national curriculum to its circumstances, giving the possibility for individualization. This plan contains the arrangement of the hours foreseen for each subject, the teaching methods that will be used and the activities that the school will organize to fulfill this plan.

Decisions about admitting pupils

The Constitution guarantees the right to education to everyone. The Law "On Pre-university Education System" specifies that "Citizens of the Republic of

Albania enjoy equal rights to education at all levels of education according to this law, regardless of social status, nationality, language, sex, religion, race, political beliefs, health status and economic level"[21].
The Normative Provisions[22] set the admitting criteria and procedures for public institutions.
Registration of children in kindergarten and pupils in 9-year schools, as a rule can be made in a kindergarten or a school defined by residential areas imposed by local government with the proposal of Regional Educational Department. Children and pupils can enroll in an institution outside the area of his/her residence when conditions and capacity of the premises permit this.

Registration of pupils in a part time program normally can be done at the school within the area of his/her residence. There are schools where admissions are competitive. MoES determines which 9-year schools and secondary schools may have competitive admissions and the competition takes place according to regulations and guidelines formulated and approved by the MoES.

Decisions about staff

Employment in the education sector is regulated under the rules of the public sector. Besides the Labour Code[23], there are specific legal documents that regulate the procedures of the recruitment, selection and appointment. A job in the education sector can be obtained on the bases of competition.
All teachers, in public and non-public schools, must meet state requirements. Teaching is a profession that is regulated by the Law "On Regulated Professions in the Republic of Albania"24. The purpose of this law is: a) to determine the criteria for practice of some important occupations, which are related to the protection of public interest, public safety and health, while respecting the principle of professionals independent scrutiny and the autonomy; b) to protect and guarantee the fulfilment of standards for certain important professions, so the qualified persons who meet criteria by this law or other laws are those that practise these professions.
A person who is seeking to practise a regulated profession must have completed an appropriate accredited program of study and /or professional qualifications in the profession, which are certified by official documents issued within or outside the country and recognized in the Republic of Albania in accordance with the legislation in power.

Criteria for practising a regulated profession including teaching are:

a) To perform professional practice;
b) To take the state exam;
c) To be registered in the respective Professional Order.

Article 4, paragraph 4/4 of the Collective Agreement dated 25.05.2010, signed among the Ministry of Education and Science, the Federation of Unions of

Education and Science and the Independent Union of Education of Albania clearly presents the employment criteria for all jobs and positions in the education system.

According to the above-mentioned collective agreement to be employed as a teacher a person must meet the following requirements:

a) A bachelor diploma (3 years of study) in teaching for pre-primary and primary education of compulsory basic education (Kindergarten/ grades 1-5). For the specific conditions of the districts are allowed two exceptions. A person who has completed pedagogical, foreign languages, music or physical education secondary school and has earned all three degrees of qualification can be employed as a teacher. This level of qualification is considered sufficient to have a permanent contract of employment. A person that possesses a diploma of the secondary pedagogical education can be employed as a teacher, on one year job contract.

b) A bachelor and a professional master diploma in teaching (3+1 years of study) for the lower secondary education of compulsory basic education (grades 6-9).

c) A bachelor and a professional master or a master of sciences diploma in teaching (3+1/ 3+2 years of study) for the upper secondary education and vocational education. Exception is made for the cases of vocational schools, where an employee must have a bachelor diploma in the relevant subject.

When two or more candidates apply for a single job, the employer (who is director of the Regional Educational Department or director of the Educational Office) creates a special commission with the participation of trade unions representative and they make a decision on the basis of these criteria:

- level of diploma, GPA, seniority in education.
- training courses and qualifications recognized by the Ministry of Education and Science.

The priority is given to those candidates who have served for a period longer than 3 years far away from their residence or in disadvantaged areas; and to the candidates that have the status of "working disabled", certified by the decision of the relevant official committee.

Recruitment of teachers in special schools is based on the criteria presented in the Chapter XIII of the Normative Provisions (2002). According to the article 58, paragraph 2, letter b and c of this document[25], selection procedures are organized by the school based on the criteria set by the Ministry of Education and Science. The school commission selects three best candidates and presents them to the Regional Educational Department that makes the appointment decision. Each selected candidate initially works as a teacher assistant for one year.

Accountability for school quality

Accountability for school quality belongs to the National Inspectorate of Pre-university Education (NIPE). It was established based on the Decision of the Council of Ministers No. 56, date 03.02.2010 as an institution that depends directly on the Minister of Education and Science. Before 2010 an inspection sector operated within the Ministry of Education and Science. Meanwhile the

Regional Educational Department and the Education Offices don't have their inspecting function as before.
National Inspectorate of Pre-university Education University aims to guarantee the quality of educational service to all students in the pre-university sector, through external evaluation of educational institutions.
NIPE inspects educational institutions, public and private, secular and religious, and complementary institutions of the pre-university education system. The National Inspectorate of Pre-university Education has these main functions: monitoring, evaluation, control, advice, and informative/reporting. NIPE evaluates quality of the service provided by the educational institutions; it is responsible for the quality assurance of the teaching process, monitors textbook issues, controls the compatibility of the activities of educational institutions with the legislation in effect, monitors the implementation of the Normative Provisions by the school, monitors the implementation of the teachers' code of ethics; inspects the performance of schools; monitors the implementation of regulations of the Matura exams and School living exams; offers advice for school improvement and educational policies, and publishes information and reports on the quality findings.

For the purposes of the national or regional level inspections, institutions to be inspected are determined by lot. NIPE inspects by priority the institutions that have shown weaknesses in previous inspections, which have been given improvement tasks, or which have low student achievements in national tests.

In Albania there are foreseen some rules on controlling the private schools that offer religious subjects. The following are two main articles related to this issues taken from the Law "On Pre-university Education System"[27].

Article 45

> 45.1 MoES determines equivalency for recognition of the transcript of a . . . private school. If the private school offers religious subjects as well, the MoES determines the equivalency for the recognition of the secular part of the curriculum at the end of a . . . private school.

Article 47

> Ministry of Education and Science and its education organs in districts control regularly the secular education process in the private school in order to verify accomplishment of the requirements of the curricula and the education programs approved by the Ministry of Education and Sciences.

More detailed requirements related to the control are included in the Decision of Council of Ministers No. 248, date 28.05.1999 "On Criteria and Procedures of Giving Permission for Functioning of Non-public Education Institutions and Complementary Education Institutions that Offer Religious Subjects or Instruction Teaching in a Foreign Language".

Teaching of values

The teaching of values is described in the legal documents and in the school curricula and school educational plan. In the legal and educational documents are described the following values: personal, cultural, national, moral, and spiritual values.
The Law "On Pre-university Education System"[28], describes in three articles the values that can be developed by the educational institutions.
Article 2: Education has the mission of spiritual emancipation, material progress and social development of the individual.

Article 21: Compulsory public education aims to develop intellectual and creative abilities, practical and physical skills of students, to develop their personality and provide them with basic elements of general culture and civic education.
Article 26: Public secondary education aims to develop fully the students' personality and potential in order to enable them to contribute actively in the economic, political, social, and cultural development of the country.
Normative Provisions[29], through the aims of the school and kindergarten presents the values that these institutions are required to develop.
Article 4: The aims of the school

School in all its activities aimed at:
- personal spiritual emancipation and development;
- development of independent, critical, creative, constructive and tolerant thinking and acting;
- development of patriotic, human, moral and democratic values;
- creating equal opportunities for all pupils and enabling them to cope with life.

The aims of the kindergarten
In its activities kindergarten aims:
- to develop the personality of the child and prepare him/her for the school;
- to ensure equal education opportunities for each child;
- to educate a child as sociable person who can establish relationship with other people.

Each educational institution must establish the goals of its educational program. The goals and the way to realize them are part of the subject matter curricula, cross curricula and projects realized through the extra-curriculum activities.

References

1. National Strategy on Development of the Pre-university Education (2009-2013). www.mash.gov.al
2. Albania in figures 2010, page 22. www.innstat.gov.al
3. Viertel, E. & Nikolovska, M. Albania. Review of Human Resources

development. 2010, page 13.
4. Albania in figures 2010, page 22. www.innstat.gov.al
5. National Strategy on Development of the Pre-university Education (2009-2013), page 5. www.mash.gov.al
6. Integrated Plan of Ministry of Education and Science, 2010. www.mash.gov.al
7. Albania in figures 2010, page 19. www.innstat.gov.al
8. Ibid, page 19.
9. Law No. 7952, "On Pre-university Education System" approved on 21.06.1995 and changed on 30.07.1998 by the Law No 8387, "On Some Amendments and Changes in the Law No. 7952 'ON Pre-university Educational System'". www.mash.gov.al
10. Constitution of the Republic of Albania, 1998. www.president.al
11. Law No. 7952, "On Pre-university Education System" approved on 21.06.1995 and changed on 30.07.1998 by the Law No 8387, "On Some Amendments and Changes in the Law No. 7952 on Pre-university Educational System". www.mash.gov.al
12. Paragraph 4 of Article 10 of the Constitution of Republic of Albania. www.president.al
13. Law No. 7952, "On Pre-university Education System" approved on 21.06.1995 and changed on 30.07.1998 by the Law No 8387, "On Some Amendments and Changes in the Law No. 7952 on Pre-university Educational System". www.mash.gov.al
14. Idem.
15. Idem.
16. Albania in figures 2010, page 19. www.innstat.gov.al
17. Law No. 7952, "On Pre-university Education System" approved on 21.06.1995 and changed on 30.07.1998 by the Law No 8387, "On Some Amendments and Changes in the Law No. 7952 on Pre-university Educational System". www.mash.gov.al
18. Ibid, article 9.
19. Decentralization policies in pre-university education. www.mash.gov.al
20. Article 28, Law No. 10011, dated 30.10.2008 "On some amendments to Law No 8872, dated 29.03.2002 'On the Vocational Education and Training in the Republic of Albania". www.mash.gov.al
21. Ibid, Article 3
22. Normative provisions 2002. Chapter III, www.mash.gov.al
23. Labor Code, www.mpcs.gov.al/ligje-legjislacioni
24. Law No.10 171, date 22.10.2009 "On Regulated Professions in the Republic of Albania", changed by the Law No. 10357, date 16.12.2010. www.mash.gov.al
25. Normative provisions, 2002, article 58. www.mash.gov.al
26. Ibid, article 64/4
27. Article, 45, 47. Law No. 7952, "On Pre-university Education System" approved on 21.06.1995 and changed on 30.07.1998 by the Law No 8387, "On Some Amendments and Changes in the Law No. 7952 on Pre-university Educational System". www.mash.gov.al

28. Article 2,21,26. Law No. 7952, "On Pre-university Education System" approved on 21.06.1995 and changed on 30.07.1998 by the Law No 8387, "On Some Amendments and Changes in the Law No. 7952 on Pre-university Educational System". www.mash.gov.al
29. Normative provisions, 2002, article 29 www.mash.gov.al

Argentina
[from 2004 edition, updated by Cara Stillings Candal]

by Hugo Chavez, Rodrigo Agrelo and Cara Stillings Candal

Overview

During the second half of the nineteenth century, Argentina experienced an extraordinary evolution of its educational system, reaching levels comparable to those of the most developed countries in the world. Domingo F. Sarmiento, President of the Argentine Republic from 1868 to 1874, laid the foundation for subsequent progress in education, introducing free and obligatory schooling for children between 6 and 12, increasing enrolments four-fold, and creating normal schools for the training of elementary and secondary teachers, among many other important means of encouraging science, culture, special education, and research.

The Common Education Law 1420, enacted in 1884, was the organizing standard for education in the entire country for more than a century.

Education progressed rapidly in Argentina. The rate of illiteracy fell from 78 percent in 1869 to 39 percent in 1908 and, supported by the economic progress which the country experienced until 1930, Argentina found itself in the educational vanguard of all of Latin America.

The country's political instability between 1930 and 1983, with successive civilian governments interrupted by military coups, affected the development of the educational system, the adequacy of its financing, its planning, and its organization. Throughout this period, the agenda and priorities of the educational system kept changing from one decade to another in accordance with the changes in the country from dictatorial to elected governments.

With the arrival of Democracy, a National Pedagogical Congress was set up on the initiative of the national government, with responsibility for undertaking the urgent and necessary reforms of the education system. The Congress was so organized that the participation of both public and private schools and of

all the organizations of society concerned with education was guaranteed. The Catholic Church, through its schools, had a strong presence in the discussions and conclusions of the Congress. Nevertheless, the conclusions of the Congress were not translated into normative form until the beginning of the 1990s.
The Argentine Republic accomplished during the 1990s major structural reforms in major aspects of the state, all of them oriented toward privatization, deregulation, and decentralization of government activities and inspired by neoliberal policies consistent with the recommendations of international organizations. The education sector did not escape from the current of changes; in 1991 a law authorized the transfer of secondary schools from the national government to the provinces, and in the 1993 was followed by the Federal Education Law which established the organization, governance, and allocation of rights and responsibilities for the education system at all levels, from pre-school to post-university. The Higher Education Law was adopted in 1995.

These laws implied an increase in the responsibilities and competencies of the provinces which, until then, under the terms of the National Constitution, had responsibility only for primary education; indeed, there was also a parallel system of primary schools dependent upon the national government created in the course of the 20th century to supplement the inability of the provinces to respond to the demand for education. With the laws enacted in the 1990s, a new organizational framework was created for the whole country and for all levels of education.

Some aspects of the 1990s reforms were changed, however, in 2006, when government passed a new Federal Law on Education. The law gives a Federal Council of Education, a body comprised on provincial education ministers, the education minister of the Federal Capital Buenios Aires, and the National education minister, the power to set broad educational goals for the entire country. Those goals are known as the Common Basic Contents (CBC) and outline expectations for what all students should know and be able to do. In addition to establishing these curricular expectations, others overarching aims of the 2006 law are to decrease drop out rates at the secondary level, increase graduation rates overall, and provide for a students an education better aligned with the demands of the labor market. The law extends compulsory education to 13 years (the entirety of secondary school) and places a renewed emphasis on the availability of vocational technical education across the provinces.[1]

More than six years after the passage of the 2006 law, debate continues in Argentina about how raise the quality of education in the country. High school attrition rates remain high and access to quality schools remains unequal between the provinces and throughout the country. Although enrollment in school at the primary level remains near universal across the provinces, at 94 percent,

---

1 Auguste, Echarte,& Franchetti (2008), The Quality of Education in Argetina, Inter-American Development Bank.

enrollment still drops sharply at the secondary level, to 74 percent across the provinces.[2]

The Character of the Educational System

The Argentine educational system, although legally defined as "regulated and organized, in a cooperative and coordinated form, by the national government and the provinces," and, despite the reforms of 2006, is regulated primarily by the provincial governments. The provinces must, under the Constitution, "provide for primary education," and by authorization of the national law 24,049 of 1991 the national government transferred to their administration the secondary schools previously under its control.

Education, whether state-managed or privately managed, is obligatory. Since 2006, this obligation extends from age five to age seventeen, although the process of implementation of this obligation is gradual and the rhythm of implementation is different in each province.

State schooling is free of charge at all levels, while private schooling is not free of charge and, in general, receives subsidies from the state. Private schools may be administered by religious organizations, NGOs, private enterprises, or individuals. The subsidies which they receive from the state in all parts of the country reduces the tuition costs and facilitates, in part, the ability of parents to choose schools. The state also has the right to regulate these schools.

By virtue of the constitutional right to teach and to learn, the system is organized on the basis of "freedom to teach" (*libertad de cátedra*) and the right to choose the education of one's children in accordance with the convictions of parents.

The Federal Education Laws 24,195 of 1993 and 2006 established mandatory basic curricula (Common Basic Contents) which the provinces must adapt to regional realities. Each school, in turn, may develop its institutional project, which complements the basic curriculum. As a results of these recent laws, an estimated 70 to 80 percent of what is taught in schools is prescribed by a state authority.

According to 2006 statistics, the Argentine provinces and the City of Buenos Aires have altogether 12.2 million pupils in the pre-school, primary, and intermediate or secondary levels. It should be noted that, based on the disparate distribution of the population, the number of pupils by province varies considerably. More than half of the provinces have fewer than 200,000 pupils, while Buenos Aires

---

2 UNESCO Institute of Statistics, Statistics in Brief, Education Profile—Argentina, 2011.

has nearly five million, or roughly 40 percent of the total, making it the second-largest sub-national educational system in Latin America.

The private education sector, though regulated, functions with considerable independence of the public school sector and is supervised by the provinces through separate offices from those that supervise public education. Despite this separation between publicly-managed and private schools, both systems collaborate to provide education in geographically-isolated parts of the country.

It is important to note that private education is on the rise in wealthier provinces and cities in Argentina. This seems largely due to two factors: public perception of the inferior quality of public schooling and the increased availability of full day schools offered by private institutions. The vast majority of public school students in Argentina, primary and secondary alike, attend school for four hours every day, 20 hours every week. In the private sector, the number of instructional hours can be double that of the public sector.[3]

Structure of the Educational System

In accordance with the structure designed by the Federal Education Law, which most of the provinces have adopted, the present educational system is composed of various levels of instruction: Initial, General Basic Education, 'Polimodal' Education, and Higher Education and Special Arrangements (*Regímines Especiales*). Obligatory education consists of thirteen years.

Initial Education consists of the education of children from three to five years of age, of which only the final year is obligatory.

General Basic Education, which is obligatory, includes three cycles of three years each, with specified curricular, pedagogical, and organizational characteristics, for children and youth between six and fourteen.

'Polimodal' Education, which became obligatory in 2006, is three years, and undertakes the education of youth from fifteen to seventeen. This education includes two types of formation, general and oriented. The first involves teaching basic common content for all pupils, and the second involves content oriented to different areas of knowledge and of social and productive competencies of five types: natural sciences, economics and organizational management, humanities and social sciences, production of goods and services, and communication, arts, and design.

The national government maintain's responsibility for the public and private

[3] Auguste et. al, 2008

university system. Higher education is, properly speaking, post-secondary education and includes both institutions which provide university education and those which provide non-university education, through programs which require five or six years in the case of the former and three or four years in the case of the latter.

Special Arrangements includes (a) Special Education for pupils with special needs, (b) Adult Education to supplement the education of those who did not complete General Basic Education, and (c) Artistic Education, which must comply with the mandatory basic curriculum prescribed by Federal Education Law 24,195 of 1993, differentiating itself only by the content of the artistic and pedagogical disciplines.

The Legal Framework

The National Constitution, the nation's supreme law, contains concrete references to education, establishing the undelegatable responsibility of the State and incorporating the right of the family and of society to participate in the education system. The Constitution adopted in 1853 was revised in 1860, 1898, 1957, and 1994.

In accordance with this last reform, the (Inter-) *American Declaration of the Rights and Duties of Man* (1948) has constitutional status in Argentina. Article 12 states that "Every person has the right to an education, which should be based on the principles of liberty, morality and human solidarity. . . . The right to an education includes the right to equality of opportunity in every case, in accordance with natural talents, merit and the desire to utilize the resources that the state or the community is in a position to provide."

The *International Covenant on Civil and Political Rights* (1966) also has constitutional status, guaranteeing "respect for the liberty of parents . . . to ensure the religious and moral education of their children in conformity with their own convictions" (article 18.4), while the *Convention on the Rights of the Child* (1989), obligates signatory governments to "make primary education compulsory and available free to all" (article 28.1a).

Among the rights of all residents of Argentina, the Constitution establishes the equality of all before the law (article 16) and the right to learn and to teach (article 14). This right is one of the pillars on which has been developed the freedom of teaching in universities as well as the organization of private education.

With respect to foreigners, article 25 provides that "the Federal Government will promote European immigration, and may not restrict, limit, or burden with any fees the entrance into Argentine territory of strangers who intend to till the soil, improve industry, or introduce and teach the sciences and arts."

The revised Constitution makes repeated reference to organizational aspects of education. Thus, for example, it charges Congress with "providing what is conducive to the prosperity of the country, to the advancement and welfare of all the provinces, and to the progress of enlightenment, prescribing plans for general and university education" (article 75.18).

The Supreme Court of Justice has interpreted this to mean that, when the National Congress, in fulfilling its obligation to prescribe "plans for general and university education," the provinces and their constitutions must comply with these norms in virtue of the supremacy established by article 31 of the National Constitution.

Congress is also charged with "approving organizational and foundational laws on education which consolidate national unity while respecting provincial and local particularities, which ensure the undelegatable responsibility of the State, the participation of the family and of society, the promotion of democratic values and equal opportunities and possibilities free of any discrimination, and which guarantee the principles of gratuity and equity in state public education and the autonomy and independence of the national universities . . ." (article 75.19).

The reform of 1994 incorporated environmental and consumer education (articles 41 and 42) and at the same time recognizes the ethnic and cultural pre-existence of Argentine indigenous peoples and ordered the National Congress to guarantee respect of their identity and the right to a bilingual and intercultural education.

Article 5 of the *Carta Magna* establishes among the fundamental obligations of the provinces to ensure that primary education is provided.

María Rosa Albornoz affirms that "On this point an intense debate has developed about the role of the State in relation to education. Some positions place the emphasis on the right to learn and, in consequence, stress the principle of the State as guarantor of this right, while others emphasize a more limited role of the State under the principle of subsidiarity, stressing the rights of those who educate."

Even though not referring exclusively to education, the Constitution charges the Congress with promoting means of positive action which guarantee a real equality of opportunities and treatment, to prescribe a system of social security in order to protect children in situations of neglect from pregnancy to the completion of the period of elementary education.

The Constitution enables the provinces, among other activities, to promote economic progress, human development, the creation of employment, education, science, knowledge and culture (article 25). National Law 24,049 authorizes the national government to transfer to the provinces the secondary schools which it previously administered.

The Federal Council on Culture and Education issues non-binding resolutions which are then adopted individually by each of the provinces.

The provincial education laws regulate the exercise of all the recognized powers of the provinces, including the administration of the system and of its schools. Some provinces enact laws regulating the functioning of privately-managed education.

Each province's "statute of the teacher" regulates the careers of teachers and their rights and obligations among other matters. The great majority of provinces have followed the spirit and the letter of the national Statute of the Teacher adopted in 1958.

Freedom to establish non-state schools

Private education (or privately-managed public education, as it is officially called) has been recognized and supported by the Argentine State ever since the genesis of the national educational system. This recognition has implied the establishment of specific norms for this sector, among then notably the historic Law 934 (1878) and Law 13,047 (1947). The articulation between the public education sectors under state and under private management acknowledges its antecedents in the Law 1,420 (1884) and the Decree 940/72 and . . . [el relacionado sobre gestión propia ello se reafirma por medio de los artículos 3° y 7° de la Ley 24.195.]

The federal education law 24,195 of 1993 (chapter V, articles 36-38) accords to the Catholic Church and other religious confessions registered in the *Registro Nacional de Cultos*, to societies, associations, foundations, and enterprises with a juridical personality, and to persons, the right to create, organize, and maintain schools. This law maintained the recognition extended for more than a hundred years to private schools, and extended this obligation to all the provinces, which must legislate in accordance with its principles.

In actuality, more than two million two hundred thousand pupils, 25 percent of the national total, attend private schools. 63 percent of those students are enrolled in Catholic schools. Private school enrollment is much higher (almost 50 percent) in the City of Buenos Aires, 45 percent of students attend private schools. Private school enrollment is also higher in the wealthier provinces.

During the 1990s, in medium and large cities, there was a significant growth of privately-managed non-confessional and non-subsidized schools, initiated by individuals or groups of parents or teachers who sought approaches not considered by state schools. Most of these schools were organized as non-profit foundations or civil associations. Other educational projects, intended for families with greater resources, were organized as for-profit commercial societies.

At the end of the 1990s and the beginning of the 21st century, many privately-managed schools were forced to close as a result of the inability of families to continue to pay school fees. The state-managed educational system received some of these pupils, while others went to subsidized private schools.

While non-state schools must comply with many requirements, they enjoy more freedom to plan their activities. Within the minimum requirements established by each province, and under its supervision, these schools can appoint and remove their administrators, teachers, and support staff, and elaborate their study plans. The main obligations upon these schools are to fulfill the guidelines of the educational policy of their provinces and to provide information for the oversight of pedagogy, finances, and personnel. They must offer programs approved by the provincial government, with teachers who possess qualifications recognized by the government.

The law refers to these non-state schools as "educational services under private management." On the one hand, this description assimilates both types of schools – government-operated and non-governmental – in the sense that both provide officially-recognized education; on the other hand, it notes the difference between the two types of schools in that the non-governmental ones are privately managed or administered. The bottom line is that, in Argentina, all recognized schools are public, but some are under state management and others under private management.

In order to operate, privately-managed schools require previous recognition and authorization from the public authorities of each province. Without this state recognition, these schools are not considered an integral part of the educational system and studies undertaken in them are not recognized as valid. Education in privately-managed schools which have been recognized is accepted as equivalent in validity to that received in state schools. Pupils can change from state schools to private schools or vice versa without any sort of limitation or obstacle. The certificates and diplomas issued by recognized private schools have full official validity.

With respect to recognition procedures, there are no substantial differences among the 24 provinces. In the course of the education reforms initiated by the Federal Education Law, many provinces enacted their own laws, decrees, and resolutions to adapt to the criteria of the federal law.

Once officially recognized – and in order to maintain the authorization to operate – schools are supervised by state authorities.

The Federal Education Law, in article 37, establishes a state subsidy for officially-recognized private schools, limited to financing teacher salaries. Receipt of this subsidy is based upon "objective criteria consistent with the principle of distributive justice in the framework of Social Justice and taking into account, among other aspects, the social function which [the private school] fulfills in its zone of influence, the type of school, and the fees which it charges."

Privately-managed schools are authorized to charge fees or tuition to finance their functioning and may, at the same time, receive a state subsidy if they turn out to be eligible, but in order to receive the subsidy they must limit the amount of the tuition per pupil to the amount authorized by each province. The system of subsidies and the limits on the level of tuition facilitates access by pupils from families with medium or low incomes to privately-managed schools.

The government subsidy can finance entirely or partially the salaries of the privately-managed school, consistent with the economic realities of the school community.

Schools which receive no subsidies – those which serve families with a higher income level – are not required to limit the level of tuition which they charge.

Families who choose privately-managed schools do so for religious reasons, because of the distinctive educational mission of the school, through identification with the school community, or seeking educational quality.

Home Schooling

Education in Argentina is obligatory, which implies that pupils must attend the school chosen by their parents among the alternatives offered by those schools recognized by the State, whether state-managed or privately-managed. Although there are indeed arrangements for cases of illness or of absence from the country, when the authorities allow parents to take charge of the education of their children, provided that the pupils are evaluated from a distance, parents or guardians responsible for the education of minors are not permitted to secede from the official education system.

The City of Buenos Aires, for example, takes into account home schools which have the mission of educating children who for reasons of health or physical limitation cannot attend schools. By this means, although the pupils are studying at home, they are being educated by the obligatory education system.

Law 1420 of Common Education (1884) lays heavy penalties upon parents who do not send their children to a school recognized by the State. At that time, Argentina was a country which received immigrants, mostly from Europe, and it was necessary to integrate them with the rest of the population through the educational system. At present, article 45 of the Federal Education Law establishes among the obligations of parents or guardians that they have their children comply with the requirement of ten years of General Basic Education, or with the requirements of Special Education for children with special needs.

The obligation is also a right of children to receive a quantity and quality of education sufficient to develop their knowledge, skills, and sense of social responsibility and solidarity; they have a right to an education which respects their freedom of conscience and their religious, moral, and political convictions within the framework of democratic coexistence (article 43).

The reasons which at present justify this obligation are of a political nature and are expressed in the objectives of the education law as “the strengthening of national identity, taking into account local, provincial, and regional idiosyncracies, the guarantee of the sovereignty of the Nation and the consolidation of democracy in its representative, republican, and federal form.” This obligation is also founded on the duty of parents, responsible for the well-being of their children, to provide them with opportunities to integrate themselves and progress in the social environment.

The obligation to study in schools recognized by the State limits the constitutional right to learn and to teach in the form that and by the means through which parents consider that most suitable if they consider that the existing supply of schooling does not represent the model that they seek.

In 1998, a case with great public resonance tested the capacity of the provincial and national governments to enforce this obligation when the Mennonite Colony of Guatraché in the Province of La Pampa maintained its decision not to send the children of the community to schools recognized by the province. The isolation of the Mennonite Colony is such that the provincial authorities did not even know the number of children of school age. The fact that the children of the Mennonite community had been born in Argentina and were Argentine citizens moved the government of La Pampa to determine that these children should be integrated into the process of obligatory schooling. The authorities started an administrative process to require them to attend provincial schools where they would have to learn Spanish.

Despite notifications from the Ministry of Education that they must comply with obligatory school attendance, the Mennonite leaders remained firm in their traditions and warned that the families might leave if the provincial authorities build schools in their locality. The subsequent negotiations centered on the possibility that the teachers chosen by the Ministry would teach Spanish and minimal notions of social science, natural science, history, and geography, using the church as a school. This idea didn’t work, either, and the discussions turned to the possibility that education could occur in homes. Finally, the provincial government signed an agreement compatible with the interests of the Mennonite community. The children of the Mennonite Colony of Guatraché, it was agreed, would learn the Spanish language at home, taught by their families and not by teachers designated by the provincial Ministry of Education. The instruction would consist of lessons in reading and writing Spanish; the curriculum materials would be analyzed jointly by government and Mennonite representatives, and provincial educators would develop a system of evaluation. If the parents did not know Spanish, the children could be taught by their relatives. The leaders of the community were given six months to put these arrangements into practice.

This conflict, with great public repercussions nationwide, included the intervention of federal authorities concerned to ensure that the obligation of schooling was complied with. It tested the possibility of enforcing this obligation and the flexibility of the system to respond to special situations presented by particular communities. The warning of the Mennonite community that it might leave the country, in which it arrived in 1921, if its children were required to attend schools recognized by the State, forced the education authorities to find a way to satisfy the requirement of minimal educational competencies and the teaching of the national language outside of schools recognized by the State. In this case they adopted an ad hoc solution which avoided the emigration of the Mennonite community or a judicial process to obligate the parents to send their children to recognized schools.

School choice not limited by family income

Argentine law and jurisprudence recognizes the right of parents to choose the school where their children will receive education consistent with their religious, philosophical, and ethical convictions. The Federal Education Law incorporates expressly the right of parents to choose schools as a general principle, and in practice this right can be exercised by choosing between publicly-managed and privately-managed schools.

With respect to the choice of state schools, the limitations are not economic, because public schools are free of charge and are prohibited from any sort of fees, but rather geographic, because of zoning; the general norm has been – though differing from province to province – that pupils who live within a determined geographical area have priority in choosing a school over those who live outside. Children of the teachers and employees of each school are an exception, as are siblings of pupils already attending the school.

In the Province of Buenos Aires, fox example, 15 percent of secondary school seats are reserved for pupils who live outside of the geographic area of each school, but the difficulty of getting students to schools outside of the geographical area of their home is an economic challenge for parents. In the Province of Córdoba, in the case of state schools, residency requirements no longer exist, and pupils can choose the school of their preference. Cases of excess demand for a school are resolved by a random lottery. Nevertheless, from the point of view of the economic resources of families, even when there are no zone limitations on the choice of schools, the cost and time for transportation to a school far from the residence of the pupils serves as an objective limit on the ability to choose. It must be kept in mind that in Argentina the government does not bear the cost of transportation required by pupils.

Most privately-managed schools, as has already been explained, receive subsidies. The basis for the allocation of subsidies is the National Decree 2543 of 1991, which in its first article states that "in order to ensure the ability of parents to choose a school for their children, within the framework of the freedom to teach and to learn which is guaranteed by the National Constitution, the State will contribute to the financing of schools incorporated into Official Instruction, in conformity with the norms of the present decree."

This decree was enacted almost simultaneously with the law 24,049, transferring schools to the provinces, and the criteria of this decree were incorporated into the norms of each of the provinces.

Among privately-managed schools we can distinguish, as already explained, between those that do not receive public subsidies and those that do. In the second group, the size of the subsidy is determined by the level of the fees charged to parents; there are cases – schools that serve communities with very low resources – in which privately-managed schools do not charge any fees at all.

The level of the subsidy, under Decree 2452/91, can be of 40, 60, or 80 percent of the costs of the teachers at each school. Subsidies of 100 percent are provided for schools that charge no fees at all.

Decisions about admitting pupils

Argentine schools may not refuse to admit pupils on the basis of religion, sex, race, nationality, sexual orientation, or ideology. Admission of pupils on the basis of where they live still exists in many provinces, but in others has been eliminated.

Selection of pupils, on the basis of their academic ability, is in general not practiced in state schools. Nevertheless, in some state schools with distinctive educational programs, such as for example schools oriented toward the arts, music, or languages, there are objective mechanisms to select pupils who demonstrate better potential to take advantage of these programs.

In addition, the secondary schools connected with the national universities, which are considered among the oldest and the most demanding in the country, implement very demanding mechanisms of academic selection.

In 1995, the **Justicia Federal** intervened in a conflict involving sex equity at the Colegio Monserrat, a secondary school connected with the Universidad Nacional de Córdoba and thus by its nature public. Although the High Council of the University had ordered the inclusion of female students in this school, which selects its pupils by academic merit, the Colegio Monserrat resisted doing so. The **Justicia**, in response to an appeal by the Colegio that the decision of the university authorities not be applied, found that the Universidad de Córdoba had authority to order the inclusion of female students, upon which they were admitted to the school.

Privately-managed schools may establish procedures of academic selection, provided that these do not involve discrimination; the selection must be based upon the identification of the applicants with the educational mission of the school. Confessional schools may limit the admission of pupils who are not identified with the religion professed by the school.

In several instances, the courts ordered the readmission of female students who had been expelled from Catholic schools because they were pregnant. This frequent occurrence led to the prescription of Law 25,584 of 2002, which prohibits schools providing public education (thus including privately-managed but state-authorized schools), of any level or type, from any action which prevents the beginning or the continuation of studies by any pregnant student or for any other circumstance connected with pregnancy which produces the effect of marginalization, stigmatization, or humiliation.

For the same reason, in November 2001, the City of Buenos Aires approved a special arrangement of support for pregnant students (Law 709), applicable to public and private schools, with the intent of avoiding that such students lose a year of schooling as a result of their condition.

Decisions about staff

In the state-managed system, teachers must be appointed in accordance with the procedures which each province establishes, which are in general similar because aligned with the Statutes of the Teacher of each province which, as we have seen, are based on the national statute of 1958. These Statutes are the principal norms which regulate the activities of teachers in the education system, establish their rights and obligations, the teaching career (entry and advancement), boards of qualification of personnel, disciplinary boards, and so forth.

In this system, teachers enter through competitions which are intended to guarantee their professional suitability and their respect for the obligations of educators. Promotion or advancement in a professional career should occur on the basis of individual merit and professional accomplishment. Teachers are appointed by the education authorities on the basis of the action of the qualification boards which determine the order of merit of the teachers for promotion, based upon academic preparation, the value of the courses taken and the undergraduate and graduate degrees earned, publications, and so forth.

School authorities have no role in the designation of the teachers that the provincial Ministry of Education assigns to them, on the basis of this elaborate system of qualifications.
The Statutes of the Teacher in general provide teachers with a high degree of stability, since state-managed schools do not appoint teachers nor remove them and their disciplinary authority is very limited; school directors can only apply minor sanctions, such as warnings, while major sanctions are applied through indictments carried out by provincial ministries of education.

On the other hand, in privately-managed schools, it is the authorities of the individual school who appoint and remove teachers. The State does not intervene in the process of appointment of teachers in privately-managed schools, by the Federal Education Law, article 38, establishes the required condition that the teachers appointed must have qualifications recognized according to the norms of each province.

Private schools may base their decisions about teachers on the basis of the identification of teachers with the religious or educational identity of the school.

It should be noted that while most aspects of the country's education norms were reformed during the decade of the 1990s, the norms which regulate the work of teachers remain those established in the 1950s, despite the intention to reform them.

Teachers in state-managed schools are public employees and their working relationships are regulated by the norms of administrative law, while those in privately-managed schools are regulated by the common labor laws. Salaries in the state sector are determined, not by the education sector but by the political authorities of each province. Schools have no role in this matter, nor are there provisions to provide rewards for effort.

Privately-managed schools pay the salaries established in the collective work contracts for the private education sector; it must also be remembered that subsidized schools receive these funds from the State specifically to pay salaries. Nevertheless, these schools have no restrictions against setting salaries higher than those established in the contracts. In practice, very few private schools – those which do not receive subsidies and serve populations with high incomes – in some cases pay higher salaries.

Teaching Values

The national Constitution contains an ensemble of principles and values based upon fundamental human rights. Among these, the right to teach and to learn and the other provisions cited previously establish the axiological framework for Argentine education.

The Federal Education Law, article 5, establishes as an objective of education "the strengthening of national identity, taking into account local, provincial, and regional idiosyncracies, the guarantee of the sovereignty of the Nation and the consolidation of democracy in its representative, republican, and federal form."

Article 6 stipulates that "the education system shall make possible the integral and permanent education of men and women, with a commitment to the nation, orientation to the region and the continent, and a universal vision, which they will realize as persons in the cultural, social, aesthetic, ethical, and religious dimensions, in accordance with their abilities, guided by the values of life, freedom, goodness, truth, peace, solidarity, tolerance, equality, and justice. Capable of elaborating, by their existential decisions, their own life-projects. Responsible citizens, critical protagonists, creators and transformers of society through love, knowledge, and work. Defenders of democratic institutions and of the environment."

And article 8 says that "the educational system will ensure for all inhabitants of the country the effective exercise of their right to learn, on the basis of equality of opportunities and possibilities, without any discrimination."

Among the rights of pupils is recognized the right to "be respected in their freedom of conscience, their religious, moral, and political convictions within the framework of democratic coexistence" (article 43). Parents are guaranteed the right "to choose for their children or wards the educational institution whose worldview corresponds to their philosophical, ethical, or religious convictions" (article 44).

The rights and guarantees established in the National Constitution and the Federal Education Law apply in the entire country. In addition, the provincial constitutions and laws have included provisions related to education which are consistent with the National Constitution.

Australia

by Brian J. Caldwell[1]

Overview

There are several seemingly intractable problems in education in Australia and efforts to address them are gathering momentum even though educational reform and strategies for school improvement have been underway for nearly four decades. These problems include the disparity in achievement between high and low performing students,[2] including distressingly low levels of success for the nation's indigenous students;[3] a fragmented approach to school governance across the six states and two territories, where constitutional powers to make laws in relation to education lie; continuing and often debilitating debates about school choice, especially in relation to public (government, state) schools and private (non-government, independent) schools; and the content of curriculum and approaches to learning and teaching. Despite these problems, Australia's students generally perform well in international tests of student achievement such as the Program for International Student Assessment (PISA) and the Trends in Mathematics and Science Study (TIMSS).[4] There is, however, a general view that the country could do much better, not only in addressing the aforementioned problems, but in ensuring that schools help ensure that Australia will thrive in an era of globalization. The economic crises as the first decade of the 21st century drew to a close impacted Australia to a lesser degree than comparable countries. However, the need to set priorities in how to address the problems is critical.

In this chapter I will describe the policy framework for current efforts in school reform, with a focus on the emergence of what has been termed 'new federalism'; summarize trends in decentralization, community engagement, choice and accountability; highlight what are emerging as 'hot topics' in policy discourse – the funding of schools and student outcomes; and assess the significance of these developments in the international arena. The first part of the chapter draws in part from a more detailed account in Caldwell (2011a) while the last part draws extensively from Caldwell (2010) and Caldwell (2011b).

---

1 Managing Director and Principal Consultant, Educational Transformations; Professorial Fellow, University of Melbourne

2 PISA, 2006

3 MCEETYA, 2008; MCEETYA, 2009

4 Gonzales, 2008; PISA, 2006; TIMSS, 2007

Policy framework

Much of the reform effort is connected with the challenge of achieving what has been termed 'new federalism'. As noted above, constitutional powers to make laws in relation to education lie with the states but the federal or commonwealth government has a very important role to play because of its financial powers. For example, it is the only level of government that has the power to raise funds through an income tax, and it must make decisions on how grants will be disbursed to the states and territories. There can only be a truly national approach if there is broad agreement across both levels of government and an arguably unprecedented effort is being made to achieve such an outcome through what are known as National Partnerships Agreements.

International observers in most other countries will be surprised that a national framework is not already in place, since this is the normal arrangement elsewhere. In this respect, considering nations around the Asia Pacific, Australia is more like Canada and the United States. Indeed, the constitution that established Australia as a nation in 1901 is in many respects modeled on that of the United States, including education, with the challenge of developing a national perspective much greater in the latter, with 50 states, than in Australia, with six states and two territories. There is, for example, no national curriculum in the United States and the likelihood of developing one is remote, whereas Australia is close to introducing one. Canada presents another contrast, with the federal government in that country having virtually no role in school education except for indigenous students and children of military personnel.

It has proved to be politically difficult for Australia to create a national framework but there was a major breakthrough in late 2007 when the Rudd Labor Government took office. This framework is critically important in the overall reform agenda across the nation.

It is important to note that 'national' in this context has a different meaning to 'federal' or 'commonwealth'. The former refers to an outcome that reflects a consensus or agreement among different levels of government, federal as well as state and territory. 'Federal' or 'commonwealth' refers exclusively to decisions of the government at that level. For many years, that level of government was known as the Federal Government or the Commonwealth Government, although, in recent years, Australian Government has been adopted, whereas the state and territory governments use the names of their jurisdictions, such as the Victorian

Government or Government of Victoria.

Given the alignment of powers in Australia's constitution, efforts to create a national framework in education can only succeed if there is agreement among governments at the state and territory levels. The Australian Government must be party to such agreements because of its power to make grants to the states and territories. Broad funding for schools from the Australian Government is normally in four-year quadrennial periods but particular grants through National Partnership Agreements may be of shorter duration. The Australian Government is the major source of public funds for private schools whereas state and territory governments are the major source of public funds for public schools.

New federalism

The idea of 'new federalism' gained currency in early 2008 and is in part an outcome of all governments in Australia at that time being of the same political persuasion (Labor), as well as palpable need, given the fragmented nature of much of the existing policy framework across the nation (this party political alignment has since been broken with Labor governments defeated in state elections in New South Wales, Queensland, Victoria and Western Australia).

Arrangements from 2008 reflected an intention of the Labor Government to lead an 'education revolution'. An explanation of what constituted an education revolution was provided by former Prime Minister Kevin Rudd and Deputy Prime Minister Julia Gillard, who also served at the time as Minister for Education, Employment and Workplace Relations[5], framed by the following rationale[6] that highlights economic, social and individual benefits:

> The Rudd Government is committed to creating an education revolution to build a world class education system, which would establish Australia as one of the most highly educated and skilled nations.
>
> This commitment recognizes the central role that education plays in the economic, social strength of our nation. Education not only drives productivity but also empowers individuals to reach their full potential, and helps overcome disadvantage.
>
> Beyond economic growth, education creates social benefits that help build social capital. Societies with a strong commitment to education enjoy higher

---

5 Gillard replaced Rudd as leader of the Australian Labor Party and Prime Minister in June 2010. She led the Labor Party to a narrow win in the federal election of August 2010. Rudd became Minister for Foreign Affairs but resigned in February 2012 to unsuccessfully challenge Gillard for leadership of the Labor Party.

6 Rudd & Gillard, 2008, p. 5; see also Rudd, 2008

> levels of civic participation, greater social cohesion, lower levels of crime and disadvantage, and a more trusting, equitable and just society.

An early illustration of the new federalism in action was the establishment of the National Curriculum Board (NCB) in April 2008. The NCB was re-named with expanded powers in 2009 and is now the Australian Curriculum, Assessment and Reporting Authority (ACARA). ACARA brings together, for the first time, the functions of curriculum, assessment and reporting. The Australian Institute for Teaching and School Leadership (AITSL) was established in January 2010.

Rudd and Gillard acknowledged that there were many excellent schools in Australia and that 15 year-olds did significantly better than the OECD average in PISA. However, they drew attention to decline in reading literacy from 2003 to 2006, the 'long tail' of underperformance linked to disadvantage, the drop in performance at the top end of achievement from 2003 to 2006, and the concentration of the 'tail' among indigenous students and students from low socio-economic status families. They built the case for reform in terms of the nation's productivity and declared that improving student outcomes is a national priority. Priorities in three 'core areas' were set: (1) raising the quality of teaching; (2) strategies based on high expectations and engagement and transitions for every student, especially those in disadvantaged communities; and (3) improving transparency and accountability of schools and school systems at all levels.[7]

Agreement was reached on strategies and funding arrangements. Outcomes include agreements with the states and territories on a national curriculum from 2013, increased funding for school buildings (Building the Education Revolution),[8] the adoption of ICT (the Digital Education Revolution),[9] greater transparency in the reporting of student achievement and school performance (National Assessment Program – Literacy and Numeracy) (NAPLAN), the creation of a web site (My School)[10] to provide a higher level of transparency on the performance of schools, standards for teaching and school leadership, and higher levels of autonomy for public schools.

Decentralization, community engagement, choice and accountability

A famous commentary on the assumptions underlying Australian education was offered in 1955 by Freeman Butts, a distinguished Fulbright Scholar, visiting from Columbia University, who undertook an extensive and comprehensive study of

7 Rudd & Gillard, 2008, p. 12
8 DEEWR, 2009a
9 DEEWR, 2009b
10 www.myschool.edu.au

education in Australia. Butts observed:

> I have been struck by the fact that the centralized Departments of Education in Australia, for all their power, are hemmed in by parliament, by cabinet, by ministers, by public service boards, by teachers' tribunals, by appeals and arbitration boards, by public works departments, and by treasury and budget officials. These are all outside the fold of professional educators. It is assumed that these groups are qualified to make decisions about education, but it is also assumed that other non-professional persons in the community are not expected to be able to make qualified or valid judgments about education.[11]

Butts acknowledged that 'it is true, of course, that much discussion and conferring may go on between top officials and lower ones, but the impression I received is that there is relatively little of it, although there is a variety of practice here'.[12] Butts wondered 'whether you miss something of the vitality, initiative, creativeness and variety that would come if the doors and windows of discussion were more open up and down the educational edifice'.[13] The following is a brief summary of developments since 1955 in relation to decentralization, community engagement, choice and accountability.

Decentralization was a common element of the restructuring movement that began in the 1980s and continues to the present. Some like Victoria have gone further than others, with more than 90 percent of the state's recurrent education budget now decentralized to schools for local decision-making within a centrally-determined framework of policies, priorities and accountabilities. It is noteworthy that the Bracks Labor Government increased this proportion following the earlier initiatives of the Kennett Liberal-National Coalition Government in a parallel to what the Blair Labour Government did in Britain in extending the local management program of the Thatcher Conservative Government.

Australia is working to an unfinished agenda in relation to community engagement. Limited engagement was described by Butts (1955) as noted above. Questions were still being raised in 1973 with the Interim Committee of the Australian Schools Commission (1973) observing that 'after almost one hundred years of public education a reappraisal of relationship of the school to the wider society is taking place in Australia, as it is in most industrialized nations. The isolation of schools is being questioned', but declaring that 'antipathy towards and apathy about community participation in the governance of schooling is widespread throughout Australia'.

The idea that the school should be 'the nucleus of the community' in the sense

11 Butts, 1955, p. 14
12 *Ibid.*, p. 15
13 *Ibid.*, p. 17

described above, has not taken hold to any great extent and it is still regarded as an innovation. The Prime Minister and Deputy Prime Minister's statement on the education revolution in 2008 drew attention to initiatives elsewhere, noting that 'The United Kingdom's full service extended schools initiative demonstrates the importance of allowing schools to develop tailored plans to meet the priorities of the local area by bringing different strands of extended service provision together into a coherent approach' and flagging further reform to 'achieve stronger links between schools and the services available in local communities that will support their students' engagement in learning'.[14]

Recent years have been characterised by the inter-twining of four issues: needs-based funding, the exercise of choice, the appointment of staff, and the nature of public education. There has been general acceptance of needs-based funding across the political spectrum and more generally within the Australian community. The debate has been largely about what constitutes need, how it is measured, and what quantum of funds should be delivered. Some stakeholders have preferred a mainly per capita approach (that is, a basic grant for all) with a needs-based component, but a pure form of a per capita approach along the lines of a voucher has been rejected, either on ideological or pragmatic grounds, and there appears little prospect of it being adopted. Determining need and the quantum of support has been the focus of much of the debate in recent times, with the complex categorization in the Education Resources Index (ERI) giving way to the Socio-economic Status (SES) model introduced in the Howard Liberal-National Coalition years and sustained by the Rudd-Gillard governments, at least until 2014 after a review set up in 2010 (see below). Until the election of the Rudd Government, the Labor Party has sought to limit (or even eliminate) funding to what are portrayed by some as 'wealthy independent schools', a stance described in some public commentary as maintaining the 'class divide' or continuing to fight a 'class war'. It seems unlikely that it will adopt this stance in the future.

There has always been agreement that Australian parents have the right to choose a non-government school for their children.[15] However, there now seems to be broad acceptance of the view that all those who choose a non-government school should receive some financial assistance by way of government grants. Nevertheless, the issue is the extent to which the exercise of choice in favor of a non-government school should result in the allocation of public funds, particularly if the non-government school that is chosen charges high fees and is resource-rich. This may be the clearest example in the contemporary setting of education policy and education funding reflecting a broader development in society. The same development is evident in health care and, increasingly, in all human services. At the federal level, both the Liberal-National Coalition and

---

[14] Rudd & Gillard, 2008, p. 29

[15] see Wilkinson, et al., 2006, for an historical account of choice and state aid to private schools

Labor accept the notion of choice. At issue is how the exercise of choice should be supported with public funds and, in particular, where this leaves government schools that are losing market share in all states.

While there is broad agreement among the major political parties that public schools should have a higher level of autonomy, operating within a broad central framework, arrangements vary across the nation when it comes to the appointment of staff. In Victoria, cited above, schools have a high level of discretion in the selection of staff even though the formal contract, as it were, lies with the state. Indeed, teachers apply directly to individual schools when there are advertised vacancies, and selection panels are set up at the local level. Appointments are limited by the overall school budget and by salary levels and other conditions that are the subject of collective agreements between the Australian Education Union and the Victorian Government. This approach has been in place in Victoria for nearly 20 years. In only one other state is there the same degree of autonomy in respect to the appointment of staff. Western Australia has established a new class of schools, which are known as 'independent public schools', which can select staff in a similar manner to Victoria.

Elsewhere around Australia the appointment of staff in public schools remains contentious. In some instances the reasons are straightforward, for example, in remote locations or highly disadvantaged settings where it is not possible to have local selection. Union opposition to local selection remains.

The Australian Government has entered into National Partnership Agreements with each state and territory government, systems of non-government schools, and independent private schools to implement projects across the country under the rubric of Empowering Local Schools. Implementation is to be achieved by 2018 with acknowledgement that there will be a variety of approaches in different jurisdictions.

These arrangements in respect to staff place public schools at a comparative disadvantage to private schools which generally have freedom to select whom they will employ subject to appointees having the required qualifications for teaching. Independent schools generally have a higher level of autonomy than, for example, systemic Catholic schools, but the discretion enjoyed by the latter exceeds that for public schools.

The nature of public education remains an issue. For some, the concept of 'public education' should extend to all schools that are in receipt of public funds, with an expectation that there should be a common framework of accountability. For others, public education is still synonymous with government education, that is, schools that are funded, built, owned, operated and staffed by the state. They maintain their opposition to the steady increase in funding for non-government schools in its different forms and the quantum of funds in the allocation. They see the apparent neglect of the government sector as manifested, for example, in the quality of facilities and the disparity in services and support for staff and students.

A notable development is the strengthening of frameworks for accountability. Funds will not be granted by government at any level unless pre-conditions are agreed and rigorous reporting is required to demonstrate fidelity in implementation. Although recipients of federal aid have always been required to be financially accountable, the nature of state aid to non-government schools today would be unrecognizable to early proponents.

The federal government more than ever before is a major distributor of public funds for all public sector services in Australia. It has played a major role for decades through its sole power to levy income tax and re-distribute some of the proceeds through the work of the Commonwealth Grants Commission. The states levy a range of smaller taxes to support their efforts in areas of state responsibility. The picture changed in dramatic fashion in 2000 with the advent of the Goods and Services Tax, levied and collected by the federal government, but delivered in entirety to the states.

These views of the role of the federal government in matters of policy prescription, service provision and rigorous accountability, suggest that there is a larger issue to be resolved, namely, the nature of federalism in Australia and the role of the federal and state governments in the provision of education in government and non-government sectors. There are several scenarios for how this issue will be played out.

In summary, there appears to be broad acceptance in Australia that needs-based funding and choice should be the basis of state aid to non-government schools, although differences in policy and practice on the emphasis to be given to each of these may change with a change in government. The mechanisms for determining need and the associated quantum of funds will be the subject of more-or-less continuous refinement, as they are in systems of government schools that operate with a high degree of decentralization, as is the case in Victoria.

Key policy issues

The hottest topics at the time of writing (early 2012) are the funding of schools, especially the allocation of public funds to public and private schools, and educational outcomes in relation to other countries.

As illustrated in Table 1, the trend to private schooling has been sustained over four decades. The global financial crisis has had no discernible impact.

Table 1: Enrollment changes by sector, expressed as a percentage of all enrollments, 1970-2008[16]

Year	Public	Private		
		Catholic	Independent	Total
1970	78 percent	18 percent	4 percent	22 percent
1980	78 percent	18 percent	5 percent	23 percent
1990	72 percent	20 percent	8 percent	28 percent
2000	69 percent	20 percent	11 percent	31 percent
2008	66 percent	20 percent	14 percent	34 percent

The shift to private schools is most evident at the secondary level, especially for the final years. Table 2 shows the distribution of students by sector in Year 12 in 2008. In large capital cities such as Brisbane, Melbourne, and Sydney, public schools now serve a minority of students in year 12. In the Australian Capital Territory (ACT) which includes the capital of Australia (Canberra), the majority of secondary students now attend schools in the private sector, the first time that this has occurred in the nation.

Table 2: Percentage distribution of students by sector in year 12 in 2008[17]

Public	Private		
	Catholic	Independent	Total
57.3 percent	22.6 percent	20.1 percent	42.7 percent

Funding for public and private schools is under review. This process occurs every four years, but the current review is the most far-reaching since 1973 when the Karmel Report[18] was released. In 2010 the Australian Government established an expert panel chaired by David Gonski, an eminent businessperson and former board member of a private school, to conduct the review, which reported in December 2011 (Gonski Report).[19] Recommendations included the continued

16 Independent Schools Council of Australia, 2009
17 Australian Bureau of Statistics, 2009
18 Interim Committee of the Australian Schools Commission, 1973
19 Australian Government, 2011

support of public and private schools to the point that no school should be funded at a lower level than is currently the case. A National Schools Resourcing Body was proposed that will establish a 'resource standard' on the basis of an evidence-based determination of the funds required to offer an outstanding education for all and close the gap between high and low performing students. A needs-based funding mechanism was advocated that takes account of parents' capacity to contribute to the costs of private schooling. There was a particular focus on financial support for students in highly disadvantaged settings (the SES model will be maintained) and for students who have special needs.

Initial response from the profession was generally positive but some state and territory governments were critical because implementation from 2014 will require a substantial injection of funds from all levels of government in a time of fiscal constraint. The mixed response from states and territories was divided on political lines between Labor and non-Labor governments. There was no assurance at the time of writing that implementation will proceed as recommended or, if it does, that traditional lines of often-heated debate will not continue.

The Gonski Report noted how the performance of Australian students had declined relative to high performers in PISA such as Hong Kong, Korea, Shanghai and Singapore. The same evidence was cited in a report of the independent Grattan Institute,[20] released shortly before the Gonski Report, but it was suggested that, while funding is important, a high priority must be given to improving the quality of teaching, as has been done in the East Asia countries mentioned in both reports.

Requirements for transparency and accountability are especially contentious. As noted above, the performance of all public and private schools is available on the My School web site. The web site reports student performance on national tests of literacy and numeracy (NAPLAN) and basic descriptive and demographic data. But the web site also reports the performance of each school in years 3, 5, 7, and 9 and compares them to 'like schools' anywhere in the country and schools in the same geographic location. The March 2011 version reported changes in performance of students who took the tests two years ago, thus providing a value-added measure for each school. Significantly, the report for each school describes its sources of revenue and the current state of its finances. The financial reports are particularly contentious. Indeed, a first attempt to launch the latest version of My School was aborted in December 2010 when many schools, especially private schools, challenged the financial reports.

Whereas 'cooperative federalism' was the mantra from 2008, terms like 'coercive federalism' or 'competitive federalism' are now cropping up in policy discourse. National testing and creating long lists of standards for teachers and school leaders may not be the answer. Rebuilding large numbers of run-down public

---

20 Jensen, 2012

schools hasn't reversed the trend of students attending private schools. The jury is still out on whether granting public schools higher levels of autonomy will make much of a difference, despite international evidence that the best-performing public school systems tend to grant relatively high levels of autonomy to their schools in budgeting and staffing. Little progress is being made in the reform of teacher education.

International significance of developments in Australia

Developments in Australia have international significance because four major issues are also faced by other nations. These are (1) the roles and responsibilities of different levels of government; (2) the funding of public and private schools, (3) the balance of centralization and decentralization in the governance of schools; and (4) related to (3) securing an optimal balance of autonomy, accountability and choice. Addressing these issues in Australia as elsewhere is important in establishing a framework to successfully achieve school reform, a major theme of which is securing improvement, given the gaps in achievement of high and low performing students.

Australia has wrestled with these issues for more than four decades and there is a constantly shifting settlement depending to some extent on policies of government but also because of fundamental changes in society and the nature of schooling. The situation that has been reached at the start of the second decade of the 21st century is that, while constitutional powers in relation to education lie with the states, far-reaching if not unprecedented agreements have been reached between governments at all levels on a framework within which reform will proceed. This is a significant achievement.

How public and private schools shall be funded from the public purse has been at the centre of policy debates for more than a century. Whereas constitutional arrangements and a broad community consensus have led to a settlement in most nations, a comprehensive sustainable framework has yet to be reached in Australia. There is general support for the view that both sectors should be funded but the mechanism for delivering this support remains contentious. What is arguably unique about the current situation in an international context is that both sectors are supported and schools in the private sector can charge fees. In fact, Australia's tradition of 'free, compulsory and secular' public education is itself under threat as more governments levy fees and charges that are 'borderline' in respect to whether they support or do not support the costs of tuition. One way of interpreting the current situation is that Australia has a de factor voucher system. These developments warrant attention in other nations.

Note

An earlier version of this chapter was presented at the Asia Leadership Roundtable on the theme 'Education Reform and Change in the Asia Pacific Region', hosted by the National Institute for Educational Development of Teachers and Educational Personnel (NIDTEP) of the Ministry of Education, Thailand, and the Asia Pacific Centre for Leadership and Change (APCLC) of the Hong Kong Institute of Education, Bangkok, March 12-14, 2010.

References

Australian Bureau of Statistics 2009, *Schools 2008*, Australian Bureau of Statistics, Canberra,

Australian Government 2011, *Review of School Funding – Final Report.* Report of the Expert Panel (David Gonski, Chair), Department of Education, Employment and Workplace Relations (DEEWR), Canberra.

Butts, R.F. 1955, *Assumptions Underlying Australian Education.* Australian Council for Educational Research, Melbourne.

Caldwell, B.J. 2011a, 'Educational reforms and school improvement in Australia' in Lee, J.C.K. & Caldwell, B.J. (Eds) *Changing Schools in an Era of Globalization.* Routledge, New York and London, Chapter 4, pp. 67-84.

Caldwell, B.J. 2011b, 'Private schools and the future of public education in Australia', *Phi Delta Kappan.* May.

Caldwell, B.J. (2010), 'Is private schooling becoming the preferred model of school choice in Australia?' *Journal of School Choice.* Vol 4, No 4, pp. 378-397.

Department of Education, Employment and Workplace Relations (DEEWR) 2009a, *Building the Education Revolution: National Coordinator's Implementation Report,* February-September 2009. DEEWR, Canberra.

Department of Education, Employment and Workplace Relations (DEEWR) 2009b. *Digital Education Revolution – Fact Sheet.* DEEWR, Canberra.

Gonzales, P., Williams, T., Jocelyn, L., Roey, S., Kastberg, D & Brenwald, S 2008, *Highlights From TIMSS 2007: Mathematics and Science Achievement of U.S. Fourth and Eight- Grade Students in an International Context.* National Center for Educational Statistics (NCES), Department of Education, Washington, DC.

Independent Schools Council of Australia (ICSA) 2009, *Snapshot 2009.* ISCA, Deakin West ACT.

Interim Committee of the Australian Schools Commission 1973, *Schools in Australia.* Peter Karmel (Chair) (The Karmel Report). Australian Government Printing Service, Canberra.

Jensen, B 2012, *Catching up: Learning from the best school systems in East Asia.* Melbourne, Grattan Institute.

Ministerial Council on Education, Employment, Training and Youth Affairs (MCEETYA) 2008, *National Assessment Program Literacy and Numeracy. Achievement in Reading, Writing, Language Conventions and Numeracy.* MCEETYA, Melbourne.

Ministerial Council on Education, Employment, Training and Youth Affairs (MCEETYA) 2009, National Assessment Program: Literacy and Numeracy. NAPLAN Summary Report. MCEETYA, Melbourne.

Rudd, K 2008, 'Quality education: The case for an education revolution in our schools'. Address by the [former] Prime Minister to the National Press Club, Canberra, 27 August (see also Rudd and Gillard, 2008).

Rudd, K. & Gillard, J 2008, *Quality Education: The Case for an Education Revolution in our Schools.* Commonwealth of Australia, Canberra.

The Program for International Student Assessment (PISA) 2006, PISA 2006 results: Executive Summary. OECD, Paris.

Trends in International Mathematics and Science Study (TIMSS), 2007, TIMSS Results 2007. National Center for Educational Statistics (NCES), Department of Education, Washington, DC.

Wilkinson, I.R., Caldwell, B.J., Selleck, R.J.W., Harris, J & Dettman, P 2006, *A History of State Aid to Non-Government Schools in Australia.* Department of Education, Science and Training, Canberra.

Belarus

by Iryna Ulasiuk[1]

Overview

The 1990s were marked in Belarus by a recent dissolution of the Soviet system of education due to the collapse of the Soviet Union and a common understanding of the need to introduce changes into the national system of education in light of the changed status of a newly independent Belarusian state. Since then, Belarus has been engaged in reforming its educational system. The most significant changes comprised the transition to a 12-year schooling system in 1998, the introduction of the 10-point pupil assessment scale in 2002, the transition to the two-level higher education system in 2007 and the introduction of the competence-based approach in 2011.

It should be noted, however, that because of the high degree of centralisation and often the absence of a clear understanding of necessary changes in education, these reforms have not been implemented successfully.

That said, the education in Belarus is repeatedly referred to as an important resource and a condition for technological progress, social and economic development of the country.[22] The long-term objective is to create an educational system which meets the needs of individual person's development, society and the State, creating conditions for further development of the system and preparing new generations for life and work in a civil society with the sustainable market economy.[33]

The educational system of Belarus is comprised of preschool education; primary education followed by lower secondary, which together constitute the basic or compulsory cycle; upper secondary education, which may be academic, vocational or specialized (also known as technical or professional) education; and higher education.

---

1 Robert Schuman Center for Advanced Studies, European University Institute, Florence, Italy

2 Programme of Development of Secondary Education in the Republic of Belarus for the period of 2007-2016 (Decision of the Council of Ministers of the Republic of Belarus □ 725 of 31.05.2007), part 2.

3 National Strategy for Sustainable Socio-economic Development of Belarus up to 2020, Minsk, 2004

The entrance school age is six years old. The general education cycle is eleven years, of which nine, the basic education, are compulsory. Since 1 September 2002 schools have been using a five-day working week, and a ten-point grading system.

The Structure of Schooling

The educational system of Belarus is characterized by highly centralized mechanisms of governance and control of educational establishments at all levels by the State. The system of educational administration and control follows a strictly hierarchical model.

The Ministry of Education of Belarus has overall responsibility for the development of the education system. It is accountable for the proper functioning of the system of education, elaboration of educational standards, curricula and educational programmes, control of the quality of education, implementation of experimental and innovative programmes, implementation of the state policy concerning teaching staff and coordination of international cooperation in the sphere of education.

Most educational establishments, all other levels of educational administration and all support services (including research and training institutions) are subordinated to the Ministry.

For general educational establishments, curricula are passed by the Ministry of Education on a yearly basis regulating schooling in detail. Other major players in the governance of the education system at the national level are the Department of Quality Assurance, the National Institute of Education (pre-school and general school education), the Institute of Higher Education, the Institute of Professional Education(vocational education)and the Academy of Post-Diploma Education.
In a framework of a clear-cut of top-down model of decision making school administration has a three-tiered structure including the national, the regional and municipal levels.

Below the national level, each of the seven regions of Belarus has its own regional educational department. These departments design the programmes of development of pre-school and general secondary education, assess the human resources' needs, and organise retraining and in-service training programmes. Their departments are accountable to the Ministry of Education, whereas municipal educational departments report to regional educational departments.

The Legal Framework

The main legislative documents governing the field of education in Belarus include the Constitution, adopted in 1994 and amended by the Republican

Referendum in 1996, the recently adopted (2011) Education Code, laws and government decrees.

At the constitutional level, two specific provisions have direct reference to the right to education. Article 49 guarantees the actual right to receive education by everybody, free primary education as well as general and equal access to secondary education. It further specifies that secondary special and higher education shall be accessible to all according to the capabilities of each student. The right to choose the language of instruction and tuition, and thus be educated in one's mother tongue in accordance with the existing legislation is stipulated by Article 50 of the Constitution.

The Education Code (2011) is the principal legislative instrument which spells out the main features of the structure of education and educational policy in Belarus and is aimed at providing an overall education strategy regulating all levels of the education system. It deals with social relations in the field of education, defines the levels and types of education, its objectives, and also determines the role of teachers, their rights, functions and responsibilities.

The Code is based on the approved laws regulating the education system and it is not designed to introduce conceptual changes. The Code has thus incorporated the provisions of the main legal documents governing the field of education such as:

- Law on Education (1991, with amendments in 2002) which defined the general principles of the state policy in education and its principles, the system of education, requirements and relations between involved actors, including the rights and obligations of teachers;
- Law on General Secondary Education (2006, with amendments in 2009) which regulated the process of education at this level, established educational standards, clearly defined the types of secondary education institutions, requirements and tasks of teachers;
- Law on Special Education (2004) which determined the system of special education, requirements to teachers' qualifications and skills
- Law on Higher Education (2007) which introduced the two-level system of higher education: Specialist degree level (4-5 years) and Master's degree level (1-2 years), admission procedures, forms of education and types of higher education institutions.

According to the Code, the milestones of education policy are compulsory basic education and the transition towards compulsory general secondary education, continuity in education, priority of human values, human rights and the human character of education, which means free choice in teaching methods for trainers and educational institutions.

Educational legislation also includes Cabinet decisions and Presidential decrees.

The Ministry of Education also adopts many normative documents, decisions, instructions and recommendations.

Freedom to establish non-state schools

Non-state educational institutions in Belarus are subject to the regulation provided in the Code for Education. The Code refers to private education on several occasions. It clearly states in Article 19 (6) that in Belarus 'educational establishments can be both public and private'. The Code further stipulates that apart from the President, the government; government agencies etc. educational institutions can be founded by legal entities and private persons holding Belarusian citizenship (Article 21), excluding religious organisations. The Code for Education stresses that the state policy in the field of education is based on the secular character of education (Article 2(1.10)) . Thus, religious education is not taught as a school subject, either in State or private schools. The principle underlying the law is the separation of secular and religious education, and this disallows any form of religious or atheist education, in fact it bans even the use of school areas for Sunday religious schools. According to Article 2(4) only optional extra-curriculum courses can take place in schools - after school time, for those who have expressed the desire in writing to attend such courses. Thus, it basically means that religious organizations are not eligible to open a secondary school with a religious mission. Churches can have the so-called "Sunday schools" in parishes or ecclesiastical centres.

Financing of private educational institutions is done at the expense of the founders, the funds derived from income-generating activities, donations by legal entities, individual entrepreneurs and other sources that are not prohibited by law (Article 137 (2).)

In order to carry out their activities, non-state educational institutions must first obtain a special licence from the Ministry of Education (Article 109). A licence is issued in light of the curricula and syllabi proposed, the potential availability of the teaching staff and of technical and other supplies etc. Furthermore, non-state educational institutions in Belarus are obliged to follow educational standards developed by the Ministry for Education (Article 109). As Article 92 (3) of the Code stipulates these standards are applicable 'to all educational institutions, other organizations, individual entrepreneurs, which in accordance with the law are granted the right to carry out educational activities'. These standards concern requirements for the content of education, organization of educational process, the maximum workload for students and the level of knowledge the pupils should have on the completion of the studies in a given educational institution (Article 154).

The development of private education emerged in Belarus as one of many consequences of the breakup of the Soviet Union. However, the proportion of private general education institutions has remained quite low. Thus, in 1995 there were five non-state general education institutions, their number rose to nine in 1998[44] and remained the same at the beginning of 2009/2010 school year with the enrolment of 586 pupils.[55] The overall share of pupils in private schools is about 0.1 percent which is the lowest in all the CIS countries. The main reasons for this trend are the absence of government support both financially and politically.

Home schooling

In accordance with Article 158 (1.2) of the Code for Education the educational process in the framework of general secondary education can be organized in educational institutions, *at home* or in health care organizations.

Article 1 (16) of the Code defines homeschooling as the organisation of the educational process during which the curriculum of general secondary education is learnt by a pupil who temporarily or permanently can't attend educational institutions at his home rather than in other formal settings of public or private school.

Further, the Code on Education specifies that the acquisition of general secondary education at home is organized for students who for medical reasons, temporarily or permanently unable to attend an education institution (Article 160(1)). The educational process is then organized by a state educational institution located close to the home of a child or by an educational institution the child used to attend before medical complications preventing him from going to school emerged. (Article 160 (2)). The decision on homeschooling in the above mentioned situations is taken by the department of education of the local executive body on the submission of the application of the child (his representatives) and the certificate of the medical board.

A list of medical conditions required for the application for homeschooling was established by the Decree of the Ministry of Health of Belarus in May 2011.[66]

Thus, the State authorizes homeschooling for medical reasons. However, a closer look at the Code reveals that although not explicitly mentioned homeschooling is also possible on two other conditions:

- if a child is exceptionally talented, or
- if a child cannot attend school temporarily or permanently 'for good reasons'.

---

4 World Data on Education, Belarus 2006/07
5 World Data on Education, Belarus 2010/11
6 Resolution of the Ministry for Health of the Republic of Belarus of 26.05.2011, No. 44

In such cases a child is entitled to studying following an individual plan of studies (Article 167 (1). The right to studying in accordance with an individual educational plan is reiterated by Article 31 (1.5) which among the principal rights of the pupils names the right to study in accordance with an individual educational plan. In that case a child is registered with a school and is allowed to attend any additional classes he/she wishes. According to the Code, home education should meet the requirements of the curriculum for public schools and thus the home schooler is required to come to school for regular tests. Homeschooling can be an option for families living temporarily abroad, and allows for more travelling. Also young athletes, poets, artists and actors can be taught at home.

Several questions arise, however, as to the practical implementation of the forenamed right. Given the vagueness of the formulation of 'the good reasons' and 'exceptionally talented child', and that homeschooling is rather broadly categorized as a specific form of education, there are no guarantees that permission to educate a child at home will be provided in case of demand. In practice, such matters are left to the sole discretion of local educational authorities. Outside the outlined two reasons, which are not always easy to justify, a parent cannot just come to school and say that he/she opts for home schooling. As one of parents said: "In practice, to justify one's wish to follow an individual plan of studies is not always easy. It is good if the child has musical or other talent, or if the parents travel a lot. And if not? To openly claim that 'we just want to develop our child in a different way, we want to give the child more possibilities is just impossible ".[77]

Interestingly, commenting on the possibility of transfering a child from attending a school regularly to studying in accordance with the individual plan because of parents' religious beliefs, Chairman of the House of Representatives Standing Committee on Education, Culture, Science and the Scientific and Technical Progress, Vladimir Zdanowicz noted that 'Religious beliefs should not interfere with the integrity of the child's education. If a school allows parents to educate their children individually because of their religious beliefs, it is a violation of the law by the school administration. This should not happen. " [88]

Finally, while not restricted by law, education provided otherwise than through the schooling system is not very much socially acceptable, considered undesirable by school authorities and is virtually non-existent.

School choice not limited by family income

The Code for Education specifies in Article 2(1.4) that the state policy in education is based on the principle of ensuring equal access to education to all. Among the main directions of the state policy in education, the Code mentions in Article 2 (2.2

7 'Home Schooling: Rare but Precise' 16.12.2011, http://sb.by/post/124477/

8 'Belarusian Code for Education will not Introduce any Novelties with Regard to Home Schooling and Schooling in Accordance with Individual Plans' 19.10. 2010 ; http://news.open.by/country/38669

, 2.4) providing access to education and creating the conditions necessary to meet the needs of the individual to education. The right to education is guaranteed, among other things, through (Article 3 (7.6.)) the creation of conditions for education in accordance with national traditions, as well as individual needs and abilities of students and (Article 3 (7.7.)) through granting an opportunity to select an institution of education, specialization, forms of education, level of studying of academic subjects, educational areas, topics. Moreover, the state undertakes the responsibility to provide, albeit in vague termss, pupils living outside the area of the institution they are attending with accommodation on a campus for the period of studies. However, this refers primarily to several disadvantaged categories of people, although low level of income of parents does not give rise to the right to free accommodation. Moreover, this right can be used only when studying in a state educational institution (Article 44(3.5)), no reference is given whatsoever with regard to non-state educational institutions. Transportation to and from school (either by public transport or by school buses) is yet another right mentioned in the Code (Article 47). Free transportation is provided to pupils of basic secondary education living in rural areas. Interestingly, the Code mentions that such transportation is provided to children to go to kindergartens but only in case the place in an educational institution in the area the child lives in was not granted. (Article 47 (3))

School distinctiveness protected by law and policy

Distinctive character

The Belarusian education system has undergone substantive changes since the end of the Soviet era. Secondary education is now 11 years instead of 10 (twelfth grade education was an initiative tried and abandoned in the late 2000s), the grading system has changed to allow teachers a wider spectrum for evaluating student performance (a 10-point grading system replaced the 5-point system), and system wide testing has been introduced to assess student learning at the end of their basic education (9th grade) and upon completion of secondary education (11th grade). The format of university entrance exams has also been changed to a more objective system, which includes standardized testing rather than oral exams. These changes parallel a global shift toward standardization in education and a move away from Soviet-style testing and student performance assessment. Notwithstanding these changes they do not fundamentally affect the organization of schools or the centralization of education that has always characterized education in Belarus. The content of education and forms of control are based on the curricula developed according to state requirements, as well as regional and national peculiarities. The Communist indoctrination programs, which were a significant part of the curricula during the Soviet times, have been replaced by more diversified courses that allow room for alternative points of view and personal opinions, but the state control of education is strong and reveals itself in the requirements of the content of education, which are prescribed by the executive organs of the Republic. The state standards include an obligatory list of subjects and the minimum number of hours assigned for them. Thus the curriculum to be taught is developed by the Ministry of Education and is relevant for all the schools in the country. In some subjects there are several options for textbooks that the teachers may choose from, but for most subjects there are no choices for textbooks. Teachers however are able to supplement the textbooks with materials of their choosing, although the problem may arise because the state-mandated curriculum is so rigorous that there is little opportunity to add substantively to the required materials.

Until 2008, Belarusian schools were able to provide specialized subjects area courses to students adding to the mandated state curriculum. As a matter of fact, in addition to the traditional general education secondary schools, the 1990s saw the development of new types of institutions—gymnasiums and lyceums. Gymnasiums provide comprehensive humanistic education, often centered on the study of foreign languages. They are expected to have a highly qualified teaching staff, use innovative textbooks, and to have modern methods of teaching. Lyceums offer professionally oriented education and are usually affiliated with higher educational or research institutions. For example, students could attend a school with intensive English language study or one specializing in mathematics. Many cities and towns had schools that specialized in different subjects and disciplines and these schools were really important since they offered diverse educational opportunity. Under new education legislation, all schools must now provide the same educational opportunities. Specialized schools have been forced to redistribute or eliminate extra subject hours that had previously been allocated to specialized subjects. Despite that requirement, many schools have found ways to retain their legacy in education quality. Today, many schools continue to offer the same classes with the rigor of subject specialization as in the past, but it is now done as elective courses or during extracurricular hours, outside the curriculum.

Decisions about admitting pupils

Article 159 of the Code for Education deals in detail with the requirements for the admission of persons to institutions of general secondary education. Most generally, the admission of pupils is done upon the submission of a written request together with the required supporting documents by parents or caregivers of the child. The school selection and consequently the admission to a school is dependent on the residence of the applicant. Thus most applications will be sent by parents to a neighbourhood school. Article 159 of the Code foresees that pupils can be admitted to institutions of general secondary education on the basis of the results of admission tests, tests of aptitude, for example, tests of abilities to engage in an individual sport (in a particular field of art), and (or) taking into account health conditions, sports performance. The Code refers to several types of institutions of general secondary education to which entrance examinations are permitted and the selection process is dependent upon the results of such examinations. These are gymnasiums, state run boarding gymnasiums, gymnasiums - art schools.

The list, terms and order of the entrance examinations/tests are determined by the statute of the institution or its type.

Several exceptions are envisaged in the law with a view to enable disadvantaged children to receive positive discrimination. Thus, orphans and children left without parental care; children from large families and children living in rural communities with populations of less than 20,000 people are admitted to state-run boarding schools (gymnasiums) outside the competition provided that the mark they receive in the admission test is not lower than 6 (a ten-mark system is used in Belarusian schools with marks ranging from 1 to 10).

Decisions about staff

Articles 20 (1), 26(1.3) and 28 (1) of the Code on Education stipulate that educational institutions of different ownership are free to choose the teaching staff and the assignment of the teaching load within the limits envisaged by the law. Article 51 briefly touches upon the requirements towards the teaching staff, noting that several categories of persons are not allowed to conduct teaching activities, among them persons who have lost such a right, those having a criminal liability, etc.
While formally granted freedom to choose teachers who will be engaged into the teaching process, school directors rely almost exclusively upon formal qualifications of the applicants. This holds true both for state and private schools. Religious beliefs of the teachers do not act as an advantage in the selection process as religion is excluded from the national curriculum.
Article 53 of the Code of Education delineates a range of responsibilities that teachers have and in accordance with which they must carry out their activities. The failure to comply with these requirements might lead to firing a teacher. Among such responsibilities the Code lists professionalism, proper realization of educational programmes and programmes of student upbringing, and respect for pupils and other participants of the educational process. In point 3 of Article 53 the Code prohibits engagement of teachers in political actions which run counter to the Constitution and the laws of the republic. Involvement in such activities will have adverse effect in the decision of hiring or not hiring a teacher.

Accountability for school quality

In compliance with Article 91 of the Code on Education, among the main requirements for the organisation of the educational process are:

- the provision of good-quality education
- competency-based approach

- protection of the students' health
- compliance with the established duration of the scholastic year, school holidays, periods and forms of the attestation of school children

In accordance with a Programme of the Republican Monitoring of the Quality of Secondary Education in 2009-2014, several aspects of the teaching/learning process are the focus of attention of the monitoring bodies. First and foremost is the level of the knowledge acquired by school children in various subjects and their readiness for the final exams which are also the entrance exams to higher educational institutions. Since one of the primary goals of the school education is the development of the talents and special gifts of students, schools are monitored from the point of view of the conditions they provide in order to develop creative abilities of the students (effectiveness of the optional classes, tutorials, etc. offered to talented students is assessed). Other factors taken into consideration are didactic (distribution of class hours on a studied topic, discrepancies in the curricula and requirements of the entrance exams, the quality of the school books etc.), methodological (level of the methodological qualifications of the teachers, etc). To what extent the school complies with the state standards of education and curricula developed by the Ministry of Education) is yet another important criterion is the evaluating school performance. Schools are also monitored from the point of view of the teaching staff they employ, their level of education, qualification categories acquired by the teachers, timely provision of teacher training and the rate at which the teaching staff changes. Protection of students' health is yet another burning issue the Belarusian educational system is confronted with in view of the negative consequences the Chernobyl disaster had on the health of the Belarusian population generally and on the health of the young Belarusians. Thus, monitoring is done with regard to the compliance with a five-day learning week, the observance of the minimum and maximum volume of the work load of the students in accordance with the requirements of the educational standard of the secondary education; school meals; organisation of the physical training and promotion of a healthy standard of living.
The state bodies are directly appointed by and accountable to the President of Belarus (Article 124(2)) which is in itself yet another indicator of a tight oversight of the system by the state characteristic of the functioning of the system of education.

Teaching of values

Article 2 of the Education Code prescribes, among other principles, the following ones upon which the state policy in education is based: the priority of human values, human rights, humanistic nature of education, secular character of education. It further states that state policy in education aims at ensuring that educational institutions promote the formation of students' spiritual and moral values, develop a conscious attitude towards concepts of citizenship, patriotism, responsibility and hard work. The main components of teaching of values comprise (Article 18 (5) of the Education Code): civic and patriotic education, ideological education, aimed at developing students' knowledge of the ideology practiced by the Belarusian State. As mentioned in various parts of the report, the educational system in Belarus is extremely centralized and is characterised by strict administrative and ideological control by the state. School is also seen as one of the most important propaganda venues. Non-state actors in education (private schools, independent universities, educational NGOs, business education) are comparatively small in number, and are not influential. **http://www.bti-project.org/country-reports/pse/blr/** Academic freedom is not a given thing in Belarus and it comes as no surprise that the recent years have witnessed the return to classrooms of such activity as 'political information' (a feature of the Soviet-time school) used primarily to 'brain-wash' students and 'enlighten' them on the 'positive' developments in the Belarusian state. That is why the free-thinking private European Humanities University in Minsk became too dangerous for those in power in Belarus and was forced into exile. It is the only university in the history of Belarus to retain real autonomy, despite various forms of pressure by the authorities and one of the few, if not the only University in Europe, in exile.

References

Borisova, G., Kuusela, T., 2009, Review of Education Sector Developments in Belarus, ETF, available at: http://nwaip.ru/doc/library/1.Review%20of%20education%20sector%20development%20in%20Belarus.pdf

Belarus: national report. 48th session of the International Conference on Education, ICE: "Inclusive Education:
The Way of the Future", Geneva, 25-28 November 2008
Minsk, Ministry of Education, 2008

Challenges of curriculum development in the XXI century: perspectives from Belarus, Moldova, Russia, and Ukraine; final report, 2004

Code for Education of the Republic of Belarus of 13 January 2011 No.243-3
Education for Some More than Others? UNICEF REGIONAL OFFICE FOR CEE/CIS 2007

Liseychikov, O.A., Teacher design course content and the basic plan for a 12-year school in different levels of training, 2001

Order of the Ministry of Education of the Republic of Belarus of 29.05.2009 No.674 'Criteria of Assessment of the Scholastic Activity of School Children in Secondary School Institutions'

Programme of Development of Secondary Education in the Republic of

Belarus for the period of 2007-2016 (Decision of the Council of Ministers of the Republic of Belarus № 725 of 31.05.2007)

World Data on Education, Belarus, UNESCO, 2010/11, seventh edition

Regional Workshop on Challenges of Curriculum Development in the XXI Century: Perspectives from Belarus, Moldova, Russia, and Ukraine; Minsk, Belarus; 2003

Vetokhin, S.S., Education in Belarus: national report of the Republic of Belarus, International Conference on Education; 47th; Geneva; 2004, UNESCO
UIS Statistics in Brief. Education (all levels) profile – Belarus, UNESCO, 2011
World Data on Education, Belarus, UNESCO, 2006/07, sixth edition

Brazil

by Nina Ranieri[1]

Overview

Brazil is one of the most complex countries with respect to education policies and regulations. The biggest country in Latin America, it has a very large population (approximately 190 million inhabitants in 2010) and strong economic differences among states and regions, reflected also in the disparities and inequalities of the educational systems, as a result of a combination of extreme poverty and low education levels, among other factors. Although the processes of social reform in Brazil - launched by the Federal Constitution of 1988 – are showing significant progress when compared to previous periods and especially in the educational area, the reforms are still incomplete and there is ample scope for improvement in efficiency and equity.

The positive changes were promoted by the Constitution of 1988 under four basic conditions: the strengthening and universalization of social rights; the decentralization of competences; the new parameters for resource allocation and the redefinition of public-private relations with regard to funding and providing goods and social services. In education, the rationale of this model is the allocation of specific and concurrent responsibilities to each level of government (local, regional and federal), from whom the Constitution stipulates mandatory minimum revenue investments. Municipalities are responsible for the lower levels of basic education (nurseries, kindergartens and fundamental schooling, from 0 to 10 years old), the States for the intermediate and higher levels of basic education (from 11 to 17 years old), and the Federal government for higher education as well as offering technical and financial support to all entities that need it. The financial system through which education is funded is regulated by an excellent legal system to ensure regular flows of public money. As such, considerable progress has been reached in the last twenty years. The educational levels of the population, in general, and of children in particular, have been increasing: during this period, Brazil has achieved some encouraging results, including almost full enrollment in fundamental education and less disparity between rural and urban areas in accessing education, though, apparently, with some sacrifice of quality for quantity.

---

1 University of São Paulo Law School, Coordinator of the UNESCO Right to Education Chair, Vice-President of the São Paulo State Education Council

According to official Brazilian data, in 2010 there were around 195,000 elementary schools, with approximately 51,500,000 enrolled students of whom 85.4% were in public schools and 14.6% in private schools. Furthermore, an analysis promoted by UNESCO between 2005 and 2007 – *A view inside primary schools* – demonstrates that one out of two students is enrolled in schools where most students, or all, come from families where parents had not completed primary education. Other initiatives, such as the quantitative expansion of technical courses in the upper educational levels through student scholarships and tax exemptions in benefit of education expenditures have also contributed to promoting equity of access and staying in school. The education policies in this period have particular relevance when considering the educational delay in Brazil, notably of public education, in comparison to other Latin America countries such as Argentina and Uruguay which had already universalized fundamental education at the beginning of the 20th century.

The results of the recent education policies are also remarkable when we take into account that in 1982 only 51% of the pupils entered public schools (in contrast to 87% of those entering private schools) at the prescribed age of seven,[2] and that in the early 1990s, only 36 % of the pupils completed the former eight grades of elementary schooling, while in the Northeast the rate was only 20%, with only 3% doing so without repeating a grade.[3] The dropout rate between third and fourth grade was 10% in 1997 and the primary schooling completion rate was 70% for the period of 1995-2001. Repeating grades has been a major issue and cost factor, while the fact that many rural schools offer only two grades makes it inevitable that many pupils do not have a realistic opportunity to complete elementary schooling, much less go on to secondary school.[4] A study in the 1980s of schools in high-poverty areas found that

> the state schools meet the standards of a minimally decent school in a poor country, with most of the essential ingredients necessary for basic operations. . . . The municipal schools hardly qualified as schools.[5]

The challenge for the first decades of the 21st Century is to assure quality in education to all, which is no simple task, considering the extreme heterogeneity and complexity of the Brazilian education system as well as its bureaucratic characteristics.

2 Mello e Souza and Valle Silva, 375

3 Plank, Amaral Sobrinho, and Ressurreição Xavier, 24

4 Gomes-Neto and Hanushek, 435

5 Maura Castro, Pinto Guimarães, Araújo e Oliveira and Costa Ribeiro, 498a

The Structure of Schooling

The Brazilian schooling system is decentralized and quite complex at each level of activity. As a Federal State, the educational system comprises all 26 states and 5,561 municipal systems, besides those of the Federal government and of the Federal District; thus the educational systems in the country could reach the amazing number of 5.589 units. All the federal entities are entitled to legislate for their own education systems, under the Federal Constitution, the National Education Law – NEL[6] and the National Education Plan - NED[7] guidelines; as such, the education systems, both in private and public schools, have the autonomy to decide how to provide education in response to local needs and to provide the right services for each community (albeit this 'autonomy' is severely limited in the case of public schools because of lack of infra-structure and human resources). Nevertheless, the NEL imposes a minimum standard to be upheld all over the country, which includes not only a basic national syllabus at each level of education (fundamental and secondary), but also standards for teacher education, since the Constitution demands a guarantee of standards of quality.

The levels of Brazilian schooling are structured as follows: basic education, with four levels: nurseries (zero to three years old), pre-school (three to five years old), fundamental education (from six to 14 years old) and secondary education (from 15 to 17 years old). Basic education is compulsory and free (except for nurseries) and must be accessible to all, at any age.

Higher education (undergraduate and graduate programs) should become equally accessible to all, based on each one's capacity, by all suitable means and especially by the progressive implementation of free lower education.

Legal Framework

The right to education is inserted in the Federal Constitution as a social and an individual right.[8] In this light, education is a duty of the State and will be provided by all the federate entities, as set forth in Article 205:

> Education, which is the right of all and duty of the State and of the family, shall be promoted and fostered with the cooperation of society, with a view to the full development of the person, his preparation to exercise citizenship and his qualification for work.

The universalization of access to basic education, based on the fundamental

---

6 Law 9394/1996
7 Law 10.172/01
8 Federal Constitution, Articles 6 and 205

principles of non-discrimination and equality of educational opportunities, also guaranteed by the Constitution,[9] is also extended to the minorities under special conditions. In relation to children and adolescents, the right to education has absolute priority;[10] as such, access to free and compulsory education is seen as a subjective right,[11] the universalization of which and the responsibility of the public authorities ensured in case of not providing or offering it irregularly.[12]

The Brazilian educational legal framework is a consequence of these constitutional norms and principles, to which the State Constitutions, State laws, municipal laws and regulations are subject. Overall guidelines are determined at the national level under the NEL[13] and the NEP.[14] Many other federal laws give substance to the set of provisions relating to the enforcement of the right to education, namely: (a) the Child and Adolescent Statute – ECA,[15] and procedural laws such as (b) the Civil Action Law,[16] (c) the Administrative Probity Law,[17] (d) the administrative liability laws,[18] in addition to the procedural rules established by the Civil Procedures Code, the Writ of Mandamus and the Popular Action. This framework sees education as an individual and a social right.

In Brazil, over the last 100 years, five Constitutions (1891, 1934, 1946, 1967 and 1988) and at least six education reforms have faced educational challenges in the fields of equity, finance, access and quality. This legislation, until the Federal Constitution of 1988, is mostly characterized by the absence of educational policies and planning, by the adoption of measures in response to immediate conditions, and by normative over-detailing. Besides, during the first centuries, from Colony to Republic, education was not valued as an individual right, but marked by the dominant traits of our Catholic, agricultural, and slavery-based culture. Considered a regal right (*jus regio*), education was centralized by the Crown, which granted the authorization to teach and the appointments of professors, but kept then in penury. A study notes that throughout the 19th century, and throughout the country, education no longer met the needs of instruction even for the restricted groups of the dominant classes. The Country became independent with virtually the entire population illiterate. Authority under the Empire, between independence from Portugal in 1822 to the inauguration of the Republic in 1889, was relatively centralized, but the First Republic (1889/1930) developed a federal structure with significant powers devolved to the states. This was not maintained,

9 *Ibid.*, Article 206, I
10 *Ibid.*, Article 227
11 *Ibid.*, Article 208, § 1
12 *Ibid.*, Article 208, §2
13 Law 9394/1996
14 Law no. 10.172/01
15 Law 8.069/1990
16 Law No. 7,347 of 24 July 1985
17 Law No. 8,429 of 11 June 1992
18 Law No. 1,079 of 10 April 1950, and Decree-Law No. 201, 27 February 1967

however, in the context of the Vargas dictatorship (1930–1934, 1937–1945) which established a centralized administrative structure, continued and intensified by the military regimes (1964–1985).

On the other hand, the Constitution of 1934 recognizes education as a social right and a duty of the State, guaranteed to all, as a result of the discussions and educational initiatives promoted in previous years by Member States (notably in São Paulo, with Sampaio Doria; Lourenço Filho in Ceará; Anísio Teixeira in Bahia and Fernando de Azevedo in the Federal District, among others, who were part of the reform group called *Pioneiros da Educação Nova),* as did the democratic Constitution of 1946. The Federal Constitution of 1946 adopted numerous measures to expand access to primary education and a federalist organization of education systems, this time with greater freedom of organization for the Member States, under supplementary activities of the Federal government to the extent of local and regional needs.[19]

After 1964, under the military regime, the imposition of authoritarianism sacrificed civil and political rights, but expanded social rights, which seems to prove that this kind of political regime sought to compensate the lack of political rights with social paternalism. Between the Constitution of 1967 and the Constitution of 1988, one of the key legal education provisions was the first National Education Law,[20] enacted in 1961, which gave the country common guidelines.

As already mentioned, the Constitution of 1988 was a step forward in the field of education due to the strengthening and the universalization of social rights, the decentralization of competences and the new parameters for resource allocation. If at the outset, decentralization did not diminish rooted regional differences and disparities, it led the federal government to understand that the educational system required reform at a national level. The government started to work on new guidelines for education in 1988, but it was only in 1996 that a consensus was reached and the National Education Law – NEL[21] was approved, under the banner of decentralizing education and the flexibility of the educational process.

The NEL enactment occurred within the context of a strong international movement for education reform focusing urgently on education outcomes. After the 1990 Conference on Education for All, held in Thailand and promoted by many international organizations, nine countries – including Brazil – with weak education systems started the E-9 group, focused on designing a ten-year plan to achieve improvement in education. This international movement was another important impetus for reform and for a National Education Plan - NEP, launched by Law no. 10,172/ 2001 with a program covering 10 years.

19 Federal Constitution of 1946, Articles 170 and 171

20 Law no. 4024

21 Law no. 9.394/1996, the so called *Lei de Diretrizes e Bases da Educação* – LDB

The NEP, among other provisions, establishes the distribution policy of public resources for mandatory schooling and determines cooperation between the Federal entities for the development of education. However, despite the guidelines established by the Plan, which aim at a coherent and effective public policy all over the country, they do not guarantee solutions to recurrent educational problems, such as the improvement of the quality of education, which implies technological and economic development. What's more, as the Constitution considers the coordination of educational policies mandatory, this gives new leverage to the National Plan as long as the conditions of its implementation are guaranteed by the State. Now there is a new National Plan of Education for the next 10 years to be discussed by the National Congress, and as of the enactment of Law 10,172, in the next few years, all states and municipalities will have to develop their own new plans for education with guidelines, objectives and evaluation criteria, according to the national plan and to the unique characteristics of the different regional or local situations, taking into account cultural and religious differences and socio-economic disparities.

The Federal Constitution, the NEL and the NEP, given the heterogeneity of the country, give special attention also to other forms of education such as special education, distance education and indigenous education by providing laws and procedures recognizing special forms of instruction within the framework of the national education objectives and evaluation criteria.

Financial system

Public education is funded by a complex fiscal system which combines federal, state and municipal tax revenues in a redistributive fund (Fundeb). As provided by Article 212 of the Federal Constitution, the Federal government shall apply no less than 18%, and the States, the Federal District, and the Municipalities, at least 25% of the tax revenues in education, annually. These percentages are mandatory and when not applied accordingly, interference from the federal government in the states, and likewise the states in the municipalities, is permitted by the Constitution. This is one of the rare situations where the federal autonomy of each entity can be breached.

Education and health are the only public social areas which are specifically treated by binding resources to tax revenue.[22] Article 167, of the Federal Constitution clearly makes an exception of the prevailing prohibition of binding tax revenues to a public agency, fund or expense. Article 218 also provides that the States and the Federal District may allocate a share of their budgetary revenues to public entities which foster scientific and technological education and research.

22 Federal Constitution, Articles 167, IV and 218, paragraph 5

The FUNDEB - Fund for Maintenance and Development of Basic Education – is a temporary fund for the maintenance and development of education with a redistributive objective. The financial mechanism used in FUNDEB obliged the federal government, the states and the municipalities to invest 60% of the resources allocated by the Constitution - the federal government 18% and the states and municipalities 25% of tax revenues - to basic education, through the fund. The resources are distributed according to the number of students enrolled annually in the public schools maintained by each governmental entity, based on a minimum value per student established by the federal government. The federal government is obliged to supplement the fund whenever, in each state and in the Federal District, the nationally set minimum value per student is not reached by the responsible government entities. The distribution of the resources will also prioritize enrolments from the 1st to the 9th grade of basic schooling. The core of the idea of establishing a single educational fund was to rationalize the allocation of public educational resources, as well as to distribute the responsibilities and resources among the states and the municipalities, as stated in Article 211 of the Constitution.

The FUNDEB was created in 2006[23] to replace the FUNDEF - Fund for the Maintenance and Development of Fundamental Education, originally aimed solely at fundamental education.[24] The new educational fund – FUNDEB – is foreseen to last fourteen years, when the target of 50 million students enrolled in basic education is achieved; and does not disoblige the states, the Federal District and the municipalities from applying the remaining 40% of the stipulated percentage in Article 212, of the Federal Constitution.

The former FUNDEF experience deserves some consideration. Despite the criticism that the impact of FUNDEF was less than expected, due to difficulties and limitations arising both from its conception and structure, as well as more general circumstances inherent in the social and political context of Brazil, FUNDEF achieved many of its goals. There was a significant increase in the total number of enrolled pupils: according to the Brazilian Institute of Geography and Statistics (IBGE), between 1995 and 2005 the percentage of children between the ages of seven to 14 not at school decreased from 9.8% to 2.6%; from the ages of 15 to 17, the decrease was from 33.4% to 18%. It also had an important impact on basic education, principally by changing the educational level of teachers, increasing the school periods, the number of teachers, as well as reducing the number of students falling behind. FUNDEF also prioritized expenditures on teachers and students instead of expenditure on infrastructure, and has especially made it possible for the areas lagging behind the rest of the country, like the North East and the cities with a low Life Condition Index – ICV. FUNDEF was an important and successful case of decentralizing fiscal resources in a country with

[23] Constitutional Amendment 53, of 20 December 2006
[24] Constitutional Amendment 14, of 12 September 1996

a long tradition of centralized federalism. In 2009, the national expenditure on education reached 4.3% of the GDP, which corresponds approximately to US$ 1,700 per student in public systems annually.

Private schools can also receive public resources,[25] if they are non-profit-making and reinvest their financial surplus in education only; it is indifferent for the purpose of receiving public funds whether they are religious, communal or philanthropic schools. The NEA[26] adds other conditions for public funding of private schools: in case of closure, the funds have to be reverted to other non-profit-making religious, communal or philanthropic schools or the government. The Public Ministry controls the allocation and expenditure of these resources in the schools.

Freedom to Establish Non-state Schools

Under the Federal Constitution of 1988 non-state schools have ample freedom to be established. This is a result of the principle of freedom of teaching, which implies the freedom of learning, researching and expressing opinion, as well as a pluralism of ideas and of pedagogical ideas and conceptions. As such, the coexistence of public and private schools are guaranteed in article 206. Furthermore, article 170 ensures the free exercise of any economic activity to everyone, regardless of authorization from government agencies, except in the cases set forth by law; private education is one of these cases as set in article 209:

> teaching is open to private enterprise, provided that the following conditions are met: I - compliance with the general rules of national education; II - authorization and evaluation of quality by the Government.

This means that powers are constitutionally imparted to the federal government and the states to control non-public education through National and State Boards of Education, respectively, as set by the NEL.[27] According to these provisions, private schools can be opened in any state and municipality, subject to compliance not only with national guidelines but also with state and municipal rules regarding education and schooling.

The NEL classifies non-State schools as: (a) private schools owned and operated by one or more private persons, under civil law; (b) private schools owned by a community, including nonprofit cooperatives that include community representatives on their boards; (c) private religious schools; (d) philanthropic schools.

---

25 Federal Constitution, Article 213

26 NEA, Article 77

27 NEL, Articles 9 and 10

As already mentioned, private education does not receive public funds directly but is sustained by private contributions and student fees, together with various tax advantages and government scholarships for pupils from low-income families. Students may receive scholarships for private school tuition from a variety of public sources at both state and federal levels, under Article 213 of the Federal Constitution.

Although not usually funded directly by government, private schools are extensively regulated, especially with regard to the tuition they charge parents: "approximately 240 different regulations concerning school tuitions were introduced in Brazil between 1986 and 1990 ".[28] A study conducted by Brazilian researchers in the late 1980s compared the regulatory structure imposed upon public schools with that upon a group of private schools operated by an organization providing schooling under contract with large employers for the children of their employees, including a broad spectrum of social class. In the public schools, they found,

> there is virtually nothing to be managed. . . . The state or the municipality hires teachers, and the principal has no authority in these matters. . . . The most important function of principals seems to be managing the battalion of janitors jammed on the payroll of what are generally decrepit schools. . . . In the [corporate] schools, by contrast, the principal is accountable to the sponsoring corporation [which] receives pressure from the employees to provide a decent school. Principals report that this pressure comes particularly from the more highly qualified workers, for whom a good school is part of their contractual arrangements. . . . In short, the appearance, inputs and patterns of management of the [corporate] schools are comparable to those of the typical private elite schools.

Teacher salaries in these schools are at least three times as high as those of teachers in public schools, in exchange for which they offer significantly more hours of instruction to their pupils; the researchers report that public school teachers average about ten hours of instruction a week.[29] This scenario hasn't changed very much in the last twenty years: the Brazilian government tends to be bureaucratic and regulates education excessively, in spite of the decentralization and flexibility guaranteed by the NEL.

That's why in the early 1990s, law suits concerning the State control of schools fees prevailed in the Brazilian Supreme Court – STF. The legal control of the augmentation of school fees was established by Law No. 8,039/90, under article 173, § 4 of the Federal Constitution which establishes that

---

28 James, Primo Braga, and Afonso de Andre, 485

29 Maura Castro, Pinto Guimarães, Araujo e Oliveira and Costa Ribeiro, 502-505

the law shall repress the abuse of economic power that aims at the domination of markets, the elimination of competition and the arbitrary increase of profits.

In the vast majority of cases, the STF ruled in favor of State control of private school fees, establishing jurisprudence to safeguard the right to education from economic abuses on the part of private initiative.

Home Schooling

Home schooling is not regulated by law in Brazil. Nevertheless, as ruled by the Federal Courts, home schooling is not allowed as a legal consequence of compulsory attendance of basic education. The constitutional fundaments of this jurisprudence reside basically in the national effort to eradicate illiteracy and to reduce school absenteeism, with the resulting benefits of removing children and teenagers from the streets, promoting awareness and preventing the exploitation of children, among others. Since the emergence of the ECA[30] penalties are imposed on parents and the Penal Code defines "stopping to provide primary education without a reason for a school-age child" as a crime.

In the most significant case involving home schooling,[31] the Superior Court of Justice – STJ examined various issues related to fundamental rights, namely: the right to education, the rights of the family, the rights of children and adolescents, the duty of the State and the family in providing education and its relationship with the freedom of learning, teaching, researching and expressing opinions; the prevalence of parental choice of education offered to children; the criminal repercussions of non-school enrollment. But what was at stake, fundamentally, was the primacy of the family *status*, as the base of society,[32] *vis à vis* the constitutional obligation of providing care in elementary school institutions.

The grounds for the decision of the STJ focused basically on three main aspects: a) school attendance as a right of the child laid down in the Constitution and regulated by the NEL and by the ECA; this regulation cannot be challenged by the philosophical beliefs of parents. b) Though recognizing the ability of parents to provide good education, it is not sufficient grounds to deprive the child of the right to school life. c) The judiciary system cannot neglect the legal system in favor of the philosophical and political convictions of parents. In this light, the Courts stated that the link between individual and collective participation in social life and in the public space require the formal transmission of a set of values and democratic principles to each generation. Therefore, in the Brazilian legal system, the freedom of learning is related to the choice between private or public school, pedagogical method of formal education and possible religious

30 Law No. 8,096/90
31 Writ of Mandamus no. 7.407 – DF
32 Article 226

orientation, among other possible options, but not between schooling and home education.

School Choice Not Limited by Family Income

Under article 206 of the Federal Constitution, basic and higher education are free in public schools and universities (as seen above, basic education includes nurseries, pre-schools, fundamental education and secondary education).

The Federal Constitution also entitles all children in fundamental school (six to 14 years), and at no cost to their parents, to be assisted by means of complementary programs providing school material, food and health care; government authorities and school officials can't refuse to provide these services, under the penalty of law.[33]

On the other hand, because of the cost of private education, private schools are not accessible to all families; in general, attendance is correlated with social class. This makes it impossible to talk about equity in education respecting the values of each family. Choice is limited by family income at fundamental and secondary level schools, where only the more prosperous classes can afford private education.

In Brazil, the debate is not on school choice but it is about education choice: the opportunity to receive an education rather than the opportunity to choose among the schools in which such education is provided. The priorities of the NEP are to guarantee access to education for all and to promote strategies to increase the completion rate at all levels of education, especially at the secondary levels, where the completion rate reached 34% in terms of age/grade distortion in 2009.

School Distinctiveness Protected by Law and Policy

The NEL is the law which governs education autonomy and school distinctiveness. Each school is free to decide for itself regarding programs and pedagogical approaches as well as being independent in the administration and management of its finances and resources. Each school has to respond to public administration regarding programs and student performance and to build programs according to national plans, state rules and municipal directives, in relation to the teaching level. This is true both for public and private schools, the only difference being that public funds are provided only to public schools, while private schools, under the Constitution, can not access public funds. On the other hand, the NEL allows the organization of courses or experimental education institutions, under its provisions,[34] which means that there is room for innovation and distinctiveness.

---

33 Federal Constitution, Article 208

34 NEL, Article 81

Distinctive Character

One important aspect of the Brazilian education system concerns the protection of different cultural expressions, i.e., popular, Indian, and Afro-Brazilian, as well as those of other groups participating in the nation building process. In this light, article 231 guarantees the Indians their social organization, customs, languages, creeds and traditions, as well as their original rights to the lands they traditionally occupy. Concerning linguistic diversity and the fundamental role that education plays in the protection and promotion of cultural expressions, Article 78 of the NEL was also designed to ensure bilingual education to the Indians, aiming at strengthening the cultural content and the mother tongue of each Indian community. Special attention is to be given to creating and implementing schooling systems for the indigenous community, and to create special books and didactic materials to sustain school programs consistent with the cultural framework and values of the indigenous community itself. The government also created special criteria for indigenous teaching and special evaluation criteria.

This is the most striking example of how the Brazilian government is trying to build a flexible system, under the control of the central government, respecting the autonomy of each state and giving attention to the local level by leaving significant decisions up to municipalities and schools. Indigenous education has always presented a problem for the Brazilian government, given the structure of indigenous communities and the cultural differences from the other ethnic groups in the country. The NEL also states that History and Afro-Brazilian Culture have to be part of the basic education curricula, as well as the teaching of the History of Africa and the Africans, the struggle of the Black people in Brazil, the Black Brazilian culture, and the role of the Black people in the construction of the Brazilian society.

Another distinctive character of Brazilian education system is the role of the Public Ministry in protecting and promoting the right to education. The Public Ministry is an independent governmental institution, both in federal and state spheres, whose function is the protection of the rule of law, the democratic regime, the public interests and fundamental rights.[35] Its members – the public prosecutors – represent society against the Federal government, States and Municipalities demanding the implementation of the laws and international treaties ratified by the country,[36] acting on behalf of an indefinite number of citizens whose rights – including the right to education, naturally - have been or could be jeopardized. In this complex context of judicial activities it is important to remember that the prosecutors do not protect individual rights directly but collectively, thus they usually deal with the representatives of the civil society such as union leaders, community leaders, NGOs, the media etc. In the fledgling Brazilian democracy

[35] CF, Article 127

[36] CF, Articles 127 e 129, III

– established in 1988 under the Federal Constitution - the role of the Public Ministry is crucial in all spheres that affect society, including education and the rights of disabled people.

Decisions about Admitting Pupils

Admission is free for basic education in public schools but, of course, this is subject to the size of the school and its capacity to serve a certain number of students. In this matter, a problem that education authorities have been recently facing is the legal obligation to enroll the child in the closest school to his home. This obligation comprises special education and nurseries, although this level is not legally classified as compulsory education.

Concerning special education, disabled students are entitled to the following basic rights: (i) free and inclusive public education, preferably in the regular education system, private and public;[37] (ii) a guarantee of equal conditions of access and permanence in school, giving an adequate opportunity for each student, depending on their singular needs;[38] (iii) priority in the fulfillment of the right to education by the government authorities;[39] (iv) to be protected from all forms of negligence, discrimination, exploitation, violence, cruelty and oppression.[40]

Regarding private schools, decisions about admitting pupils are made by each school autonomously and with independent criteria, under the constitutional and legal framework, and, of course, depend upon the family income and the shared values of the family and school. Recently Courts have decided that a student cannot be dismissed for not paying the school fee.

Decisions about Staff

Teacher training and the quality of teaching are among the most discussed issues in Brazil education policies. Teacher training varies according to the level of education: for lower education, a higher education degree is required; for higher education a post-graduate degree is necessary. A B.A. or post-graduate degree in Pedagogy is required for the administration, planning, inspection, supervision and pedagogical counseling for primary education. Among the innovations introduced by the NEL, Education Colleges (called *institutos superiores de educação*) were created to prepare teachers for fundamental and secondary education, only.[41] More specifically, the Brazilian legislation accepts the following degrees in the exercise of teaching: degrees in Religious Science; Pedagogy; History,

---

37 CF, Article 205
38 CF, Article 206, I
39 CF, Article 227
40 CF, Article 227
41 NEL, Article 63

Philosophy, Social Sciences, and Psychology; diploma in Education, issued by the *institutos superiores de educação*. There are special categories of teachers such as the indigenous group teacher, and special education teachers. They have to qualify by following special courses and training before being admitted to teach.

The problem is that it is very difficult to implement these teachers' requirements in the interior and poorer regions of the country, especially at the first levels of education, and guarantee, at the same time, quality of education. The NEL tried to enforce these measures in the so called Decade of Education (1997/2007), the purpose of which was to only admit teachers with higher education or with supervised teacher training.[42] This last requirement can substitute, in extraordinary circumstances and taking into consideration the enormous disparities that exist in a huge country like Brazil, the requirement of higher education for teaching in primary schools, as long as the teacher has had teacher education at secondary school level.[43]

Access to the public teaching career is provide by each federal entity, by public competition through which only successful candidates will be admitted to become teachers or professors in the grade they have competed for. Teachers and professors come under public administration and are managed by the state government or the municipal government according to the school grade they teach in. Private schools have independent recruitment procedures and criteria, linked of course to the values or mission of the school.

Accountability for School Quality

Quality is still, together with equity and evaluation, one of the aspects of the Brazilian education policy framework most under debate. Before the 1990s, Brazil was far from establishing a national evaluation system, because of the heterogeneity of the different educational views in the country and the absolute lack of control of the differences among municipalities and states. There were at least three factors: the first was the autonomy of states and municipalities in education, established by the 1988 Constitution; the second was the differences in culture and socio-economic structure among regions, the third was the role of the central government that, for primary and secondary education, was only supplementary, providing financial and technical assistance if required.

The decision to reform the education system and provide a new policy framework was strictly related to the role of the central government, designated by the Constitution of 1988 to head the process by providing national guidelines and by implementing a quality control system (indeed, a further role of the federal government is to take responsibility for evaluation and quality control of the system

42 *Ibid.*, Article 87

43 *Curso Normal*, cf. Article 62

and keep track of the national situation by providing statistics and information). The Government created the National Institute for Education Studies and Research (*INEP Instituto National de Estudos e Pesquisas Educacionais*), in charge of all education statistics and evaluation at the national level. Once a year, INEP carries out a census of fundamental and secondary education, requiring the participation of all public and private schools in the country. The census allows the government to better implement national strategies and monitor the changes and demands in the country. In addition, the census is the basis for the distribution of public funds by the FUNDEB.

Although the work carried out by INEP is absolutely important and strategic for the country, Brazil still faces obstacles in reaching high quality standards in all the country. Contributing to that is the weakness of teacher education and training and the socio-economic problems faced in many regions of the country. To identify areas in which quality can be improved Brazil is investing a lot in evaluation and information flows.

Concerning basic education, the most important assessment tool is the SAEB - National System of Evaluating Basic Education (*Sistema Nacional de Avaliação da Educação Básica*). Administered by the Ministry of Education - MEC, it is given to students from public and private schools in the country, in rural and urban areas, enrolled in basic education from the 1st to the 8th level of fundamental schooling and also in the 3rd year of high school. For students of the 1st to 3rd grades of fundamental education, the test is called *Prova Brasil*; the students are selected randomly and tested on Portuguese and Mathematics. The results of the SAEB compose the IDEB – Development Index of Basic Education, a tool to define public polices nationwide. On a scale of 0 to 10, the Ministry of Education has established an average grade of 6, to be achieved, nationwide, by 2021; this grade was defined based on the proficiency average of the developed countries of OECD. In 2009, the IDEB results show that the SAEB index had increased 8.5%, from the 1st to 4th grade: it was 175.8 in 2007 and 184.3 in 2009. In mathematics, the grade rose 10.8% on average. These results are very important considering their impact on the following school years.

Teaching of Values

The independence given to schools and their autonomy in designing programs and a distinctive pedagogical approach leaves the door open to freedom of teaching values. Under the Federal Constitution, the teaching of religion is optional and shall be offered during the regular school hours of public fundamental schools.[44] As such, the NEL states that religion is considered part of the school curriculum but is not compulsory and has to take religious differences into account and

44 Federal Constitution, Article 210

avoid proselytism.[45] Municipalities and states, after promoting hearings with the civil society, have the responsibility of deciding on the religious content and establishing criteria for the accreditation of teachers and professors.

The regulation of religious education in Brazil presents peculiarities compared to other disciplines of the syllabus. Firstly, it is the only case of exemption from federal jurisdiction in establishing national guidelines and provides differentiated regulations in states and municipalities. Secondly, though the teaching of religion is part of the content of the right to education as much as is Portuguese or mathematics, it is an optional subject unlike the other disciplines.

References

Birdsall, Nancy, Barbara Bruns and Richard H. Sabot, "Education in Brazil: Playing a Bad Hand Badly," in Birdsall and Sabot, 1996.

Birdsall, Nancy and Richard H. Sabot, editors, *Opportunity Foregone: Education in Brazil*, Washington, DC: Inter-American Development Bank, 1996.

EFA 2000, Education for All: evaluation of the year 2000. National Report – Brazil, UNESCO 2000.

Gomes-Neto, João Batista and Eric A. Hanushek, "The Causes and Effects of Grade Repetition," in Birdsall and Sabot, 1996.

Guimaraes de Castro, M.H., *Brazil's National Education Plan*, INEP (Instituto Nacional de Estudos e Pesquisas Educacionais) 2002.

Guimaraes de Castro, M.H., *Evaluation : an Educational Reform Strategy in Brazil*, INEP (Instituto Nacional de Estudos e Pesquisas Educacionais) 2002.

Hanushek, Eric A., João Batista Gomes-Neto and Ralph W. Harbison, "Efficiency-Enhancing Investments in School Quality," in Birdsall and Sabot, 1996.

James, Estelle, Carlos Alberto Primo Braga and Paulo de Tarso Afonso de Andre, "Private Education and Public Regulation," in Birdsall and Sabot, 1996.

Mello e Souza, Alberto and Nelson do Valle Silva, "Family Background, Quality of Education and Public and Private Schools: Effects on School Transitions," in Birdsall and Sabot, 1996.

Moura Castro, Claudio de, Sonia Dantas Pinto Guimarães, João Batista Arauja e

[45] *Ibid.*, Article 33

Oliveira and Sergio Costa Ribiero, "Dealing with Poor Students," in Birdsall and Sabot, 1996.

Plank, David N., José Amaral Sobrinho, and Antonio Carlos da Ressurreição Xavier, "Why Brazil Lags Behind in Educational Development," in Birdsall and Sabot, 1996.

Rigotti J and Fletcher P., *Growth of Educational Opportunities in Brazil during the 1980s and 1990s*, 2001.

Wolff L. and De Moura Castro C., Public or Private Education for Latin America?, IADB Interamerican Development Bank, Washington DC 2001. Available on www.iadb.org/sds/edu
also

INEP www.inep.gov.br

Ministry of Education www.mec.gov.br

Unesco www.unesco.org

World Bank www.worldbank.org

Interamerican Development Bank www.iadb.org

Canada

by Derek J. Allison[1], Deani A. Neven Van Pelt[2]

Overview

Canada is a federal state of ten provinces and three territories, each of which is responsible for education within its borders. This is a common division of powers but, unlike most other federations, Canada's federal government does not exercise significant authority over education. There is no Canadian minister or department of education, no comprehensive national education policy and, with a few important exceptions, no national standards governing the establishment and operation of schools. The federal government does have constitutional responsibility for First Nations education and provides some financial support for minority and second language instructional programs, but provincial legislatures exercise exclusive jurisdiction over elementary and secondary education, subject only to conditions imposed by constitutional protections, judicial rulings and available resources. The territorial governments of Yukon, Nunavut, and the Northwest Territories have no inherent jurisdiction, their authority over education deriving from constitutive legislation passed by the Canadian (federal) Parliament. They have nevertheless developed their own education structures (or are doing so in Nunavut), which they administer under official, essentially benevolent, federal supervision. There are thus thirteen discrete education jurisdictions in Canada, each with its own distinct system of compulsory, publicly funded, regulated, and supervised elementary and secondary schooling, and each with its own, often quite different, policies concerning non-public education.

There are commonalities across the different jurisdictions, which are largely rooted in a common history and shared geography. Public schools are largely financed through centrally administered grants funded through a combination of property taxes and general revenues, are governed and administered by local authorities responsible for defined geographic districts and are formally free. Details nonetheless vary across jurisdictions, particularly with regard to the extent of the geographical areas served and the ways schools are organized. So too with non-public education: while all jurisdictions allow children to be educated outside of the state system, there are differences in how non-public schools are

---

1 The University of Western Ontario
2 Redeemer University College

regulated, and even in how they are officially regarded. The pertinent legislation in British Columbia and Saskatchewan provides for "independent" schools, for example, while that in Ontario and Alberta addresses "private" schools, and that in New Brunswick mentions neither, remaining silent on the possibility of non-state schools. Given these and many other variations it is tempting to regard education in Canada as being decentralized, but such a view can divert attention from the high levels of centralization within each of the thirteen jurisdictions, a condition which is more accurately captured by Elboim-Dror's (1973) notion of deconcentration.

Matters are complicated further by constitutional protections for publicly operated religious and linguistic schools. Currently, the protections for religious schools only apply to Roman Catholic or Protestant minorities in Ontario, Saskatchewan and Alberta, while those provided for minority language instruction extend to all provinces and territories, but are applied differently in Quebec. In each case the differential access to public schools results in instances of asymmetrical federalism.[3] Less tractable geographical asymmetries concerning area, population, industry, and income also influence school variety and access. Although the three territories span 40 percent of Canada's landmass, less than 0.5 percent of Canadians make their home there. The markedly asymmetrical population distribution across the provinces is more significant, with 93 percent of the national population residing in the six geographically largest provinces of (in order of decreasing population) Ontario, Quebec, British Columbia, Alberta, Manitoba, and Saskatchewan. Moreover, over half of all Canadians live within one of the 17 largest cities, ten of which are located in southern Ontario or Quebec. Given these settlement patterns the review which follows is primarily focussed on schools and schooling in the six most populous provinces as given above.

One final asymmetry needs mention. As noted by Mark Holmes "the lack of consistency and, in many cases, of important data makes informed provincial comparison and national discussion difficult".[4] Over the past decade or so cooperation between Statistics Canada and The Council of Ministers of Education has enhanced the range and quality of internationally comparable data available, but in some important instances this advance has blurred rather than improved internal comparisons, which are inherently difficult given jurisdictional differences in structures and operational definitions. Non-public schools are a pertinent case in point. At the time of writing national level enrolment data for non-state schools by jurisdiction were not available, although they were scheduled to be released at the end of 2011.[5] Given this limitation efforts have been made to generate up-to-date and comparable state and non-state school statistics from data available *via* provincial and territorial Department or Ministry of Education

[3] Simeon & Robinson, 1990

[4] Holmes, 1998, p. 40

[5] Statistics Canada, personal communication, 3 March 2011

websites and, unless otherwise noted, it should be assumed that the enrolment numbers, school counts and related statistics presented in this review were collected or calculated from such sources.

Structure

Each of the thirteen jurisdictions has enacted a legislative framework to govern the establishment and operation of elementary and secondary schools. In all cases this legislation divides duties and responsibilities between a central (provincial/ territorial) Ministry or Department of Education, and various forms of local and regional education authorities. Division of responsibilities broadly conforms to Kandel's[6] classic characterization of state centralization in which school *interna*, such as admission, curriculum, finance, teacher certification, and examinations are controlled centrally, with responsibilities for operational *externa*, such as staff employment and remuneration, pupil transportation, building maintenance, equipment and supplies, being assigned to local authorities.

With the exception of the very few special purpose schools operated directly by governments, public schools are established, operated and closed by local authorities that have been assigned responsibility for defined geographical districts, usually coterminous with city or other municipal boundaries. These local authorities typically take the form of an elected board of trustees with an administrative staff. The size and complexity of the areas administered varies considerably, some rural school districts in the prairie provinces serving fewer than five thousand students distributed across a dozen or so schools spread over thousands of square kilometres, while the larger city districts serve hundreds of thousands of pupils in hundreds of schools in a much more densely settled, as well as socially and ethnically varied, milieu. Numbers of administrative staff vary accordingly, ranging from half-a-dozen or less to hundreds, although the number of elected trustees governing any district typically numbers less than twenty or so. School board elections, it should be noted, are not contested by established political parties, candidates usually running their own campaigns, with elections focused on local issues and personalities.

Although accurate statistics are not readily available, approximately eight percent of all school aged children in Canada are currently educated outside of state schools. This relatively small proportion by comparative international standards is largely accounted for by the wide range of options available within the provincial schooling systems, especially the publicly funded Roman Catholic separate schools in Ontario, Alberta, and Saskatchewan, which account for some 15 percent of total Canadian elementary and secondary enrolment. In addition, all jurisdictions have established school boards which operate publicly funded minority language

6 Kandel, 1933, pp. 215-218

schools for eligible francophones or anglophones, these accounting for a further five percent or so of total public enrolments. Most public school districts outside of Quebec also allow parents to choose to have their children educated in a French immersion program. These have proven popular, with demand exceeding available spaces in many districts, current enrolments amounting to some eight percent of total public enrolments. Many larger urban school districts also provide access to publicly financed alternative schools and programs of various kinds.[7] In 2010-11 there were also some 7,800 students attending one of 19 publicly funded charter school campuses operating in Alberta, the sole Canadian jurisdiction permitting this form of school choice.

Section 93 of the Canadian constitution guarantees the continued provision of separate schools and governing boards for Roman Catholic and Protestant minorities in Ontario, Alberta, and Saskatchewan. Almost a third (30.2 percent) of Ontario elementary and secondary pupils attend such schools, which are operated by 37 Roman Catholic Separate Boards, eight of which are also French language instruction boards. There is also one Protestant Separate Board (officially designated a School Authority) operating a single elementary school, enrolling some 250 pupils in 2005-06. In 2010-11 there were 16 Roman Catholic separate boards in Alberta, enrolling a total of 127,500 pupils, as well as a further 6,500 students in 14 schools operated by the single Protestant separate board. Total 2011 Alberta separate school enrolment amounted to 23.4 percent of students in public elementary and secondary schools. Saskatchewan has the smallest number (34,250) and proportion (21 percent) of separate school students, distributed across 117 schools operated by ten boards, including a sole Protestant board enrolling less than 100 pupils in a single school. The Yukon, Northwest Territories and Nunavut Acts each provide for minority Catholic or Protestant separate schools. There were three Catholic schools in Yukon in 2011, accounting for 19 percent of total public enrolments. As is the case with all except the minority language public school in the Yukon, these three are operated directly by the Department of Education, with elected school councils providing a forum for parent advice and involvement. There is one Catholic separate board in the Northwest Territories, operating a secondary and two elementary schools. Nunavut currently has no separate schools or boards.

As discussed further in the next section, Canada's separate schools are a legacy from the country's founding. As the rise of state secularism displaced the original non-sectarian Christian character of the majority public schools with a growing official commitment to religious neutrality, social discourse and legal opinion has come to uncritically view Canada's public schools as secular institutions. This appears to imply that the separate schools in Ontario, Alberta, Saskatchewan and the Territories are not public schools: that is are not publicly funded, managed and controlled schools. This is incorrect: Canada's separate schools are an

---

7 CUP, 2004, pp. 29-59

integral part of the public school systems in the jurisdictions concerned. More accurate yet cumbersome usage would distinguish between denominational separate public schools and secular public schools, but such usage would not hold for the community of St. Albert, the location of Alberta's sole Protestant school board, where the majority public board is the Greater St. Albert Catholic Schools Regional Division.

Consonant with the deconcentrated character of Canadian schooling, the separate schools and systems embody important differences. In all three provinces only members of the minority faith can elect separate board trustees. In Ontario separate board supporters must officially direct their property taxes to support separate boards, or they otherwise default to the public board, but in the districts where separate schools exist in Alberta and Saskatchewan, property taxes paid by members of the religious denominations concerned automatically support the separate schools. In Edmonton, Calgary and Saskatoon non-Catholic pupils may enrol in Catholic separate schools and Catholic children enrol in public schools at no financial cost, but in Ontario non-Catholic children are only allowed to attend Catholic elementary separate schools at the discretion of the school board concerned and are normally required to pay fees which compensate for the property taxes they are unable to direct to the separate board. Such requirements do not hold for secondary level Catholic schools in Ontario, which have been open to all students since 1985.

Prior to joining Canada in 1949, Newfoundland's distinct history had created a comprehensive denominational system of public education which, in the early 1960s, was composed of schools operated by the Roman Catholic, Anglican, United, Salvation Army, Presbyterian, Seventh Day Adventist, and Pentecostal churches. After a hard fought campaign the provincial government eventually secured a constitutional amendment which enabled it to institute a single non-denominational system in 1998.

Section 23 of the *Canadian Charter of Rights and Freedoms* provides a constitutional right to publicly funded primary and secondary instruction in the language of the English or French linguistic minority of a province, where numbers warrant. All jurisdictions have created dedicated public school boards or similar governing agencies to establish and operate minority language schools for eligible pupils. In six provinces and each of the territories there is a single francophone board governing all French language schools in that jurisdiction. During 2010-11 numbers ranged from a single school in each of the Yukon and Nunavut, to 38 in British Columbia, 24 in Manitoba, 20 in Nova Scotia, six in Prince Edward Island, five in Newfoundland and Labrador, and two in the Northwest Territories. Provinces with larger francophone minority populations have established multiple boards with responsibility for defined geographic areas. Ontario has 12 francophone boards (eight of which are also RC separate boards) serving almost 92,000 pupils, while Alberta has five francophone regional authorities enrolling almost 6,000 pupils. New Brunswick, Canada's only officially bilingual province, established a dual school system with separate English and French sectors in 1971, each with its own central administrative department, curriculum, and assessment systems, and each with its own regional management structures. In 2011 New Brunswick's five French District Education Councils accounted for almost 30 percent of total public enrolments in that province.

French is the official and majority language in Quebec. Although the province is not currently bound by the Section 23 minority language guarantees, its *Charter of the French Language* allows a publicly funded English language education for Canadian anglophones, as discussed further in following sections. Public schools are currently operated by 60 French and nine English boards. Schools operated by the English language boards enrolled 130,000 pupils in 2006-07, representing 10.8 percent of the provincial elementary and secondary public enrolment. There were an additional 13,160 pupils enrolled in English language private schools in that year, accounting for 11.9 percent of Quebec's non-preschool and non-adult private school students.

Excluding pre-school and junior colleges (CGEPs), there were 119,300 pupils enrolled in Quebec private schools in 2006-07, accounting for 12 percent of total elementary and secondary enrolment in that province, the highest of any Canadian jurisdiction. Quebec has long had the highest level of non-public school enrolment in Canada, the proportion of the province's elementary and secondary pupils attending private schools having risen from 8.6 percent in 1988 to 12.2 percent in 2007.[8] Enrolment in private secondary schools is three times that in elementary schools, a pattern almost entirely accounted for by French language schools, reflecting the continued influence of the surviving classical colleges founded by religious orders. Overall, English language private schools account for some 12 percent of total private school enrolments in Quebec. Many of the English schools integrate non-subsidized elementary school sections with subsidized secondary grades.

Legal Framework

Modern Canada came into being with the proclamation of the *British North America Act, 1867*. Initially composed of only Ontario, Quebec, New Brunswick and Nova Scotia, provisions were made for future inclusion of the remaining British colonies and possessions in North America, all but one of which had joined the federation by 1905. Following a close referendum the Dominion of Newfoundland became the tenth Canadian province in 1949.

Although drafted by representatives of the emerging country, the *BNA Act* was

---

8 Statistics Canada, 2001, p. 2, & Quebec, 2008a, p. 140

passed by the parliament of the United Kingdom which, because of internal disagreement between representatives from Quebec and the other provinces, retained sole authority to amend Canada's constitution until it was patriated in 1982. This was accomplished through the *Canada Act, 1982* which, in addition to ending the UK parliament's residual legislative responsibilities, consolidated subsequent amendments to the original *BNA Act* into a renamed *Constitution Act, 1867* as well as the *Constitution Act 1982*, which entrenched an amending formula and the *Canadian Charter of Rights and Freedoms* into the constitution.

There are two particularly important provisions regarding education in these constitutive laws. The most fundamental is Section 93 of the renamed *Constitution Act, 1867* which, as previously touched upon, assigns exclusive legislative authority over education to the provinces and protects the continued operation of minority denominational boards and schools in the three provinces where they still exist. As also outlined earlier, Section 23 of the *Charter* guarantees minority language education rights of English or French-speaking citizens. Both sets of protections are complementary facets of the French fact in Canada's history and politics, the passage of 115 years between the entrenchment of Section 93 and Section 23 spanning a period which saw a rebalancing of the saliency of religion and language in forming and preserving French identity. Rebalancing, not displacing. As illustrated by the shared official identity of many francophone and Roman Catholic schools in Ontario and Alberta, and by the more informal religious character of francophone schools in New Brunswick and elsewhere, language and Catholicism mutually reflect and support the distinctiveness of Canada's French communities and their schools, and have done so from before Confederation.

Although Section 23 contains the only specific reference to education in the *Canadian Charter of Rights and Freedoms*, other provisions have indirect bearing. The most obvious is Section 59 which exempts Quebec from sub-section (1)a of Section 23, the major practical outcome being that while French-speaking Canadian citizens are entitled to enrol their children in a French language public school anywhere in Canada where numbers warrant, in Quebec only those anglophone parents who are Canadian citizens and who were themselves educated in Canada in English or have at least one child who has been educated in Canada in English are entitled to enrol their children in a public English language school. Other parents have been able to send their children to English language public schools by enrolling at least one child in a non-subsidized English language private school for a year. Quebec sought to close this so-called *ecoles passerelles* (bridging schools) exception in 2002, but the legislation was struck down by the Superior Court and finally quashed by the Supreme Court of Canada in 2009. New 2010 legislation extended the qualification period at *écoles passerelles* to three years and instituted a points system which is to be used by state officials to assess eligibility on a case by case basis.

Other *Charter* provisions have indirect influence on education. Section 2 guarantees the fundamental individual freedoms of conscience, religion, thought, belief, peaceful assembly and association, all of which have a bearing on the content of education and the conduct of schools, as clearly demonstrated by the *Zylberberg* and *Elgin* cases as discussed below. Judicial reasoning concerning education in those and other *Charter* cases was and will continue to be strongly influenced by Section 1, which limits the rights and freedoms set out in the *Charter* "to such reasonable limits prescribed by law as can be demonstrably justified in a free and democratic county," and by Section 27, which requires the *Charter* to be "interpreted in a manner consistent with the preservation and enhancement of the multicultural heritage of Canadians." Although Canada is a signatory to the United Nations Universal Declaration of Human Rights – indeed, a Canadian, John Peters Humphrey, was the principal drafter of the document and the first Director of the UN Division of Human Rights[9] – the Canadian *Charter* makes no explicit mention of the right to an education, nor to a parent's prior right to choose his or her child's education. Section 27 nonetheless acknowledges that the contents of the *Charter* "shall not be construed as denying the existence of any other rights or freedoms that exist in Canada". In this respect Canada's ratification of the United Nations *Convention on the Rights of the Child* carries with it an obligation to accept the right to an education and the related provisions concerning parental choice in Sections 29 and 30. More directly, Canadian jurisprudence acknowledges the broad, but by no means absolute, right of parents to raise their children as they choose. In *B.(R.) v. Children's Aid Society of Metropolitan Toronto*, [1995] four Supreme Court justices found that the Section 7 right to liberty in the *Charter* includes the right of a parent to care for, nurture and make fundamental decisions for a child, observing that,

> While parents bear responsibilities toward their children, they must enjoy correlative rights to exercise them, given the fundamental importance of choice and personal autonomy in our society. ... This role translates into a protected sphere of parental decision-making which is rooted in the presumption that parents should make important decisions affecting their children both because parents are more likely to appreciate the best interests of their children and because the state is ill-equipped to make such decisions itself. While the state may intervene when it considers it necessary to safeguard the child's autonomy or health, such intervention must be justified. ...
> If one considers the multitude of decisions parents make daily, it is clear that in practice, state interference in order to balance the rights of parents and children will arise only in exceptional cases. The state can properly intervene in situations where parental conduct falls below the socially acceptable threshold, but in doing so it is limiting the constitutional rights of parents rather than vindicating the constitutional rights of children.[10]

---

9 Morsink, 1999

10 *B.(R.) v. Children's Aid Society of Metropolitan Toronto*, [1995], p. 5-6

Quebec has had its own *Charter of Human Rights and Freedoms* since 1976 which originally included the following provisions regarding education:

> 40. Every person has a right, to the extent and according to the standards provided for by law, to free public education.
> 41. Parents or the persons acting in their stead have a right to require that, in the public educational establishments, their children receive a religious or moral education in conformity with their convictions, within the framework of the curricula provided for by law.
> 42. Parents or the persons acting in their stead have a right to choose private educational establishments for their children, provided such establishments comply with the standards prescribed or approved by virtue of the law.

As part of the project to secularize education in Quebec Section 41 was amended in June 2005 to read as follows:

> 41. Parents or the persons acting in their stead have a right to give their children a religious and moral education in keeping with their convictions and with proper regard for their children's rights and interests.

The Quebec Charter only has effect within that province and these provision can be overridden by the legislature, as was the case with Section 41. Further, the *Canadian Charter* is supreme and in *Gosselin v. Quebec* (2002) the Supreme Court held that a failure to respect rights declared in the Quebec *Charter* may attract a judicial declaration of violation.

Section 29 of the *Canadian Charter* explicitly declares that "Nothing in this Charter abrogates or derogates from any rights or privileges guaranteed by or under the Constitution of Canada in respect of denominational, separate or dissentient schools". The rights and privileges referred to are those in Section 93 of the *Constitution Act 1867*, which reads as follows:

93. In and for each Province the Legislature may exclusively make Laws in relation to Education, subject and according to the following Provisions:
(1) Nothing in any such Law shall prejudicially affect any Right or Privilege with respect to Denominational Schools which any Class of Persons have by Law in the Province at the Union:
(2) All the Powers, Privileges and Duties at the Union by Law conferred and imposed in Upper Canada on the Separate Schools and School Trustees of the Queen's Roman Catholic Subjects shall be and the same are hereby extended to the Dissentient Schools of the Queen's Protestant and Roman Catholic Subjects in Quebec:
(3) Where in any Province a System of Separate or Dissentient Schools exists by Law at the Union or is thereafter established by the Legislature of the Province, an Appeal shall lie to the Governor General in Council from any Act

> or Decision of any Provincial Authority affecting any Right or Privilege of the Protestant or Roman Catholic Minority of the Queen's Subjects in relation to Education:
> (4) In case any such Provincial Law as from Time to Time seems to the Governor General in Council requisite for the Execution of the Provisions of this Section is not made, or in case any Decision of the Governor General in Council on any Appeal under this Section is not duly executed by the proper Provincial Authority in that Behalf, then and in every such Case, and as far as the Circumstances of each Case require, the Parliament of Canada may make remedial Laws for the due Execution of the Provisions of this Section and of any Decision of the Governor General in Council under this Section.

By granting exclusive legislative powers over education to the provinces while protecting existing legal rights concerning denominational schools, Section 93 has fuelled, framed and constrained a series of political debates and judicial reviews influencing school diversity in Canada, and resulted in the denominational separate schools in Alberta, Ontario, and Saskatchewan discussed earlier. In the founding provinces religion was widely accepted as an integral part of education throughout the nineteenth century and into the twentieth, especially in rural areas, particularly those settled by homogenous groups of European immigrants. As such, early public schools characteristically embraced the religious character of the community they served, which was predominately non-Catholic Christian outside of Quebec and some scattered francophone communities elsewhere, and predominantly Roman Catholic within Quebec. As originally conceived and implemented, publicly funded minority denominational schools not only provided a supportive milieu where children could be educated in their family faith, they provided protection from compulsory participation in public schools defined or permeated by a competing religion, while also not forcing their parents to financially support such schools through their property taxes.

At Confederation all four founding provinces had developed arrangements for accommodating adherents of the minority religion within their embryonic public schools, but only Quebec and Ontario had enacted these into law. The arrangements in those two provinces were consequently protected under Section 93(1), whereas the informal arrangements that had emerged in New Brunswick and Nova Scotia were not.

Quebec had adopted a dual school system composed of Roman Catholic and Protestant branches representing the two Christian confessions, schools for the minority being called dissentient schools. Until the extensive reforms implemented during and following the Quiet Revolution in the 1960s each of the two confessional systems controlled its own curriculum, school inspection and teacher training. Quebec replaced its confessional system with the current linguistic system after securing the 1997 amendment to the constitution that inserted Section 93A, which reads as follows: "Paragraphs (1) to (4) of section 93 do not apply to Quebec".

A system of common and separate public schools had emerged in Ontario prior to Confederation. Under the terms of the 1863 Scott Act—which has been called the charter of denominational schools—Roman Catholics were able to establish school boards separate from those governing the common schools and to direct their property taxes to support those boards. The Scott Act accorded these separate boards the same powers as those governing the common schools, and granted them shares in legislative and municipal grants made in support of education. In return, separate schools became subject to inspection by the then Department of Public Instruction, which also assumed control over curriculum and teacher training in and for the separate schools. In addition to ensuring the continued existence of Ontario's separate schools as provided for in the Scott Act, the application of Section 93 had the effect of perpetuating features in place at the time of the Union. The most egregious effects severely limited Ontario separate boards' access to business property tax revenues and denied access to both legislative grants and property revenues for senior level secondary school students (Grades 11 – 13).

Redress of the secondary funding limitation was famously sought through the poetically named *Tiny Separate School Trustees v. The King* test case which, after evenly dividing the Supreme Court of Canada, was finally decided by the Judicial Committee of the Privy Council in Westminster in 1928. Following a detailed interpretation of Section 93 and a thorough review of the legislative and administrative history of state schooling in Ontario before and after Confederation, the Privy Council decided that when Section 93 came into effect in 1867, Ontario's separate schools were a special kind of common school and thus not authorized to provide the pre-university instruction available in the grammar schools of the day. In consequence, their Lordships ruled that the Section 93 rights of Ontario's separate boards were not prejudicially affected when the legislature subsequently introduced a new high school system in 1871 which made no provision for Catholic separate schools. Their Lordship's ruling continued to deny public funding for Catholic Grade 11-13 high schools for a further half century, although Ontario did continue to fund Catholic junior level secondary enrolments (Grades 9-10), but at the elementary rather than the secondary per pupil grant rate. The practical consequences of this forced Ontario separate boards to operate and fund senior high school classes as fee-charging private schools. While Catholic communities typically subsidized these schools in various ways, substantial numbers of students were nonetheless forced to transfer into the increasingly secular state secondary schools to complete their secondary education. Moreover, these financial and organizational strictures essentially restricted Catholic secondary schools to urban locales.

In his written judgement on the *Tiny* case, Viscount Haldane went to some length to explain how the Privy Council's ruling was based on a strict legal interpretation of Section 93(1). He nonetheless observed that subsection (3) clearly contemplated the possibility of provincial legislatures establishing systems of minority denominational schooling which either did not exist when a province entered Confederation, or which provided rights and privileges beyond those in place at that time. In short, there was no constitutional impediment to the Ontario legislature—or that in any other province—funding Catholic schools—or any other kind of school—should it choose to so do. The Ontario legislature finally moved to provide equivalent finding for separate secondary schools with the passage of Bill 30 in 1985, which comfortably survived a challenge to its constitutionality in a 1987 ruling by the Supreme Court of Canada. Bill 30 amended Ontario's *Education Act* to allow Roman Catholic boards to operate and receive full equivalent grant support for integrated Grade 9-13 high schools. This extension of 'full funding', as it is often but erroneously called, was warmly welcomed at the time but brought with it restrictions on the autonomy of the Catholic high schools that have come to be regretted in some quarters. And while the new policy distributed per-pupil legislative grants equally to separate and public Boards, disparities in the administration of property taxes resulted in less than fully equal funding for separate schools. These discrepancies were largely resolved in 1997 with the passage of Bill 160—the *Education Quality Improvement Act*—which introduced broad structural reforms and centralized the administration of property taxes for education under the Ministry of Finance.

A modified but essentially parallel version of Section 93 was included as Section 22 of the *Manitoba Act 1870*, under which the Red River Settlement and associated territory became Canada's fifth province. A substantial French presence resulted in the establishment of a confessional system of public schools modelled on that in Quebec, but substantial immigration from Ontario drastically reduced the proportion of French Catholics in the population, prompting an Anglo-Protestant dominated provincial legislature to withdraw funding from the Catholic schools in 1890. This precipitated a major constitutional crisis known as the Manitoba Schools Question. Section 93(3) [22(2) in the Manitoba Act] provides for such infringements of denominational education rights to be appealed to the Canadian government, which is empowered to pass remedial legislation under 93(4) [22(3)]. The Canadian parliament and people were deeply divided on the issues, leading to the only national election fought ostensibly over school policy. Ostensibly because the schools were only the battleground, the battle itself being fought over the religious, linguistic and cultural identities and futures of the English and French 'founding peoples'. The incumbent conservatives lost that landmark 1897 election to Wilfrid Laurier's Liberals who promised a new "sunny ways" compromise. The practical outcome for Manitoba's public schools saw non-compulsory religious instruction being allowed for half-an-hour at the end of the school day and for instruction in French or another language to be allowed where ten or more students spoke that language.

On the broader political stage, the length and bitterness of the conflict over Manitoba's schools illustrates the deep divisions between the two founding peoples that have surfaced from time to time in the unfolding of Canada's story, typically with consequences for education policy. Over the past half-century these divisions fuelled the rise of a separatist movement in Quebec, which very nearly triumphed on a 1995 referendum to secede from Canada. Separatist and other French Canadian aspirations have had profound effects on schools and schooling in Quebec, and are at the root of the asymmetrical linguistic education rights outlined earlier.

The immediate resolution of the Manitoba Schools Question preserved limited religious education rights for Catholics within a unitary public school system. Although this was a loss for the French Canadian cause in Manitoba and the nation, it helped ensure the preservation of separate schools in Alberta and Saskatchewan when they entered Confederation in 1905, and laid the groundwork for the subsequent extension of these rights to the three territories.

British Columbia joined Canada in 1871 without the long legacy of French-English tensions and compromise, and with an unitary system of non-sectarian public schools which reflected a commitment to separation of church and state which was not then embraced across Canada. In the other provinces education had been historically viewed as more of a partnership between state, church and family. Indeed, this principle animated the emergence of the denominational school compromises discussed above, as well as the multi-denominational system that became established in Newfoundland before it joined Canada in 1949.

Section 17 of the terms of Union under which Newfoundland entered Canada embodied the applicable principles of Section 93, thus protecting Newfoundland's unique religious schools from changes prejudicial to the rights of supporters, although various reforms were adopted in search of enhanced administrative efficiency. Adoption of the amending formula in the *Constitution Act 1982* eventually led to Section 17 being amended in 1998 to read as follows: "the Legislature shall have exclusive authority to make laws in relation to education, but shall provide for courses in religion that are not specific to a religious denomination," thus clearing the way for Newfoundland's long standing system of denominational state schools to be replaced with the current nondenominational system. Various religiously defined private schools were subsequently established, including Holy Cross Community School in St. Alban's and St. Bonaventure's College in St. John's.

In modern times, two influential court cases significantly contributed to a *Charter* derived enforced secularism in Ontario's non-separate public schools. In 1988 the Ontario Court of Appeal ruling on *Zylberberg et al. v. Sudbury Board of Education* struck down a long standing regulation which had authorized recitation of the Lord's Prayer and other Christian devotions during opening and closing exercises in public schools as an unreasonable infringement on freedom of religion. Two years later in *Elgin County (Canadian Civil Liberties Association) v. Ontario [Minister of Education]* the same court ruled that another regulatory provision allowing two half-hour periods of religious instruction each week in elementary schools also violated the freedom of religion. In this case the court held that the intent of the regulation itself, as well as the school activities it authorized, indoctrinated pupils into the religious tradition of the majority, which was ruled unacceptable under the *Charter*. The court nonetheless noted that education *about* religion would be acceptable provided it did not indoctrinate into a specific faith.

Both the *Zylberberg* and *Elgin* cases brought detailed responses from the Ontario Ministry of Education. The 1993 Ministry document outlining current expectations for opening and closing exercises includes sample readings and a list of desirable values. Religious readings are deemed acceptable if precedence is not given to a single faith and if non-religiously derived moral and spiritual texts are also used. Interestingly, the Lord's Prayer is deemed permissible provided it is read and not recited. The 1994 Ministry document on education about religion provides a bland history of religious instruction in the province's public schools, together with a discussion of the form and content of currently acceptable education about religion. Current law is set out in Sections 27 – 29 of *Ontario Regulation 298: Operation of schools: General*. Non-separate boards may provide optional programs of education about religion if such programs promote respect for freedom of conscience and religion, provide for the study of different religious beliefs, giving primacy to none, and do not exceed one hour a week. Under section 29(3) boards may also allow "a person to conduct religious exercises or to provide instruction that includes indoctrination in a particular religion or religious belief in a school" provided this is not done under the auspices of the board, no one is required to attend, and the activities take place outside of the school's instructional program. It is not known how many non-separate boards provide instruction about religion or allow religious instruction, but both are probably rare. Even so, *The Globe and Mail* reported that the Toronto District Board had been allowing Friday prayers in some schools with high proportion of Muslim students.[11]

In these *Charter* cases and others, Ontario courts have reasoned and ruled that the province's non-separate public schools are to be secular. The precedents set by these cases, together with generally compliant legal and administrative policies in other jurisdictions, have influenced expectations and practices across the country, the constitutional amendments in Quebec and Newfoundland providing particularly momentous examples of the strength of the secularist tide. More recent opposition to a new mandatory *Ethics and Religious Culture* program in Quebec has brought the clash between secular and religious values in education into the courts, as discussed later.

These developments have led to a backlash on the part of some religious groups. As a distinguished Canadian educator observed the mandated secularization of Canada's public schools was "a sad day for the influence of parents over their

11 Hammer, 2011

children's education and a disgrace in a society that prides itself on its tolerance and multiculturalism".[12] It has nonetheless been uncritically welcomed by many teachers and others who "look back in horror to an age when religious training was mandatory, but have no inhibitions about the state-ordered inculcation of contemporary majoritarian values (or even those held by an expert minority)".[13]

Freedom to establish non-state schools

Education is compulsory from five or six to sixteen, seventeen or eighteen years of age, depending on jurisdiction. In all cases the compulsory attendance requirements can be satisfied through home instruction or by attending a non-public school, but there is considerable variation in the regulatory procedures and standards in the different jurisdictions. All jurisdictions require non-public schools to be registered in some way, a requirement upheld when the Supreme Court of Canada ruled this was appropriate for even religiously based independent schools in *Jones v. The Queen*, provided the registration process respects freedom of conscience and religion in education and the principles of fundamental justice.

There has been a steady but slow increase in the numbers of children and youth being educated in non-public settings in each of the six most populous provinces, the proportional increase being amplified by declines in public school enrolments over the past decade or so.

British Columbia and Quebec are distinguished by specific legislation governing non-state schools. Quebec's 1968 *Act Respecting Private Education* came about as part of the massive modernization of education in that province during the Quiet Revolution in the 1960s. Prior to the establishment of the modern, integrated system of public schooling brought about by those reforms, private education had long been an essential feature of Quebec's educational landscape, especially at the secondary level where ecclesiastically affiliated colleges had provided publicly subsidized access to post-secondary study. The new universal public system threatened the very existence of those revered institutions, all of which suffered substantial reductions in enrolment as families opted for the newly expanded, free public secondary schools. Fears of collapse were allayed by the preamble to 1964 legislation laying the foundations for the new state system which recognized the right of parents to choose a system of education for their children as well as the right to establish autonomous educational institutions. These rights are currently recognized in the preamble to the statute establishing Quebec's Ministry of Education which reads as follows:

> ... every child is entitled to the advantage of a system of education conducive to the full development of his personality;

12 Holmes, 1998, p. 201

13 *Ibid.*, p. 83

> ... parents have the right to choose the institutions which, according to their convictions, ensure the greatest respect for the rights of their children;
> ... persons and groups are entitled to establish autonomous educational institutions and, subject to the requirements of the common welfare, to avail themselves of the administrative and financial means necessary for the pursuit of their ends.[14]

As noted earlier, Quebec's 1976 *Charter of Human Rights and Freedoms* also acknowledges parents' right to choose private schools for their children.

Passage of the *Act Respecting Private Education* preserved many of the established private secondary colleges by authorizing government subsidies which initially approached 80 per cent of public school instructional grants, declining to around 45 percent in recent times. In its current form the *Act* allocates extensive discretionary powers over private sector schools and post secondary establishments to the Minister of Education, who is to be advised by an appointed *Commission consultative de l'enseignement privé* [CCEP] which exercises wide supervisory powers through a permanent administrative staff and reports independently to the legislature. All private schools are required to have a valid permit which will only be granted to schools conforming to state curriculum requirements and participating in provincial examinations. Section 12(2) further stipulates a permit applicant must demonstrate "to the Minister's satisfaction that the institution will have at its disposal the adequate human and material resources required for dispensing the educational services for which the permit is issued and sufficient financial resources for that purpose". Given that private schools must, unless exempted, teach the authorized program of studies, the CCEP has interpreted these criteria as requiring that all private school teachers must normally hold provincial qualifications. One long standing implication of delivering the full provincial curriculum is that Quebec private schools must typically adopt an extended schedule in order to present additional curriculum content integral to their purpose.

To qualify for financial support Quebec private schools must be accredited as well as registered. Section 78 of the *Act* lists seven standards that are to be "taken into account" when granting accreditation, including "(1) the quality of the institution's educational organization and the criteria governing the selection of the teaching and managerial personnel; ... (5) the specific contribution to be made by the institution in terms of enrichment, complementarity or diversity; ... (7) the compatibility between the institution's objectives and the policies of the Minister or the Government." More unequivocally Section 125 stipulates that subsidies will only be paid to schools in compliance with Quebec's 1976 *Charter of the French Language*. This means that, as in the public schools, subsidized private schools can only provide instruction in English to students previously educated in English

14 Quebec, 2006

in Canada, or to those who have a sibling or a parent who is a Canadian citizen who was educated in English in Canada. These requirements are administered by means of eligibility certificates issued by the Ministry of Education. Under the original legislation it was possible for a certificate of eligibility to be issued to otherwise unqualified children who had completed a year in an unsubsidized English language private school in Quebec. Once one child in a family had qualified for a certificate by this route, all others in the family were eligible. In 2002 Quebec's National Assembly sought to close this 'loophole' with Bill 104, which declared education obtained in an unsubsidized private school in Quebec was to be disregarded when issuing eligibility certificates. After wending its way through the appeals process this legislation was finally struck down by Canada's supreme court in 2009 as an unreasonable denial of the very existence of English private schools and the reality of the education they provide. New 2010 legislation established a points system under which students will normally be required to accumulate three years of English instruction in a unsubsidized private school to qualify for a certificate of eligibility. The new system accords considerable discretion to CCEP officials when awarding points to individual students, raising the spectre of future litigation. While the new system preserves the so-called *écoles passerelles*, it also represents a qualified triumph for parental choice given that the Parti Québécois opposition advocated unconditional application of the rules in the Language Charter, which would have restricted access to private English language schools to anglophones born in Canada, as is the case in Quebec's public schools.

Quebec has long had the highest level of non-public school enrolment in Canada, the proportion of the province's elementary and secondary pupils attending private schools having risen from 8.6 percent in 1988 to 12.2 percent in 2007.[15] Enrolment in private secondary schools is three times that in elementary schools, a pattern almost entirely accounted for by French language schools, reflecting the continued influence of the surviving classical colleges founded by religious orders. Overall, English language private schools account for some 12 percent of total non-public school enrolments in Quebec. Many of the English schools integrate non-subsidized elementary school sections with subsidized secondary grades.

In sum, while Quebec has the highest proportion of private school students in the country, the government has a firm grip on the non-public schools it permits to operate, forcing parents who choose this option to see their children studying the mandated state curriculum in its entirety. As discussed further later, even unsubsidized Christian, Jewish and Muslim private schools are required to follow the new and controversial *Ethics and Religious Culture* course which is designed to provide non-preferential descriptive accounts of religions.

British Columbia's non-public schools are regulated under the *Independent School*

[15] Statistics Canada, 2001, p. 2 & Quebec, 2008a, p. 140

Act which was originally enacted in 1977 as the *School Support (Independent) Act*. Before then all private schools in British Columbia were unregulated and unfunded, although they had access to free government approved text books. The number and variety of private schools had been increasing since midcentury despite escalating costs which were a challenge to many, particularly denominational schools. Initial passage of the *School Support (Independent) Act* provided partial funding for schools agreeing to conform to provincial curriculum, staffing and other standards. This was a boon for the Catholic, protestant and other non-public schools that had long voluntarily taught the core of the provincial curriculum.

This policy was reviewed by the Sullivan Royal Commission which issued its report and recommendations on education in the province in 1988. In the course of a balanced yet succinct review of the commonly voiced arguments for and against public support of non-public schools the British Columbia Royal Commission on Education (1988) offered the illuminating sketch of the diversity of British Columbian private schools at that time:

> ... we listened to staunch advocates of public schooling suggest that independent schools are synonymous with elitist education, that they do not serve well the diversity of provincial learners, and that they are essentially exclusionary in character. ... Granted, ten or so of the more than 300 British Columbia independent schools emulate the curricular interests, character, and style of old world institutions. However, by far the greater number of the funded non-public schools – Roman Catholic, Evangelical, Protestant, Seventh Day Adventist, Jewish, Mennonite, Sikh, Lutheran, and Fundamentalist Christian Schools, as well as the secular Waldorf and Montessori schools – exercise considerable social reach and include in their enrolments youngsters with diverse interests and needs from a variety of ethnic backgrounds and from various parts of the social and economic spectrum. The focus on the small number of 'elitist' or 'wealthier' schools which implicitly cater to a clientele desiring university entrance, the Commission feels, has diverted attention from the larger denominational and special needs independent school sector and the importance of fiscal support to the educational programs of such institutions.[16]

The Commission concluded its review and presaged its recommendations by linking diversity to choice.

> In framing a perspective on the issue of support for independent schools, the Commission recognizes the importance of diversity and choice and their value as sound educational principles. At the same time, the Commission recognizes that other principles equally basic to the system should serve to balance diversity and choice – notably principles of access, equality, and accountability.

[16] British Columbia Royal Commission on Education, 1988, p. 250

> Simply put, the provincial system envisioned by the Commission should be marked by both 'loose' and 'tight' properties. It should accommodate the demand for diversity that exists in both public and non-public sectors; it should allow pupils, parents, and other participants in schooling the right to make educational choices and to provide reasonable levels of resources for them to do so; it should, at the same time, seek to promote equality of opportunity and equality of educational access for all children to the extent that it is feasible; and, it should, in the interests of children's welfare and the common good, monitor the levels of service delivered in efficient and effective ways.[17]

The subsequent *Independent School Act* of 1989 amended the existing legislation in broad conformity with these principles and the specific recommendations made by the Commission. Under this statute a provincial inspectorate oversees and administers the establishment and operation all independent schools in the province. Independent schools are defined as those offering "an educational program to 10 or more school age students" that does not solely consist of religious instruction, language instruction, social or cultural activities or recreational or athletic activities.[18] Independent schools are free to establish programs of study consistent with their philosophy, provided they satisfy an inspector that "no program is in existence or proposed at the independent school that would, in theory or in practice, promote or foster doctrines of

> (i) racial or ethnic superiority or persecution
> (ii) religious intolerance or persecution
> (iii) social change through violent action, or
> (iv) sedition."[19]

Independent schools are classified into one of four categories. Group 1 schools receive provincial funding equal to half of the per student operating grants received by their local public board. They must be operated by a non-profit authority and are required to provide instructional programs that meet provincial learning outcomes and comply with Ministry instructional time and program requirements, employ provincially certificated teachers, file regular reports, participate in the provincial testing program, satisfy all applicable municipal by-laws, be inspected every two years and undergo a external evaluation every six years. In 2010 there were 54,901 students enrolled in 252 Group 1 schools, including 6,335 students enrolled in 12 distributed learning schools, defined as those where instruction "relies primarily on indirect communication between students and teachers, including internet or other electronic-based delivery, teleconferencing or correspondence".[20]

17 *Ibid.*, p. 207
18 *Independent School Act* of 1989, Section 1(1)
19 *Ibid.*, Schedule 1(a)
20 *Ibid.*, Section 1(1)

Group 2 schools must meet the same requirements as those in Group 1, but receive lower operating grants (35 percent) to compensate for higher operating costs. There were 66 Group 2 schools enrolling 14,317 students in 2010.

Group 3 schools must meet all of the common standards outlined above with the key exceptions of not being required to employ certificated teachers or to satisfy Ministry curriculum or instruction requirements. They are nonetheless required to receive a satisfactory initial evaluation by an inspector and are inspected at least once every two years. Group 3 schools receive no public funding There were 19 Group 3 schools enrolling 544 students in 2010.

Group 4 schools primarily cater to "off-shore", non-Canadian students seeking secondary graduation certificates for admission to university and are thus required to fully conform to applicable Ministry program requirements. Group 4 schools receive no financial support and may operate as for profit ventures, but must be bonded. There were 10 Group 4 schools enrolling 943 students in 2010.

Provincial teaching certificates are normally issued by the British Columbia College of Teachers (scheduled to be dissolved and replaced with a new government department in 2012) but under the *Independent School Act* the Inspector is authorized to issue teaching certificates to applicants who satisfy guidelines developed by an appointed Independent School Teacher Certification Committee. This provides a regulated way in which teachers who do not meet domestic qualification requirements but do satisfy specific program or philosophical emphases in Group 1 and 2 schools can become certificated.

As indicated by the summary statistics above, virtually all (98 percent) independent schools in British Columbia receive partial public support, more than three quarters (77 percent) at the Group 1 level of 50 percent support and one-fifth at the Group 2 level of 35 percent support. The Group 3 schools accommodate less than one percent of the province's non-public enrolment and are quite small, with average enrolments of 28 pupils. Over half of British Columbia's independent schools are religiously defined, approximately 30 percent being Roman Catholic and 26 percent Protestant.

British Columbia has long had the second highest proportion of Canadian students enrolled in non-public schools, 7.9 percent attending private schools in 1988, rising to 10.8 percent in 2011.[21] Although Group 1, 2 and 3 schools are required to satisfy provincial outcomes as given in the provincial curriculum and conform to instructional time allocations and other operational standards, they "have freedom to address the curriculum from their own religious, cultural, philosophical or pedagogical perspectives" subject to the prohibitions quoted

[21] Statistics Canada, 2001, p. 2, & British Columbia, 2011, p. 1

above.[22] While this provides much greater latitude for independence than is allowed in Quebec, Jean Barman (1991) has argued that by bringing all private schools under the control and regulation of the state and subordinating them to its "social and economic priorities" the 1989 *Independent School Act* ensured that "British Columbia's remaining 'private' schools were in effect legislated out of existence".[23]

In the remaining seven provinces and three territories non-public schools are regulated under the statutes governing public education. Largely as a consequence of the settlement of the Manitoba Schools Question as touched on earlier, Manitoba has the third highest proportion of students enrolled in non-public schools, approximately a third of which are Roman Catholic or Eastern Rite. In 2010, 7.7 percent of students attending elementary and secondary schools were enrolled in non-public schools, compared to 4.8 percent in 1989.[24] More than 90 percent of these students attend funded non-public schools, which are referred to as private schools in Manitoba's *Public School Act*, but usually called funded independent schools in official literature. Although they are officially recognized, non-funded independent schools are neither defined nor recognized in provincial legislation, their existence being implicitly subsumed in a reference to children deemed to be "receiving a standard of education at home or elsewhere equivalent to that provided in a public school" in the Section 242(b) protection from prosecution under the compulsory attendance provisions in *The Public School Act*. A "private school" is formally defined in the *Education Administration Act* as "any school, other than a public school, which provides a curriculum and a standard of education equivalent to that provided by the public schools, but does not include any home or place to which clause 262(b) of *The Public Schools Act* applies",[25] such a place being what is referred to as non-funded independent school as discussed above.

The standards deemed appropriate to ensure educational equivalence to public schools and thus qualify for funded status are laid out in Section 60(5) of *The Public Schools Act*. These include official approval of the school's core curriculum contingent on appropriate adherence to the provincial program of studies, employment of teachers and a principal who hold "valid and subsisting teaching certificates", governance by a legally incorporated Board of Directors and the presence of an elected advisory board that includes at least three parents or guardians of students. Funded independent schools are also required to participate in provincial testing, accept regular inspection, and submit appropriate reports including annual audited financial statements. Non-funded independent schools that do not satisfy these requirements are nonetheless monitored by officials from

22 British Columbia Ministry of Education, 2011, p. 4
23 Barman, 1991, p. 17
24 Manitoba, 2011 & Statistics Canada, 2001
25 *Education Administration Act* , Section 1

Manitoba Education, Citizenship and Youth to ensure the education provided is appropriate as required under Section 242(b). Department officials also provide support services.

There were 35 such non-funded independent schools enrolling 1,119 pupils in 2010-11, accounting for 7.5 percent of total non-public enrolment. None of these schools enrolled more than 100 students, 29 enrolling less than 50. At least 12 (34 percent) were protestant Christian and 7 Mennonite. There were also four Mennonite funded independent schools as well as two Islamic, three Jewish and at least 13 other Christian schools among the funded independent schools. Under the regulations private schools can be granted permission to modify the provincial program of study to "reflect the unique religious perspectives, cultural objectives, or values of the private school".[26]

New Brunswick's *Education Act* defines 'school' as "a structured learning environment through which *public* education is provided to a pupil" (emphasis added) and makes no mention of private, independent or any other kind of non-public schools. Section 16(2) nonetheless declares that "the Minister shall, on application of the parent of a child, exempt in writing the child from attending school where the Minister is satisfied that the child is under effective instruction elsewhere". Approximately 1,000 students (1.06 percent of total) receive such permission to attend some 20 non-public schools each year, all of which are currently within the anglophone sector. The Department of Education normally pre-prints application forms for families that had enrolled children in an independent school the previous year, and sends them to the school for distribution to parents to verify or modify, sign and return to the school, which then forwards the forms to the Department.[27] There are no official regulations or policy documents governing the establishment and operation of non-public schools. The Department of Education collects basic operational data, distributes an annual memorandum listing elements of an effective instructional program, and invites non-public schools to participate in its testing program, but non-public schools are not required to implement the provincial curriculum, employ provincially certificated teachers or conform to any other official educational expectations. The Minister will nonetheless investigate complaints or other indications which imply pupils are not receiving effective instruction and act accordingly.

Nova Scotia has a more explicit and extended set of requirements. The *Education Act* defines public and private schools separately, the later being "a school, other than a public school, that serves school-age children and has a curriculum comparable to that provided by the public schools but does not include a home-

[26] Manitoba Reg. 267/97, 14(2)
[27] personal communication, 3 March 2011

education program".[28] A subsequent section explicitly states "a private school may offer a religious-based curriculum"[29] and under the heading of "Right to attend private school" Section 130 declares "A child may attend a private school". Section 113 exempts children from attending public schools if they attend private schools "operating in compliance with this Act". Requirements for compliance are minimal unless the school applies to be recognized as providing a program meeting the requirements for a Nova Scotia high school leaving certificate, in which case the school must demonstrate it is offering appropriate courses taught by appropriately qualified teachers. Considerable latitude is allowed in comparison to other jurisdictions, applicants being able to seek approval for school specific courses different from those included in the provincial curriculum to be accepted for equivalent credit, and for teachers not holding provincial certificates to be accepted as appropriately qualified. There were 34 private schools in Nova Scotia enrolling 3,414 students in 2010-11, representing 2.6 percent of the total elementary and secondary population. While modest, the proportion of pupils being educated in Nova Scotia's non-public schools has doubled over the past two decades.

As noted earlier, Newfoundland and Labrador secured a 1998 constitutional amendment to replace its long established system of church affiliated schools with a secular system within which provision is to be made for non-denominational religious education. Section 43 of the *Schools Act 1997* provides for persons to "establish and operate a private school in the province" on receipt of written permission from the Minister, subject to three relatively modest but open requirements as follows: (a) the use of appropriate premises, (b) "courses of instruction ... as prescribed or approved by the minister" and (c) employment of teachers holding valid provincial qualifications. Elsewhere the *Act* further stipulates that private school students are subject to provincial testing programs. Departmental statistics identified only six private schools enrolling a total of 830 students in 2009-10, representing 1.2 percent of total school enrolments. While relatively small, this proportion represents a threefold increase since 1998. Four of the six schools are religiously defined, three of these being Roman Catholic, these latter accounting for 67 percent of the total private school enrolment. One of these six establishments is essentially a privately operated public school serving a small community of workers and their families operating a large yet isolated hydro-electric generating complex in Labrador.

Prince Edward Island has half as many private schools as Newfoundland and Labrador; two of the three are protestant Christian, the other a very small cooperative school. Together the three account for a little over one percent of the total elementary and secondary enrolment on the Island. All private schools must be licensed in accordance with the requirements set out in a regulation

[28] Education Act, Section 3(1)(x)

[29] *Ibid.*, Section 131(3)

made under the *School Act*. The chief requirement is the provision of effective instruction, which is initially decided through assessment of a written submission including an outline of a school's goals, a description of the proposed program of study including a grade by grade course outline, and staffing plans. All teachers and administrators must be eligible for provincial certification. The Minister of Education is authorized to "inspect, annually and as often as the Minister determines is necessary, any private school, including examination of the physical facilities and course materials and the observation of classes taught by the school, and the Minister shall also have the right to administer tests to the students".[30]

Each of the three territories provides for non-public schools in its educational legislation, but none are currently operating. Section 19 of the Yukon *Education Act* declares that "parents may choose home schooling, private schooling or public schooling for their children", although Section 29(7) explicitly prohibits public funding of private schools. Section 29(1) provides that private schools may be operated by religious denominations and Section 29(3) provides that any official regulation "shall take into account the religious preferences of the private school." Private schools are required to be registered or accredited, to demonstrate their teachers are properly certificated, and agree to monitoring and evaluation by the Department. The North West Territories *Education Act* also states parents are entitled to choose a public, private or home education for their children,[31] but in this jurisdiction private schools are entitled to partial public funding equivalent to approximately 40 percent of the public rate. While private schools must be registered and offer an acceptable program of studies, neither the *Act* nor the subsidiary Regulation specifically requires adherence to the official curriculum or the employment of certificated teachers, although the Minister may require such. One requirement for registration is a statement declaring the school will not promote objectionable social doctrines which mirrors the wording in British Columbia's *Independent School Act*. A unique provision exempts private schools from offering instruction in a designated Official Language (of which there are eleven in the NWT). Nunavut's new *Education Act* contains no reference to parental choice and provides minimal requirements for the registration of private schools, which are nonetheless required to follow "a curriculum approved by the Minister" and ensure acceptable standards of student achievement.

The remaining three provinces all have substantial proportions of pupils attending publicly funded separate schools. The preamble to Alberta's *School Act* declares "parents have a right and a responsibility to make decisions respecting the education of their children" but also includes a strong commitment "to the preservation and continuation of its one publicly funded system of education through its two dimensions: the public schools and the separate schools". Section 28 of the *Act* nonetheless provides for registered and accredited private schools.

---

30 Prince Edward Island, 2010, Section 4

31 North West Territories *Education Act*, Section 11(1)

Registered schools must seek approval to operate and agree to regular inspections. Provided the premises satisfy all applicable health, safety and building codes and the school complies with the goals and standards for education established by the Minister and is considered to deliver acceptable levels of instruction, then it is "entitled to be registered as a private school". In addition to meeting the standards for registration, accredited schools must be non-profit enterprises governed by an elected board, must enrol at least seven students from two or more families, teach the provincial curriculum, participate in provincial testing, and employ teachers holding valid Alberta teaching certificates but who are not necessarily eligible for participating membership in the Alberta Teachers' Association. Schools satisfying these standards are eligible for Level 1 funding at a rate of 60 percent of public school per pupil grants. At their discretion schools can qualify for Level 2 (70 percent) funding by accepting additional accountability requirements. A official 2010 list of private schools identified 148 as holding accredited status and thus eligible for partial public funding, with only four being designated as being simply registered. From their names three of these were protestant Christian schools and one a Mennonite school. At least 57 (39 percent) of the accredited schools were protestant Christian, 18 (12 percent) were culture and language schools, two were Jewish, two Islamic, and two Sikh. Despite Alberta's publicly funded separate schools there was also at least one accredited private school offering a traditional Catholic education. Overall Alberta's private schools accounted for four percent of total provincial enrolment in 2010, which is a decrease from the 4.5 percent reported by Statistics Canada (2001) for 1998-99, the only such decrease in any province over that period. Even so, this apparent decline does not reflect the increased enrolment in publicly funded charter and alternative schools as discussed more fully in a subsequent section.

Section 1 of Saskatchewan's *Education Act* defines an independent school as an institution "(i) in which instruction is provided to pupils of compulsory school age; and (ii) which is controlled and administered by a person that is not a public authority". As in other jurisdictions all independent schools must be registered and may also be accredited. To qualify for a certificate of registration applicants are required to affirm that the facilities satisfy recognized standards, the school is governed by a properly incorporated board comprised of at least three adults from three different families, and the school will enrol pupils from at least two families. Applicants are also required to submit a statement of the school's philosophy and goals, which is reviewed by officials. Saskatchewan's (1991) *Independent School's Policy Manual* stresses that the legal criterion for acceptance is that the goals of an independent school are "not inconsistent" with official provincial goals, and that the onus to demonstrate inconsistency is on Department officials. Further, Section 18(1) of *The Independent Schools Regulation* clarifies that "Each registered independent school has the freedom to add to the goals of education for Saskatchewan and to define responsibility for their achievement among the school, the home, the church, and the community", this requirement not being "intended to diminish or infringe on the religious conscience of the owner or operator of any registered independent school". Section 10(1) of the Regulation requires registered independent schools to employ provincially certificated teachers, but provisions are made for otherwise qualified teachers who do not satisfy normal provincial certification requirements to be granted appropriate probationary certificates at the discretion of the Department. Accreditation requires schools to subscribe to – rather than be consistent with – the official goals of education, to implement the official curriculum, and accept supervision by the Department or local board officials. Schools may seek accreditation for one, two or all of the elementary, middle and secondary curriculum levels.

Prior to 2012 accreditation did not confer eligibility for funding, but Saskatchewan had traditionally funded what are known as historical high schools which are long established, religiously-affiliated secondary schools granted special status in recognition of their invaluable educational contributions in the province's early years, when public secondary schools were not widely available. Since 1991 the province has also provided financial support for associate schools which are religiously-based independent schools that have entered into a joint operating agreement with a public board. Such schools must be operated by a non-profit corporation and conform to provincial curriculum policy, but they retain their freedom to educate from a philosophical perspective different from the public schools. There were ten such associated schools in 2010, accounting for almost half of the total enrolment in independent schools. In December 2011 Saskatchewan announced increasing funding for associate schools. More significantly the Minister of Education also announced a new category of qualified independent schools. This initiative will provide accredited schools with financial support equivalent to 50 percent of provincial per student funding beginning in 2012-13. Qualified independent schools will be required to employ only teachers with a Professional "A" teaching certificate, implement the Saskatchewan Curriculum, participate in the provincial accountability framework, submit to inspection and supervision, and comply with ministry policy and directives.

Overall, Saskatchewan's independent schools enrolled 2.5 percent of all elementary and secondary students in 2010-11, as compared to 1.6 percent in 1990-91, although total enrolment has declined slightly in recent years.[32] The new category of qualified schools should re-establish the upward trend.

Ontario is the most populous province by far, with more than 2.2 million pupils enrolled in public and non-public schools in 2010-11, compared to 1.4 million in Quebec, 0.65 million in British Columbia and 0.59 million in Alberta. It also has the least restrictive and least sophisticated polices toward non-public schools. Section 1(1) of Ontario's *Education Act* defines a private school as "an institution at which instruction is provided at any time between the hours of 9 a.m. and 4 p.m. on any school day for five or more pupils who are of or over compulsory school

[32] personal correspondence & Statistics Canada, 2001, p. 2

age in any of the elementary or secondary school courses of study." Section 21(2) excuses pupils from attending public schools if they are "receiving satisfactory instruction at home or elsewhere". Satisfactory instruction is not defined in the *Act* or elsewhere, although Bernard Shapiro[33] recommended promising wording in his Royal Commission report on private schools in the province. Section 16 of the *Act* provides that all private schools must file an annual notice of intent to operate which "shall include such particulars as the Minister may require". The required particulars are minimal as are the operational expectations outlined on the official form on which schools submit the details. A private school is expected to have common, school-wide policies on attendance, assessment and evaluation and a common procedure for reporting to parents. Private schools are also required to have open admission policies and to be open to official monitoring and inspection. Ontario does not require private schools to adhere to the provincial curriculum, although most if not all publicly declare they do; nor are private schools required to submit curricula for approval, demonstrate compatibility of goals and philosophies with those of the provincial system, or employ provincially certificated teachers. Except, that is, for private schools seeking to offer course credits for the Ontario secondary graduation diploma, in which case they must request and pay for provincial inspections and conform to any appropriate requirements. Private schools are not required to participate in provincial testing programs, but may do so for a fee. This almost total absence of prescription is accompanied by a total lack of financial support. As discussed in more detail later, a recent Conservative government introduced a tax credit for parents paying fees to private schools, but this was repealed by the successor Liberal government. Given the relative lack of official scrutiny and the absence of any per-pupil funding, enrolment data for Ontario private schools are unreliable and less than timely. We estimate of there were approximately 145,000 or more students attending almost 1,000 Ontario private schools in 2010-11, representing a little more than six percent or so of total public and non-public enrolment. There is nonetheless no doubt that Ontario private school enrolments have increased substantially over the past half-century, rising from slightly less than 2 percent in 1960, through 3.3 percent in 1990-91, to perhaps 6.7 percent in 2011. Approximately half of the students attend religiously defined private schools, including at least twenty schools offering a traditional Roman Catholic education.

Home Education

As noted earlier, home education in all Canadian educational jurisdictions satisfies compulsory education requirements. Yet while the right for parents to choose to home educate their children has been protected since confederation, the regulatory framework within which home education has been delivered in Canada has varied over time and across educational jurisdictions.

[33] Bernard Shapiro, 1985, p. 42

As in most Western countries the first phase of modern era Canadian homeschooling was initiated by critics who questioned the correspondence between the institutional processes of schooling and the child's natural approaches to learning. Legal provision for the freedom to home educate, however, implied neither general awareness of the practice nor accessible expertise to support the practice. Thus first phase of modern homeschooling in Canada—protected by residual regulation from pioneer times—was often met with attempts to either shut down individual instances of the practice, naively subject the practice to hostile interrogation, either formally or informally, or simply marginalize the practice by regarding it as a curiosity.

The second phase homeschooling in Canada begun in the early 1980s and lasting to the mid-1990s, resulting in a comparative explosion of adherents. Homeschooling families were often dealt with by the authorities on a case by case basis, their treatment ranging from lenient to invasive. Even where provincial policies existed board by board application varied. A festering discontent emerged over the prevalence of unevenly applied vague laws and policies which resulted in many families hesitating to declare their status and be counted in official statistics. The variation in accountability measures during this phase—many of which resulted in provincial inquiries and several of which moved into the courts—could not be sustained. Combined with the increasing numbers of students that had to be somehow incorporated into the educational framework, Ministries became more invitational in their approach to homeschooling.

In contrast to the two earlier phases, the current third phase of home education in Canada is marked by normalization of the practice. From the mid to late 1990s until the present, not only were regulations and policies standardized within each province, but the aura of suspicion surrounding the practice in many provinces was lifted and Ministries conveyed an authentic desire to record how many and which families were home educating and in some jurisdictions—especially the western provinces— to offer authentic practical financial and/or resource support towards its success. An atmosphere of freedom and trust began to surround the practice as a new phase of long term reporting and standardized regulation came into place in most jurisdictions.

In the four most western provinces regulatory changes occurred in the late 1990s and early 2000s—and since then some have been further updated—resulting in each province's legislation not only mentioning home education in some form, but several also providing separate detailed regulation of the practice. For example, in Ontario a new 2002 Ministry of Education Policy Program Memorandum[34] ushered in a new era of official accommodation toward home education, as did a new 2003 section of the Prince Edward Island *Education Act*.

[34] PPM 131

This process of normalization has primarily moved from west to east, with Quebec and Newfoundland and Labrador remaining anomalies as both jurisdictions continue to evidence an inhospitable disposition towards home education. In Quebec some have argued that coherence with continental European educational ideals for equality rather than liberty for diversity appears to serve as inspiration. A hesitation to risk any form of parallel societies being shaped through diverse approaches to education results in a constricted view of acceptable approaches to homeschooling and thus the form of homeschooling that is tolerated is doing that which occurs at school at home.

Smith (1996) discusses how home schooling was first "recognized as an acceptable educational option within the education acts of Saskatchewan, Alberta, British Columbia, and Yukon Territory",[35] with other jurisdictions simply allowing exemption from compulsory public school attendance where a child was under "efficient", "equivalent", "satisfactory", or "adequate" instruction at home or elsewhere. Although they allowed for it, the statutes in those provinces did not then make specific reference to homeschooling. But over the past 15 years or so, notable changes have been made. Eleven provinces and territories now specifically recognize the option of home schooling (by some such similar name) within their statutes. Four distinctive labels are used in the respective Education or School Acts to describe the practice: "home education/home education program" (British Columbia, Alberta, Nova Scotia, Prince Edward Island, Yukon Territory), "home-based education" (Saskatchewan), "home school/ home schooling/homeschooled/home schooling program" (British Columbia, Manitoba, Quebec, Northwest Territories and Nunavut Territory), and "home instruction" (Newfoundland). These Education or School Acts not only specifically name the practice but include varying amounts of detail on its governance. Only in Ontario and New Brunswick is the practice not recognized in legislation, these two jurisdiction simply allowing for the fulfillment of compulsory attendance requirements by a student being under either "satisfactory" or "effective" instruction "elsewhere", additional policy documents in these two provinces completing the specifications. In New Brunswick parents must annually complete an Annual Home Schooling Application Form that includes their instruction intentions regarding curriculum, assessment, field trips and resources. In Ontario educational authorities are instructed in PPM 131 to accept from parents a notification of intent to home school and are subject to conditions under which they may conduct any investigation. The gradual recognition of home schooling in the governing education legislation of all but two of Canada's provinces and territories effectively entrenches this educational option as a legitimate choice. Furthermore, a growing number of jurisdictions have developed regulations governing the practice of home education. In general these regulations cover such issues as the responsibilities of the various parties, the notification process, and assessment and funding arrangements, where applicable, thus increasing

[35] Smith, 1996, pg. 1

official recognition of the practice. In short, the practice is increasingly regarded as acceptable and no longer is viewed with suspicion.

Ontario is similar to most Canadian educational jurisdictions in that funding is not provided for home educating parents. Section 21 of the *Education Act* simply allows for "satisfactory instruction at home or elsewhere" and an official directive instructs officials to collect basic information from home educators in their school districts. Although this has not been the case in the past, the atmosphere surrounding the practice is as accepting as it is of private schooling. Freedom is given to follow the educational program of the parent's choice. Slim accountability measures are in place. Home educators function as autonomous educators and unless evidence is presented otherwise, they are deemed to be providing satisfactory instruction. Numbers of home schooled students in the province increased steadily from 3,170 in 2005/2006 to 3,502 in 2009/2010 with the number of home schooled secondary students almost doubling in that period from 575 to 986 students.

Manitoba's *Public School Act* is considerably more demanding than Ontario's *Education Act*. Section 260 requires the parent or guardian of a child who is a pupil in a home school to annually notify the minister of the establishment of the home school in an approved format, providing the name and birth date of each pupil, the name of the school or school division each pupil would otherwise attend, and an outline of the education program and grade level for each pupil. The educational programs are completed according to a Notification Form Template and are typically submitted by October 1 of each year for each student. The parent or guardian is also required to provide the Minister with periodic progress reports on each pupil in the home school in January and June of each year. Every report is reviewed, processed, and filed, and in some instances feedback is provided to the parents. Students are not required to participate in any provincial or other standard forms of assessment and no funding is offered for the home education program. The latest numbers available for Manitoba indicate that home schooling enrolments have steadily increased from 1,669 students in 2004/05 to 2,126 in 2010/11. One home schooling liaison in a homeschooling regional office suggested that the increase may be due to increased bullying in schools, an increased willingness by parents to comply with the notification requirements, and an increase in the popularity of blended school and home school models of educational delivery.

The *Education Act* of the Statutes of Saskatchewan, defines home-based education as a program that is provided to a pupil between the ages of 6 and 18, that is started at the initiative of and is under the direction of the parent or the guardian of the pupil, and in which the pupil is receiving instruction at and from the home of the pupil. In striking contrast to the definition of student in the Ontario *Education Act*, the definition of pupil in the Saskatchewan Act includes a person who is receiving instruction in a registered home-based education program. Section

157(1) of the *Act* allows that a pupil may be exempted from attendance at a school ... where the pupil is receiving instruction in a registered home-based education program. The Home-based Education Program Regulations, first promulgated in 1994 and revised in 2000, specify that registration of home-based pupils will, in the first instance, be with the pupil's resident board, but if necessary may be with the Department of Education. Notification of intention to provide home-based education must be given by August 15 before instruction begins. The home-based educator is deemed to have accepted the control, direction and management of the home-education program and the responsibility for the education of the student. In what appears to be the more detailed approach to reporting, a written education plan is required as is a portfolio of student work as well as annual report of student progress. Only the portfolio need not necessarily be submitted to the authorities annually. Access to standardized testing and special needs assessments are made available. School divisions receive up to 50 percent of the regular per pupil funding amount per registered home educating student with some of the funds being redistributed to the parent through items such as books, facilities use, or waived distance learning fees. The number of students enrolled in home-based learning in Saskatchewan was 1,810 in the 2008/09 school year with modest increases to 1,940 in September 2010 and to 1,996 students by September 2011. As the province has seen recent increases in population it thus appears that the percentage of home educated students has remained constant.[36]

The Department of Education in Alberta claims that "school choice is a key strength of Alberta's education system...[and that] the updated Home Education Regulation (2006) ensures home education in Alberta continues to be a meaningful option for students and their parents". Section 29 of the *School Act* states that a parent of a student may provide a home education program for the student if the program meets the requirements of the regulations and is under the supervision of a board or an accredited private school. Associate school boards and associate private schools will evaluate the performance of home-educated students based on education programs planned and provided by parents. Home-educated students will be visited at least twice each year by a teacher from the associate school board or associate private school. These teachers will assess progress by reviewing samples of students' work and by observing students while they perform learning tasks. Information gathered from these visits will be shared with parents. Funding is provided for both the associate school and the parents. Student enrolment in home education in Alberta have increased slightly from 9,976 in 2007/2008 to 10,461 in 2011/2012. These numbers include home schooled students enrolled in blended programs and all are registered with Public, Separate, Francophone, Charter, Early Childhood Service Private Operators or Private School Authorities.

In British Columbia parents must enroll their home schooled child with a public

36 personal communication, 28 December 2011

school or independent school of their choice. The school is paid a nominal fee (slightly more if it is a public school) for accepting the enrolment, maintaining contact with the family and offering evaluation and assessment services as well as instructional resources for the pupil. The number of homeschooled students *enrolled* in public and independent schools in British Columbia declined from 2,811 in 2006/07 to 2,228 in 2010/11. In contrast the number of students enrolled in Distributed Learning Programs (in which students are *registered* with a school and most of the learning takes place at a distance) increased by almost 300 percent during the same period, from 16, 876 to 49,601 students. During this period the number of students enrolled in all forms of schooling in the province decreased from 655,732 to 649,366, but independent school enrolment increased from 67,916 to 70,272.[37]

The Quebec *Education Act*, Article 15, states that, "a student who receives home schooling and benefits from an educational experience which, according to an evaluation made by or for the School Board, is equivalent to what is provided at school", is exempt from compulsory attendance. If applicable, a child must have a Certificate of Eligibility for English Instruction under the *Charter of the French Language* in order to be homeschooled in English, and must be registered with a local school board. Parents must annually complete an Application Request for Home Schooling and provide a detailed Home Schooling Education outline that reflects the Quebec Education Program and demonstrates on educational experience equivalent to that provided by the School Board on or about May 31 of the year prior to home schooling. Approvals are signed contracts between the parents and the School Board. Evaluation that the child is meeting expectations by the School Board takes place on an annual basis by a teacher in the school in the student's Board attendance zone. Students must also participate in any Ministry of Education end-of-cycle assessments. Parents must maintain a portfolio of the teaching, learning and assessment experiences during the term of the approval. Any compliance failures become legal matters. Consistent with this rigid view towards home schooling, Quebec is the only Canadian jurisdiction where recent legal action has taken place surrounding a family's right to home educate their children.

As part of home schooling registration process in the Yukon Territory, parents are required to submit a three year education plan which includes the teaching methods and resources to be used for the subjects of literacy and numeracy. There is no requirement to provide this information for other subject areas. Home education is described by the Yukon Department of Education as one of the educational "alternatives outlined in the *Education Act*". Section 31 gives extensive detail on the Home Education Program requirements.

Section 139 of Prince Edward Island's *School Act* states

---

[37] British Columbia, 2011, p. 1 & 30

> (1) A parent who intends to provide a home education program for his or her child shall, before the commencement of the school year, provide the Minister with (a) a notice of the parent's intention to provide a home education program; and (b) a copy of the proposed home education program.
> (2) The Department may provide to the parent advice and comments on the home education program.
> (3) A student attending a home education program may attend courses offered by a school board as permitted by the regulations.

The Private Schools and Home Education Regulation provides more detail, for example, on the name and address of a teacher advisor who is eligible for an instructional license under the Act and who would be available to the parent to provide advice or guidance to the parent on the child's home education program. Further details about textbooks availability and extracurricular opportunities with the school board are also given.

New Brunswick education statistics reveal that the numbers of notifying home educators in the province are remaining steady with, for example, 565 notifying students in 2007/08 and 597 in 2011/12. (Approximately 30 to 50 per year are francophone, the great majority anglophone.) In some sense the number of notifying home schooled students is surprising given that not even twice the amount are enrolled in independent schools in the province per year. In all, the province currently has approximately 102,000 students thus just over half of a percent of the New Brunswick students are home educated. The education official who shared these statistics is confident that they represent 90 to 95 percent of all home educated students in the province, so that the number of students being home educated "underground" is very small.

Canada is one of only three nations—the others being the United States of America and South Africa—that hosts a privately funded organization with fulltime lawyers on staff that serves the legal needs of home educators. Such organizations not only contribute to the protection and standardization of the practice of home education, they serve educative and support functions that contribute to the legitimization and maturation of this relatively new form of education. Thus it could be argued that statutes and policy surrounding the governance and practice of homeschooling within most Canadian jurisdictions might be regarded as unique from an international perspective. The ongoing active participation and presence of such organizations might well have contributed to exemplary, if not at minimum, satisfactory regulatory environment (in almost all provinces) within which to deliver home education. The role of such organizations may well have contributed to increasing not only public confidence in the practice of home education but also of home educators' confidence that they will be treated fairly and with respect. Even so, with the increasing confidence in the practice of home education in Canada it is hard to say whether the modestly increasing numbers of enrolled/registered/notified home educated students in Canada simply reflects an increased comfort level with reporting or does indeed indicate an increase in the numbers of students being home educated in Canada.

Given the most recent available numbers reported above for registered home educating students in British Columbia (2,228), Alberta (10,461), Saskatchewan (1,996), Manitoba (2,126), Ontario (3,502), and New Brunswick (597), we have evidence for almost 21,000 home educating students in Canada. Imputing missing numbers for Quebec, the other three Atlantic provinces, and for the three territories, a modest estimate of registered home educated students in Canada in 2011/2012 would be 25,000. With an estimated additional unreported 10 percent of total home educating students that are not registered (a reasonable percentage proposed in conversation with a number of home education officials in various provinces), it is likely that at minimum 27,500 Canadian students are currently being home educated. While these numbers are small, and appear in no jurisdiction to exceed one percent of the student population, the choice to home educate in Canada remains a steady, if not somewhat increasingly popular, option over recent years.

School choice not limited by family income

Six of Canada's thirteen education jurisdictions offer direct per-pupil financial support to non-public, child-enrolling schools that satisfy their accountability standards. Leaving aside the North West Territories, where there are currently no non-public schools in operation, the five remaining jurisdictions that currently provide public funds supporting eligible non-public schools (Alberta, British Columbia, Manitoba, Quebec and Saskatchewan) account for 54 percent of the total Canadian population, 54 percent of national Gross Domestic Product, and 63 percent of total non-public school enrolment in Canada. If Ontario—which is home to 38.7 percent of the Canadian population, accounts for 39.7 percent of national GDP and approximately 35.7 percent of all non-public school students—were to be excluded from this calculation, then the provinces that provide some direct financial support for non-public schools would account for approximately 97 percent of the total non-public school enrolment. Even after adjusting for the relatively few private schools in those provinces that do benefit from government funding, it is fair to say that if Ontario were to be excluded from consideration then some 90 percent of parents with children enrolled in Canadian non-public schools would be recognized as benefitting from partial public subsidies of the schools concerned. While this statistic may appear somewhat obscure, it gains significance when it is realized that Ontario did provide limited financial support for non-public school parents from 2001 - 2003, as discussed later.

The level of support in the five provinces currently providing direct financial support ranges from 35 to 70 per cent of the per-pupil operating grants made to public schools, with the subsidies usually being paid directly to recipient non-public schools. Various forms of ancillary financial assistance are provided by jurisdictions that do and do not provide direct support through such grants. Some jurisdictions, Prince Edward Island for example, allow private schools access to authorized textbooks on the same fee basis as public schools, while Manitoba provides an annual $60 per-pupil grant to unfunded private schools for textbook purchases. Non-public schools also benefit from property tax exemptions and from gifts and contributions that donors can deduct from their income tax as charitable donations. While this can be viewed as a notable subsidy, public school boards, post-secondary institutions, churches and other agencies considered to contribute to the public good—including government entities— are also exempt from property taxes. Many publicly funded educational organizations (including school boards and some public schools) have established foundations or made similar provisions which allow them to benefit from tax-deductable charitable donations.

Some non-public schools also share in the modest Federal grants made to support second language instruction programs. These funds originate from the national government but are administered and distributed under agreements negotiated with each province and territory. This allows for some very minimal, indirect federal support for non-state schools in the seven jurisdictions which do not provide direct subsidies. Indirect financial assistance is also available in the form of several Federal income tax benefits. Parents with children attending non-public schools that provide religious instruction may be able to claim a charitable contribution tax credit for the portion of the tuition fee attributed to religious, as distinguished from other academic, instruction. Parents may also be able to claim a child care tax deduction for any portion of school fees charged for supervision before or after the regular school day. Recent Federal budgets have introduced two new tax credits for children enrolled in eligible fitness and arts programs. These are available to all parents of children under sixteen and are usually used to offset costs of out-of-school programs, but they do provide opportunities for non-public schools to seek tax credit eligibility for parts of their instructional programs. The new Children's Arts Tax Credit introduced in the 2011 Federal budget is particularly interesting in this regard as eligible expenses include fees for activities such as language, music, dance and visual arts instruction. Parents may claim up to $500 of eligible expenses for each child under 16 each year, but the tax credit only amounts to 15 percent of the sum claimed. Tuition fees for children enrolled in Nursery, Junior Kindergarten and Kindergarten may also qualify as tax deductable child care expenses. Tuition fees for Nursery and Junior Kindergarten pupils are fully tax-deductible, but only 57.3 percent of Kindergarten fees are eligible.

Ontario's brief flirtation with partial funding for non-public schools extended from 2001 to 2003, but sprang from roots extending much deeper in time and which must be expected to bring forth new initiatives in the future. The immediate history begins with then Premier William Davis' 1984 announcement to the legislature that his Progressive Conservative government intended to extend public funding to the senior grades of Roman Catholic high schools which, as discussed earlier, had continued to be operated as private schools following the final 1928 decision in the Tiny Township case. When making the his announcement Davis observed that

> ... what we have decided to do legitimately raises questions about the place of independent schools in our province. While rights are not at issue, the diversity and quality of our society is affected and served by these schools. ... Thus, a commission of inquiry will be established by the Ministry of Education:
>
> • to document and comment on the role of independent schools;
> • to assess whether public funding, and its attendant obligations, would be desirable and could be compatible with the nature of their independence; and
> • to identify possible alternative forms of governance for these schools and make recommendations for changes deemed to be appropriate.[38]

Bernard Shapiro was appointed the sole Commissioner and submitted his report (which includes valuable appendices reporting research undertaken for the Commission) the following year. He observed that while there was a clear constitutional obligation to fund separate schools, there were no constitutional restrictions on other kinds of schools the province might choose to fund, noting that when the constitution is read along with the

> antidiscrimination provisions of The Canadian Charter of Rights and Freedoms [they] provide a strong argument for the extension of public funding to private schools [and that] the strength of this argument is increased ... by any extension of public funding to the secondary Roman Catholic schools since this appears to be more clearly an act of political will than a fulfillment of a constitutional obligation. The government is, of course, clearly entitled to exercise this political will but not on a discriminatory basis.[39]

Even so, Shapiro declared he did not "believe that such [non-public] schools have a right to public funding in any way commensurate with that provided to the Province's public schools".[40] He consequently recommended two forms of financial subsidy, the first a modest program of limited support for non-public schools that wished to preserve their independence, the second an associated school design which would see non-public schools negotiating agreements with public boards which would allow them to share in provincial per-pupil operating grants. The limited support option would have given non-public schools preferential opportunities to purchase or lease surplus public board facilities, allowed access to public school bussing services, and would have provided direct

38 Davis, 1984, p. 76
39 Shapiro, 1985, p. 49
40 *Ibid.*, p. 51

grants for the purchase of instructional materials. Shapiro's associate school model was similar to that currently in place in Saskatchewan except that it would not have been restricted to religious schools and participating schools would have been prohibited from charging tuition fees.[41] These recommendations were not adopted by the Liberal government in office when Shapiro presented his report.

The underlying issues lay dormant until 1992 when they were thrust back onto the public stage by *Adler v. Ontario* in which a group of Jewish and Reformed Christian parents alleged their *Charter* rights to freedom of religion, conscience and equal benefit of the law were being violated by Ontario's failure to fund private religious schools. The trial judge found the parent's equality rights had been infringed but that the discriminatory effect of the *Education Act* was a reasonable limitation under Section 1 of the *Charter*. Ontario's Court of Appeal upheld this decision in 1994 and an appeal to the Canadian Supreme Court was dismissed in 1996, the majority holding that "the appellants, given that they cannot bring themselves within the terms of s. 93's guarantees, have no claim to public funding for their schools".[42] Madame Justice L'HeureuxDubé J. dissented, observing that,

> The legislature creates a distinction between the appellants and others who are able to access publicly funded education in the surrounding social context. As found at trial, remaining a member of the particular religious communities in question and acting in accordance with the tenets of these faiths required that the children be educated in a manner consistent with the faith and therefore outside of the public or Roman Catholic schools. Control over the education of their children was essential to the continuation of the religious communities in question. This distinction results in the denial of the claimants' s.15 right to equal benefit of the law on the basis of their membership in an identifiable group. ... Denial of any funding to the appellants constitutes not only a financial prejudice, but also a complete nonrecognition of their children's educational needs and the children's and parents' fundamental interest in the continuation of their faith. In applying s.15 in the context of the denial of funding for education to those who cannot access it for religious reasons, s.27 of the *Charter* [dealing with the preservation and enhancement of a multicultural heritage] supports a finding that the interests at stake, the preservation and continuation of the communities in question, form interests fundamental to the purposes of the *Charter*. The *Education Act* funding scheme represents a *prima facie* violation of the s.15 guarantee of equal benefit of the law. ...[43]

All sources of legal recourse having been exhausted, in 1996 Arieh Hollis Waldman complained to the Human Rights Committee of the United Nations that Ontario's failure to fund religious schools other than the Roman Catholic separate

[41] *Ibid.*, p. 53
[42] *Adler*, 1996, p. 4
[43] *Ibid.*, p.12 & 14

schools violated sections of the International Covenant on Civil and Political Rights.[44] Waldman specifically complained that he had paid $14,050 in tuition fees for his children to attend Hebrew Day School, while the Roman Catholic separate schools were free. He acknowledged that this amount was reduced by a federal tax credit to $10,810.89, but also pointed out he was required to pay local property taxes to support state schools he did not use.[45] The State party (Canada as the UN member state) responded that the distinction was not between Catholic and other religious schools, but between public and private schools, since the subsidized Catholic system was "subject to state supervision" and thus part of the public system in a way that private schools were not. The State response further argued that Ontario had a legitimate interest in promoting "a tolerant society that truly protects religious freedom," and that this goal was best served by secular public schools. "The State party argues that if it were required to fund private religious schools, this would have a detrimental impact on the public schools and hence the fostering of a tolerant, multicultural, non-discriminatory society in the province".[46]

The Human Rights Committee concluded that Waldman had "sent his children to a private religious school, not because he wishes a private non-Government-dependent education for his children, but because the publicly-funded school system makes no provision for his religious denomination, whereas publicly-funded religious schools are available to members of the Roman Catholic faith".[47] Providing only a secular public education was consistent with the International Covenant on Civil and Political Rights, but "if a State party chooses to provide public funding to religious schools, it should make this funding available without discrimination".[48] As a result, "the State party is under the obligation to provide an effective remedy, that will eliminate this discrimination".[49]

This decision has no legal force or effect but does bear moral force. According to one correspondent, Janet Ecker, the Ontario Minister of Education at the time, stated the government had "no plans to extend funding to private religious schools or to parents of children that attend such schools, and intends to adhere fully to its constitutional obligations to fund Roman Catholic schools".[50]

Discontinuing funding for Catholic public education would bring Ontario into line with the United Nation's Covenant, and this option has typically been supported by some 40–50 percent of respondents in recent public opinion polls. Perhaps

44 United Nations, 1999
45 *Ibid.*, para. 1.3.1
46 *Ibid.*, para. 4.4.3
47 *Ibid.*, para. 10.5
48 *Ibid.*, para. 10.6
49 *Ibid.*, para. 12
50 personal communication, January 2011

curiously, there were 22 private Catholic schools among the 972 private schools in Ontario in 2010, each receiving no direct public financial support. The number of private Catholic schools has been steadily increasing over recent years implying that a growing number of Catholic parents do not consider the publicly-funded Catholic schools to be sufficiently 'religious', preferring to pay for an alternative education which better meets their expectations. These private Catholic schools are preponderantly elementary schools: 12 are elementary only and a further nine are elementary and secondary, while only one school is exclusively secondary. This is particularly interesting, since it can be argued that publicly-funded Catholic elementary schools have remained reasonably well-defined, while the secondary schools have changed considerably since the extension of funding which brought with it mandatory open admissions. In consequence, while the separate elementary schools continue to limit admission to at least nominally Catholic students, the student population of separate secondary schools are by no means exclusively Catholic, although all students are normally required to participate in religious education courses. The very nature of Ontario's Catholic secondary schools has consequentially changed substantially—some would say drastically—since the extension of funding to the senior grades, encouraging many to wonder whether the influx of state money was worth the price. Elementary schools, on the other hand, have remained much more distinctively Catholic; yet this is the level where there has been most growth in the private sector.

In April 2001, less than two years after the 1999 finding of discrimination by the United Nations Human Rights Committee, then Conservative Premier Mike Harris introduced a measure to provide tax credits to parents who chose to send their children to non-public schools. Tax credits for private school tuition were to be phased in over five years, up to a maximum of 50 percent of the independent school tuition, to a limit of $3,500. With this provision Ontario would join the five other provinces financially supporting non-public schools, but unlike the other provinces this scheme would transfer money to parents rather than schools. This partial voucher scheme was very short-lived. Harris' government had waged a lengthy, largely successful, battle to reform public education in the province which had been decried by the Liberal and New Democratic Party opposition and bitterly resisted by the teacher unions. The 2003 provincial election was won handily by the Liberals with the active support of the teacher unions and the new government immediately cancelled the tax credit retroactively, vowing to deny any future funding to private schools.

This was by no means the end the of the story. In 2005 the United Nations committee revisited their original decision and issued a second report condemning Ontario for having failed to "adopt steps to eliminate discrimination on the basis of religion in the funding of schools in Ontario".[51] John Tory, the aptly named new leader of the Conservative party, sought to respond to the issues in the

51 United Nations, 2006, p. 6

subsequent 2007 election by promising to fund all faith-based schools provided they hired provincially licensed teachers, participated in provincial testing, taught the provincial curriculum, and accepted supervision by local public school boards. The details of the proposal involved absorbing private faith-based schools into the public system as alternative schools, in which religious content would be permitted in addition to the provincial curriculum, essentially mirroring Shapiro's original 1985 recommendation. The proposal was widely condemned by those who opposed all alternatives to public schooling, but it was also condemned by some independent school supporters and viewed with suspicion by many others on the grounds it demonstrated a fundamental misunderstanding of what faith-based schools are about. The public controversy raised by the proposal contributed to the defeat of the Conservatives.

As sketched earlier, the population affected by the funding issue is not insubstantial, and has been increasing steadily for many years. In 2010, an estimated 145,000 pupils attended 972 private schools in Ontario, representing about six percent of the total provincial student population, up from 3.7 percent in 1990. Of the 972 schools, 53 percent offered only elementary grades, 22 offered only secondary, and 24 percent offered both. Approximately half of the schools were defined by a specific religion or denomination, including 340 Christian schools, 48 Jewish schools, and 53 Islamic schools, the latter having grown explosively in over the first decade of the new century. There were also about 190 private schools catering to specific populations, primarily special education groups, or offering on-line and/or tutorial services, the latter being another area of growth.

While there is no government funding for non-public schools in Ontario, there is a private charitable foundation which provides financial support. Children First, a project of the Fraser Institute which also operates in Alberta, provides funds to parents wishing to send their elementary-aged children to independent schools. Grants are awarded to cover half of the cost of tuition, up to a maximum of $4,000, with no restrictions on the choice of school. In 2010, the foundation gave grants to 1,000 children, attending more than 200 Ontario independent schools. Grants are awarded based entirely on the financial need of parents, with no academic, prior achievement, or other criteria considered. The fund is limited, and if there are more applicants than grants in any given year—which is typically the case—a simple lottery is used to select families. Once a family is funded, the funding usually continues throughout the elementary years.

Saskatchewan has long funded its separate and other public schools equally. As touched on earlier the province has also funded two kinds of non-public schools—associate schools and historical high schools—and recently announced plans to fund a new category of qualified independent schools at 50 percent of the average public per capita rate beginning in the 2012-13 academic year.[52] Associate schools,

[52] Saskatchewan, 2011

which enrolled 2,028 of Saskatchewan's 4,088 (49.6 percent) non-public students in 2010, are funded at the same level as the public schools administered by the school division with which they are associated, but receive only the proportion of the grant amounts agreed to in the contract negotiated with the division, the balance being retained to fund services provided. The associate schools, which remain independently governed, retain the right to charge tuition and other fees. Agreements are negotiated independently between public or separate divisions and eligible non-public schools. Independent schools are eligible for funding as associate schools if they are religiously-based, governed by a non-profit board, and have been in operation for at least two years. Agreements are expected to address governance, recruitment and employment of staff, facilities, transportation, special needs pupils, curriculum and supervision. Eight of the ten associate schools operating in 2010 were Christian, the remaining two Islamic.

Saskatchewan's historical high schools are long-established, Christian affiliated schools granted special status in recognition of their significant historical contributions. They receive basic per-pupil operating grants at the same rate as public schools, but do not share in the transportation, targeted funding and other selective grants available to public schools. Only permanent resident pupils are eligible for grant support which, given that out-of-province students make up more than half of the total enrolment in these schools, substantially reduces the overall subsidy. Historical high schools are also eligible for capital construction grants amounting to 20 percent of recognized costs. There were seven designated historical high schools operating in 2010, two of which were also associated schools and were funded as such. Total 2010 enrolment for the remaining five historical high schools was 1,185, of which 636 were resident students eligible for basic grant support. Adding together the 2,028 pupils attending associate schools and the 636 resident students enrolled in historical high schools, Saskatchewan provided partial but relatively generous financial support for some 65 percent of the province's non-public school students in 2010. Saskatchewan also funds several independently operated special-needs schools designated as alternative schools. Students are normally placed in these schools by school boards or social and justice agencies. As touched on earlier, the new category of qualified independent schools will be required to employ as classroom teachers only those with a Professional "A" provincial certificate, implement the Saskatchewan Curriculum, participate in the provincial accountability framework, permit inspection and supervision by Ministry officials or designates and comply with Ministry policy and directives. They must also be incorporated non-profit organizations and have been in operation for a minimum of two consecutive years

Alberta also funds its public and separate schools equally, the province having made a commitment to maintaining a single publicly funded system with what it refers to as "two dimensions". Alberta also funds private schools, charter schools and alternative programs operated by public or separate boards. The province began funding private schools with a $100 per pupil grant in 1967 which had increased to $173 by 1973, after which funding was changed to a proportion of the foundation grants allocated to public schools. Initially, eligible private schools received a third of the foundation per-pupil amount, but this was increased at various times culminating in the current (2011) rates of 60 or 70 percent, depending on the accountability measures accepted by governing boards. Child enrolling accredited schools other than designated special education private schools and various language and culture schools are eligible for funding, accreditation requiring adherence to the provincial curriculum, employment of certificated teachers, and participation in provincial testing. To qualify for 60 percent Level 1 funding private schools must agree to regular reviews by provincial officials which include on-site visits, and to the development and maintenance of publicly posted three year plans which include test results and financial statements. The 70 percent Level 2 grants require governing boards to commit to more detailed planning and evaluation activities including participation in Alberta's quality of education accountability surveys, which are standard in all public and separate schools. A major difference is that whereas provincial reviews identify deficiencies to which Level 1 schools can respond as they choose subject to some limited follow-up, Level 2 schools are required to correct any deficiencies identified in provincial reviews. The 60 and 70 percent funding allocations are not calculated on the full range of grants available to public and separate boards: grants for student transportation, administration and socio-economic conditions are not included. Some other targeted grants are fully funded at 100 percent of the public board amount, including grants for students with severe disabilities and registered home education students.

Since 1994 the Alberta *School Act* has authorized the establishment of charter schools, a option unique to this Canadian jurisdiction. The *Charter Schools Handbook*[53] available on the Alberta Education website provides a detailed account of legal requirements and the procedures to be followed by individuals or groups seeking to establish such schools. The *Handbook* describes these schools as "autonomous public schools" which "provide innovative or enhanced means of delivering education to improve student learning".[54] They are autonomous in that they are governed by their own non-profit board and authorized to provide an innovative or enhanced form of education which is different from what is available in local public or separate schools. The specific nature of the education provided is described in the charter agreement proposed by the founders and approved by the Minister of Education. In addition to specifying how the school will be established, and administered the charter is expected to describe "the unique educational service the school will provide",[55] present "the particular teaching philosophy, vision and purpose of the school with the goals of the school written as measurable outcomes" and describe "the improved student learning outcomes

53 Alberta, 2011

54 *Ibid.*, p. 1

55 *Ibid.*

to be attained by the students".[56] Alberta's charter schools are public in that they are licensed by the Minister, are eligible for the same grants as public schools, open to all students eligible to attend public schools (even to those who do not reside locally), required to build their curriculum around the Alberta program of study, employ provincially certificated teachers, and participate in all provincial testing and accountability measures. They must also be non-religious in the sense that "they may not be affiliated with a religious faith or denomination",[57] although they "may provide religious instruction and exercises under section 50 of the Act, as may any other public school".[58] Section 50 of the Act permits boards to prescribe religious and patriotic instruction or exercises as they may decide within their local political environment, subject to the prohibition of religious intolerance as required by Section 3 of the Act. The *Handbook* attempts to reconcile any confusion that may remain by explaining charter schools are not "intended to replace the services offered by private religious schools".[59]

In essence, then, Alberta's charter schools are officially regarded as public rather than private schools, but they are encouraged to be–and endowed with the ability to be—independent of the educational apparatus operated by the state. As such they are clearly schools of choice that, by definition, provide an independently operated, comparably funded form of education not available in the local public schools. While they enjoy equal access to provincial operating grants, they are not eligible for public assistance with capital costs, so that facility costs must be funded through loans and donations. Nor are they permitted to charge tuition fees, although they may levy fees for instructional supplies and materials, as do public schools. To encourage financial viability a minimum enrolment at opening is set at 100 pupils, although this may be varied if considered appropriate. Even so, as Bosetii (2001) put it, Alberta's charter schools "do not operate on a level financial playing field with other public schools".[60]

As discussed further in the following section, Alberta also allows public and separate boards to establish and operate alternative programs requested by parent or community groups. Such programs can emphasize a particular religion and are fully funded. Applicants seeking to establish a charter school must have previously made an unsuccessful attempt to establish an alternative program within their local school board, a requirement which both illustrates Alberta's commitment to accommodating parental choice within its publicly controlled schooling system while also highlighting the combination of independence and (non-religious) choice distinctive of this iteration of the charter school model.

56 *Ibid.*, p. 18
57 *Ibid.*, p. 2
58 *Ibid.*, p. 2
59 *Ibid.*, p. 2
60 Bosetii, 2011, p. 116

There were 12 charter school authorities operating 19 school campuses in 2010, with a total enrolment of 7,800 or so elementary and secondary pupils, representing 1.3 percent of total provincial enrolment. There were 146 accredited private schools eligible for Level 1 or 2 funding in 2010 with a total enrolment of approximately 23,000, representing 3.9 percent of provincial enrolment. Taken together, the fully funded charter school and partially funded private school enrolments amounted to 5.2 percent of total provincial enrolments.

Manitoba began partial funding of non-public schools in 1990, a full century after the legislature had ended funding for Roman Catholic schools and precipitated the provincial-federal crisis known as the Manitoba Schools Question discussed previously. While the Laurier-Greenway resolution to the Question allowed limited religious and French instruction in public schools, it was widely resented by French-Catholics in Manitoba and elsewhere. Resentment deepened with the passage of the 1916 *Education Act* which eliminated French instruction in Grades 1-9 and limited the time available for religious instruction. School district consolidation in the 1960s further exacerbated matters by eliminating many of the small schools which had allowed denominationally homogeneous communities to provide religious education in their local school. The 1959 MacFarlane Royal Commission on Education had perceptively anticipated a consequent increase in demand for non-public religious schools and recommended partial public funding to a maximum of 80 percent of the provincial grant. Despite vigorous lobbying successive governments declined to adopt the Commission's recommendations. After obtaining an encouraging legal opinion in 1985, the Catholic community petitioned the Federal Government to intervene through an interpretation of the 1895 School Question Remedial Order that implied a right to public funding for Catholic schools. This move raised the political stakes, but there was a widely shared preference for a provincial as opposed to an imposed Federal resolution. The 1988 election of a new Conservative government led to negotiations with the Manitoba Federation of Independent Schools which resulted in the 1990 "Letter of Comfort" which extended partial public funding to all approved Catholic and other independent schools and, in doing so, brought the Manitoba School Question to a full close.

As Mrs. Vodrey, then Minister of Education and Training, explained in response to a question in the Legislature:

> the letter of comfort was a mechanism to assist the province and assist the Federation of Independent Schools in coming to terms with an agreement, which avoided a court case and which, we have been led to believe, at that point would require 100 percent funding of independent schools. This agreement was reached in order to avoid that immediate 100 percent funding and to provide a phasein up to a maximum of 80 percent on the operating side, and does not include capital.[61]

[61] Hansard, Monday, May 4, 1992

The initial 80 percent commitment was contentious and subsequently renegotiated in 1996 to the current (2011) equivalent of 50 percent of the net per-pupil operating costs of public boards. To be eligible for funding, schools must be in compliance with the provincial curriculum and offer all mandated compulsory courses, employ provincially certificated teachers, participate in provincial testing and comply with all pertinent regulations and policies. Independent schools—both funded and non-funded—are also eligible for $60 per-pupil curricular materials grants. For non-funded independent schools this amount is made available as a credit for purchases made through the Manitoba Textbook Bureau, whereas funded schools receive half of the amount as cash and the balance as a credit redeemable at the Bureau. Funded independent schools are also eligible for grants for registered special education students at the same rate as are public boards. At their discretion school boards can enter into agreements with funded independent schools to provide shared service agreements providing access to established school bus routes, home economics and industrial arts instruction, and school clinicians. Eligible independent schools must meet the required standards over a three year period before qualifying for grant support.

Manitoba (2011) reported a total of 94 independent schools enrolling 14,594 pupils in September 2010, representing 7.7 percent of total provincial enrolment. The 59 funded independent schools accounted for 92.5 percent of total independent school enrolment, and seven percent of total provincial enrolment. Some of the 35 non-funded independent schools would be serving their three year qualification period preparatory to receiving funding. There were 17 Roman and Ukrainian Catholic schools among the funded independent schools, accounting for 34.5 percent of funded independent enrolment. All of these schools are located in the greater Winnipeg area and are administered by a diocesan school board. As such Manitoba's partially funded Catholic schools are more similar to parochial schools in the United States than they are to separate schools in Alberta, Ontario or Saskatchewan. There were also two Jewish, two Islamic and, judging by their names, at least four Mennonite and 14 other Christian schools among the funded independents in 2010.

British Columbia began funding independent schools in 1977. As discussed in a previous section, independent schools are classified into one of four categories, two of which receive financial support. Group 1 schools receive provincial funding equal to 50 percent of the per student operating grants received by their local public board; Group 2 schools are supported at a rate of 35 percent. Schools in both groups must meet the same accountability requirements, assignment to Group 1 or 2 depending on whether a school's operating costs exceed those of local public schools. In both cases schools must be operated by a non-profit authority and are required to employ provincially certificated teachers, participate in provincial testing, file reports and participate in regular inspections, provide programs that satisfy provincial learning goals and comply with Ministry program requirements. Grants are calculated by multiplying (1) the per-pupil operating grant amount received by the public school board serving the area in which the independent school is located, (2) the number of eligible FTE students enrolled in the school, and (3) the applicable percentage rate which, in turn, is determined by comparing an independent school's average per pupil operating costs with the local board's grant amount. Grants for independent schools which spend more per-pupil than the local public board are calculated at the 35 percent Group 2 rate, all others at the 50 percent Group 1 rate. Calculation of public boards' operating grant amounts include a range of supplementary grants recognizing enhanced instructional costs associated with unique student needs and variable salary, transportation and housing costs, with capital costs being excluded. Independent schools can charge whatever tuition fees they choose, but by basing the grant percentage factor on actual operating costs the state creates a partial defence against accusations of funding elite schools patronized by wealthy families.

In 2010, 318 of the 347 independent schools in British Columbia (92 percent) received government funding, 252 at the Group 1 level and 66 at the Group 2 level. These 318 funded independent schools enrolled 69,218 students, representing 10.7 percent of total public and non-public enrolment in 2010. Group 1 schools enrolled 54,901 and Group 2 14,317 pupils, equating to 79 percent and 21 percent of funded independent enrolment respectively. Nineteen of the 29 non-funded independent schools enrolling 544 students were classified as Group 3 schools that are not required to employ certificated teachers or satisfy provincial curriculum standards . The remaining ten schools with 943 students were Group 4 schools catering to secondary level, off-shore students.

More than a quarter of all British Columbia's non-public school students attend Catholic independent schools and a similar proportion attend other Christian schools. British Columbia's five Roman Catholic Dioceses have each established support systems providing guidance and administrative support for Catholic independent schools within their regions. Details vary but these organizations assist parishes and schools by coordinating financial, operation and personnel policies and procedures. The Catholic Independent Schools of Vancouver Archdiocese is by far the largest of these non-public schools systems, with 49 schools, 900 teachers and some 14,000 pupils. The CISVA sets common tuition fees annually and administers common salary and benefit schedules for teachers and principals, but each school is vested in and operated by a single parish. Each school hires its own staff and, subject to approval by the parish priest, establishes and administers its own budget, which typically includes a subsidy from the parish in addition to revenues from fees and government grants.
Unlike other Canadian jurisdictions, Quebec has provided some form of financial support to private schools throughout much of its history. Funds provided prior to passage of the *Private School Act* in 1968 were distributed in a somewhat inconsistent and inequitable manner: for a time Roman Catholic classical colleges providing secondary education for boys were subsidized, for example, while those educating girls were not. Passage of the *Private Schools Act* established a statutory

basis for funding all non-public schools that were recognized as being, in the wording of the original legislation, "in the public interest". Initially the level of grant support was a remarkable 80 percent of the per pupil grant to public schools. This initial generosity preserved many of the classical colleges operated by religious orders which had provided pre-university education to generations of Catholic Quebecers, and which had been struggling to compete with the new public secondary schools and junior colleges (GEGEPs).

Private school funding was an issue in Quebec's landmark 1976 provincial election campaign with the separatist Parti Québécois (PQ) led by René Lévesque advocating the complete elimination of government subsidies for private schools. After being swept into power with a stunning majority, Lévesque's new government abandoned its policy of elimination in favour of reduced support and by 1990-91 grant support to private schools had fallen to 52 percent of the public school per pupil grant. Quebec separatism has been in remission since the close-run 1995 referendum and the province reverted to a Liberal government in 2003. Financial support for private schools increased somewhat over the past decade or so to stabilize around 55-60 percent of the per pupil public school grant.

Overall, Lefebvre & Merrigan[62] report that approximately 90 percent of primary and secondary schools are subsidized. Under current rules only accredited private schools are eligible for government subsidies. As discussed earlier, accreditation requires compliance with the *Charter of the French Language* and delivery of the provincial curriculum, the former limiting admittance to English instruction schools to anglophone Canadians and the latter requiring, in part, delivery of the secularized new Ethics and Religious Culture curriculum. Eligible private schools receive per-pupil grants to subsidize basic operating costs plus an "allocation in lieu of rental value" to cover "acquisition of furniture, equipment and tools, major repairs, and the improvement and refurbishing of buildings used for the institution's educational projects".[63] Schools may also receive various additional grants to support government priorities and/or subsidize unusual operating costs. Subsidized private schools that provide school bus transportation for their students are eligible to a share of transportation grant allocations.

Per-pupil grant amounts vary by curriculum level. In 2005-2006, the basic operational per-pupil private school grant at the pre-school level was $3,064, at the primary level $2,808 and the secondary level $3,612: per-pupil grants in lieu of rental value were $95, $95 and $139 respectively.[64] Financial reports for 2006-2008 show total government contributions accounted for 43.7 percent of total private school expenditures, with student contributions accounting for 28 percent, donations five percent, auxiliary businesses two percent and other

62 Lefebvre & Merrigan, 2009, p. 6
63 Quebec, 2009, p. 18
64 Lefebvre & Merrigan, 2009, Table 2, p. 19

revenues (primarily bank and investment interest and rental income) 21 percent. Subsidized private schools are prohibited from charging admission fees exceeding the basic operational per-pupil grant amount. Even so, Lefebvre and Merrigan (2009) report that only a handful of subsidized schools set tuition fees at the maximum level, the average student fee charged in 2004-2005 being 68 percent of the authorized maximum,[65] although fees in unsubsidized 'elite' schools such as Lower Canada College and Selwyn House School are much higher. As noted earlier, private secondary schools are considerably more popular than private elementary schools, a pattern unique to Quebec. Further, a high proportion of Quebec's non-public schools are concentrated in and around Montreal. An eminent student of Quebec's private school sector commented on their religious variety as follows:

> Inexplicably, Ministry of Education data are silent with respect to the denominational character of private schools. However, it is common knowledge that many French-language institutions have Roman Catholic ties. For example, of the 100 private secondary schools belonging to the Association des institutions d'enseignement secondaire (AIES), 64 of them are governed by diocesan clergy or religious communities.[66]

School distinctiveness protected by law and policy

While the Section 93 protections for "any Right or Privileges with respect to Denominational Schools" enjoyed by "any Class of Persons" appear to guarantee religious distinctiveness, the guarantees conferred are limited in various ways. First and most unequivocally this protection has never applied to the five provinces where denominational distinctiveness was not enshrined in law at the time of confederation. Various kinds of public supported religious schools had existed in New Brunswick and Nova Scotia prior to 1867, for instance, but because their status was not codified into law when these two original confederation partners entered the union, these schools did not survive. The more dramatic curtailment of Roman Catholic schools in Manitoba as discussed earlier provides a more draconian example of the historical limitations of the Section 93 protections, as does the limitation of Catholic secondary schools in the wake of the Tiny Township decision in Ontario. In more modern times the 1997 constitutional amendments gained by Quebec and Newfoundland to free their governments from the constraints imposed by Section 93 illustrate how coordination of political interests and public sentiments can mobilize the support needed to revoke even constitutional guarantees. In each case the changes wrought were significant. Prior to the amendments five—fully half—of Canada's provinces representing 77 percent of the national population had state funded, regulated and legitimated denominational schools, whereas nowadays such schools are

65 *Ibid.*, p. 6
66 Magnuson, 1993, p. 5

present in only three of Canada's ten provinces accounting for 53 percent of the population. Newfoundland's 1997 constitutional amendment replaced public schools characterized by religious diversity with bland, secular, uniformity, while Quebec's amendment relegated religious distinctiveness to non-state schools.

Even so, the courts have consistently interpreted Section 93 in ways that have protected the distinctiveness of publicly funded and governed denominational schools where and when the protections applied. Moreover, the legal reasoning and rulings supporting the constitutionality of Ontario's 1985 decision to extend funding to senior high school grades in Roman Catholic separate schools unequivocally upheld a provincial government's powers to extend greater rights and privileges to minority denominational schools should it choose to so do—as the Privy council had recognized in its 1928 ruling that had restricted funding to Grades 1-10. In a less obvious way, the prospect of a legal challenge invoking a retrospective reinterpretation of Section 93 protections for francophone-Catholic public schools in Manitoba was apparently decisive in encouraging the government to adopt the current partial funding arrangements for non-public schools, as illustrated by Mrs. Vodrey's 1992 statement to the Legislature quoted earlier.

Prior to the adoption of Canada's *Charter of Human Rights and Freedoms* rights to French or English language education were implicitly and only loosely protected through the shared identity of religion and language, especially in Quebec. Although various developments in the 1970s gave increasing prominence to the issue of minority language education rights, the Section 23 *Charter* right to a public funded primary and secondary education in the language of the English or French minority added a new form of school distinctiveness to Canada's educational landscape. As discussed earlier, Section 23 does not yet apply fully to Quebec, so that the protections for school distinctiveness that emerged apply primarily to francophone schools outside of Quebec.

The *Charter* right granted in Section 23 "applies wherever ... the number or children who have such a right is sufficient to warrant to them out of public funds of minority language instruction".[67] In its unanimous 1990 ruling in *Mahé v. Alberta* the Supreme Court declared "Section 23 encompasses a 'sliding scale' of requirements ... [which] guarantees whatever type and level of rights and services is appropriate under s. 23 in order to provide minority language instruction for the particular number of students involved". "What is essential", continued the court,

> is that the minority language group have control over those aspects of education which pertain to or have an effect upon their language and culture. So, where the number of s. 23 students does not warrant granting an independent school board (the maximum level of management and control), but is significant

[67] *Charter of Human Rights and Freedoms*, Section 23(3)(a)

> enough to warrant moving towards the upper level of the sliding scale, it may be sufficient to require linguistic minority representation on an existing school board. In this latter case: (1) the representation of the linguistic minority on local boards or other public authorities which administer minority language instruction or facilities should be guaranteed; (2) the number of minority language representatives on the board should be, at a minimum, proportional to the number of minority language students in the school district, i.e., the number of minority language students for whom the board is responsible; (3) the minority language representatives should have exclusive authority to make decisions relating to the minority language instruction and facilities, including: (a) expenditures of funds provided for such instruction and facilities; (b) appointment and direction of those responsible for the administration of such instruction and facilities; (c) establishment of programs of instruction; (d) recruitment and assignment of teachers and other personnel; and (e) the making of agreements for education and services for minority language pupils.[68]

This quite sweeping interpretation resulted in a series of extensive modifications to provincial and territorial education laws to provide francophone communities with meaningful control over the character of their schools, modifications which generated various levels of political opposition in different anglophone provinces. Because *Mahé* concerned the francophone community in the relatively large city of Edmonton, the court's ruling did not specifically address the quantitative aspect of the "where numbers warrant" issue, but this was unavoidable in the 2000 Supreme Court decision in *Arsenault-Cameron v. Prince Edward Island* which turned on the nature of the education the province was obligated to provide for the 59 francophone students residing in the small city of Summerside (population 14,654 in 2001). The province contended it could satisfy Section 23 by transporting the students to a existing French language school, the average bus journey being 57 minutes. In deciding in favour of the francophone appellants the court noted the Minister of Education had failed to allow for increases in enrolment that could follow establishment of a French language school, and had also

> failed to recognize that the s. 23 children were faced with a choice between a locally accessible school in the majority language and a less accessible school in the minority language, a choice which would have an impact on the assimilation of the minority language children.[69]

Taken together the *Mahé* and *Arsenault-Cameron* rulings not only served to strongly protect the distinctiveness of second language instructional education in Canada, they have facilitated the establishment of well appointed schools in relatively

[68] *Mahé v. Alberta*, p. 4-5

[69] *Arsenault-Cameron*, p. 4

small francophone enclaves. A recent case in point is the 2011 ruling of Yukon Supreme Court which requires the government to build a new high school for the territory's only school board, which was established specifically to govern and manage education for Section 23 children. The Commission scolaire francophone du Yukon currently educates some 184 students in its sole elementary school: the new secondary school will likely enrol less than 50 students.[70] The government has appealed the decision alleging bias on behalf of the presiding judge, who once served as president of an Alberta francophone board.

In the policy realm, at least five provinces have official statements in legislation or policy documents recognizing the legitimacy of non-public education options which offer at least implicit protection for school distinctiveness. Educational legislation in British Columbia and Alberta commits each province to maintaining a strong public education system, but it also includes statements recognizing the importance of parental choice and educational diversity. Saskatchewan's *Independent Schools Policy Manual* (1991) contains the following statement:

> Independent schools have the right to exist in Canada. Churches, denominations, and religious societies have an authority separate from the state to operate schools, not always in complete accordance with public education practices.[71]

Distinctive character

As illustrated above, the factors which have led to educational diversity in Canada are unusually varied with language, religion, and pedagogical philosophy all having shaped the development of publicly-funded schools, non-public schools and home education provisions.

One remarkable feature particularly prominent in Alberta has been the development of choice options within the regular public school systems. Section 21 of the province's *School Act* defines an alternative program as "an education program that (a) emphasizes a particular language, culture, religion or subject-matter, or (b) uses a particular teaching philosophy, but that is not a special education program, ... or a program of religious education offered by a separate school board." The Section authorizes a board to establish such programs if it "determines that there is sufficient demand for a particular alternative program." The Edmonton public school currently operates over 100 alternate programs some of which, such as the Amiskwacity Academy and various Christian schools among others are stand-alone schools, and others programs within other "regular" schools, such as the many language and culture programs which include Arabic, Mandarin and German bilingual programs, as well as the non-sectarian Logos

70 McMahon, 28 July 2011
71 Independent Schools Policy Manual, 1991, p. i

Christian programs. This diversity of choice dates from the early 1970s when the Edmonton public board began responding to requests from parent groups by establishing alternative schools tailored to their specific preferences. The first alternative programs included a Talmud school (officially listed as a language and culture program), a fine arts program, a Waldorf school and a program for Cree language speaking children. The board decided to allow faith-based alternatives in 1996. This was primarily in response to parental demand, but public debate surrounding the development of Alberta's non-religious charter schools was influential. The first faith-based alternative program, Logos, was so successful that two well-established private Christian schools thereafter joined the public system as alternative programs.

A different pattern emerged in Calgary, Alberta's other large city, where the development of alternative programs has been much more limited. Distinctively faith-based alternatives were forbidden by the public board, but alternative schools were allowed to provide religious instruction outside of the regular curriculum. This, of course, was unsatisfactory to many parents, since the essence of a faith-based education is that faith informs all aspects of teaching and learning and cannot be relegated to "after hours". The ensuing controversy generated intense political wrangles, with trustees campaigning—and winning election— with the declared intent of abolishing faith-based alternatives within the public system. As of 2011, Calgary has a wide variety of alternative programs, but none are faith-based.

Public alternative programs do exist in other provinces, but generally only in small numbers, and larger urban large centres.[72] Saskatchewan's ten associate schools are perhaps the most obvious, but there are others. Most large boards in Ontario, for example, offer fine arts school and various alternative programs for at-risk students. Occasionally a high-profile alternative, such as a recently established program for black students in Toronto, excites much media attention, but alternative programs are usually quietly introduced and many existing programs are usually not well known. The First Nations School of Toronto, the board's first alternative school opened in 1977, for example , and the Toronto public board currently operates some 100 alternative and specialized programs of varying sizes but minimal publicity. There are a few faith based—or at least affiliated – alternative programs operating under the aegis of a public authority elsewhere in Canada, but outside of Alberta and Saskatchewan this form of school distinctiveness is almost exclusively the domain of non-public authorities.

Decisions about admitting pupils

Discrimination is broadly forbidden under the *Charter*, but the Section 93

[72] see CUP Research Team, 2004

protection for rights and privileges of denominational schools allows Roman Catholic separate schools to restrict admittance to baptized children and members of a church in union with the See of Rome, usually understood as including Greek, Ukrainian and other Eastern rites. As a consequence of the extension of public funding to Catholic secondary schools in Ontario as discussed previously, those schools are required to admit all resident pupils who choose to attend on the understanding they will participate in mandatory religion courses and respect the Catholic religion. This is not the case in Ontario's elementary (K-8) separate schools where admittance is usually restricted to children baptized in the faith or members of a recognized church. Nevertheless, separate boards can and do admit other students on a case-by-case basis when requested, but because non-Catholics are not allowed to direct their property taxes to support separate schools in Ontario, the parents are usually required to pay a fee to compensate for the lost revenue.

Open admittance to Ontario's separate secondary schools has undoubtedly diluted their religious identity, spirit and distinctiveness—to the point of irrelevance in the view of some. Even so, non-Catholic pupils continue to enrol in these schools primarily because their parents believe these schools have more disciplined academic and social cultures. In response to the diluted religious character of these publicly funded Catholic schools more independent, non-publically funded Catholic schools have been established over the past decade or so. Interestingly, though, most of these have been elementary rather than secondary schools.

Resident pupils baptised in the Roman Catholic and associated churches have a right to enrol in separate schools in Alberta and Saskatchewan, but these school also accept other pupils subject to space, program suitability and a commitment to respect the religious identity and character of the school. When public funding was originally extended to various faith-based alternative schools by the Calgary public board, those schools were required to admit any pupils, and were only allowed to provide religious instruction at certain times, and could not make it compulsory. In contrast, the Edmonton public board which, as discussed earlier, has an extensive range of alternative schools, operates various explicitly religious alternatives within the public system.

There are some indications that provincial policies that subsidize non-public schools result in a higher proportion of low-income children attending these schools, as could be expected. "Canadian experience shows that lower-income families are as likely or more likely to take advantage of independent schooling when a public subsidy is available. ... remarkably, children from better-off western families were three percent *less* likely to send their children to independent schools",[73] presumably because they lived in affluent residential communities with good public schools. The obvious inference is that such public funding

---

[73] Robson & Hepburn, 2002, p. 29

promotes equal educational opportunity.

Decisions about staff

As a general rule non-public schools receiving public funding are usually required to employ teachers holding officially approved qualifications, but where there are no public subsidies, there are usually no such requirements. Hence, while teachers in British Columbia's funded independent schools (Groups 1 & 2) are required to hold provincial certification, those employed in the unfunded Group 3 and 4 school do not need to be so qualified, unless a Group 4 school wishes to offer the province's high school graduation certificate, and similar provisions hold in other jurisdictions. Even so, provisions exist for teachers in independent schools who do not meet provincial qualification requirements to obtain acceptable certification on the basis of specialist qualifications obtained elsewhere, such as Montessori or specialist arts training. Ontario, which provides no public funding to independent schools, has no qualification requirements except, again, in the case of secondary schools wishing to offer credits toward provincial secondary school graduation certificates. Even so, non-public schools in Ontario and other Canadian jurisdictions often choose to hire teachers with provincial teaching qualifications, while also providing appropriate preference to qualifications consistent with the philosophy of the school (such as Waldorf training or qualifications from a Christian university).

Canada has strong protections against discrimination on the basis of the race, religious beliefs, colour, gender, physical or mental disabilities, age, ancestry or place of origin and sexual orientation, both in the *Charter* and human rights legislation. Nonetheless, the *Canadian Human Rights Act* and similar provincial statues allow employers to hire selectively for *bona fide* reasons of identify or mission.

The central legal case in the education sector is the Supreme Court's decision in *Caldwell et al. v. Stuart et al.* (1984). Margaret Caldwell had been employed by the Catholic Public Schools of Vancouver Archdiocese, but her contract was not renewed after she married a divorced man in a civil ceremony. The court ruled that this was allowable under the British Columbia Human Rights Code, observing

> ... the Catholic school is different from the public school. In addition to the ordinary academic program, a religious element which determines the true nature and character of the institution is present in the Catholic school. To carry out the purposes of the school, full effect must be given to this aspect of its nature and teachers are required to observe and comply with the religious standards and to be examples in the manner of their behaviour in the school so that students see in practice the application of the principles of the Church on a daily basis and thereby receive what is called a Catholic education. Fulfillment

> of these purposes requires that Catholics observe the Church's rules regarding marriage. It must be celebrated in the Church and the marriage of divorced persons is not recognized. The Board found that Mrs. Caldwell knew this when she was employed, that inquiries were made respecting these matters before she was hired to insure her eligibility for employment in this respect. It was therefore open to the Board to find that when Mrs. Caldwell in contravention of the Church's requirements married a divorced man in a civil ceremony, she deprived herself of a *bona fide* qualification for the employment.[74]

Interestingly, the Catholic school in this case was part of the Catholic Public Schools of Vancouver Archdiocese, and thus a Group 1 category independent school rather than a separate school. Still, the crucial issue in this and similar cases is whether the discrimination is a *bona fide* requirement. The test for this, the court observed, has both subjective and objective branches, the first concerning whether the discriminatory requirement was established honestly, in good faith and with a sincere belief that it is necessary for the work in question to be conducted properly; the second whether the grounds for a selective hiring or dismissal are reasonably necessary to secure the objectives of the enterprise. The importance of satisfying the objective standard was illustrated in a 2000 decision of the Ontario Superior Court which hinged upon the clarity with which employment expectations were articulated to staff. An employee of Christian Horizons, a large provider of residential and support services to the disabled, was dismissed for living in a same-sex, common-law relationship. The employee claimed discrimination to an Ontario Human Rights Tribunal arguing her lifestyle was acceptably Christian, producing Christian authorities to support her point. After hearing depositions from many interested groups, including Catholic Bishops and evangelical organizations, the Ontario Superior Court ruled that religious organization do have the sight selectively hire and fire under the province's human rights code, but must clearly establish reasonable and specific requirements that are properly articulated to prospective employees.

In Alberta, where a number of previously private schools opted to become alternative schools within public boards, the right to require religious conformity has caused problems. The Logos School in Calgary (discussed above) required that teachers "affirm their active membership within a Christian church, and acceptance of the creedal (Apostles' and Nicene Creeds) basis of the Christian faith." This requirement, essential to the definition of the school, was nonetheless unacceptable to a newly elected Calgary public board which cancelled their contract with Logos.[75] Selection of principals was another challenge. In the case of the Edmonton Christian School, already in existence for fifty years, the agreement under which it was integrated into the public system specified that the principal would be hired by the superintendent of the public system, who would consult

74 *Caldwell et al. v. Stuart et al.*, 1984, p. 619-20
75 Hiemstra, 2001, p. 14

with the Edmonton Society for Christian Education Board, and must be bound by the school's definition, whether or not he or she agreed with this.

Accountability for school quality

As in the United States, there has been a difference of opinion in Canada between professional educators and the broader public with regard to the quality of (public) schooling provided and the means of assessing that quality. This difference was illustrated by Holmes's (1998) Ontario survey which found that "while only 11 per cent of directors of education agreed with annual achievement testing of elementary students, the proposal was supported by 59 per cent of a similarly educated comparison group of non-educators".[76] Moves by provincial governments to introduce provincial testing and standards over recent decades have not been popular within the educational establishments. As with all other aspects of education policy and practice, different jurisdictions have adopted different approaches and techniques, with varying degrees of rigour and success and, although the Canadian Council of Ministers of Education has encouraged provinces to participate in international comparisons such a PISA, there are no national educational standards or examinations, and no prospects of such in the future.

As would be expected, the extent to which each jurisdiction requires non-public schools to participate in its assessments programs and conform to its educational standards varies considerably. As a general rule access to public funding depends on a non-public school participating in a province's pupil testing program. Some provinces require non-public schools to demonstrate acceptance of official educational goals and to submit to inspection, but others do not, as discussed in more detail earlier. Alberta goes several steps further requiring its charter and funded independent schools to participate in its school accountability program which includes publication of test results and improvement plans and regular reviews.

Teaching of values

In his wide-ranging criticism of the vague standards bedeviling Canadian education and, in particular, its failure to accurately reflect the true diversity of Canadian society, Mark Holmes (1998) does not spare the way in which the schools approach questions of deeply-held values. While conceding that this partially reflects a failure of broader cultural agencies and actors to address such matters, Holmes argues "the values of the larger society . . . should not be imposed on children by the power of the state against the will of their parents." Nor, he insists, is the claim of value-neutrality often made by and for the public sector at

[76] Holmes, 1998, p. 142-43

all credible given the threats its quasi-monopolistic position creates:

> It is wrong for the state to determine, deliberately or not, that young children should be raised, for example, on the basis of high self-concept and the pursuit of personal self-fulfilment in a morally and socially permissive . . . climate, unless there is a clear consensual support for these values.[77]

The only way out of this dilemma, and the only way to ensure that schools can operate with a clear and distinctive mission, Holmes insists, is to allow for parental choice among state-supported schools. "An important part of the problem facing schools today is simply that people want different and sometimes contradictory things, with the result that teachers face vague ambiguity and high-minded platitudes from the bureaucracies they serve".[78]

When it comes to values and worldviews, it is less problematic for governments to mandate what should not be taught in their quasi-monopolistic schools than to mandate what should be taught. A good example is found in the Alberta *School Act*, where Section 2.01 (which applies to all schools), states

(1) All education programs offered and instructional materials used must reflect the diverse nature and heritage of society in Alberta, promote understanding and respect for others and honour and respect the common values and beliefs of Albertans.
(2) For greater certainty, education programs and instructional materials referred to in subsection (1) must not promote or foster doctrines of racial or ethnic superiority or persecution, religious intolerance or persecution, social change through violent action or disobedience of laws.

Even so, and as we have seen, publicly financed and governed schools in Alberta may include religiously-based alternative programs as well as non-religious emphases.

In 2002 Canada's Supreme Court rendered a long awaited decision in *Chamberlain v. Surrey School District No. 36*, ruling against a decision by the Surrey, British Columbia, public school board that had denied the use of books portraying samesex parent families in lower primary classes. James Chamberlain, a primary level teacher employed by the board, had requested permission to use three books portraying same-sex families in his Kindergarten and Grade 1 classes. The Board declined permission by a 4-2 vote and Chamberlain, with the support of the Civil Liberties Association and a gay advocacy group, challenged the decision in court. The trial judge upheld the school board's decision, which was subsequently quashed by the BC Supreme Court and then reinstated by the Court of Appeal.

---

77 *Ibid.*, p. 240
78 *Ibid.*, p. 85

The trial judge found the Board had concluded the books would "engender controversy in light of some parents' religious objections to the morality of samesex relationships". The judge further noted that the provincial curriculum objectives could be achieved without use of the books and that books' content was not age appropriate.[79]

Although the case had been initially been framed as turning on Charter rights and the lower courts had indeed treated it as such, the ultimate ruling from Canada's Supreme Court relied on administrative law principles, observing "The *School Act*'s insistence on secularism and nondiscrimination lies at the heart of this case".[80] The court reasoned that

> The Board was authorized to approve or not to approve books for classroom use. But its authority is limited by the requirements in s. 76 of the *School Act* to conduct schools on "strictly secular and nonsectarian principles" and to inculcate "the highest morality" while avoiding the teaching of any "religious dogma or creed". The words "secular" and "nonsectarian" in the Act imply that no single conception of morality can be allowed to deny or exclude opposed points of view. Disagreement with the practices and beliefs of others, while certainly permissible and perhaps inevitable in a pluralist society, does not justify denying others the opportunity for their views to be represented, or refusing to acknowledge their existence. Whatever the personal views of the Board members might have been, their responsibility to carry out their public duties in accordance with strictly secular and nonsectarian principles included an obligation to avoid making policy decisions on the basis of exclusionary beliefs. Section 76 does not prohibit decisions about schools governance that are informed by religious belief. The section is aimed at fostering tolerance and diversity of views, not at shutting religion out of the arena. It does not limit in any way the freedom of parents and Board members to adhere to a religious doctrine that condemns homosexuality but it does prohibit the translation of such doctrine into policy decisions by the Board, to the extent that they reflect a denial of the validity of other points of view.[81]

This was nonetheless a majority decision. In their dissenting opinion justices Gonthier and Bastarache based their analysis of the reasonableness of the School Board's decision within both the local context as well as *School Act* requirements and *Charter* standards.

> The privileged role of parents to determine what is in their children's well-being, including their moral upbringing, and their right to raise their children in accordance with their conscience, religious or otherwise, is

79 *Chamberlain*, p. 3
80 *Ibid.*, p. 4
81 *Ibid.*, p. 5-6

> central to analyzing the reasonableness of the School Board's decision. The common law has long recognized that parents are in the best position to take care of their children and make all the decisions necessary to ensure their well-being providing they act in accordance with the best interests of their children. This Court has reiterated the paramount parental role by construing the nature of the authority schools and teachers have over children as a delegated authority. The notion of a school's authority being delegated, if it allows parents to remove their children from the public school system, must also guarantee to parents the role of having input with regard to the values which their children will receive in school. This is generally brought about by electing representatives to school boards who will develop consensus and govern on matters pertaining to public education. These local school boards are empowered by the School Act to approve or not approve complementary educational resource materials. They do not, however, have an unfettered discretion. They must act in a manner consistent with the School Act and the evaluation, selection criteria and procedures adopted by the Board. Here, the Board's criteria for approving complementary educational resource materials contained reference to concepts such as "age-appropriateness" and envisaged that the existence of parental concern in the community would be a factor to be considered.[82]

Justice Gonthier, for the minority, consequently concluded the Board's decision was indeed reasonable as it was well within its purview, consistent with its own policies, provincial law and Ministerial directions. He further observed that by "striking an acceptable balance and a position which is respectful of the views of both sides" the Board's decision was also consistent with the *Charter*.[83] The minority opinion further observed that whereas "the best interests of children includes education about 'tolerance', 'tolerance' ought not be employed as a cloak for the means of obliterating disagreement".[84]

From its earliest days British Columbia's school legislation adopted a non-sectarian emphasis that contrasted to the assumed partnership between school, family and church reflected in early school legislation in central and eastern Canada. As such, and because, once more, of the exclusive legislative powers over education accorded to Canadian provinces under Section 93 of the constitution, the Supreme Court's disposition of *Chamberlain* on administrative rather than Charter principles has had little immediate application outside of British Columbia. Even so, the more pragmatic approach taken in the dissenting analysis offers a tantalizingly plausible application of Charter standards to the parental, pedagogic and local governance concerns animating *Chamberlain*, the logic of which may yet have implications for the teaching of values nation-wide.

---

82 *Ibid.*, p. 8-9
83 *Ibid.*, p. 10
84 *Ibid.*, p. 10

More recently the Supreme Court issued what will likely be the first of several rulings concerning Quebec's new *Ethics and Religious Culture* [ERC] course, which marks the current high water mark of the laicisation of schooling in the province. The course was developed in accord with the 1999 report of the *Task Force on the Place of Religion in Schools in Quebec*, more popularly known as the Proulx report, established to address religious curriculum legacies inherited from the confessional system. Although Quebec's state schools had been restructured along linguistic lines in 1998, the *Education Act* continued to extend parents the right to choose Catholic or Protestant religious instruction—or non-denominational moral education—for their children. Proulx recommended replacing these options with the compulsory "study of religions from a cultural perspective" in both elementary and secondary schools.[85] The ERC program of study[86] flowed directly from this recommendation and the Proulx Commission's accompanying reasoning. After several years of consultation and development the new curriculum became compulsory in all Quebec schools in 2008. The course seeks to provide non-preferential, solely descriptive accounts of the province's religious heritage structured around the two major themes of *Recognition of others* and *Pursuit of the common good*. Teachers are enjoined to be "discreet and respectful, and to not promote their own beliefs and points of view" in delivering the material.[87]

As may be imagined, the development and introduction of this ostensibly unbiased approach to studying religion as a cultural phenomenon, albeit with due attention to the contributions of Catholicism and Protestantism to the history of Quebec, generated considerable controversy. Various groups organized protest marches and polls have shown public opinion to be deeply divided. Media reports suggest that some 1,700 parents sought official exemptions for their children. All such requests were denied. Indeed, the Minister of Education publicly announced that no exemptions would be allowed. Two Roman Catholic parents sought exemption for their children from their local school board on the grounds the ERC program would cause harm to their children and interfere with their obligation to pass on their religious beliefs. When this was refused they appealed to the Superior Court of Quebec which ruled participation in the ERC program did not violate their freedom of religion or conscience because they had been unable to demonstrate their children would suffer harm as a result of participating in the program. No fewer than eight additional parties were granted intervener status for the Supreme Court hearing, including the Canadian Civil Liberties Association and the Canadian Catholic School Trustees' Association. The court denied the appeal in two concurring judgments, Justice Deschamps expressing the views of the majority, Justice LeBel those of the minority.[88]

---

85 Quebec, 1999, p. 222
86 Quebec, 2008b, 2008c
87 Quebec, 2008b, p. 28
88 *S.L. v. Commission scolaire des Chênes*, 2012

Deschamps crisply concluded that the majority could find no error in the original denial of the appeal, concurring with the trial judge's assessment that the new program essentially presents different religions and encourages pupils to talk about the themes of recognition and the common good, declaring this is not "in itself an indoctrination of students that would infringe the appellants' freedom of religion".[89] She then went on to consider the appellants' concern that that exposing children to various religions is confusing, especially when differing beliefs are presented "on an equal footing".[90] In response she observed

> Parents are free to pass their personal beliefs on to their children if they so wish. However, the early exposure of children to realities that differ from those in their immediate family environment is a fact of life in society. The suggestion that exposing children to a variety of religious facts in itself infringes their religious freedom or that of their parents amounts to a rejection of the multicultural reality of Canadian society and ignores the Quebec government's obligations with regard to public education. Although such exposure can be a source of friction, it does not in itself constitute an infringement of s. 2(a) of the *Canadian Charter* and of s. 3 of the *Quebec Charter*.[91]

Justice LeBel was more guarded in his presentation of the concurring minority view, noting that "The evidence concerning the teaching methods and content and the spirit in which the program is taught has remained sketchy".[92] Given this, LeBel concluded it was not possible to decide whether the ERC program will enrich student's knowledge of diversity and build respect for differences, or whether it is "an educational tool designed to get religion out of children's heads by taking an essentially agnostic or atheistic approach that denies any theoretical validity to the religious experience and religious values".[93] Consequently he was "unable to conclude that the program and its implementation could not, in the future, possibly infringe the rights granted to the appellants and persons in the same situation",[94] leaving the door wide open for future, better grounded, legal challenges.

Drawing on the 2004 Supreme Court's ruling in *Syndicat Northcrest v. Amselem*, Deschamps and LeBel both provided clear guidance on the standard required for any such challenges to succeed. To establish that the ERC program or any other law, policy or action violates freedom of religion under the Canadian *Charters*, claimants will have to demonstrate significant interference with a sincerely held religious belief which carries an obligation to engage in a religious practice, such as parental commitment to induct their children into their faith. The justices made it clear that while the standard for determining a religious belief is

89 *Ibid.*, para. 37
90 *Ibid.*, para. 38
91 *Ibid.*, para. 40
92 *Ibid.*, para. 57
93 *Ibid.*, para. 53
94 *Ibid.*, para. 58

essentially subjective, the standard for showing interference with the practice of that belief must necessarily be objective, the onus being on a claimant to prove, on the balance of probabilities, state interference with their religious obligation. The justices did not doubt the sincerity of the parents' religious beliefs in *S.L. v. Commission scolaire des Chênes,* but they could find no evidence that the ERC program had infringed on their right to educate their children in their faith.

As outlined earlier, Quebec's private schools are required to conform to provincial curriculum requirements, including the *Ethics and Religious Culture* program. This obviously creates difficulties for the many religious private schools, not the least of which is the expectation that teachers will refrain from promoting their own beliefs. Loyola High School, a long established boy's private Catholic school in Montreal, sought to substitute its own locally developed course that approached the ERC material from a Roman Catholic perspective. When permission was denied the school sought a legal remedy. This was obtained in June 2010 when Justice Gerard Dugre of Quebec's Superior Court found the Minister of education had erred when ruling Loyola's locally developed course was not equivalent to the ERC program.[95] Dugre further found the imposition of the ERC curriculum violated the school's freedom of religion under Quebec's *Charter of Rights and Freedoms.* More colourfully and pointedly Dugre concluded his extensive analysis by observing that "the obligation imposed on Loyola to teach the ERC course in a secular manner is totalitarian in nature and essentially tantamount to the command given to Galileo by the Inquisition to abjure the cosmology of Copernicus".[96]

In his judgement Dugre carefully separated this case from *S.L.* as discussed earlier, stipulating the central issue in *Loyola* as being a clash between the desire of the Minster of Education to have the ERC course taught "in a lay manner" and the obligation of Loyola to "teach it in a denominational manner so that the school complies with the precepts of the Catholic religion that governs it and that it has applied since it was founded in 1848".[97] The immediate issue was the Minister's refusal to grant Loyola an exemption from following the ERC program of studies as allowed under Regulation. Justice Dugre disposed of this through a detailed analysis of applicable administrative law principles that led him to conclude the Minister had exceeded her jurisdiction and Loyola was entitled to the exemption on the grounds that its locally developed program was equivalent to the provincially prescribed program of studies. On the trial judge's analysis "The teaching of the Loyola's program in accordance with the Catholic faith does not change its nature or make it lose its status as an equivalent program".[98] On the freedom of religion question Dugre applied the two point test used *Amselem*

95 *Loyola High School v. Courchesne*

96 *Ibid.*, para. 331

97 *Ibid.*, para. 15(i)

98 *Ibid.*, para. 182

as outlined above. On the first question of holding a sincere religious belief the trial judge held there was clear and unequivocal evidence that Loyola's officials, staff, parents and students believed the school must "teach the ERC with its own program and according to the precepts of the Catholic religion".[99] On the second question of interference, the improper refusal of the Minister to grant the requested and lawful exemption obviously satisfied the required objective standard. As observed by Dugre, "The fundamental principles of the Quebec *Charter* are aimed precisely at protecting people from such interference and such coercion by the law or an act of an administrative decision maker who derives his or her power from the law".[100] So too, of course, for the Canadian *Charter*, even though the trial judge had delimited his consideration to the Quebec *Charter*. Quebec has appealed this decision. Oral arguments before the Quebec Court of Appeal are scheduled for 7 May 2012.

Envoi

Choice, accountability and, to a more variable extent, autonomy in schooling have been increasing in those provinces west of Ontario—the younger, energetic, economically optimistic future heartland of the country. Canadians living east of Quebec have experienced little change to the quite limited school choices made available by provincial governments, although the situation in Nova Scotia is not as bleak. In particular, Newfoundland and Labrador's rush to supplant its denominational schools with a modernized, non-sectarian, centralized system in the name of all the usual vaunting promises of equity and social justice have cast a stifling blanket over parental freedom and school autonomy, at least for the present. Similar regressions are evident in Quebec, although the resilience of religious and anglophone communities has arguably strengthened many non-public schools in some respects. The pressing future threats to freedom and autonomy in Quebec education flow from the governing establishment's seemingly blind commitment to its laicization project. In this respect the final disposition of the *Loyola* case will be of overwhelming importance for all the issues animating these volumes. Should the Supreme Court of Canada eventually rule on the *Charter* issues inherent in this case, the decision may also bear heavily on Ontario politics and school policy. Currently, the Canadian province with the largest population and largest share of the national GDP appears paralyzed by the challenges and promises inherent in enhanced school choice, autonomy and accountability, remaining sleepily content with the most unsupportive and uninterested policies toward non-public schools in the entire country, although its official stance on homeschooling is more enlightened. Despite the crushing logic and humiliation of the United Nations ruling condemning the province's refusal to provide even token financial support for parents choosing faith schools other than the separate schools created in and for another age and set of political

99 *Ibid.*, para. 265

100 *Ibid.*, para. 272

circumstances, Ontario's current governing elites remain stubbornly committed to the *status quo*, with public opinion divided and confused. Yet innovative educational models abound in this country and it may well only be a matter of time before this province embraces what its younger siblings have found to be the way forward on the road to respecting difference, embracing diversity, and improving choice, accountability and autonomy.

References

We gratefully acknowledge the invaluable help provided by Patricia Allison. We are also indebted to Charles Glenn's chapter on Canada in Volume 3 of the original *Balancing freedom, autonomy and accountability in education* on which we drew freely in various places.

Adler v. Ontario. (1996) 3 S.C.R. 609. Retrieved from http://scc.lexum.org/en/1996/1996scr3-609/1996scr3-609.pdf

Alberta. (2011). *Charter Schools Handbook.* Alberta Learning. Special Programs. Retrieved from http://education.alberta.ca/media/434258/charter_hndbk.pdf

Arsenault-Cameron v. Prince Edward Island, (2000). SCC, [2000] 1 S.C.R. 3. Retrieved from http://scc.lexum.org/en/2000/2000scc1/2000scc1.pdf

B.(R.) v. Children's Aid Society of Metropolitan Toronto, (1995). SCC [1995] 1 S.C.R. 315 *(Sheena B.)*. Retrieved from http://scc.lexum.org/en/1995/1995scr1-315/1995scr1-315.pdf

Barman, J. (1991). Deprivatizing private education: The British Columbia experience. *Canadian Journal of Education, 16*:(1) 12-38.

Bosetti, L. (2001). The Alberta charter school experience, pp. 101-120 in Hepburn, C. (Ed.). *Can the market save our schools?*. Vancouver, The Fraser Institute.

British Columbia. (2011). *Overview of Independent Schools in British Columbia.* Ministry of Education Office of the Inspector of Independent Schools. Retrieved http://www.bced.gov.bc.ca/independentschools/geninfo.pdf

British Columbia Royal Commission on Education. (1988). *A legacy for learner : The report of the Royal Commission on Education.* Victoria : Queen's Printer for British Columbia.

Caldwell et al. v. Stuart et al., (1984), SCC, [1984] 2 S.C.R. 603 (Retrieved from http://scc.lexum.org/en/1984/1984scr2-603/1984scr2-603.pdf).

Canadian Charter of Rights and Freedoms. (1982). Part I of the *Constitution Act, 1982*, RSC 1985, app. II, no. 44.

Chamberlain v. Surrey School District No. 36, (2002), 4 S.C.R. 710, 2002 SCC 86. Retrieved from http://scc.lexum.org/en/2002/2002scc86/2002scc86.pdf)

CUP Research Team. (2004). *Choice and accountability in Canadian education: Technical report.* Edmonton, AB: University of Alberta, Community-University Partnership for the Study of Children, Youth, and Families. (Retrieved from http://www.cup.ualberta.ca/component/option,com_docman/task,cat_view/gid,13/Itemid,5/)

Davis, W. G. (1984). Statement to the Legislature, June 12, 1984, in Shapiro, B. (1985). *The report of the commission on private schools in Ontario.* Toronto: Commission on Private Schools in Ontario.

Elboim-Dror, R. (1973). Organizational characteristics of the educational system. *Journal of Educational Administration,* 11(1), pp. 3-21.

Hammer, K. (2011, July 5). Toronto District School Board defends hosting Muslim prayer sessions. The Globe and Mail. Retrieved from http://m.theglobeandmail.com/.

Hansard, Manitoba Legislature. (Monday, May 4, 1992). Education and Training. Retrieved from http://www.gov.mb.ca/legislature/hansard/3rd-35th/vol_58a.html

Hiemstra, J. (2001). From Constantine to naked public square: Any room in the public school inn for Alberta's alternative religious schools? Paper presented at the *Christians in Political "Science Conference,* Point Loma Nazarene University, San Diego, California, June 7-10, 2001.

Holmes, M. (1998). *The reformation of Canada's schools.* Montreal: McGill-Queen's University Press.

Kandel, I. L. (1933). *Comparative education.* Westport, Connecticut: Greenwood Press

Lefebvre, P. & Merrigan, P. (2009). Public subsidies to private schools do make a difference for achievement in mathematics: Longitudinal evidence from Canada. Laval, Quebec: *Centre interuniversitaire sur le risque, les politiques économiques et l'emploi* (CIRPÉE) Working Paper #09-35. Retrieved from http://www.cirpee.org/fileadmin/documents/Cahiers_2009/CIRPEE09-35.pdf

Loyola High School v. Courchesne. (2010. Superior Court (S.C.), Montréal, QC, CANADA, 500-17-045278-085, Justice Gérard Dugré, retrieved from https://secureweb.mcgill.ca/prpp/sites/mcgill.ca.prpp/files/loyola_judgment_english.pdf .

McMahon, T. (28 July 2011). Court orders Yukon to build $15M school for 41 francophone students. *National Post.* (Retrieved from http://news.nationalpost.

com/2011/07/28/court-orders-yukon-to-build-15m-school-for-41-francophone-students/)

Mahe v. Alberta. (1990). [1990] 1 Supreme Court Reports. 342. Retrieved from http://scc.lexum.org/en/1990/1990scr1-342/1990scr1-342.pdf

Magnuson, R. (1993). A profile of private schools in Quebec. *McGill Journal of Education, 28*(1), 3-12.

Manitoba. (2011). Enrolment report, September 30, 20010. Manitoba Education, Schools' Finance Branch. Retrieved from: http://www.edu.gov.mb.ca/k12/finance/sch_enrol/index.html

Manitoba Regulation 267/97. *Private Schools Grants Regulation.* Registered December 24, 1997.

Morsink, J. (1999). *The Universal Declaration of Human Rights: Origins, drafting and intent*: Philadelphia: University of Pennsylvania Press.

Ontario Ministry of Education. (1993). *Opening or closing exercises for public schools in Ontario, 1993.* Toronto, Author. http://www.edu.gov.on.ca/eng/document/resource/ecu93105.pdf

Ontario Ministry of Education. (1994). *Education about religion in Ontario public elementary schools, 1994.* http://www.edu.gov.on.ca/eng/document/curricul/religion/religioe.html

Prince Edward Island. (2010). *Private schools and home education regulations.* Legislative Counsel Office, Department of Justice and Public Safety. Retrieved June 11 2011 from http://www.gov.pe.ca/law/regulations/pdf/S&2-1-06.pdf

Quebec. (2009). Funding for education in Quebec at the preschool, elementary and secondary school levels. Ministère de l'Éducation, du Loisir et du Sport, December 2009.

Quebec. (2008a). *Education Indicators, 2008 edition.* Ministère de l'Éducation, du Loisir et du Sport: Direction de la recherche, des statistiques et de l'information.

Quebec. (2008b). *Quebec Education Program Elementary Education Update May 2008.* [ERC Elementary] Ministère de l'Éducation, du Loisir et du Sport: Retrived from https://www7.mels.gouv.qc.ca/DC/ECR/pdf/ecr_elementary.pdf

Quebec. (2008c). *Quebec Education Program Secondary Education Update May 2008.* [ERC Secondary] Ministère de l'Éducation, du Loisir et du Sport: Retrieved from https://www7.mels.gouv.qc.ca/DC/ECR/pdf/ecr_secondary.pdf

Quebec. (2006). *An act respecting the Ministère de l'éducation, du loisir et du sport*, R.S.Q., chapter M-15 (preamble R.S.Q. 2006, c. 52, s. 24.).

Quebec (1999). *Religion in Secular Schools: A New Perspective for Quebec*. Task Force on the Place of Religion in Schools in Quebec [Proulx Report]. Quebec City: Ministry of Education. Retrieved from http://www.mels.gouv.qc.ca/REFORME/religion/Integ-an.pdf

Robson, W. & Hepburn, C. R. (2001). *Learning from success: What Americans can learn about school choice from Canada*. Vancouver, B.C. Milton and Rose D. Freeman Foundation and the Fraser Institute.

Saskatchewan. (2011). Education minister announces funding for new category of independent schools, changed funding for associate schools. News Release - December 21, 2011. Retrieved from http://www.gov.sk.ca/news?newsId=92fd507e-7e47-45ad-aaf4-4cebd32981fb

Saskatchewan. (1991). *Independent Schools Policy Manual*. Saskatchewan Learning. Retrieved from http://www.education.gov.sk.ca/adx/aspx/adxGetMedia.aspx?DocID=10522,10519,10477,144,107,81,1,Documents&MediaID=18948&Filename=Preface.pdf

S. L., et al. v. Commission scolaire des Chênes, et al. 2012 SCC 7. (Retrieved from http://scc.lexum.org/en/2012/2012scc7/2012scc7.html)

Shapiro, B. (1985). *The report of the commission on private schools in Ontario*. Toronto: Commission on Private Schools in Ontario.

Simeon, R. & Robinson, I. (1990). *State, society, and the development of Canadian federalism* (Toronto: University of Toronto Press, 1990).

Smith, D.S. (1996). Parent-generated home study in Canada. *The Canadian School Executive*, 15 (8). Retrieved May 13, 2005 from http://user.fundy.net/fplace/overview.htm.

Statistics Canada. (2001). Trends in the use of private education, 1987/88 to 1998/99. *The Daily*. Wednesday, July 4.

United Nations. (1999). Communication N° 694/1996 : Canada. 11/05/1999. CCPR/C/67/D/694/1996. (Jurisprudence). Human Rights Committee. Retrieved from http://www.unhchr.ch/tbs/doc.nsf/0/b3bfc541589cc30f802568690052e5d6?Opendocument

United Nations. (2006). Concluding observations of the Human Rights Committee. Canada. CCPR/C/CAN/CO/5. Retrieved from http://www.unhchr.ch/tbs/doc.nsf/898586b1dc7b4043c1256a450044f331/7616e3478238be01c12570ae00397f5d/$FILE/G0641362.pdf

Chile

by Francisco J. Leturia and I. Francisca Vallejo

Overview

During colonial times, public education was not a priority in Chile. It would, however, become an important objective during the first years of Chile's independence. In 1813 the government created the National Institute (Instituto Nacional) and, in the same year, the first education law, which stipulated there should be at least one school for boys and one for girls in every town in Chile. Implementation of the law was stalled for twenty years, when the Spanish once again took control in Chile.

In 1833, Chile established its own constitution, which mandated that "public education is a priority concern of the state," meaning that education should be provided by the state and in a centralized manner. It was this constitutional mandate that began to shape the "teaching state" (*estado docente*) in Chile, which would solidify during the second half of the nineteenth-century, in 1860, with the Organic law of Primary and Normal Education (*Ley Orgánica de Enseñanza Primaria y Normal*). The law stated that education would be free and government-directed. Another act that would contribute to strengthening the state's role in education was the Organic Law of Secondary Education of 1879, which established that public secondary education would be free. It also required the creation of free public schools in each province of the country.[1]

Years later, in 1920, the Compulsory Primary Education Act was passed, and so "education for children between the ages of 7 to 13, or until completion of the fourth year of elementary schooling," became obligatory. This act was amended in 1929, increasing the mandatory age to 15 years or until the completion of six years of school.[2]

Chile's 1925 Constitution reaffirmed the state's role in education. This Fundamental Law also instituted one of the guiding principles in Chile: educational freedom. Two years after the consecration of this important principle, the Chilean Ministry of Education was created (hereafter referred to as MINEDUC). The Ministry's

---

1 Beyer, 2000
2 Freeburger & Haugh, 1964

charge has been to establish an integrated educational management structure.[3]

The 1965 reform eventually modified other reforms. It made primary compulsory education last eight years and decreased secondary education from six to four years. It also divided secondary education into two tracks:"technical-vocational" education and "scientific-humanist " education.[4]

In 1971, Salvador Allende's socialist government developed a project called the National Unified School. The project sought to turn primary and secondary school into one continuous general and polytechnic education cycle of 12 years. The project, however, was never fully implemented, as after 1973 the military government implemented a series of reforms with a totally different approach.

The military reforms addressed what the regime believed to be the two main problems in Chilean education at the time—high repetition of grades and dropout rates due to limited capacity of schools and to a highly centralized system that failed to recognize and accommodate a growing demand for education.[5]

In 1979 the government transferred authority for public schools to the municipalities, which became responsible for the provision of resources and personnel. Teachers, therefore, ceased to be public employees.[6] Municipalities could manage schools by implementing one of two systems: either creating municipally controlled non-profit corporations called "*corporaciones municipales,*" which were private law organizations governed by their own rules, or by establishing Municipal Education Administrative Departments (Direcciones de Administración de Educación Municipal, hereinafter DAEM).[7]

A second modification had to do with the funding of the institutions. Until then, the Ministry of Education in Santiago had a budget for resourcing schools derived from general tax revenues. The Ministry then distributed funds to the entire school system, specifying the amount each school could spend. Under the new funding system each school was allocated a budget based on the nuber of students in attendance.[8] The amount of resources was to be determined on an annual basis and paid monthly. Budgets were weighted to consider grade level and special student needs.[9]

"Along with this change in the way of allocating resources, the market supply of

3 Amar, 2007
4 Soto R., 2000
5 Beyer, 2000
6 *Ibid.*
7 *Ibid.*
8 Medlin, 1997
9 González, 1998

education was completely deregulated, allowing private, nonprofit and for-profit, organizations to collaborate in educational management".[10] In effect, this meant that any person or body approved to run a school could have access to these allocations as well.[11] As a result, the number of private schools financed with public funds increased by 50% between 1980 and 1990.[12]

In this voucher-like system, families chose educational establishments according to perceptions of quality, and were not limited by income. The system was also meant to ensure competition.[13] Although in some ways well-structured, the system lacked a fundamental element—there was little to ensure that parents had the information necessary to make informed choices about schools. It wasn't until 1995 that the first results of the System for the Measurement of the Quality of Education (Sistema de Medición de la Calidad de la Educación, hereinafter SIMCE), created in 1988, were made public.[14] That system did provide one indicator of school quality.

The cycle of educational reforms implemented by the military government culminated in the enactment of the Constitutional Organic Law of Education (Ley Orgánica Constitucional de Enseñanza, hereinafter LOCE) published on March 10, 1990.[15] This law described the minimum requirements that had to be fulfilled within the different levels of education and established that it was a duty of the State to ensure that municipalities complied with the requirements. Secondly, it stated that education was a right of all people, and also that it was both a "preferential right" and a duty for parents to educate their children. Lastly, educational freedom (libertad de enseñanza) was also consecrated in this new law.[16]

In 1990 a left-center coalition was elected to govern the country. Even though it didn't modify the essential structure of the educational system it had inherited from the military government, it did seek to introduce educational reforms.[17] These reforms can be described in terms of two groups, the first concerned with guiding the educational process, and another with implementing structural reforms.[18]

Among those belonging to the first group was the "Nine Hundred Schools Program" (Programa de las Novecientas Escuelas, hereinafter P-900). The idea of

---

10 Beyer, 2000
11 González, 1998
12 Cox, 2003, p. 7
13 González, 1998
14 Beyer, 2000
15 Cox, 2003
16 Articles 2 and 3, LOCE
17 Gauri, 1998
18 Beyer, 2000

the P-900 was to support the nine hundred worst performing and under-resourced schools to improve educational quality by better educating and equipping teachers and school leaders.[19] "Courses of action implemented to improve the educational process and working conditions included: the implementation of teacher training workshops, the creation of classroom libraries, the provision of educational materials, the strengthening of educational management, and the implementation of training workshops and the provision of special attention to children at higher risk".[20]

Other programs regarding educational processes aimed at the Improvement of the Equity and Quality of Education (Programas de Mejoramiento de la Calidad y Equidad de la Educación, hereinafter MECE).

In discussing this group of reforms, it is important to mention that the new government also put forth curricular reforms, which replaced existing programs that had been created in the early 80's and involved the reorganization and introduction of cross-disciplinary subjects, and the incorporation of skills development plans and contents regarding values.[21]

Among reforms concerned with the structure of education, in 2002 Law 19532 created the "Régimen de Jornada Escolar Completa" or "Full School Day regime," which sought to lengthen the weekly teaching hours from 30 to 38. Another reform mandated a "shared financing system" (sistema de financiamiento compartido). Until 1993 it was possible for subsidized schools to charge families a school fee, though doing so would cause schools to lose up to 40% of their government subsidies. The new system provided that schools coud charge fees, but that doing so would involve a variable decrease in the subsidy, according to the amount of the fee charged.[22] This system of shared financing has been widely criticized because it is believed to contribute to segmentation and social segregation within the school system, undermining a push toward systemic equity.[23]

To fully understand the Chilean system of education today, it is important to point out that from 1990 to 2003 spending on education steadily increased, ranging from 3.8% to 7.4% of the GDP.[24] Moreover, in 2003, a constitutional reform was passed making secondary school compulsory, thus extending mandatory schooling from eight to twelve years.[25]

---

19 *Ibid.*
20 Colegio de Profesores de Chile, 2005, p. 343
21 OCDE, 2004
22 González, 1998
23 *Ibid.*
24 OCDE, 2004
25 *Ibid.*

Finally, in recent years, the Chilean educational system has not been free of criticism. In 2006 students joined in a massive, well organized protest to express their objection to the high levels of segmentation and social segregation that characterize the system. Within this context, students demanded the right to receive an education of quality under equal conditions. The government decided to respond to these demands by introducing changes that many believe should be interpreted as a new educational reform—an institutional reorganization of the school system that is best compared to the neoliberal reforms of the early '80s.[26] The proposals elaborated as a result of these protests were embodied in a project that would replace the LOCE: the General Law of Education (Ley General de Educación, hereinafter LGE).

Indeed, the current government has regarded the improvement of education in Chile as one of its fundamental objectives. That is why a series of reforms have been announced, some already materialized, among which are:

- providing scholarships to those students obtaining high scores on the University Selection Test (Prueba de Selección Universitaria, hereinafter PSU)
- setting up 60 schools of excellence to cover all cities
- "modifying curricula by incorporating more effective technologies and teaching methods
- evaluating teachers and providing financial compensation to those who perform well while training those who do not achieve the expected results
- granting greater powers and autonomy to principals which in turn must meet performance targets
- and informing parents to so that they can make better decisions about their children's education.[27]

[Editor's note: a study released in July 2012 found that the rate of improvement in test score performance over the past 14 years in Chile was among the highest in the developed world and more than twice that in the United States; at the associated conference at Harvard's Kennedy School, Professor Gregory Elacqua attributed this strong progress, in part, to a much improved framework of accountability for the system of school vouchers.[28]]

[26] Bellei, Contreras, & Valenzuela, 2010

[27] Emol, 2011

[28] Hanushek, Peterson, and Woessmann.

The Structure of Schooling

i. External structure:
  a. An OECD report found that there are different administrative categories for schools in Chile:[29]
    i. Municipal schools: administered by the 345 municipalities of the country through one of two systems:
      a. Through Municipal Education Administrative Departments (hereinafter DAEM): "They respond directly to the mayor and are subject to more inflexible standards regarding staff management." (OCDE, 2004) Until 2004, 80% of the municipal education was administered by these departments.[30]

      - Through municipally controlled non-profit corporations: they are "governed by less stringent rules regarding staff recruitment and use of resources".[31]
    ii. Subsidized private schools, financed by a public subsidy or grant, based on per-student attendance.32
    iii. Private paid schools: completely financed by parents, they receive no subsidies.33
    iv. Non-profit corporation schools or delegated administration schools: during the 80's agreements were signed with private non-profit corporations linked to business organizations, so that they would take over the administration of vocational-technical schools.34 The government finances these through especially assigned funds.35
  b. Funding: School establishments can be categorized according to how they are financed:36
    Subsidized: these schools are funded through a state per student grant. This grant is paid monthly to the sponsor on a per-student basis, according to the average attendance of each student during the last 3 months prior to payment. The value of the grant is expressed as a factor of the School Subsidy Unit (Unidad de Subvención Escolar, hereinafter USE), varies depending on whether the establishment has adopted the "full school day" program (JEC), and depends on the level of schooling the student attends to (preschool, primary and scientific-humanistic

29 OCDE, 2004
30 *Ibid.*
31 *Ibid.*
32 *Ibid.*
33 *Ibid.*
34 González, 1998
35 OCDE, 2004
36 Ministerio de Educación de Chile

secondary or technical-vocational secondary).37

According to how subsidized schools are administered, they can be divided into:

- Municipal subsidized schools: Administered by "sponsors," (sostenedores) who can either be Municipal Education Administrative Departments or municipally controlled non-profit corporations.
- Private subsidized schools: Formerly administered by a person or a legal entity. Today, according to the LGE they can only be administered by legal entities.[38]

Shared financing subsidized schools: these schools are funded through a state grant and the economic contribution of parents who have to pay a monthly fee.39 This system works based on a tiered reduction of subsidies, depending on the amount contributed by the families (the maximum amount that can be charged to parents is of 4 USE, if this is exceeded, the establishment shall abandon the subsidized system to become a private paid school)40. Sponsors of either primary or secondary schools may voluntarily opt for this mode. Municipal schools however, have limits: those providing primary education cannot, by law, comply with this system. Secondary municipal schools can, but require parents' approval.41

According to article 9 of law no. 19247 of 1993, private schools providing preschool education from the 2nd level of transition as well as those providing general basic and secondary education may ascribe to this system when complying with certain requirements.

Schools administered by DAEMs or by municipally controlled non-profit corporations can only opt for this system if they provide secondary education and if the majority of parents and guardians of students attending the establishment agree to it.

Delegated Administration schools (Decree Law 3166 of 1980): these are technical-vocational schools, owned by the State, funded through agreements signed by legal entities linked to business and industry (Ministerio de Educación de Chile). Most nonprofit corporations administering these schools are owned by guilds and other trade associations.[42] Each year the Ministry

37 Aedo & Sapelli, 2001

38 Ministerio de Educación de Chile

39 *Ibid.*

40 González, 2003

41 Aedo & Sapelli, 2001

42 González, 2003

of Education may allocate resources to these schools, in order to finance their operation.[43]

i. Fiscal Schools: Administered directly by the Ministry of Education, funded by the state (There is currently only one school subject to this system called Villa Las Estrellas de la Antártica).
ii. Paid schools: They are funded entirely through monthly payments made by parents.[44]
    c. Staffing:
    d. Education professionals are governed by different rules depending on the administration of the establishment at which they work. Thus:
        a. Law 19,070, which most people refer to as "Teachers' Statute", governs education professionals working at public schools. This law provides, in its article 2 that "Educational professionals are persons holding the title of professor or educator, awarded by "normal" schools, universities, or Technical-Vocational Institutes. All persons lawfully authorized to exercise the teaching profession and those authorized to perform it according to legal regulations currently in force will also considered to be Educational professionals."

ii. Internal Structure:
Formal or regular education is organized into four levels: preschool, primary, secondary and tertiary education, and into different models of delivering education, aimed at addressing specific groups.[45] Different models of educational delivery consist of "organizational and curricular options within one or more the referred levels (of education) which seek to respond to special learning needs, personal or contextual, in order to ensure an equal right to education".[46] Modalities can be divided into:
    a. Special or differential education: aimed at students with special temporary or permanent educational needs, as a result of a deficit or specific learning difficulty.[47]
    b. Adult education: aimed at young people and adults who wish to start or complete their studies. This modality is intended to ensure compliance with compulsory education and to provide education opportunities throughout peoples' lives.[48]

---

43 Article 4, Decree Law 3166
44 Ministerio de Educación de Chile
45 Article 17, LGE
46 Article 22, LGE
47 Article 23, LGE
48 Article 24, LGE

Legal Framework

The Chilean Constitution guarantees all people the right to education. Article 19 No. 10 states that "Parents have the preferential right and duty to educate their children. The state shall provide special protection to the exercise of this right. Moreover, It is an obligation of the state to promote early preschool education and ensure free access and government funding, although preschool shall note be a prerequisite for primary schooling.

Primary and secondary education are compulsory, the state must finance a free system for that purpose, aimed at ensuring access for all. Secondary education, in accordance with the law, shall be available to students until 21 years of age.

In recent years, the Chilean education system has undergone many changes. Most are the product of an intense debate concerning the deficiencies observed in the school system, such as "high levels of social segmentation and segregation".[49]

Freedom to establish non-state schools

Historically, the Chilean education system has had a mixed character. "Education has been provided both by public schools and by private entities of philanthropic or religious nature".[50]

The mixed nature of which we speak is enshrined in Article 4 paragraph 4 of the LGE as follows: "The education system is of mixed nature, including one of ownership and management of the state or its organs, and private one, subsidized or paid, assuring parents and guardians the freedom to choose the educational establishment for their children. "

For its part, Chile's Constitution provides in its Article 19, number 11 that "Freedom of education includes the right to open, organize and maintain educational establishments" and "An Organic Constitutional law shall establish the minimum requirements to be demanded in each of the levels of primary and secondary education, and will set the objective rules of general application that would allow the State to ensure compliance. Such law will, likewise, set the requirements for official recognition of educational institutions at all levels ".

It follows that freedom of education in Chile has two sides, or faces: one that involves the right of parents to choose the educational establishment for their children and another that includes the right to open, organize, and maintain educational establishments. This is likewise consecrated by Article 8 of the LGE.

49 Correa & Stahl, 2010, p.7
50 Biblioteca del Congreso Nacional de Chile, 2010, p. 13

Educational establishments must be officially recognized by the state in order to operate.[51] Once officially recognized, these educational institutions must meet the general objectives set out in this law, as well as the national learning standards, which are required to be complied by the entire school system.[52]

The law imposes certain requirements to be fulfilled so that an educational institution can obtain official recognition. They are briefly summarized as follows:

a. Having a sponsor (a "holder"). Sponsors are legal entities governed by public law, such as municipalities and other entities created by law, or legal entities governed by private law, whose sole purpose shall be education. The sponsor is responsible for operating the educational establishment.[53]
b. Having an educational project or program.[54]
c. Sticking to the curricular bases developed by the Ministry of Education, while applying a broader program of study.[55]
d. Having and implementing regulations that meet the national minimum standards for evaluation and promotion of students for each level.[56]
e. Committing to fulfilling national learning standards, according to the instruments established by law for such purposes.[57]
f. Having an internal regulation governing the relations between the establishment and the various people who make up the school community and ensuring fair procedures in case that sanctions are contemplated. This regulation shall not contravene the laws and other norms in force.[58]
g. Having the appropriate and necessary teaching staff and sufficient support staff to enable educators to meet their respective roles, considering the level and modality of education they provide and the number of students who attend their classes.[59]
h. Giving evidence of having paid a minimum capital.[60]
i. Proving that the facility in which the establishment operates meets the standards of general application previously established.[61]
j. Having at least the minimum appropriate furniture, equipment, teaching elements and learning materials for the levels and type of education they seek to provide.[62]

---

51 Article 45, LGE
52 Article 45, paragraph 4, LGE
53 Article 46, letter a, LGE
54 Article 46, letter b, LGE
55 Article 46, letter c, LGE
56 Article 46, letter d, LGE
57 Article 46, letter e, LGE
58 Article 46, letter f, LGE
59 Article 46, letter g, LGE
60 Article 46, letter h, LGE
61 Article 46, letter i, LGE
62 Article 46, letter j, LGE

Sponsors are required to comply with these requirements if their institutions are to be officially recognized.

Home Schooling

Article 41 of the LGE, states that "A Supreme Decree issued by the Ministry of Education will regulate the way of validating knowledge developed outside the formal system, either from personal experience or the workplace, leading to levels or degrees, and how studies equivalent to primary or secondary education completed abroad will be validated."

The above law ensures that homeschooling is permitted in Chile. The validation process for studies achieved outside the formal system is fully regulated by Supreme Decree No 2272 of 2007, and can be carried out through two mechanisms: taking a validation test or undergoing a validation process.[63]

The validation test requires the submission of certain documents and the presentation of certificates of study that provide proof of completed courses leading to the level requested to be validated. The validation process requires a homeschooler to provisionally enroll in an educational institution designated by the Regional Ministerial Secretariat of Education where he/she is to be evaluated in order to obtain a qualification for determining his /her promotion or level.[64]

School Choice Not limited by Family Income

As mentioned previously, Chile has a mixed system where schools are allowed to establish their own educational projects. Freedom of education is enshrined in a way that allows parents to choose the establishment that has the educational project that best suits their needs and beliefs.

Other factors considered by families are often related to "family income, workplaces, residential, educational and religious preferences, among other factors. Families even self-select based on their children's abilities".[65]

Unfortunately, income is often an important when choosing an educational institution. This is believed by some to have contributed to segregation within the school system.

Although the amount required to be paid by parents in the public system is near to zero, those establishments operating under a subsidy system may choose to

---

[63] Article 8, Supreme Decree No 2272 of 2007

[64] Article 9, Article 14 and Article 15, Supreme Decree No 2272 of 2007

[65] Beyer, 2007

subscribe to shared financing, which involves charging families. This system therefore entails limiting access to certain schools for certain families, according to a family's ability to pay.[66]

Two factors, however, help compensate for the lack of equity in the current system. First, the LGE provides in Article 12 that "within the admissions processes of subsidized establishments or the ones receiving regular state funds providing education between the first transition level and sixth year primary school, shall not be considered, in any case, the previous or potential school performance of the applicant for any of these levels. Furthermore, the applicant's family shall not be required to submit socioeconomic background information within these processes "

Secondly, the SEP Law mitigates differences through "increased subsidies targeted to the poorest students".[67] This benefit ensures that a sponsor cannot charge a student receiving the SEP subsidy.[68]

Distinctive character

The principle of freedom of education permeates the Chilean educational system. This involves the freedom to open, organize, and maintain educational establishments, which in turn implies the right of educational sponsors to establish and carry out an educational project and to develop plans and programs of their own in accordance with the law.[69] However, if such sponsors want their educational institutions to be able to certify validly and independently the approval of formal studies, they shall undergo the process of official recognition.[70]

The LGE, in Article 46, outlines the regulations for this procedure, "redefining, specifying and increasing the requirements for the state to grant official recognition".[71]

For their part, sponsors are required to comply with the requirements to maintain official recognition of the educational establishment they represent. They are further requied to ensure continuity of educational services during the school year, to render a public account for academic results of their students and, if they are financed by the state, to render a public account for the use of these resources and the financial status of their establishment.[72]

---

66 Mena & Corbalán, 2010
67 *Ibid.*
68 *Ibid.*
69 Article 10, letter f, LGE
70 Article 45, LGE
71 Biblioteca del Congreso Nacional de Chile, 2010
72 Article 10, letter f, LGE

Requirements set by the General Law of Education are "essential to provide compulsory education and to independently certify these processes, regardless of their ability to obtain public funding to do so. In other words, the requirements apply to what, in the Chilean educational system, are called municipal or publicly owned schools, private subsidized schools, and private paid schools, without exceptions. Those who do not meet these requirements will not be publicly recognized and will therefore not be certified.[73]

With regard to curriculum, as we explained above, while the sponsor is entitled to establish and pursue an educational project and to develop plans and programs of its own in accordance with the law, it is also requireto comply with specific objectives set in the curricular bases for preschool, primary and secondary education, and with the general objectives set by the LGE for each level in its Title II.

Curricular bases for preschool, primary, and secondary school are set by the President, by means of a Supreme Decree issued through the Ministry of Education, after the approval of the National Council of Education. These define, by cycles or years respectively, the learning objectives that will allow the achievement of the overall objectives for each of the levels specified in the LGE.[74]

Those educational institutions wishing to develop alternative plans and programs that they consider appropriate to fulfill the objectives defined in the curricular bases and the complementary goals that they independently set, must submit those plans to the regional education authority so that they can be approved by the Ministry of Education. This approval requires the explicit inclusion of the learning objectives found in the curricular bases.[75]

In this manner, while respecting the general learning objectives defined for the entire Chilean education system, each school is given a certain flexibility to emphasize the aspects of formation considered relevant based on its own plans and programs of study. Those establishments that do not have plans or programs, are bound to abide by those developed by the Ministry of Education and approved by the National Council of Education.[76]

Decisions about Admitting Pupils

The Constitution guarantees all people equality before the law and states that no law or authority may establish arbitrary differences.[77] The LGE dictates

73 Peña, 2007
74 Article 31, LGE
75 Article 31, paragraph 5 and 6, LGE
76 Article 31, paragraph 4 and Article 53, letter c, LGE
77 Article 19, No.2, Constitución Política de la República de Chile

"education is a right of all people and that it is a duty of the state to provide special protection to the exercise of this right. It is also a duty of the state to provide free quality education, based on a public education project, respectful of all religious expression and pluralistic, allowing access to the entire population and generating conditions for remaining into it in accordance with the law.[78]

The Constitutional provision is also supported by article 11 of the referred law, by stating that "Neither the State nor the educational institutions may arbitrarily discriminate regarding the treatment they should give students and other members of the educational community."

Having mentioned these laws, it is also important to point out that article 12 of the LGE tacitly allows admissions processes to be carried out by subsidized schools and by those regularly receiving state funds, referring to "admissions processes conducted by subsidized establishments or schools receiving regular state funds providing education between the first level of transition and the sixth year of basic general education...".

The aforementioned provision does not make any distinctions regarding control of these schools, which means both municipally controlled schools as well as private subsidized schools can conduct admission processes. This leads to the irrefutable conclusion there must surely exist certain factors that shall not be considered when admitting students, these are:

- Until 6th year of primary education the past or potential academic performance of the applicant shall not be regarded, nor shall the submission of the applicant's family socioeconomic background be required[79]
- change in the marital status of parents and guardians shall not prevent a pupil from continuing to study in the same establishment.[80]
- Between preschool's first level of transition and the sixth year of primary general education, students' academic performance shall not prevent future enrollment.[81]
- In subsidized schools, students have the right to repeat a grade at least once in the same primary educational establishment and once in the same secondary educational establishment. Grade repition shall not lead to expulsion from school.[82]

The LGE also established criteria seeking to prevent arbitrary discrimination in all establishments, whether private or public, these are:

---

78 Article 4, LGE
79 Article 12, LGE
80 Article 11, paragraph 2, LGE
81 Article 11, paragraph 5, LGE
82 Article 11, paragraph 6, LGE

- Pregnancy and motherhood shall, under no circumstances, constitute an obstacle to enter and remain in any level of an educational establishment, the latter shall provide academic and administrative facilities to enable the fulfillment of both objectives.[83]
- During the term of the respective academic school year, the cancellation of enrollment, suspension, or expulsion of students for causes associated to non-payment of obligations contracted by parents or to student performance will not be permitted.[84]
- Non-payment of commitments made by a student or his/her parents or guardians shall not constitute a reason for the implementation of any sanctions during the school year nor for the retention of academic documentation.[85]

Finally LGE article 13, states that:

"Processes of admission of students must be objective and transparent, ensuring respect for the dignity of students and their families in accordance with the guarantees established in the Constitution and the treaties signed and ratified by Chile.
When soliciting applicants, an institution should report:

a. Number of places offered for each level
b. General criteria for admission
c. Deadline for application and date of publication of results
d. Requirements for applicants, background information, and documentation to be submitted by them
e. Types of tests that applicants will be subjected to
f. Payment amount and conditions for participating in the process
g. The establishment's educational project "

Decisions about staff

As we have already seen, one of the requirements schools must meet to in order to obtain official recognition is to have the appropriate and necessary teaching staff so that educators are enabled to meet their respective roles, considering the level and modality of education they provide and the number of students who attend their classes.[86]

The term "appropriate teaching staff" refers to requirements educators must meet in order to teach each level and modality:

---

83 Article 11, paragraph 1, LGE
84 Article 11, paragraph 3, LGE
85 Article 11, paragraph 4, LGE
86 Article 46, letter g, paragraph 1, LGE

- For preschool and primary education: "qualified teachers are those educators holding a professional degree corresponding to the educational level they wish to teach and to the specialty they seek to impart when appropriate, or those who are entitled to exercising the teaching profession according to legal norms in force".[87]
- For secondary education, "qualified teachers are those educators holding a professional degree corresponding to the education level they wish to teach and to the specialty they seek to impart when appropriate, those who are entitled to exercising the teaching profession according to legal norms in force, or those holding a professional title or degree of at least 8 semesters from an accredited university in an area similar to the specialty imparted by them. The latter will be allowed to teach for a maximum period of three years renewable for another two, continuously or intermittently and at the simple request of the director of the establishment. After five years, if they still want to continue to teach, they must hold the corresponding professional educational degree, or pursue studies leading to such degree or certify teaching competencies according to the stipulations of the establishment's internal regulations. These regulations shall only establish assessment instruments of disciplinary knowledge and pedagogical practices as the ideal means to accredit teaching skills.".[88]

Different institutions, such as "universities receiving public funds, private universities, and professional institutes, provide initial teacher training in Chile. Their careers are defined according to levels and modalities of education that correspond to our current system: preschool, primary, secondary and differential, including some specialties that may correspond to more than one level".[89]

Usually university careers tend to be longer, lasting about 10 semesters, while careers offered by technical institutes have a shorter duration of approximately 8 semesters.[90]

As well explained by Manzi (2010), the choice of a teaching career is more common among those students attaining average or low results on admission tests to universities. This demonstrates that there is a lack of appreciation of the teaching profession by students, an issue related to low salaries and other issues. Strengthening of the profession through the implementation of various policies has become a priority in recent years.

The INICIA program, created in 2008, has been identified by some education experts like Manzi (2010) as one of these policies, seeking to transform institutions,

87 Article 46, letter g, paragraph 2, LGE
88 Article 46, letter g, paragraph 2, LGE
89 Ávalos, 2010
90 Consejo Superior de Educación en Ávalos, 2010

curricula and practices involved in initial teacher training.[91] To that end, the program includes three lines of implementation: the application of a diagnostic evaluation of the knowledge acquired by students of education in various teacher training institutions (universities and institutes) in the country; the definition of disciplinary and educational standards and national curriculum guidelines for the formation of teachers; and the creation of a special fund for financing projects for the strengthening and renewal of teacher training institutions.[92]

Another improvement policy is the provision of the "teacher vocation scholarship" for those who choose the teaching career. All students and professionals with an educational vocation can apply for it. There are no considerations regarding age, high school year of graduation, secondary education grades, socioeconomic status, or school of origin (municipal, private subsidized or private). On the other hand, having achieved a good score, that is, over 600 points on the University Selection Test (Prueba de Selección Universitaria, hereinafter PSU) is an important requirement for obtaining this grant.

Accountability for school quality

There are two different systems for evaluating education in Chile:

1. The Ministry of Education's National Evaluation System of Quality of Education (hereinafter SIMCE): Its main purpose is to help improve the quality and equity of education by reporting on student performance in different segments of the national curriculum and relating them to the school and social context in which they learn.[93]

   SIMCE tests measure the learning achievements of students set out in the Curricular Framework (now call by the LGE "Curricular Bases"). These test are applied nationally, every year, to students who attend a certain educational level.[94]

   In addition to tests related to curriculum, the SIMCE also collects information about teachers, students, parents and/or guardians through context questionnaires. This information is used for contextualizing and analyzing the results these tests.[95]

   The SIMCE publishes learning outcomes at a national, regional, and communal level. It also publishes the results of each individual establishment

91 Ministerio de Educación de Chile

92 *Ibid.*

93 *Ibid.*

94 *Ibid.*

95 *Ibid.*

in the country.[96]

SIMCE results have diverse uses: They provide parents with information about their children's school performance thus helping them to make informed decisions. They also allow teachers, among other things, to assess whether the initiatives implemented in schools have a positive effect on the level of students performance. Finally, the results are a tremendously useful tool for the Ministry of Education, as they allow it to identify establishments presenting consistently low scores and therefore in need of external support to improve teaching and learning.[97]

2. The National Performance Assessment System for Subsidized Educational Establishments (hereinafter SNED): This system was created in 1995, by Law 19,410, and began operating in 1996. It belongs to the set of initiatives aimed at strengthening the teaching profession. The main objective of the SNED is to help improve the quality of education provided by the subsidized educational system in the country through recognizing and incentivizing teachers and institutions that perform well. The SNED provides a Performance Excellence Subsidy, which is a monetary bonus divied among teachers in high-performing schools.[98]

   In order to measuring a number of factors related to the performance of educational institutions, groups of establishments with similar characteristics (called "homogeneous groups") are formed in each region of the country. Once these groups are structured, a performance assessment based on various indicators or effectiveness is made.[99]

Teaching of values

The LGE in its article 2 includes the definition of education and also prescribes those values that should be included within the learning process:

> Education is a lifelong learning process that encompasses the various stages of people's lives and aims to meet their spiritual, ethical, moral, emotional, intellectual, artistic and physical development, through the transmission of values, knowledge and skills. It is based on respect and appreciation for human rights and fundamental freedoms, multicultural diversity and peace, and our national identity, enabling people to lead their lives fully, to live and participate in a responsible, tolerant, united, democratic and active way in a community and to work and contribute to national development.

96 *Ibid.*
97 *Ibid.*
98 *Ibid.*
99 *Ibid.*

The foregoing is supported by article 4 of the same law, which states: "without prejudice to its other duties, is the duty of state that the system integrated by educational institutions owned by it, provides free education of quality, founded on a public educational project, secular, that is, respectful of all religious expression, and pluralistic, allowing access to the entire population and to promote social inclusion and equity."

The inclusion of these articles in the LGE is due to our legislators' conviction that the educational process must be aimed towards the integral development of students and not just the achievement of learning standards.[100]

References

Aedo, C., & Sapelli, C. (Otoño 2001). El sistema de vouchers en educación: Una revisión de la teoría y evidencia empírica para Chile. *Estudios Públicos*, , 35-81.

Amar, M. (2007). Equidad, calidad y derecho a la educación en Chile: Hacia un nuevo rol del Estado.(Serie Estudio N° 09-07) Retrieved from www.bcn.cl/bibliodigital/pbcn/estudios/estudios.../nr009-07.pdf

Ávalos, B. (2002). In Ministerio de Educación (Ed.), *Profesores para Chile : historia de un proyecto.*

Ávalos, B. (2010). Formación inicial docente en Chile: calidad y políticas. In C. Bellei, D. Contreras & J. P. Valenzuela (Eds.), *Ecos de la revolución pingüina : avances, debates y silencios en la reforma educacional* (pp. 257-284). Santiago: Universidad de Chile – UNICEF.

Bellei, C., Contreras, D., & Valenzuela, J. P. (2010). Viejos dilemas y nuevas propuestas en la política educacional chilena. In C. Bellei, D. Contreras & J. P. Valenzuela (Eds.), *Ecos de la revolución pingüina : avances, debates y silencios en la reforma educacional* (pp. 11-27). Santiago: Universidad de Chile – UNICEF.

Beyer, H. (2000). Entre la Autonomía y la Intervención: Las Reformas de la Educación en Chile. In F. Larraín, & R. Vergara (Eds.), *La Transformación Económica de Chile* (pp. 643-708). Santiago: Centro de Estudios Públicos.

Beyer, H. (2007). Algunas notas sobre selección educacional. In J. J. Brunner, & C. (. Peña (Eds.), *La Reforma al Sistema Escolar: Aportes para el Debate* (pp. 221-237). Santiago de Chile: Universidad Adolfo Ibáñez y Universidad Diego Portales.

Biblioteca del Congreso Nacional de Chile. (a). *Establece la Ley General de*

[100] Biblioteca del Congreso Nacional de Chile, 2010

Educación. Retrieved 4/02/2011, 2011, from http://www.bcn.cl/resumenes-de-leyes/ley-general-educacion

Biblioteca del Congreso Nacional de Chile. (b). *Ley general de educación*. Retrieved 4/02/2011, 2011, from http://www.bcn.cl/guias/ley-general-educacion

Biblioteca del Congreso Nacional de Chile. (2010). *Historia de la Ley N° 20370 que establece la Ley General de Educación*. Santiago: Biblioteca del Congreso Nacional de Chile. Retrieved from http://www.leychile.cl/Navegar/scripts/obtienearchivo?id=recursoslegales/10221.3/3824/7/HL20370.pdf

Biblioteca del Congreso Nacional de Chile. (2011). *Historia de la Ley N° 20501 sobre Calidad y Equidad de la Educación*. Santiago: Biblioteca del Congreso Nacional de Chile. Retrieved from http://www.leychile.cl/Navegar/scripts/obtienearchivo?id=recursoslegales/10221.3/34031/1/HL20501.pdf

Consejo Nacional de Educación. *Qué es en CNED*. Retrieved 04/13/2011, 2011, from http://www.cned.cl/public/secciones/SeccionAcercaDe/acerca_de.aspx

Colegio de Profesores de Chile. (2005). La reforma educacional en los '90. In CTERA, CNTE, COLEGIO DE PROFESORES, AFUTU – FENAPES, LPP. (Ed.), *Las reformas educativas en los países del Cono Sur: un balance crítico*. (Primera Edición ed., pp. 341-349). Buenos Aires: CLACSO Libros.

Ley 18962 que establece la Ley Orgánica Constitucional de Enseñanza. (1990)

Ley 19247 que Introduce modificaciones a la Ley sobre Impuesto a la Renta; modifica tasa del impuesto al valor agregado; establece beneficio a las donaciones con fines educacionales y modifica otros textos legales que indica. (1993).

Ley N° 20370 que establece la Ley General de Educación, (2009).

Correa, R., & Stahl, G. (2010). Presentación. In C. Bellei, D. Contreras & J. P. Valenzuela (Eds.), *Ecos de la revolución pingüina : avances, debates y silencios en la reforma educacional* (pp. 7-9). Santiago: Universidad de Chile – UNICEF.

Cox, C. (2003). Las políticas educacionales de Chile en las últimas dos décadas del siglo XX. In C. Cox (Ed.), *Políticas educacionales en el cambio de siglo: la reforma del sistema escolar de Chile* (pp. 19-113). Santiago: Editorial Universitaria.

Emol. *Piñera apuesta a que reforma educacional sea aprobada antes de marzo de 2011*. Retrieved 5/25/2011, 2011, from http://www.emol.com/noticias/nacional/detalle/detallenoticias.asp?idnoticia=448666

Espínola, V., & Claro, J. P. (2010). El sistema nacional de aseguramiento de la calidad: una reforma basada en estándares. In C. Bellei, D. Contreras & J. P. Valenzuela (Eds.), *Ecos de la revolución pingüina : avances, debates y silencios en la reforma educacional* (pp. 51-83). Santiago: Universidad de Chile – UNICEF.

Eyzaguirre, S. (2010). Hacia reformas de segunda generación en educación. *Puntos de Referencia,* Retrieved from www.cepchile.cl/dms/archivo_4718_2865/pder327_eyzaguirre2.pdf

Freeburger, A. R., & Haugh, C. C. (1964). *Education in Chile.* Washington D.C.: U.S. Department of Health, Education and Welfare.

Gallego, F., & Sapelli, C. (2007). El financiamiento de la educación en Chile: una evaluación. *Revista Pensamiento Educativo, 40,* 263-284.

Gauri, V. (1998). *School choice in chile, two decades of educational reform.* United States of America: University of Pittsburgh Press.

Gobierno de Chile.*Sistema de alta dirección pública / servicio civil.* Retrieved 7/22/2011, 2011, from http://www.serviciocivil.gob.cl/sistema-de-alta-dirección-pública-0

Constitución Política de La República de Chile (1980).

Decreto Ley 3166 de 1980 que autoriza la entrega de la administración de determinados establecimientos de educación técnico profesional a las instituciones o a las personas jurídicas que indica. (1980a). Retrieved from http://www.leychile.cl/N?i=70774&f=1997-11-19&p=

Decreto Exento N° 2272/ 2007: Aprueba procedimiento para el reconocimiento de estudios de enseñanza básica y enseñanza media humanístico-científica y técnico-profesional y de modalidad educación de adultos y educación especial. (2007).

DFL N° 1 de 1997 que fija texto refundido, coordinado y sistematizado de las ley 19070 que aprobó el estatuto de los profesionales de la educación, y de las leyes que la complementan y modifican.

DFL N° 2, de 2010 Ministerio de Educación, Fija texto refundido, coordinado y sistematizado, de la Ley N° 20.370 con las normas no derogadas del Decreto con Fuerza de Ley N° 1, de 2005. (2010).

González, P. (1998). Financiamiento de la educación en Chile. In PREAL-UNESCO (Ed.), *Financiamiento de la educación en Latino América* (pp. 161-187). Santiago:

González, P. (2003). Estructura institucional, recursos y gestión en el sistema escolar chileno. In C. Cox (Ed.), *Políticas educacionales en el cambio de siglo: la reforma del sistema escolar de Chile* (Segunda ed., pp. 597-660). Santiago: Editorial Universitaria.

Hanushek, Eric A., Paul E. Peterson, and Ludger Woessmann, *Achievement Growth: International and U.S. State Trends in Student Performance*, Cambridge, MA: Harvard Kennedy School Program on Education Policy and Governance, PEPG Report No.: 12-03, July 2012

Mac-Clure, L. (2010). ¿ Quién está a cargo de la gestión de la educación pública escolar ? Un análisis de la regulación legal de las escuelas "municipales". *Puntos de Referencia*, Retrieved from http://www.cepchile.cl/dms/archivo_4612_2769/pder322_MacClure.pdf

Manzi, J. (2007). Selección de estudiantes en el sistema escolar chileno: ¿la buena educación debe ser sólo para los mejores? In J. J. Brunner, & C. Peña (Coordinadores) , *La reforma al sistema escolar: aportes para el debate* (pp. 203-220). Santiago: Universidad Diego Portales; Universidad Adolfo Ibáñez.

Manzi, J. (2010). Programa INICIA: fundamentos y primeros avances . In C. Bellei, D. Contreras & J. P. Valenzuela (Eds.), *Ecos de la revolución pingüina : avances, debates y silencios en la reforma educacional* (pp. 285-310). Santiago: Universidad de Chile – UNICEF.

Medlin, C. A. (1997). Aplicación de la lógica económica al financiamiento de la educación: La experiencia en Chile con el subsidio por estudiante. In E. Cohen (Ed.), *Educación, eficiencia y equidad* (pp. 91-117). Santiago: CEPAL / OEA / Ediciones SUR.

Mena, P., & Corbalán, F. (2010). La selección escolar: una cuestión de libertad, competencia, igualdad e integración. In C. Bellei, D. Contreras & J. P. Valenzuela (Eds.), *Ecos de la revolución pingüina: avances, debates y silencios en la reforma educacional* (pp. 331-363). Santiago: Universidad de Chile – UNICEF.

Ministerio de Educación de Chile. (a). *AYUDA MINEDUC - Procesos de selección.* Retrieved 4/9/2011, 2011, from http://w3app.mineduc.cl/Aplicacion600Web/cons_03Cd?Codigo=SELECCION&Tipo=1&Nivel=2&enlace=1

Ministerio de Educación de Chile. (a). *AYUDA MINEDUC - Sistema de registro de Atenciones - ¿Qué es el SIMCE?* Retrieved 7/26/2011, 2011, from http://w3app.mineduc.cl/Aplicacion600Web/cons_03Cd?Codigo=AGSIMCE &Tipo=1&Nivel=3&CodAux=SIMCE3&enlace=2

Ministerio de Educación de Chile. (b). *AYUDA MINEDUC - Sistema de registro de*

Atenciones - SNED. Retrieved 4/26/2011, 2011, from http://w3app.mineduc.cl/Aplicacion600Web/cons_03Cd?Codigo=DGSNED &Tipo=1&Nivel=3&CodAux=SNED&enlace=2

Ministerio de Educación de Chile. (b). *Cobros - AYUDA MINEDUC*. Retrieved 3/25/2011, 2011, from http://www.ayudamineduc.cl/resguardo/resg_educ/educ_cobr/index.php

Ministerio de Educación de Chile. (c). *Currículum Nacional - Planes de Estudio*. Retrieved 4/8/2011, 2011, from http://www.mineduc.cl/index5_int.php?id_portal=47&id_contenido=13293&id_seccion=3264&c=1

Ministerio de Educación de Chile. (d). *Currículum Nacional - Programas de estudio*. Retrieved 4/8/2011 from http://www.mineduc.cl/index5_int.php?id_portal=47&id_contenido=13293&id_seccion=3264&c=1

Ministerio de Educación de Chile. (e). *Enlaces - CET*. Retrieved 3/23/2011, 2011, from http://www.enlaces.cl/index.php?t=44&i=2&cc=174&tm=2

Ministerio de Educación de Chile. (f). *Matrícula y Proceso de Selección - AYUDA MINEDUC*. Retrieved 4/9/2011, 2011, from http://www.ayudamineduc.cl/resguardo/resg_educ/educ_matr/matr_preg.php#5

Ministerio de Educacion de Chile.*Para qué sirve el SIMCE*. Retrieved 3/12/2011, 2011, from http://www.simce.cl/index.php?id=286&no_cache=1

Ministerio de Educación de Chile. (g). *Programa Inicia*. Retrieved 4/14/2011, 2011, from http://www.programainicia.cl/

Ministerio de Educacion de Chile.*Qué es el SIMCE*. Retrieved 3/12/2011, 2011, from http://www.simce.cl/index.php?id=288&no_cache=1

Ministerio de Educación de Chile. (h). *SIMCE*. Retrieved 3/14/2011, 2011, from http://www.simce.cl/

Ministerio de Educación de Chile. (i). *SNED - Sistema Nacional de Evaluación del Desempeño*. Retrieved 3/12/2011, 2011, from http://www.sned.cl/appSned/Public/sobre-sned.jsp

Ministerio de Educación de Chile. (j). *Subvención preferencial*. Retrieved 3/29/2011, 2011, from http://www.mineduc.cl/index2.php?id_portal=29&id_seccion=3018&id_contenido=12011

Ministerio de Educación de Chile. (2008, 3 Enero 2008). Ley de Subvención Escolar Preferencial: un camino para mayor equidad. *Revista Nuestros Temas -*

Material de apoyo para Profesoras y Profesores, (28), 2-10. Retrieved from http://www.google.com/url?sa=t&source=web&cd=1&ved=0CBgQFjAA&url=http%3A%2F%2Fwww.mineduc.cl%2Fbiblio%2Fdocumento%2F200801031517400.NTSeparata29.pdf&ei=3SrgTeCxDqrb0QGIlu3aCg&usg=AFQjCNFddz94ZHBZrBipJUmIoj5WswurKA

Ministerio de Educación de Chile. (d). *SNED - Sistema Nacional de Evaluación del Desempeño*. Retrieved 3/12/2011, 2011, from http://www.sned.cl/appSned/Public/sobre-sned.jsp

OCDE. (2004). *Revisión de Políticas Nacionales de Educación: Chile 2004* [Reviews of National Policies for Education: Chile 2004] (Ministerio de Educación de Chile Trans.). OCDE Publishing.

Peña, C. (2007). La provisión educativa en Chile: requisitos y financiamiento. In J. J. Brunner, & C. Peña (Coordinadores), *La reforma al sistema escolar: aportes para el debate* (pp. 23-52). Santiago: Universidad Diego Portales; Universidad Adolfo Ibáñez.

Ruiz Tagle, P. (2010). Apuntes para la reforma educacional. In C. Bellei, D. Contreras & J. P. Valenzuela (Eds.), *Ecos de la revolución pingüina : avances, debates y silencios en la reforma educacional* (pp. 31-50). Santiago: Universidad de Chile – UNICEF.

Soto R., F. (2000). *Historia de la educación chilena*. Santiago: CPEIP.

Valenzuela, J. M., Pía, L., & Paula, R. (2008). Educación en Chile: Entre la continuidad y las rupturas. principales hitos de las políticas educativas. *Revista Iberoamericana de Educación*. No. 48, pp. 129-145.

Colombia

by Jorge Alberto Mahecha Rodríguez and
Luis Enrique García De Brigard[1]

Overview

Analyzing the Colombian schooling system from the perspectives of school choice, system accountability and autonomy of institutions yields a simple yet challenging conclusion: SES of families and the public-private divide account for most of the variation across said perspectives. Let us begin with school choice in Colombia. Low income families are, for the most, completely restricted to public schools in their geographical vicinity, thus having little choice as to what kind of institution will educate their children. The range of choices grows in the middle class but it is not always related to increased quality. Higher SES families, instead, enjoy expanded opportunities that include second language education, specialized schools and high-standards scholastic programs such as the International Baccalaureate.

Likewise, school system accountability varies greatly depending on SES and the public or private nature of institutions. Whereas elite, high-SES schools -which are private in its entirety- ought to remain competitive in standardized tests in order to preserve their status and reputation (an output-based accountability system), public schools rely on a solely input-based system; educational outcomes of any kind can be either seriously considered or plainly disregarded by public schools without significant consequences.

Autonomy of schools and the communities they serve is protected by law. However, most of the pedagogical innovation in Colombia has been led by private, high-SES schools; hence a high diversity of educational offer is available for high-SES households. Public schools are far more uniform and traditional, at least in urban areas. Rural public schools on the other hand, constitute a notable example of innovation in Colombia, due to the mass adoption of the widely known multi-grade program "Escuela Nueva Activa" (Active New School)[2].

Heterogeneity in Colombian schooling system has thus created a sharp divide

---

1 Co - Founders, *Enseña por Colombia*; with very helpful suggestions from Felipe Barrera-Osorio.

2 McEwan, 2001.

in educational outcomes between high-SES private urban schools and low-SES public urban and rural schools,[3] a difference which has been pervasive throughout Colombian history. This in turn has led to a quest for an overall increase in quality, especially in public schools. In that regard, and despite some progress in quality as measured by international test results, many challenges are yet to be overcome. Several national and international test results in reading and math show a disturbingly high percentage of pupils not reaching basic competency levels.[4] The school system in Colombia can be said to have overcome just recently some access issues, reaching over 95 percent attendance rates for populations between 6 and 10 years old, and over 90percent for populations between 11 and 14 years-old. Children 5 years old and less, or 15 or more, have lower attendance rates, 80.4percent for the youngest group and just 74 percent for the early-teenager population.[5]

As is the case in other Latin American countries, the education system in Colombia has undergone significant changes, partially related to the enactment of a new constitution (1991). Most notably, the school system has experienced a significant administrative transformation since 2001, allowing a decrease in the size of the system, as measured by the number of schools, and an increase in its efficiency, as measured by average spending per pupil. However, there are conflicting views on this latter issue.[6]

This chapter will further examine the Colombian schooling system by first analyzing the structure of schooling and the legal framework supporting it, in order to discuss school choice related issues such as freedom to establish non-state schools, home schooling and the degree to which family income affects school choice. We will then examine the autonomy of educational institutions focusing on aspects such as the freedom schools have to define their own mission, and to select both staff and pupils. Thirdly, we will discuss school system accountability in the light of its relation to quality. An additional reflection on the degree to which the teaching of values is influenced by state closes this chapter.

The Structure of Schooling

The school system in Colombia is made up of almost 14,000 schools, approximately two thirds of them public (9,235) and the rest (4,558) private. Regardless of their nature, all schools are controlled by 94 regional Secretariats of Education: 32 *departamentos* (departments), and 62 certified territorial entities which include every municipality with more than 100,000 inhabitants (or have obtained "certification" through the accomplishment of certain requisites, even

3 ICFES, 2011a; Nuñez, Steiner, Cadena, Pardo, 2002.

4 World Bank, 2008; PREAL, 2006.

5 MEN, 2010a.

6 Piñeros, 2010.

though their population is below the 100,000 threshold). The Secretariats have control over enrolment of pupils, hiring of teachers, payroll of all school related personnel, pupil supplemental services such as health screening and nutrition and teacher professional development. These 94 "Certified Territorial Entities" (CTE) as they are called in the legislation, follow a common framework of policies, decrees, laws and academic regulations which are centralized in the Colombian Ministry of Education. The ministry authorizes and regulates funds transfers to the CTE, oversees its performance, and provides support regarding some state or nationwide recommended teacher professional development programs. The Ministry is also responsible for signing agreements with multilateral institutions such as the Inter American Development Bank, or the World Bank, irrespective of whether projects sponsored by such organizations are of local or national level.

By 2010, this school system served approximately eleven million pupils (10,996,272). The vast majority were enrolled in public schools (78 percent), with 22 percent attending either private, independent schools (17 percent), or private institutions that receive government subsidies (5percent).[7] These eleven million pupils are taught by almost half a million teachers (451,723), more than two thirds of them women. 15 percent of the teachers in the system only reached a secondary education degree. The remaining 85 percent are distributed among 63 percent with undergraduate degrees and 22percent with graduate degrees.[8] These teachers were trained by some 1,300 teacher training undergraduate programs nationwide, of which only six percent had a "high quality accreditation" by the National Council of Accreditation, which regulates higher education in Colombia.

The school system is comprised of one mandatory preschool year, nine mandatory years of "*basic*" education, (five in primary and four in secondary school), and two final, non-mandatory years of what is called "*educación media*" (intermediate education), that precedes higher education. Together, the 4 years of mandatory basic secondary education along with the 2 of the intermediate education are called "*Bachillerato*" (Baccaulerate).

The Legal Framework

In 1991 a new constitution was adopted, in which education was defined as a fundamental right (Article 67; Colombian Const., 1991) and as a public service of social function. Three years after that National General Law 115 for Education (1994) was passed in the congress, regulating the general structure and operation of the whole educational system from preschool to higher education and from mainstream to minorities. The law also includes general guidelines about the rights and status of teachers, pupils and educational institutions, along with mandatory topics in school curricula, and goals for each of the education levels.

7 DANE, 2010a.
8 DANE 2010b.

Although including detailed guidelines, the law establishes that schools enjoy distinctive character and have a certain degree of curricular autonomy within the bounds established by law.

The General Law of Education has been further elaborated by a number of national decrees, under the competence of the National Ministry of Education, including (a) further specifications of general topics related to the school system, and (b) updates and reforms on issues such as teacher statutory tenure and academic calendars.

As for the first kind of regulations (further specifications of general topics related to the school system), the first attempt to regulate several aspects of the national general law of education was National Decree 1860 (1994), enacted just six months after the general law, concerned with two main topics. The first is the structure of schools and schooling. By "structure" we mean the organization of grade levels and cycles (groupings of grade levels) educational institutions should have, the number of years of each education level, school governance, and the structure of the "Educational Institutional Project" (*Proyecto Educativo Institucional, PEI*, by its Spanish acronym), a compendium of strategic planning, pedagogical, sociological and organizational guidelines for schools.

The second topic in the decree is the guidelines to operate in the aforementioned "structure": what kind of goals should be set for each level or cycle, national curriculum standards, and evaluation and criteria for passing or failing grade levels.

While the structure of schooling, the first topic of Decree 1860, has remained almost unchanged since its enactment, rules regarding the operation of schooling, the second topic in the decree, have been further developed and discussed since its early days. Particularly, curricular regulations have been made and remade since the late 1990's and up until now. These regulations, although not having the character of law, can be seen as further developments of law 115, as the law itself established that there would be further regulations understood as integral to it. However, the actual use of these regulations, which include national curriculum standards, is not clear in the educational community. The fact that these standards are not used either for mandatory nation-wide evaluations or actual curriculum design in schools poses doubts about its actual reach.

Other aspects of the "operation side" of Decree 1860 have been addressed more formally. Evaluation of pupils and particularly, criteria for passing or failing a given grade level, has been a central topic in Colombian legislation. Recently derogated National Decree 230 (2002) is an archetypal example. The decree created an ad-hoc school body called "commission of evaluation and promotion" including up to three teachers, a representative from the school families, and the principal of the school. This commission was to decide on the passing or failing of each individual pupil in school, and to determine which pupils were not to be promoted. The decree established that no matter which conclusions the commission reached, the proportion of pupils that could fail a given academic year was 5 percent at most. The decree defined an era, from its enactment in 2002 up to its replacement in 2009 by national Decree 1290, when it was almost impossible for a pupil in the public school system to fail a year and be held back.

Apart from these further regulations of law 115, both in the form of decrees or other lower status regulations, the legal framework for schooling in Colombia includes some updates and reforms to issues such as pupil calendars (the duration of school years, mandatory periods of vacation, mandatory numbers of schooling hours) and teacher statutory tenure. In this last regard, National Decree 2277 (1979), which regulated the teaching profession, was changed in 2002 by National Decree 1278 (2002). Although this reform was challenged as unconstitutional, the Constitutional Court deemed the decree constitutional. One important aspect of this new decree is that it allows professionals other than those specifically trained to enter the teaching profession. This opened the door for programs such as *Enseña por Colombia*, a program which recruits outstanding professionals to become public school teachers for the first two years of their career; this same idea underlies Teach for America, a pioneer program which started in the United States in 1990.

Private schools in Colombia must comply with national regulations regarding schooling. However, they are also subject to local regulations of each of the 94 certified territorial entities. Traditionally these regulations are of administrative nature and do not interfere with superseding regulations such as national decrees or Laws. For example, local regulations establish minimum areas for classrooms or playground areas for schools, based on pupil numbers, which may vary across the nation; modifications in school calendars due to local environmental or public order conditions; and administrative procedures for payroll.

Freedom to establish non-state schools

As discussed above, most education in Colombia is provided by public schools managed at the regional level, but there is a substantial percentage of pupils who attend private institutions. It is the purpose of this section to discuss the framework within which non-state schools may be established.

It is important to note that the Colombian legislation allows for non-state schools to become providers of the education at the public level. This structure is primarily directed to compensate for the lack of public-school slots in certain areas of the country. The government is thus compelled to hire the services of private schools that will enroll pupils from the public sector in exchange for a payment issued by the regional authorities. This mechanism is known as *convenios*.

A second variation of non-state schools providing public-level education is the so-called *concession* schools that essentially follow the structure of charter schools in the US. In this case, the motivation is not one of access, but rather one of quality: the government appoints private providers, via a bidding process, to administer schools with a significant degree of freedom in exchange for the payment of a fixed per-pupil amount. This framework remains very small in scale, and has become a very contentious issue, in spite of significant evidence of increased quality.[9]

Amongst non-state schools, both *convenios* and *concessions* are subject to the highest degree of government regulation. For example, *concession* schools must be administered by not-for-profit organizations of proven record in the education sector, in some cases religious organizations; they are bound by stringent regulations of financial management, as well as hiring procedures. While they are allowed to hire professionals who have not followed the traditional track to become a public teacher, they must comply with strict quotas of licensed teachers on their staff.

On the other hand, schools that operate under the *convenio* framework enjoy significantly higher levels of autonomy. These can be established under for-profit entities and have full independence in the process of hiring and firing. They must, however, apply to become part of the *banco de oferentes,* a pool of private schools that have gone through a relatively simple process in order to become eligible to enroll pupils from the public system and receive government payment in exchange. Most of these schools cater to a pupil body with a combination of private pupils whose families pay tuition and public pupils whose tuition is paid to the school by local government.

Aside from *convenios* and *concessions,* there are also a significant number of private schools that have no relation whatsoever with the public education sector. These private, independent schools cater mostly to middle and upper class pupils whose families have decided to opt out of the public education system. While there is huge variance in the quality of these private schools, almost all of the top performing schools (top one percent) in Colombia, are high-SES, private schools. The standing of these schools as top performers is determined by the results its pupils attain in a nation-wide, mandatory scholastic test which every pupil must take in his final year of secondary school, called "Saber 11". Out of the approximately 14,000 schools in Colombia, 12,273 which offer the last year of secondary education went through this testing in 2011.[10] The national testing agency (ICFES) releases data which allows only simple average comparisons of school performance, disregarding school sample sizes and the

9 Barrera-Osorio 2010; Bonilla, 2011.

10 ICFES, 2011b.

relative performance ranking of pupils ("puesto").[11] The agency however, releases data which is used in journalistic reports,[12] which attest to the wide differences between private and public sector schools in Saber 11 test: only 19 public schools rank among the top 500 performers.

However, a study on the efficiency of school education in Colombia shows that these wide differences in performance between high-SES private and low-SES private schools can be explained by more favorable socioeconomic conditions of the families and communities they serve. Even most, when these context conditions are removed from consideration, efficiency levels of private and public schools are not very different.[13] This interesting result highlights the importance of families, communities and the general environment of pupils in school achievement.

Private, independent schools enjoy great freedom in almost every aspect of their operations. They can be incorporated as for-profit or not-for-profit organizations, they can freely establish structures to hire and fire staff, and are not required to hire licensed teachers. Private schools are also entitled to establish their own curriculums, benchmarks and standards, if only making sure to abide by very general countrywide specifications such as those regarded in the general law of education. (e.g the provision of sex education, environmental education, Afro-Colombian studies, etc.). This freedom has allowed for the existence of a very diverse offer of private schools. From religious to secular, from arts to technology focused, from grade-structured to personalized approaches. While a strong history of Catholic tradition and a special diplomatic agreement between the Colombian and Vatican governments which lasted from 1887 to 1995 has led to a significant number of Catholic schools, currently there is no legal provision that favors these institutions or any other confessional institutions over secular schools. The degree of autonomy enjoyed by private schools regarding their distinctive character has allowed these institutions to become the leading pedagogical innovators: almost every innovative school, either past or present, is or was private.

Perhaps the most significant regulation to which these schools are subject relates to the amounts that can be charged as tuition. National Decree 2253(1995) established a mechanism whereby schools could determine the maximum amounts that could be charged to families, as well as the yearly increases in price. Depending on a series of criteria, schools can be classified in one of three levels of freedom: *Controlada* (controlled), *Vigilada* (supervised), *Regulada* (regulated). Belonging to either of these classifications will entail a higher or lesser degree of independence in determining and making yearly increases in tuition. Notably, none of the criteria that are used to determine the classification of the schools in

[11] ICFES 2010.
[12] Dinero, 2011.
[13] Iregui, 2006

any of the three levels of freedom is related to quality. It relies, instead in input-based indicators such as square meters per pupil and teacher-pupil ratio.

Home schooling

The issue of home schooling in Colombia is far from being a mainstream topic of interest for educational authorities. Occasionally, however, press reports document isolated histories of families that for one reason or another have decided to take education into their own hands. There is an incipient level of organization for the home-schooling community in Colombia. Home schooling is not even a legally recognized issue in Colombian legislation; as such it is nor forbidden nor encouraged; it is just ignored. If parents decide to take the option of home schooling, they are not required to inform authorities, nor do their activities receive any kind of supervision. A joint research group of the main Colombian Public University, National University of Colombia and Oviedo University in Spain have been conducting an investigation about "Education without schools" in Colombia, for which they are asking families to complete a 100-question survey. The number of families involved is uncertain.

Home-schooled children can remain completely outside schooling, even if they decide to enter the higher education system. In order to do that, pupils must take a nation-wide state scholastic test (Saber 11) which is a prerequisite for entering higher education, as it grants the title of *Bachiller* ("Bachellor"). This test is administered by a national government agency. In order to register for the test, pupils are not required to be enrolled in any educational institution. If their result matches the admission requirements of the higher education institution of their choice, they could be admitted and hence have skipped formal schooling in its entirety.

Pupils of any age or grade level can level-up with formal schooling if they have been out of the system for any reason. This is done via a special process called *validación* ("validation"), which would allow them to skip any given grade level provided that they pass a special government examination test. Then they would be able to enter the next corresponding grade level. Public and private institutions offer validation programs that also allow pupils to take two or more grade levels in a given school year. Validation is recognized by the law as a special variety of formal schooling. Although designed to be an entrance mechanism to formal education for children left out of the school system for reasons as varied as forced displacement due to armed conflict, extreme rural isolation, the repeated failure of a grade level in the private school system, or any other exceptional circumstance, validation is an entry mechanism that could also be used by home-schooled children. National Decree 2832 (2005) establishes regulations for this process.

School choice not limited by family income

The schooling system in Colombia is characteristically segregated. In spite of significant efforts by the government to guarantee universal access to public education, the differences in quality between public and private schooling remain extreme. While the focus of the public agenda has largely shifted from access to quality, the reality for most pupils remains one in which family income is the strongest predictor for the type of school that a pupil will attend, and hence the quality of the education the pupil will receive.

As a consequence of the above, there is a very limited range of options for parents in school choice not determined by family income. Practically all pupils from lower socio economic backgrounds or who live in rural areas attend public schools in the region where they live. The two exceptions to this rule were discussed above, and relate to schools that operate under the *concession* and *convenio* structures. While these mechanisms result in pupils attending *non-state* schools, the process to admission does not imply school choice on the part of families. School choice is limited to private schools that serve pupils whose families can afford to pay tuition and other costs.

The strong correlation between school choice and family income has also yielded a significant heterogeneity in the supply of private schools. Sending their children to private school remains and aspirational goal for families, who tend to opt out of public education as soon as their disposable income allows them to do so. This phenomenon is very common in the lower middle and middle class and almost universal in the upper and upper middle class. As a result, private schools cater to each of these layers, resulting in very diverse levels of quality, infrastructure, and, unsurprisingly, price. While, on average, private schools outperform their public counterparts in what relates to quality, there are a significant number of private institutions that perform at similar and even lower levels of quality than the average public schools. Predictably, these schools typically serve families that belong to the lower middle class.

In order to understand how public and private schools are distributed across socioeconomic levels in society, it is worth mentioning how socioeconomic classification works in Colombia. For the purpose of equitably charging public utilities rates, the government has classified households and public and private facilities of every kind into six socioeconomic "strata". The lower income strata are charged less for public utilities, which are in turn subsidized by increased charges to their higher strata counterparts. Socioeconomic strata are defined in terms of physical characteristics of households, availability of transportation, and the overall quality of their surroundings. With these criteria, six socioeconomic strata have been defined in Colombia (National decree 196, 1989): Lower-low (I), Low (II), Middle-low (III), Middle (IV), Middle-high (V) and High (VI). When looking at school strata, the existence of socio-economic segregation is evident: 80 percent of low stratum schools are public, while more than 95 percent of high stratum schools are private. In the middle class (middle low, middle and middle high -strata III, IV and V-) more than 80 percent of schools are private.[14] If middle class families choose to send their children to middle strata schools, they could increase their degree of choice using the private school offer. However, given the limited offer of public education for middle- low income families, this increased choice turns into a particularly heavy economic burden for a population segment which would still require some government attention. On the other hand, stratum 2 (low income families) have a nearly balanced offer of public and private schools (60 percent – 40 percent) approximately.

The Colombian government has taken some measures in the past to increase school choice freedom of families in need. Notably, the government did have a school voucher program for nearly a decade. The Plan for the Expansion of Access in Secondary Education or PACES for its Spanish acronym (*Programa de Ampliación de Cobertura de la Educación Secundaria*), sought to improve access for secondary education by taking advantage of the surplus in private education supply, which contrasted with a dramatic deficit in public capacity during the early nineties. This initiative became one of the largest voucher programs ever implemented in the world. By 1997, 125.000 vouchers had been awarded to pupils from low socio-economic backgrounds.[15]

While the primary goal of PACES was related to access, it represented a clear example of school choice and its effects went far beyond access. It remains a widely studied case on the effectiveness of school voucher policies.
Under PACES, rising sixth graders could apply to the lottery provided that they could (a) demonstrate –via public utilities receipts- that they belonged to low SES, (b) had already been admitted to a participating private school and (c) were under 15 years old. Roughly 40 percent of the private schools in the 10 largest cities in Colombia accepted vouchers – most elite private schools opted out-, which provided expanded school choice for low SES families. Research has shown that winners of the lottery "completed more years of school and had lower grade repetition, higher test scores, and a lower probability of working than did losers." [16]

While the value of the vouchers was initially designed to cover the full costs of tuition –hence providing an unbiased option to participating families-, as the program evolved through the years, the vouchers rarely kept up with increases in tuition, which implied that most recipient families had to supplement the voucher with their own private resources.[17]

PACES remains the most salient example of a school choice policy implemented in Colombia, even though its *raison d'être* was the expansion of access, rather

14 MEN, 2012b
15 Angrist et al, 2006.
16 Angirst et al, 2006.
17 Angirst et al, 2006.

than quality, or choice itself. Despite its positive results, the program fell victim of political tensions between the teachers' union and the government. Legal and management issues also became a challenge, which resulted in payments delay that became unsustainable for schools[18]. The program ceased to be a central government strategy in 1998,[19] and as the government expanded its own school infrastructure and was able to achieve universal access, the relevance of PACES slowly eroded.

School distinctiveness protected by law and policy

Distinctive character

Educational legislation requires each school to define its distinctive character. This mandate is established in both the general law of education, and Decree 1860 (1994). The legal structure that gives actual ground for school distinctiveness is known as the Institutional Educational Project, PEI by its Spanish acronym. This structure is defined in article 73 of the national general law 115:

> *In order to accomplish the integral formation of pupils, each educational institution should design and implement an Institutional Educational Project, where it will specify aspects such as the principles and goals of the educational institution, available and required didactic teaching resources, pedagogical approach, regulations for teachers and pupils and management system; all of this aimed at fulfilling the regulations imposed by this law and its further regulations*

The article further states two important issues around the PEI. The first is that the government will establish "*stimuli and enticements for research and pedagogical innovations, and for those non-for-profits which PEI has been assessed as excellent*", according to a national evaluation agency. The second is that PEIs must "*respond to context and needs of pupils, local communities, regions and the country, and be concrete, feasible and evaluatable*". National Decree 1860 further develops the topic of the PEI, devoting a whole chapter that states its minimum required contents and structure, the participatory procedure that must be followed in its development and enactment, and its mandatory nature: in order to obtain an operating license, a school must formally register and receive approval of its PEI by the local education authority. Whatever its nature, whether public or private, secular or confessional, innovative or traditional, any legally operating school in Colombia is understood to have a *PEI* which has been officially approved. On this basis, private institutions satisfy school attendance requirements and certifications provided by these schools are officially accepted and enjoy the same legal status as those of their public counterparts.

---

[18] Calderon, 1996

[19] Saavedra, 2011

The specific and even contextual nature of the PEI, which is the source of distinctiveness for each school in the country, is both encouraged and limited by the national general law of education and the national Decree 1860. On the positive side, schools are granted autonomy regarding curriculum. This autonomy is stated in article 77 of the national general law and allows institutions: "*...to organize the fundamental areas of knowledge defined for each educational level, to introduce new optional courses, to adapt certain subject areas to regional needs and characteristics, and the use of particular teaching methods...*" (Law 115).

The same law, however, opens the way for limitations on this autonomy by two different means. The first is a paragraph in article 77, stating that Secretariats of Education are responsible for advising educational institutions in their jurisdiction regarding curriculum design. In the case of large and influential Secretariats of Education such as that of Bogota, during the last 8 years the relationship between local and national regulations has been unclear.[20]

The second limitation on autonomy is article 78 of the law, which states that the Ministry of Education will design "general guidelines of curricular processes, and will establish achievement indicators for each grade level of formal education". Although this actually never happened, the ministry of education has undertaken several initiatives of curriculum regulation in the past 12 years. These initiatives begun with resolution 2343 of 1996, which extensively defined curricular goals for the 8 to 13 mandatory curriculum areas in each educational cycle (a couple f grade levels) in schooling. The following project on curriculum regulation was a set of "curricular guidelines", a 12 booklet series which presented pedagogical and theoretical considerations for curricular areas, released in 1998. These guidelines led to four booklets which define national curricular standards for mathematics, sciences, language and citizenship, released in 2006. The role of these standards as curricular guidelines for schools is unclear: how they should be "observed" is left undefined. There are no nation-wide pupil evaluations which are clearly based on these standards

This uncertainty has had widely different effects among public and private schools. While the most highly regarded pedagogical innovations in Colombia have been private, curricular autonomy in public schools is rarely attained; for the most part, their PEIs are built around a set of commonplaces, and their curriculum, even in newly established institutions, ends up being highly traditional.

Decisions about admitting pupils

As with most of the characteristics of the schooling system in Colombia, the public-private divide determines the differences in policies for pupil admission.

---

[20] Mahecha, Borda, 2009.

Private, independent schools enjoy a significantly higher level of freedom when establishing criteria for admission.

For the public system, the framework for admission rests largely on two constitutional mandates: The fundamental right to equality and the fundamental right to the free development of character. These two precepts, contained in articles 13 and 16 of the national constitution, have dominated school legislation and court rulings in relation to admission –and expulsion- of pupils from schools. As a result, public schools follow a general rule of equality, where all pupils have the right to be admitted irrespective of their race, religion, gender or intellectual ability. Public schools in Colombia are co-ed, secular and non-tracking. The obvious benefits of this rule nevertheless limits school distinctiveness.

While there has been some political pressure – especially in large cities – to establish public magnet schools with the aim of countering the pervasiveness of low quality in public schools, the legal framework of the schooling system makes it difficult to allow for such initiatives to be effectively implemented.

Private schools, on the other hand, are allowed to extend the reach of their distinctiveness into corresponding admissions policies. It is not uncommon to find private schools that are single-sex, religiously affiliated, that cater to academically gifted pupils or to pupils with special needs, and even those that admit pupils based on nationality. This characteristic of private schooling has favored the existence of highly selective private schools that can be found both at elite schools serving affluent families and at those that cater to middle class pupils.

That said, even private schools are bound by the constitutional principles of equality and free development of character, primarily in relation to decisions involving pupil expulsions. An abundant body of court rulings has established the boundaries within which private schools are allowed to expel their pupils. Motivations that were common and acceptable less than two decades ago (teen pregnancy, sexual orientation, personal appearance) have been ruled out as legitimate motivations for expulsion.

Both at the public and private levels, families can make use of the constitutional mechanism of *Tutela* – an expedited judicial action aimed to protect fundamental rights – when they feel that their children's admission to or continuance in a school is jeopardized by a policy or decision affecting their fundamental rights to equality and the free development of character. Thousands of these actions are brought to court every year.

Decisions about staff

As in many other aspects of the Colombian education system, there are notorious differences between public and private sectors in staff management. Public sector hiring of teachers is a highly regulated government process which, in accordance with the Constitution, cannot exhibit any sort of discrimination. The process in under the management of a national government agency called *Comisión Nacional del Servicio Civil* (National Commission of Civil Service, CNSC by its Spanish acronym). This agency regulates hiring for all public jobs in the Colombian government in all of its branches: health, justice, education, etc.

What CNSC does in the case of teacher staff is to determine which persons are eligible to occupy a teaching position. The agency does so by a merit competition which is aimed at producing lists of eligible people (*lista de elegibles*) for each of the 94 Secretariats of Education. The process by which a person applies for a teaching position and consequently gets included on an eligible list can take as long as two years.

The general framework for public service in education is regulated by national Decree 1278 of 2002, which establishes the statutory tenure requirements and conditions for public teaching in Colombia. Decree 1278 specifically states the requisites, conditions and steps that the merit competition by which public teaching positions are assigned should follow, along with rights, duties, and other considerations regarding public teachers in Colombia. Significantly, the decree allows the entrance of professionals other than teachers to the teaching profession.

The process of hiring public teachers can be said to rely entirely upon formal qualifications, and does not take into account a possible fit between candidates and schools. The reason for this is that teachers apply for a teaching position, so teachers select which schools they want to work in, and not the reverse: public schools have absolutely no control about which teachers they hire.

In the private sector the situation is very different: there is no state regulation regarding hiring of teachers. The absence of regulations creates a very heterogeneous pool of potential teacher applicants. Their quality positively correlates with school SES: the higher the SES, the better the teachers and vice versa. Entry requirements vary accordingly: while high-SES, bilingual schools may not even consider candidates without graduate studies specific to the teaching of their subject areas, other schools can hire professionals with no knowledge or experience whatsoever in teaching matters.

The most organized and more well-established private schools can select their teachers on the basis of religious or philosophical agreement with the mission of the school; these selection processes are not subject to any government or other regulations. Legal requirements of non-discrimination by race, beliefs, gender or any other criteria are hence almost impossible to enforce. In this regard, private schools enjoy near absolute freedom as to whom they hire for a teaching position. Private operators of public education, *convenios* and *concesiones*, have autonomy to hire and fire personnel based on internal performance evaluations.

Accountability for school quality

It has been noted previously that the biggest challenge to the Colombian schooling system remains improving its quality. Beyond documented inequalities between the private and public education systems, the nation as a whole remains one of the bottom performers in international standardized tests. The most recent available benchmark is the PISA 2009 examination, where pupils from 65 participating countries where measured in reading, mathematics and science scales. Colombia was ranked 52 and scored statistically significantly below average on all evaluated areas. The results of this evaluation are not isolated; the performance of Colombian pupils in earlier PISA evaluations, as well as in other examinations such as TIMSS and PIRLS, are consistent with the PISA 2009 results.

It is thus not surprising to find that the schooling system in Colombia has little focus on quality-based accountability. As a matter of fact there are very few mechanisms of accountability whatsoever (even those that do not relate to quality). A complex history of education policy development has favored a system that orbits around the highly unionized teacher profession. This reality has yielded a schooling system that – as in many Latin American Countries – remains unfavorable for most forms of accountability and even more so those that rely on quality measures.[21]

One of the primary obstacles for quality-based accountability in Colombia is the absence of a favorable ecosystem of standards, test taking policies and information systems. Even if the country were to adopt the very contentious policy of high-stakes testing, it would find itself with no tools whatsoever to implement such an effort. The Colombian testing service is directed by ICFES, responsible for designing and administering standardized tests at the primary, secondary and higher education levels. However, at the school level, there are only 3 tests available during the entire school-life of a pupil. The SABER exam is administered at grades 5, 9 and 11. However, several characteristics of the testing undermine this standard's ability to become an input for quality-based accountability:

- At grades 5 and 9 the test is sample-based: This means that only a sample of the pupil population at such grades is tested. While the sample is representative of the population, it fails to provide information about every pupil. Only 11th grade pupils are assessed with a census methodology. A consequence of this is that many pupils will only be tested once, and in very exceptional cases, three times during their entire school life,
- At grades 5 and 9 results are not individualized: Although individual identifiable pupils take the test, the results are only released as statistical averages of performance. This allows, at the most, assessing school-level performance on the random years when a given school forms part of the sample. The general

21 Corvalán and McMeekin, 2006.

use of the tests, however, is to provide system-level information that will allow interpreting national or regional performance results.
- The tests do not follow cohort progress: Because the tests are not administered every year to every pupil in the corresponding grade, they do not provide information that can be used to track the academic progress of pupil cohorts.

In sum, the assessment tools that the school system relies on lack the necessary characteristics –both in design and implementation techniques-, to serve as reliable sources of data for quality-based accountability. As a result, the very limited mechanisms of accountability are primarily input based and, again, have very little implications for teachers or administrators. As with most of the system characteristics, these limited expressions of accountability vary depending on the public or private nature of schools.

At the public level, most accountability is based on the fact that teachers and administrators are considered public servants and as such are subject to the regulations of the public profession. However, the teaching profession is largely seniority-based and quickly grants tenure to teachers and administrators. Most of the responsibilities to which school administrators can be held accountable relate to the fulfillment of bureaucratic requirements and the submission of input-based reports. There are, however, no legal provisions that allow the dismissal or other disciplinary actions of teachers or administrators based on their pupils' performance. However, the new tenure statutory regulations enacted in decree1278 (2002) constitute an important advance regarding teacher accountability, as the approval of qualifying tests is a condition for teachers' promotion in the tenure track, and better performing teachers receive economic stimulus.

In private schooling, the few expressions of accountability are primarily reliant on input-based indicators. Schools submit a yearly self-evaluation report that focuses on indicators such as teacher-pupil ratios, square meters of space per pupil, qualifications of staff, educational resources, etc. As discussed in section 3, above, this evaluation yields a score that grants schools three distinct levels of freedom or autonomy -*Controlada* (controlled), *Vigilada* (supervised) or *Regulada* (regulated)-. These degrees of autonomy, regulated in Decree 2253, have effect on the schools' ability to determine yearly increases on their tuition. There are no outcome-based criteria included in this self-evaluation report. More recently, private schools that are quality certified or accredited by international organizations (such as the European Foundation for Quality Management EFQM or the International Standardization Organization ISO) experience a "bonus" in the percentage points that they can increase in the yearly cost of tuition. Likewise, being ranked at the highest (*muy superior*) level at the grade 11 SABER test also yields bonus percentage points to the maximum yearly increments in the cost of tuition.

Teaching of values

Colombia is a secular state and as such does not prescribe a particular set of moral values to be taught in public schools. However, ethics and human values, religion and the national constitution, are amongst the mandatory subjects to be taught in schools in Colombia according to the general law of education. The Ministry of Education has implemented several strategies to respond to these requirements.

In regard to ethics and values, the Ministry produced in 1998 a twelve-booklet series on curricular guidelines which included a volume on ethics and values education, and another volume on the study of the national constitution. These booklets presented theoretical considerations about what education in values should be. By 2004 this latter considerations were even disregarded or not further developed, and instead the creation of a set of national curriculum standards in citizenship was underway. By 2006 the last version of the standards was released to the public. These standards are designed by groups of grade levels (from 1st to 3rd for example), and have a significant focus on the improvement of relating with each other in peaceful ways (*convivencia*: as living in community, coexistence) and peaceful conflict resolution. Some criticism that has been raised about an excessive idealism underlying the foundations of these standards;[22] nonetheless these standards have been the dominant and current perspective on issues related to morals and ethics in the country since 2004.

Citizenship competence standards have also served as basis for designing tests, that although not national in nature, have involved statistically robust samples of pupils of different grade levels. Ongoing changes in standards dating from 2003 have rendered some results of the different tests not comparable. For some years, the national testing agency has been working with IEA as an advising body, and Colombia was involved in the 2009 international comparative civics study.

Besides these citizenship competencies standards, there are no further government regulations regarding ethics and values. According to the autonomy schools enjoy by law, and in accordance to their individual PEIs, schools are free to adhere to any confession or set of values they choose. In this regard, Catholic Church enjoyed special level of influence in several state matters, particularly regarding education and morals education since colonial times. Additionally, a special diplomatic agreement between Colombia and the Vatican state known as *El Concordato* was signed in 1887, and then renewed and reformed in 1973.[23] However, as a result of changes derived form the new national constitution of Colombia, enacted in 1991, Colombia was declared a secular state. This ended the official recognition of the dominant position of the Catholic Church in regard to morals education. The Concordat was derogated after a Constitutional Court

---

22 Mejía, Perafán, 2006.

23 Martín, 1973.

ruling in 1995 and following the regulation of the right to religious freedom by law 133 of 1994.

Religious education was sued, unsuccessfully, as unconstitutional in 1994; the constitutional court ruled that pupils were free to either take the religious education of their preference or refuse. National Decree 4500 of 2006, however, introduced further regulations in this matter, and established religious education as mandatory for all pupils, and its evaluation like any other academic subject. Religious education addressed in this decree is not bound to any particular set of beliefs.

There are no ideologies or sets of values whose teaching is explicitly forbidden in Colombian legislation; denial of the Holocaust and other "hate crimes" do not exist in Colombian law, but legislative projects addressing racism and related issues are known to be underway.

References

Angrist, J., Bettinger, E. y Kremer, M., (2006). "Long-Term Educational Consequences of Secondary School Vouchers: Evidence from Administrative Records in Colombia". American Economic Review, Vol. 96, No. 3, 847-862.

Barrera-Osorio (2010). The impact of Private Provision of Public Education: Empirical Evidence from Bogotá's Concession Schools. World Bank Policy Research Working Paper 4121. Retrieved at: http://ddp-ext.worldbank.org/EdStats/COLimp07.pdf

Bonilla, J.D. (2011). Longer Term Educational Consequences of Contracting Out Public Schools: Evidence From Administrative Records in Colombia. Retrieved at: http://www.depeco.econo.unlp.edu.ar/cedlas/ien/pdfs/meeting2011/papers/Bonilla.pdf

Calderón, A. (1996). Voucher Program for Secondary Schools: The Colombian Experience. Human Capital Working Papers. WorldBank. Retrieved at: http://www-wds.worldbank.org/external/default/WDSContentServer/WDSP/IB/1996/05/01/000009265_3970619110741/Rendered/PDF/multi_page.pdf

Colombian Constitution, 1991, Art 67. Retrieved at: http://www.secretariasenado.gov.co/senado/basedoc/cp/constitucion_politica_1991_pr002.html

Corvalán, J. y McMeekin, R. (editores) (2006). Accountability educacional: posibilidades y desafios para América Latina a partir de la experiencia internacional. Santiago de Chile: PREAL. Retrieved at: http://www.rinace.net/bliblio/Accountabilitypercent20Corvalan.pdf

DANE (2010a). Formal Education Statistics for year 2010. Retrieved at http://www.dane.gov.co/files/investigaciones/educacion/educacion_formal/EFormal_alumnos_sector_2010.xls

DANE (2010b). Formal Education Statistics for year 2010. Retrieved at http://www.dane.gov.co/files/investigaciones/educacion/educacion_formal/EFormal_establecimientos_Sector_2010.xls

Dinero (2011). Los mejores colegios de 2011. http://www.dinero.com/edicion-impresa/caratula/articulo/los-mejores-colegios-2011/139064

ICFES (2010). Examen de Estado de la educación media – ICFES SABER 11°. Qué se evalúa. Cómo se interpretan los resultados individuales. Bogotá. Pp 57. Retrieved at: http://www.icfes.gov.co/index.php?option=com_docman&task=doc_view&gid=3348&Itemid=59

ICFES (2011a). Examen de estado de la educación media. Resultados del periodo 2005-2010. Bogotá. Pp 49, 50. http://www.icfes.gov.co/index.php?option=com_docman&task=doc_view&gid=4435&Itemid=59

ICFES (2011b). Resultados de los establecimientos educativos en las pruebas saber 11°, 2011. http://www.icfes.gov.co/index.php?option=com_content&task=view&id=709&Itemid=990

Iregui, A.M., Melo, L., Ramos, J. (2006). Evaluación y análisis de la eficiencia de la educación en Colombia. Banco de la República, Bogotá, Colombia. Retrieved at: http://siteresources.worldbank.org/PSGLP/Resources/MeloBecerra.pdf

Mahecha, J., Borda, S. 2009. Autonomía curricular en los colegios: contradicciones entre teoría y práctica. In *Educación para el siglo XXI, aportes del Centro de Investigación y Formación CIFE, 2001 – 2008.*
Retrieved at: http://otroblogsobreeducacion.blogspot.com/p/archivos-y-vinculos.html

Martin-Sánchez, I. (1973). El nuevo Concordato entre la Santa Sede y La República de Colombia. Revista de estudios políticos, No. 192, Pp. 165-186.
McEwan, P.J., Benveniste, L. (2001). The politics of rural school reform: Escuela Nueva in Colombia, Journal of Education Policy, 16:6, 547-559.

Mejía, A., Perafán, B. (2006). Para acercarse al dragón, para amansarlo, es necesario haberlo amansado primero: una mirada crítica a las competencias ciudadanas. *Revista de Estudios Sociales*, **23**, Pp23 - 35.

MEN (2010a). Revolución Educativa 2002-2010. Acciones y lecciones. Ministerio Nacional de Educación, República de Colombia. Bogotá. Pp 94 http://www.

mineducacion.gov.co/1621/articles-241342_memorias_RE.pdf

MEN (2010b). Revolución Educativa 2002-2010. Acciones y lecciones. Ministerio Nacional de Educación, República de Colombia. Bogotá. Pp 87. http://www.mineducacion.gov.co/1621/articles-241342_memorias_RE.pdf

MEN (2012a). National system of Information for Higher education SNIES. Retrived query: http://snies.mineducacion.gov.co/ConsultaSnies/ConsultaSnies/consultarInfoProgramasAcademicos.jsp?metodologia=&nombreIes=&codProg=&nivelFormacion=06&id=&programa=&condicionCalidad=03&area=3&nbc=313&codIes=&municipio=&6578706f7274=1&departamento=&Submit=Buscar+programa&d-49781-e=2&departamentoL=&nivel=

MEN (2012b). National system of Information for Midel and Basic Education "Buscando Colegio". Retrived at: http://www.mineducacion.gov.co/buscandocolegio/

National Decree 196 (1989). Retrieved at: http://www.minambiente.gov.co/documentos/dec_0196_260189.pdf

National Decree 1278 (2002). Retrieved at: http://www.mineducacion.gov.co/1621/article-86102.html

National Decree 1860 (1994). Retrieved at: http://www.mineducacion.gov.co/1621/article-86240.html

National Decree 2253 (1995). Retrieved at: http://www.mineducacion.gov.co/1621/article-104515.html

National Decree 2277 (1979). Retrieved at: http://www.mineducacion.gov.co/1621/article-103879.html

National Decree 230 (2002). Retrieved at: http://www.mineducacion.gov.co/1621/article-103106.html

National Decree 2832 (2005). Retrieved at: http://www.mineducacion.gov.co/1621/article-103106.html

National General Law of Education 115 (1994). Retrieved at: http://www.mineducacion.gov.co/1621/article-85906.html

National Resolution 2343 (1996). Retrieved at: http://www.iered.org/cmapserver/servlet/SBReadResourceServlet?rid=1H1GLZZ2D-N2696B-1CR

Nuñez, J., Steiner, R., Cadena, X., Pardo, R. (2002) ¿Cuáles colegios ofrecen mejor educación en Colombia?. Bogotá. Universidad de Los Andes, Documetos

CEDE. http://economia.uniandes.edu.co/investigaciones_y_publicaciones/CEDE/Publicaciones/documentos_cede/2002/cuales_colegios_ofrecen_mejor_educacion_en_colombia

OECD (2010), PISA 2009 Results: What Pupils Know and Can Do – Pupil Performance in Reading, Mathematics and Science (Volume I) http://dx.doi.org/10.1787/9789264091450-en

Piñeros, L.J. (2010). "Una Mirada a las cifras de la educación en Colombia 2002 – 2009". Educación Compromiso de Todos. Bogotá. http://www.educacioncompromisodetodos.org/ect2/index.php/publicaciones/74-2010-una-mirada-a-las-cifras

PREAL (2006). Hay avances pero quedan desafíos. Informe de progreso educativo Colombia. Bogotá. http://www.preal.org/Archivos/Bajar.asp?Carpeta=Prealpercent20Publicaciones\Informespercent20depercent20Progresopercent20Educativo\Informespercent20Nacionales&Archivo=RCpercent20Colombiapercent202006.pdf

Saavedra, J.E., Bettinger, E., Kremer, M., Kugler, M. Efectos de largo plazo de las Becas PACES para la Educación Secundaria privada en Colombia. Notas de Política, Universidad de Los andes, Bogotá, Colombia. Retrieved at: http://gobierno.uniandes.edu.co/Publicaciones/Notaspercent20depercent20Politica/notas_de_politica10_internet.pdf

World Bank (2008). "The Quality of education in Colombia. An analysis and Options for a Policy Agenda" (Report No 43906-CO). Washington D.C. http://ddp-ext.worldbank.org/EdStats/COLstu08.pdf

Cuba
From the 2004 edition

by Daniele Vidoni

Overview

The Cuban case is rather unusual, because it is a striking example of a society with *no* freedom of education. This tightly controlled society with limited choices has, however, been able to set up an effective school system, especially by comparison with some other Latin American countries.

Looking at the history of education in Cuba, it is possible to compare the present data with the information available for the Batista period. In 1953 - at the beginning of Castro's quest for power (the Revolution would not actually take place until 1959) - 55.6 percent of the children aged 6-14 did not have access to a school, there were more than one million illiterate people (22.3 percent of the population 10 to 49 years of age), primary education was available only to half of the population, middle and higher education available only to restricted minorities in the major urban centers, and there were an estimated 10,000 unemployed teachers.

Since the advent of his authoritarian regime, Castro and his entourage have included education among the primary political instruments and also objectives of the state. According to official data, 98 percent of Cuban children of the appropriate age attended pre-school in 1997-98. The enrolment rate for 6 to 16-year-olds was 94.2 percent, and primary school enrolment was 100 percent. Grade-repetition rates were 1.9 percent in primary school, 2.8 percent in secondary and 1,8 percent in pre-university school.

The result is even more remarkable if compared to the achievements obtained by the other Latin American and Caribbean countries. The results of Cuban student with regard to language achievement in third grade are superior to those of any other country in the area.

Part of the Cuban achievement success is due to its peculiar situation: Cuba is a small country (11 million people) that - until the collapse of the Soviet Union in 1989 - received heavy subsidies from the Soviets. These arrangements saved Cuba from the recession the rest of Latin America suffered in the 1980s, and allowed the Cuban government to invest high shares of the GDP in education - around 10 percent, a much higher percentage than the 6 percent recommended as adequate by UNESCO.[1] Of course, the size of GDP allocated to education alone is insufficient to define an effective education system, but the system's strict centralization implies that the Ministry, which decides the system's objectives, allocates all the money. This arrangement makes it possible to distribute money efficiently, without "informational advantages of self-interested agents . . . [that] can create adverse incentives and leeway for the agents to act opportunistically, leading to an inefficient use of given resources and to misallocations of resources across different uses."[2] When the subsidies from the former Soviet Union ceased, the Cuban economy risked collapse; it is now slowly starting to breathe again by attracting massive numbers of European and now U.S. tourists bucking the embargo.

However, this situation is posing two new burdens on the quality of Cuban education. On one side, the economic crisis has meant a serious shortage of education materials - such as textbooks and notebooks - that in the past have been widely available; on the other side, it poses a serious threat to the availability of the most important resource inside the school, well trained and qualified teachers. Carnoy notes that, until recently, teaching was a relatively prestigious profession, and wages (about 300-450 pesos per month, or $US13-18) are only somewhat lower than those of physicians and about the same as in other professions. This situation ensured the Cuban government a steady supply of potentially talented teachers, attracted to teaching mainly on the basis of wanting to work with children and adolescents in a relatively prestigious job. "Now this situation has changed, particularly in two provinces, Habana and Mantazas, the centers of the rapidly growing tourist industry. Tourists can only pay in U.S. dollars, and a parallel dollar economy has developed in the two provinces. Workers in hotels, transportation, and restaurants receive tips in dollars, and can use these dollars to purchase goods not available to other Cubans in special foreign currency stores. A chambermaid in a hotel, for example, may earn $30-50 dollars in tips per month (or more), double or triple a teacher's salary. Ironically, the competition from tourist industry jobs has drawn off highly skilled labor from teaching, creating shortages in the teaching force."[3]

The next few years will be crucial to understanding whether the Cuban system will or will not be able to overcame these growing difficulties. However, the example of a system that provides a rigid structure for family and youth choices plays the role of a devil's advocate in any attempt to promote and defend the role of freedom in education, and it raises important questions on the essence and the aims of education:

"In the Cuban restricted choice model, educational 'success' is part of that rigid

1 Ritzen 1999.
2 Bishop and Woessmann 2002, 2.
3 Carnoy and others, 21.

structure: the state 'requires' children to be as successful in school as their ability permits."[4] What is the meaning of "education" in a society where individual self-definition is limited by such a heavy structure?

Does such education just lead to a dystopia where a small group of people decide the essence and the value of the human life?

And, in more practical terms, will government continue to monopolize Cuban education? If not, who will be able to partner with government? NGOs? Private education entities?

Can Cuba maintain the coherence of its education policies in the absence of historically strong state guidance and control?

What features of the rigid Cuban structure might more democratic countries adopt for enhancing the effectiveness of their schools?

Legal Framework

In Cuba, schooling is a function of the state; this fundamental principle is affirmed by article 9 of the 1992 *Constitution of the Republic of Cuba*. The article reads: "The state . . . ensures the educational, scientific, technical and cultural progress of the country . . . [and] as the power of the people and for the people, guarantees . . . that no child be left without schooling, food and clothing; that no young person be left without the opportunity to study; that no one be left without access to studies, culture and sports." Article 39, 40, 51 and 52 also refer to education; article 39 and 40 are the basic guidelines for educational policy, and article 51 and 52 affirm the right to education.

Specifically, article 39 indicates that "the state orients, foments and promotes education, culture and science in all their manifestations." Educational and cultural policy are based on a set of comprehensive and extremely detailed principles. The first is that "the state bases its educational and cultural policy on the progress made in science and technology, the ideology of Marx and Mart, and universal and Cuban progressive pedagogical tradition;" this principle goes along with the assertion that "the state promotes the patriotic and communist education of the new generations and the training of children, young people and adults for social life." Education is a tool for the advancement of the Cuban society, and its outcomes are especially devoted to the solution of social problems. "The state encourages and facilitates research and gives priority to that which is aimed at solving the problems related to the interests of society and the well-being of the people; the stat! e makes it possible for the workers to engage in scientific work

4 Carnoy and others, 24.

and to contribute to the development of science; the state promotes, foments and develops all forms of physical education and sports as a means of education and of contribution to the integral development of citizens; . . . the state promotes the participation of the citizens, through the country's social and mass organizations, in the development of its educational and cultural policy."

Article 40 specifies that children are the first beneficiaries of the outcomes of these principles; in fact, "the state and society give special protection to children and young people. It is the duty of the family, the schools, the state agencies and the social and mass organizations to pay special attention to the integral development of children and young people."

Chapter VII, Fundamental Rights, Duties And Guarantees, specifies how the right to education is guaranteed. Article 51 says that "everyone has the right to education. This right is guaranteed by the free and widespread system of schools, semi-boarding and boarding schools and scholarships of all kinds and at all levels of education and because of the fact that all educational material is provided free of charge, which gives all children and young people, regardless of their family's economic position, the opportunity to study in keeping with their ability, social demands and the needs of socioeconomic development. Adults are also guaranteed this right; education for them is free of charge and with the specific facilities regulated by law, by means of the adult education program, technical and vocational education, training courses in state agencies and enterprises and the advanced courses for workers."

Furthermore, article 52 indicates that "everyone has the right to physical education, sports and recreation. Enjoyment of this right is assured by including the teaching and practice of physical education and sports in the curricula of the national educational system; and by the broad nature of the instruction and means placed at the service of the people, which makes possible the practice of sports and recreation on a mass basis."

These principles are realized through the *Sistema Nacional de Educacion,* the Cuban School System, which relies on a core of laws: resolution 210 (April 23, 1975), resolution 654 (October 21, 1976), resolution 656 (October 21, 1976), resolution 160 (March 17, 1981) and resolution 430 (July 24, 1981).

These laws are accountable for the features that have made the Cuban school system so strict, specific and, eventually, successful. First, the state is the only entity that can operate schools, but the entire society is required to participate in the educational process by receiving at least primary and lower secondary education, and by direct support of the schools' work through the family, the state agencies, and the social and mass organizations. Second, the only permitted form of education is co-education, on the basis of the principle that males and females should have access to the same facilities. Third, education is free; the

State provides all educational material free of charge, and maintains a widespread system of schools, semi-boarding and boarding schools and scholarships of all kinds and at all levels of education.

A peculiarity of the Cuban school system - especially because of its widespread application - is the combination of school and work. This principle is directly derived from José Martí 's theories, and it calls for the need of linking theory and practice, school with life, and teaching with production, and gives a reasonable explanation for the success of the system. In fact, "since Cuban education had been functioning at a reasonably high standard since the 1970s, secondary school average students received a higher level of math, science, and language training, which they brought with them into teacher education. By training these student-teachers in government-run pedagogical institutes to teach a well-designed national curriculum, the Ministry of Education could deliver reasonably 'good' teachers trained to teach the required curriculum to every school in Cuba, even rural schools in provinces distant from the capital, Habana."[5]

Freedom to establish non-state schools

Article 39 of the 1992 Constitution of the Republic of Cuba states that "education is a function of the state." On the basis of this principle, non-state schools are illegal in Cuba.

Home schooling

Article 39 further specifies that "the law . . . [establishes] the integration and structure of the national system of education and the extent of compulsory education and defines the minimum level of general education that every citizen should acquire. In order to make this principle a reality, general education and specialized scientific, technical or artistic education are combined with work, development research, physical education, sports, participation in political and social activities and military training." Said education may be acquired only through schooling in one of the state schools; home schooling is illegal.

School choice not limited by family income

As already stated, article 39 of the Constitution states that schooling is provided free of charge; this statement holds at all levels but it is only valid for the state schools because these are the only institutions that can legally provide the schooling service.

---

5 Carnoy and others, 21.

School distinctiveness protected by law and policy

Decisions about admitting pupils

All Cuban pupils attend state schools, and admission to the local school is automatic at the age of six. The burden this provision sets on the government is high because almost 75 percent of the six year old children live in the cities, and that only 25 percent of the schools are urban schools; in Cuba 4792 primary schools (53.6 percent of the total) serve less that 50 students each. Following the demands made by UNICEF and UNESCO, the Cuban government has started programs like "Educa a tu Hijo" (give your child an education). These programs try to involve the family and the community in infants' early education, so that children enter the school "ready to learn."[6]

Decisions about staff

The *ley de Nacionalización de la Enseñanza* (June 6, 1961) (law on the nationalization of the teaching profession) declared that the teaching function is public, and its service is free. This law established that the state exercises the teaching function as a non-transferable duty and as a right of all Cuban citizens, without distinctions or privileges, in accordance with the principles of the Revolution. This law carries-out article 51 of the Cuban Constitution that requires the protection of the right to education by creating a "free and widespread system of schools, semi-boarding and boarding schools and scholarships of all kinds and at all levels of education."

One interesting feature of the Cuban system is the *emergentes*. The *emergentes* are bright upper secondary school students with the promise of receiving a university degree in humanities while teaching in primary school; these students receive six to eight month of teacher education courses, and then become elementary school teachers. *Emergentes* sign up for five years of teaching, taking courses for their university degrees on Saturdays and during the school vacations. As noted by Carnoy, "the conversion of lower secondary education into a 'continuation' of the primary school model is also using *emergente* training. This involves a one-year teacher education course and close supervision once in the classroom by their teachers college mentor."[7] Although in the first year of practice the *emergentes* are not necessarily successful teachers, they learn fast, and they are soon able to produce results in terms of students achievements. This characteristic way of linking together theory and practice provides a large number of bright and motivated prospective teachers who can be sent to any school in the country. Such arrangement means, on one side, that also the rural schools are served with talented and trained professionals (however young they may be) and, on the other

6 *Educación para todos*, 13, 11.
7 Carnoy and others, 22.

side, it provides a possible solution for the teacher shortage that may result from the present very difficult economic situation.

Accountability for school quality

The creation of an accountability system for Cuban schools is one of the results of the enactment of the reforms established in the decade 1972 - 1981. The Ministry of Education is responsible for the entire system, and it carries out the periodical evaluation school quality and of teachers' and students' results through the *Instituto Central de Ciencias Pedagógicas* (Central Institute of Pedagogical Science) and on the Central office of Planning, Statistics, and School Inspection. Local authorities also take part in the evaluation process as local representatives of the Ministry.

Such strict system design aims at the constant improvement of educational quality. Evaluation is based on a participatory approach designed to detect and correct problems of poor educational process and achievement through a comprehensive set of indicators.

The introduction of the so called *entrenamiento metodolgico conjunto* (joint methodological training) identifies the class as the central focus of the evaluation process carried out by the *estructuras de dirección docente-metodológicas* (directive structures of teaching methodology) and by the school. This joint action allows for systematic control over the teaching-learning process, with regard both to students' results and to teaching methods.

Resolution 216 (June 7, 1989) is the framework on the basis of which Cuban teachers assess their students' achievements; the tools for carrying out the assessment process are standardized tests, in class or take home exams, or specific performance in practical activities designed by the teacher. Standardized tests determine promotion, entrance to specific secondary schools, and access to specific majors within each university. Standardized tests have been used traditionally also used to determine access to primary school, however "Cuba . . . experienced a serious 'bottleneck' effect as students entering the first grade were unable to pass the standardized exam.

The Ministry of Education recently revised the exam policy to be more consistent with early childhood education principles, eliminating this entrance requirement for first grade."[8] The exam still remains a requirement for entrance into second grade and higher.

Student achievement, diligence, and punctuality are (together with the teacher's

8 Lindahl, 48.

diligence, punctuality, commitment, and mastery of the disciplinary contents taught) the objects of the teacher assessment process. A teacher's career growth depends primarily on positive evaluations in these areas; moreover, failure in leading the students to norm results may mean cuts in the teachers' salaries. Continuous evaluation is considered a part of the teachers' professional development because it provides useful information to improve teaching practice through action research and life-long learning; in fact one of the formative outcomes of the evaluation process are recommendations for *planes de superación autodidacta o postgraduada* (teachers' self-development plans).

The teacher evaluation process is carried out mainly through inspections. As described by Gasperini, "the 'chief of the pedagogical unit' (*jefe de círculo pedagógico*) visits every teacher each month during classes, assesses his/her activities and addresses any problems detected, deciding, for example on in-service training needed for teachers in different areas. A 'municipal specialist in teaching methods' (*metodologos municipales*) helps the school address pedagogical problems. If a problem cannot be solved with the 'metodologos,' the Instituto de Capacitación Pedagógica gets involved. Administrative and pedagogical inspectors set deadlines by which time problems must be solved. Assessment takes place at all levels of the system: the nation assesses the province, the province assesses the municipality, and the municipality the school. Teachers' performance is assessed by the school director, the party, the union, the Organization of Young Communists, and the 'pedagogical guide' for each cycle (preprimary, primary, secondary)."[9]

The Cuban approach to accountability implies that test results can translate directly into action toward the teachers, "but this action comes directly from the educational bureaucracy, not from parents, who have little school choice or voice. Interestingly, it is the hierarchical bureaucratic system that seems to be able to translate the information into more effective education than systems relying on indirect market mechanisms."[10]

Teaching of values

As indicated in Article 39 of the Constitution, the objectives of the education system are indicated and shaped around the Marxist-Leninist philosophy. Specifically, the system seeks to educate the citizen to "assume its most basic social duties, . . . [it] educate[s] this being to produce material and spirituals goods that will serve society in a way that every human being participates in material production, in order to eliminate the contradiction among school and society, producer and consumers, intellectual work and physical work, and among cities and rural areas."[11]

9 Gasperini, 13.
10 Carnoy and others, 23.
11 Garcia Gallo, 62.

References

Aguirre, B. E. and Vichot, R. J., *The Reliability of Cuba's Education Statistics, Comparative Education Review*, May 1998

Bishop, J. and Woessmann, L., *Institutional Effects in a Simple Model of Educational Production*, IZA DP No. 484, April 2002.

Carnoy, M., Gove, A., and Marshall, J., *Why do students achieve more in some countries than in others? A comparative study of Brazil, Chile, and Cuba*, Stanford University (mimeo), 2004

Educación para todos: evaluación en el año 2000 - República de Cuba, by various authors, 2000.

Garcia Gallo, G., *Bosquejo general del desarollo de la educación en Cuba*, Educación, n.14, July, September 1974

Gasperini, L., *The Cuban Education System: Lessons and Dilemmas*, Human Development Department LCSHD Paper Series No. 48, December 1999

Lindahl, R. A. *Comparing the challenges facing education between the United States and Cuba*, Education (Chula Vista, Calif.) 120 no1 45-52+ Fall 1999

OEI (Observatorio de la Educación Iberoamericana), *Sistemas Educativos Nacionales - CUBA, 1996*, http://www.campus-oei.org/quipu/index.html

Ritzen, J., *Looking for Eagles: A Short Guide to Bird Watching in an Educational Context*, Washington: World Bank, 1999.

El Savador[I]

by Daniele Vidoni[2]

Background

Slowly but steadily, El Salvador is progressing in the long path towards defeating illiteracy, raising school attainment, and improving student achievement. As shown by the data collected by MINED (Salvadorian Ministry of Education), net primary school attendance increased by over 13 percent between 1992 and 2007 and reached 97 percent in 2007. At the same time, illiteracy rates went down from 15 percent to 7 percent in youth 15-24 years old and from 23 percent to 15 percent overall.

Although these results are important, much is still left to be done closing the educational gap existing with more advanced economies, and the situation remains critical especially in the rural areas. The result is that, overall, only 2 percent of the infant population is enrolled in kindergarten, only roughly 55 percent of the population attends pre-primary education (4 to 6 years of age), and only about 33.3 percent of the population has access to high school (16-18 years of age).

Moreover, equity issues are at stake as rural schools are lagging behind urban schools in many areas ranging from the availability of technological equipment, to the lack of continuing professional development for teachers, to the quality and security of school buildings, and to the existence of support services and facilities such as laboratories, theaters, or gyms and playing fields.

These problems, which are specific of the education system, are worsened by a social fabric weakened by social insecurity, delinquency, and only limited spaces for development, exchange, and social participation.

After 2 decades (1989-2009), the right-wing Nationalist Republican Alliance (ARENA) party was substituted in power by the left-wing Farabundo Marti National

---

1 The chapter rests heavily on the contents already presented in the earlier description of El Salvador produced in 2004 by Oscar Picardo Joao and Charles L. Glenn.

2 Head of the Evaluation Research Unit in INVALSI, Italian Institute of Research in Educational Evaluation.

Liberation Front (FMLN) party. Although with different focuses, both parties have tried to address these issues by adopting action plans implemented at country level.

The current action plan 2010-2014 "Vamos a la escuela" (Let's go to school) adopts a holistic approach that encompasses the schooling and the social dimension of education. In the few years of its implementation, the Ministry of Education expanded material assistance to all the children at public primary schools throughout the country. For example, the MINED (2011) reports that in 2010 over 1.3 million students received basic nutrition at school. The program involved mothers in the preparation of school meals at 3,675 schools. More attention has also been paid to providing pre-school health and nutrition services. During this same period, primary school children in all 262 municipalities (roughly 1.4 million students) received uniforms, shoes, and school supplies, which had the spillover effect of creating employment opportunities for almost 54 thousand people involved in the production of such supplies. Between 2009 and 2011, more than $52 million dollars was spent on infrastructure repair to 2,136 school buildings.

In 2010, almost 51 thousand youth and adults attained literacy. To further address access to education, a number of flexible education programs were set up to provide a variety of course delivery modes, including distance learning and accelerated courses. These programs served more than 55,000 students. The reforms have also begun to more aggressively address the needs of at risk youth, special needs and disabled children. Special attention was also given to teacher training and professional development; over nine thousand educators underwent professional teacher training.

Despite the relevance of these results, doubts exist on the actual possibility of such measures to obtain permanent results in terms of student achievement and school quality. For example, according to UNDP data, public spending on education in El Salvador remains rather low, amounting to an average of 3.6 percent in 2010, and children receive schooling for an average of approximately 5.9 years (2008).

Moreover, serious inconsistencies remain across the country with regard to institutional provisions for education, training, and research and development, as few schools are established in rural areas, and poor children are effectively prevented from attending school due to the persistence of illegal school fees. The fact that rural parents frequently withdraw their children from school by the sixth grade to work contributes to this small number and reduces by a great deal the effect of some of the key-school programs enacted that have an essentially social nature, such as the "Vaso de leche" (glass of milk) program and the "Programa de alimentacion escolar" (School feeding program).

As Fernando Reimers explains: "One of the most valuable lessons of the last decade of reform has been that education quality is not generated spontaneously as a result of the institutional or management reforms. On the contrary, quality must be actively promoted with specific initiatives directed to the improvement of teachers' competences and with well-structured educational material which allow students the gradual acquisition of new skills such as reading and writing"; in fact, results mentioned in the report itself show that there is still a lot to do: "Between 20 percent and 30 percent of first grade students are held back at least once.

Among young people who are between 15 and 19 years old, one of them out of four does not even finish six years of primary schooling. Only two out of five finish basic education. The MINED evaluations show that the majority of the students does not acquire the competences reflected in the syllabuses...", and to this we would have to add the conclusions of the "Human Development in El Salvador 2010" report, elaborated by UNDP (United Nations Development Program) which points out that, at country level, the average score in the PAES standardized test is only 4.99 out of 10 (the MINED reports that the average country score has been 4.85 out of 10 in 2011) and that the country ranked 32 out of 36 in the TIMSS international survey of 2007.

Structure of the educational system

The national educational system has two modalities: formal education which comprises the initial, nursery school, basic and middle levels and is imparted in authorized educational institutions, in a regular sequence of school years or courses, subject to progressive curricular guidelines and conducive to degrees and qualifications; and the non-formal education which is offered with the aim of implementing, updating, supplying knowledge and educating in academic or work-related aspects without being subject to the system of levels or degrees.
The initial level starts from the child's birth up to the age four, and it fosters the socio-affective, psychomotive, perceptive, language and game development, by means of an appropriate early stimulation.

Nursery school (escuela parvularia) normally comprises three years of study and it fosters the complete development of the student of the ages of four to six, involving the family, the school and society.

Basic Education (escuela basica) regularly comprises nine years of study, and it is organized in three courses of three years of duration each, normally started at the age of seven. High school (escuela media) is offered in two modalities, the general one, with two years of duration, and the technical one, of three years of duration allow pupils to continue advanced studies or to report for work. In the technical modality the following special fields are offered: commercial, health, architecture, general mechanics, automobile mechanics, electrical engineering and electronics.

Higher education comprises technological and university education. Technological education aims at training and fitting professionals and specialists for the application of knowledge and skills in the different scientific and humanistic areas. University Education is directed towards the training in multidisciplinary careers on science, art, culture and technology, which educates us scientifically and in a humanistic way and leads us to the obtaining of university degrees. In this educational level the corresponding academic degrees are those of technician, teaching, technologist, degree, engineering, architecture, master's degree and doctorate.

The main institution of the national educational sector is the MINED, which is responsible for the administration of all levels of education of the public sector and for establishing norms and supervising the educational services which the private sector renders. The MINED is in charge of establishing norms, financing, promoting, evaluating and controlling the available resources in order to get the aims of national education. At the level of Higher Education, the Higher Education Council is the institution of the MINED for the development of higher education. The development of the Salvadorian education counts on the investment and participation of the Government and the different sectors of society.

Legal Framework[3]

The core principles governing Salvadorian education are expressed in art. 53 to 64 of the Constitution (1983), which establishes that the organization of the education system and the establishment of the schools and the provision of the necessary services are a responsibility of the State (art. 54). The objectives of Salvadorian education are the following: "achieving the full development of personality in its spiritual, moral, and social dimensions; contributing to the building of a democratic society more prosperous, just, and human; nurturing the sense of respect towards all human rights and the abidance to the corresponding duties; fighting against all feelings of intolerance and hatred; being knowledgeable of the national reality and identify oneself with the values of Salvadorian nationality and favor the unity of the Central-American people. The parents shall have preferential right to choose the education of their children" (art. 55). "The teaching offered in the official education centers shall be essentially democratic. The private education centers are subject to State regulations and inspections and could receive public funded if not for profit. The State exclusively shall be entitled to organize the training of teachers" (art. 57).

There is specific reference to the need of favoring integration and avoiding any kind of segregation. In fact, the Constitution indicates that "no educational institution shall be allowed to reject pupils for reasons related to the type of

3 To a large extent, the paragraph was derived from the comprehensive descriptions of the Salvadorian legal educational framework and of the administrative structure of the educational system presented in UNDP (2010).

relationship existing between their parents or tutors, or for reasons attaining to social, confessional, racial, or political differences" (art. 58).

The Constitution also rules about the right and the duty of education for all Salvadorian citizens. Specifically, it indicates that "all inhabitants of the Republic have the right and the duty of receiving pre-school and basic education for acquiring the knowledge and skills necessary to act as useful citizens. The State shall foster the settling of special education centers. Pre-school, basic, and special education shall be free of charge when provided by the State" (art. 56).
The General Law of Education of 1996 (Chapter II, Aims of National Education) indicates that: "the national education shall attain the aims set forth by the Constitution:
- To achieve the integral development of the human personality in its spiritual, moral, and social dimensions;
- To contribute to the building of a democratic society increasingly prosperous, just, and human;
- To transmit to the people the respect of human rights and the abidance to the corresponding duties;
- To fight against any intolerance and hatred;
- To acquire knowledge of the national reality and to identify the values of Salvadorian nationality; and
- To favor the unity of the Central-American people" (Art. 2).

The same General Law of Education of 1996 also specifies the general objectives of Salvadorian education, which are:
- To develop to the maximum possible extent the physical, intellectual, and spiritual potential of all Salvadorian people, and avoiding to impose limits upon those who could reach levels of further excellence,
- To balance the education plans and programs on the basis of the relevant corpus of science to obtain an adequate image of the human person in the context of the country economic and social development,
- To establish the didactic sequences so that all knowledge acquired shall favor the development of mental functions and the creation of positive and desirable attitudes in the people,
- To nurture creativity, the habit of thinking and planning, the persistency in achieving objectives, the ability to prioritize, and the development of critical competences,
- To systematize the domain of individual knowledge, skills, habits, abilities, and attitudes to make each individual functional for working efficiently so that, overall, the quality of life of the Salvadorian people can increase;
- To favor the development of individual and social relations in a climate of respect to human duties and rights, by nurturing civic loyalties, i.e. the natural interfamiliar relationships of the citizen with the homeland and of the human being with the culture;
- To improve the relationship of the people with the environment, by using

educational tools and teaching methods that explain the processes implicit in such relationship within the framework of rationality and conscience; and
- To nurture relationships that would develop feelings of solidarity, justice, mutual support, freedom, and peace in the context of the democratic order that recognizes the human being as the origin and the objective of the work of the State. (Art.3).

Apart from the constitution, the laws that characterize the architecture of the system are:
1. General Law of Education,
2. The Teaching Career law,
3. The Professional Training Law,
4. The Higher Education Law.

The General Law of Education, Legislative Decree n. 917 of 12/19/1996, defines the aims and the basic principles lying at the core of the education system, which were reported above. Moreover, it regulates the organization and the functioning of the system. The law has been modified in different occasions (1990, 1994, 1996, 2005) accordingly to the demands of the present reform processes.
This law devises the policies related to access to education, the structure of the education system, the characteristics of the national curriculum, the organization and the contents of the national system of educational evaluation, and the administrative and monitoring processes that emphasize the role of the community in education.

The Teaching Career Law, Legislative Decree n. 665 of 3/7/1996 and reformed in 2006, regulates the relationship of the State and of the educational community with the teachers – who are employees of the former, the autonomous institutions, the municipal schools, and the private schools. The law rules about the duties, the rights, the prohibitions and sanctions to which educators are exposed. The law also lies down the organs in charge of the administration of the teaching career and their specific duties (chapter VIII, Art.41):
- Human Resources Unit (MINED),
- Headship of the Teaching Institution,
- Educational Executive Council (CDE),
- Board of Examiners (*Tribunal Calificador*),
- Teaching Career boards and Court of Teaching Career.

This group of organs guarantee the teacher a coherent filter for evaluation and administration and the due ways of access in order to get an educational process with a higher quality.

The Professional Training Law, Legislative Decree 554 of 6/29/1993, allowed the creation of the Salvadorian Institute of Professional Training (INSAFORP), which is responsible for the direction and coordination of the country's professional training system. The objective of the system is to train professionally train human resources that would support the economic and social development of the country.

The Higher Education Law, Legislative Decree 468 of 10/29/2004, regulates higher education and the creation and functioning of new public and private institutions offering higher education courses, institutes the Commission for the Accreditation of the Academic Quality of Higher Education Institutions and the Council of Higher Education, which is a body that the MINED consults for advice and proposals on how to maintain and improve the quality of higher education.

In terms of system administration, subsequent reform waves have resulted in the MINED acquiring a role, which is more regulatory rather than initiative-taking. The territorial functions are concentrated in the 14 Offices/Department Directions of Education. These offices have the duty of planning, organizing and coordinating the necessary actions for ensuring that the schools of the department are functioning and providing an adequate level of education. The Offices provide logistic, administrative and technical support to the educational initiatives of the National Directions and other central offices.

Within the framework of the Educational Reform, and as crucial part of the decentralization process, school autonomy was strengthened through the creation of the School Communal Associations (ACE), Executive School Councils (CDE) and the Catholic Educational Councils (CECE); each structure intrinsically includes the active participation of the students, parents of a family, teachers and headmasters; it is important to point out that, apart from the administrative authority delegation, quality funds and bonds have been transferred so that autonomy can be complete and they can solve their problems and needs without going through bureaucratic processes. In 2002, ACEs and CDEs were managing directly 17 percent of the total school budget and 41 percent of the budget share reserved to teacher salaries.

Home Schooling

The educational system, its politics and laws do not admit within the system educational processes outside the school or teaching institutions as alternatives; there are only specific programs of "Tele Learning" and "Interactive Radio" as complementary and reinforcement programs outside the school, which do not have complete courses in the level or degree.

School attendance not limited by family income

The Constitution, in article 56, 2nd subsection, provides that: "Nursery, Basic and Especial Education will be free when the State imparts it," a cost-free principle which is emphasized in the General Law of Education in the articles 5 and 76. However, the articles 76 and 77 of the General Law of Education allowed the voluntary collaboration of parents, which were abolished by means of the legislative decree 180, issued in October 30th, 2003. The Cost-free Status Bond eliminates the voluntary fees established as an institutional habit in order to pay operative expenses in official educational centers; such measure had the main objective of guaranteeing Salvadorian children the free access to education. Yet, recent data indicates that – especially in rural areas – illegal fees are still demanded to student families and this fact contributes to the experienced dramatically lower levels of school attendance.

The Teaching Careers Law considers in article 55 section 2 as a serious fault not obeying the orders of the Ministry of Education, which can be penalized with up to 30 days of suspension without pay. Article 56 considers as a very serious fault demand for payment, which is penalized with up to 60 days of suspension without pay.

Article 6 of the General Law of Education establishes that in the middle levels and official technological institutions, the Ministry of Education will establish school fees, bearing in mind the democratization of access policy. School fees will be established by means of a General Parents Assembly and they will send the information to the Ministry of Education for its approval.

In El Salvador there are a total of 6,162 (2009) teaching institutions with the levels of Nursery schools, Basic education and high school; in 2010 there was a total of 1.58 million students in the public schools and 320 thousand students in the private options. In general, there was a drop in the matriculation rates in 2011 (77 thousand less students in the public schools and 94 thousand less students in the private schools), and such drop can be mostly attributed to parents not enrolling their children in school for fear of violence.

Private schools have a varied character including secular, bilingual, and Catholic and Protestant schools. Their costs are varied and can range between US$ 25 and US$ 400 per month. Parents can apply for the admission of their children to these centers depending on their means, rather than on access requirements or pupil capacities.

Educational polities on behalf of the school

In the framework created by the constitution and by the laws outlined in previous paragraphs, annual or multiannual plans are established to favor the development of education in the country. On one side, the initiatives taken try to improve on the actual quality of the education provided. On the other side –and to some extent to a more basic level – the initiatives try to create the conditions for reducing the cost of schooling on families with the aim of increasing school attendance rates. The current action plan 2010-2014 identifies 5 main goals for education:

1. Universalization of initial, basic, and secondary education.
2. Establishment of an education system to which all people will have a right.
3. Increase the participation of the community in the their schools
4. Prepare students for careers in science and technology.
5. Overcome illiteracy in the population of those 15 and older.

Accordingly, a number of specific programs were devised to attain the mentioned goals. The key programs in the 2010-14 plan are:

1. The presidential program for providing students with school uniforms, shoes, and school supplies. The program targets the resources to students in nursery schools and basic education and aims at reducing the financial burden on families, as well as at improving school attendance and making local economies more dynamic. In 2010, the 1,38 million students going to state schools received school uniforms, shoes, and school supplies.
2. The School Feeding Program, which is targeted to students in nursery schools and basic education and aims at lowering dropouts, as well as at improving school attendance and reducing the levels of malnutrition. As extensively described in Bundy, Burbano, Grosh, Gelli, Jukes, and Drake (2009), the school feeding program in El Salvador was fully taken over by the government in 2008 after 24 years of partnership with World Food Program.
3. National Alphabetization Plan, which aims at making sure that 96 percent of the whole population is alphabetized by the end of 2014 (which implies a reduction of analphabetism by 13.3 percent with respect to the 2010 levels). In 2010, the program reached roughly 53,000 young and adults and 329 people with special needs.
4. National Program of Education and Integral Development of the Early Infancy, which shall benefit children between 0 and 6 years of age and shall guarantee their integral development by coordinating and integrating different action strands at national and local level (both public and private) and by enhancing the role of the family and of the community;
5. Program of Inclusive Education, which aims at building an education system more centered on the human dimension and which would contribute to promoting a culture more open to differences and more attentive to the needs of the shares of population who are in disadvantaged situations, especially with respect to education. In 2010, the program has reached roughly 70,000 students with special needs and 25 specialized centers are under construction;
6. Program of School Infrastructures, which aims at developing the environments and securing the technical and technological supplies that are key for improving the teaching-learning process. In 2010, an investment of US$52 million allowed the rebuilding or the renovation of 2,136 schools.
7. Program Science and Technology, for developing the teaching and pedagogy of science and technology. Within such program, in 2010 the initiative "Cerrando la brecha de conocimento" (Closing the learning gap) – which is active in the municipality of Nombre de Jesús, Chalatenango – distributed 1,041 Laptops OLPC XO to students and teachers.
8. Program for the Professionalization of the Teaching Career, which includes both elements that are of specific interest of the trade-unions (such as salary and working hours), and elements more specific to the professional dimension (such as specialization and continuing professional development). In 2010-11, roughly 9,500 teachers received continuing professional development and an agreement was reached for an increase of 6-10 percent to all teacher salaries.

Distinctive Character

Next, a taxonomic chart of Salvadorian schools is presented, which reflects the specific character of the different modalities.

Kind of School	Meta-Population	Ideological nature	Pedagogical Profile
State School (urban and rural)	Lower class	To follow the Official Program of the Ministry: Constructivist, Humanist and Socially Involved Curriculum	Constructivist in theory, financial in practice.
Private Catholic School (only a few are Protestant and 70 are non-religious)	Middle class	Curriculum of the MINED plus ecclesiastic principles of the Church and of the order or congregation (Jesuits, Salesianos, Maristas, etc.)	Constructivist combined with traditional approaches (good results in standardized tests)
Bilingual Private School	Upper class	They are trained to study in the United States	they hardly follow the MINED program, and they believe in North American programs.

Decisions to admit students

Going on with the previous taxonomy the following chart shows, in outline, which the entrance requirements are, depending on the kind of school:

Kind of School	Entrance Requirements
Public School	None
Private Catholic School, Protestant, and non-religious schools	Exams with rigorous processes, due to the high demand.
Bilingual Private School	Ability to pay the fees

Decisions about Staff

In private schools or institutions the decisions about the appointment of the headmaster, administrators, and teachers are made with great freedom, just as in a private company; the majority of the appointment and dismissal criteria depend on competence and achievements, generating a great autonomy. In the public sector, on the contrary, the situation is very different, since they work with official posts which the government sets at service, awarded by means of a Board of Examiners of the Teaching Course.

The state schools of the system have serious problems to hire or dismiss teachers due to the legal conditions, trade-union or union guarantees and bureaucratic processes; both Headmasters and Teachers are very protected regardless of actual results.

Responsibility for the quality of education

The Country has made a substantial effort to build a comprehensive system of educational evaluation that looks at teacher and school quality, as well as at student achievement.

The constituents of the system are:

- The PAES (test for all the students graduating from secondary education);
- Achievement Tests for the 3rd, 6th and 9th Grades;
- Evaluation of educational institutions;
- The ECAP test for all the students who have passed the initial training as teachers.

Considering teacher quality as a crucial element for education quality, the MINED has invested considerable resources assessing the quality of initial teacher training. The instrument used to this aim is the ECAP (Evaluación de las Competencias Académicas Y Pedagógicas, Evaluation of Academic and Pedagogical Competences), an exam for assessing the levels of initial teacher training. In the exam, the graduates of teacher training courses in universities or accredited technical institutions are tested on their subject knowledge and pedagogical competences.

Efforts have been devoted also to monitor school quality. As part of the National Development Plan for Education 2021(Plan Nacional de Educacion 2021, strategic line on "good management practices", actions on "information systems, monitoring and evaluation"), the MINED had devised a catalogue of indicators for monitoring progress in the Salvadorian education system. The underlying conceptual framework, which devised by UNESCO (Instituto Internacional de Planeamiento de la Educación), foresees the need of collecting data along 4 main strategic strands:

- equitable access to education;
- effectiveness of nursery school, basic education, and high school;
- competitiveness;
- good managerial practices.

Moreover, the MINED has also established the SINAE (Sistema de Información, Monitoreo y Evaluación de Aprendizajes – System of Information, Monitoring, and Assessment of learning), the unit in charge of devising the assessment instruments, of analyzing the data collected, and of producing the information used in education policy making and implementation.

SINAE carries out of regular investigations on the Factors Associated to Student Achievement and School Value Added. The objective of such investigations is to identify actions and policies that could make the student learning experiences more effective and dynamic. Information on schools, school principals, teachers, and parents are also collected by means of specific questionnaires.

To identify the actual levels of student achievement at the end of each formal education cycle, SINAE administers the PAESITA, achievement Tests for the 3rd, 6th and 9th Grades and the PAES, a set of standardized tests, which have been administered since 1997, cover 4 subject areas (Mathematics, Social Studies, Language, and Science), and currently count for 25 percent of the student final grade.

As already hinted in the introduction, student results in the PAES are unsatisfactory. The average student grade at national level is 4.85 out of 10 (2011 data, the passing grade is 6). Yet, the most alarming indicator is the distance existing between public and private institutions, and between rural and urban schools. As UNDP (2010) indicates, only 3of the 15 school with best PAES scores in 2009 were public schools. On average, students in private schools score 5.44, while public school students stop at 4.84, which suggests that less affluent students – who rely mostly on public schooling – receive an education of lesser quality.

In 2007, El Salvador participated for the first time to the Trends in International Mathematics and Science Study (TIMSS), which assesses student achievement in Mathematics and Science at 4th and 8th grade. The country ranked 32nd out of the 36 participating countries and no Salvadorian student obtained a scored that can be considered "advanced" at international level.

Values education

The General Law of Education (1996) affirms that "education is a process of permanent training of the individual's personal, cultural, and social dimensions. It is based on an understanding of the human person as a whole, with own dignity, rights, and duties" so that "the educator is the professional in charge of directing the learning and training of the student towards the development of a moral, honest, loyal, and worthy. The teaching of values occurs within any learning process, with the objective of practicing and passing on the values of equality of human rights, refusal of any discrimination, respect to all cultures."
In the last years, MINED has tried to translate these principles in practice by developing specific programs both for teachers and for students.
Looking at the most relevant recent initiatives, the MINED has started a program with the Universidad Católica de Occidente for training graduates in values education. Moreover, in a joint effort with Plan El Salvador, the U.S. Embassy and the Ministry of Domestic Affairs, MINED launched in 2009 the campaign "Aprender Sin Miedo" (Learning without fear), which shall train teachers to network for creating school safety nets aimed at contrasting school violence, harassment, and sexual harassment. As the researchers of Plan El Salvador point out, such campaign – started in the municipality of El Paisnal - is extremely relevant as 42 percent of school children has suffered some kind of psychological

violence from peers or teachers, 25 percent has been physically harassed in the previous 3 months, and 10 percent of the students were sexually harassed during their school years.

Moreover, in the context of the action plan 2010-2014 "Let's go to school", the MINED started the Program "Un Sueño Posible: Un estudiante integralmente formado" (A feasible dream: a fully nurtured student). Two action strands of the program focus on the "Education for Life" and "Citizenship". In the former, students are taught how to take decisions taking into account the value of human rights, the need of favoring social cohabitation, caring about sexual health, and valuing gender equity. In the latter, students are taught how to become active citizens who are respectful of diversity and human values, who understand social changes and look for the common good, and who are knowledgeable of their historical heritage and of the duties of living in a democracy. In 2010, 3,275 teachers and 131,512 students were trained in the "Education for Life" strand, while 1,719 teachers and 223,676 students took part to the activities of the "Citizenship" strand.

References

MINED (2006); Logros de Aprendizaje de Primer Grado; http://www.mined.gob.sv/downloads/Informes/boletin-logros-1er-Gdo_0_.pdf.

MINED (2009a); ECAP 2009; http://www.mined.gob.sv/downloads/Institucional/Documento percent20informativo percent20ECAP percent202009.pdf.

MINED (2009b) Plan social educativo Vamos a la Escuela; http://www.mined.gob.sv/index.php/servicios/descargas.html?task=finish&cid=2591&catid=235 and http://www.mined.gob.sv/index.php/servicios/descargas.html?task=finish&cid=2592&catid=235.

MINED (2011) Logros MINED 2010 -2011 http://www.mined.gob.sv/index.php/descargas.html?task=view.download&cid=2369

UNDP (2010); Informe sobre Desarrollo Humano El Salvador 2010 - De la pobreza y el consumismo al bienestar de la gente. Propuestas para un nuevo modelo de desarrollo; http://hdr.undp.org/en/reports/national/latinamericathecaribbean/elsalvador/name,20684,en.html

UNESCO (2010); Datos Mundiales de Educacion VII Ed. 2010/11; http://www.ibe.unesco.org/fileadmin/user_upload/Publications/WDE/2010/pdf-versions/El_Salvador.pdf.
http://plan-international.org/aprendersinmiedo/recursos/historias/campana-toma-la-delantera

Reimers, F. (2004); *Introducción al Diagnostico de la Educación en El Salvador de 2004*; unpublished manuscript.

Bundy, D., Burbano, C., Grosh, M., Gelli, A., Jukes, M., and Drake, L. (2009); *Rethinking School Feeding Social Safety Nets, Child Development, and the Education Sector*. Washington D.C.: The World Bank

Legal documents:

LEY DE LA CARRERA DOCENTE http://www.oei.es/quipu/salvador/Ley_carrera_docente_reforma2006.pdf

LEY GENERAL DE EDUCACION http://www.oei.es/quipu/salvador/Ley_general_educacion_reforma2005.pdf

LEY DE EDUCACIÓN SUPERIOR http://www.oei.es/quipu/salvador/Ley_de_Educacion_Superior.pdf

Iceland

by Margrét Hardardóttir

Overview

A fundamental principle of the Icelandic education system is that everyone shall have equal access to education irrespective of sex, economic status, geographic location, religion, and cultural or social background. This principle is stated in the Constitution of the Icelandic Republic as well as in the various laws pertaining to the different educational levels. The educational system is divided into four levels: Pre-primary, compulsory (single structure primary and lower secondary education), upper secondary and higher education.

The pre-primary school level is intended for children up to the age at which compulsory school begins. Education is compulsory for children from six to sixteen years of age. The upper secondary level normally includes the sixteen- to twenty-year age group. Anyone who has completed compulsory education, has had equivalent basic education or has turned sixteen is entitled to enrol in upper secondary education. Those that have the right to enrol in upper secondary school studies have a right to study in upper secondary schools until the age of 18 as a minimum.

One of the aims of educational policy in Iceland in recent decades has been to raise the general level of education. According to the laws that govern different educational levels, handicapped pupils, at pre-primary, compulsory and upper secondary school levels, are entitled to the same education as other pupils. The main policy is integration rather than segregation. Schools are expected to provide handicapped pupils with appropriate opportunities.

The legislation of 2008 on pre-primary, compulsory and upper secondary schools is being implemented. The main emphasis of the reviewed policy on the basis of the Lifelong Learning Strategy is to make all levels of education comprehensive so that the paths of pupils through the system are as transparent and direct as possible, with the emphasis always on flexibility.

In Augusti 2011, the Ministry of Education, Science and Culture, published revised general sections of the National Curriculum Guides (NCG) for pre-primary, compulsory and upper secondary schools, which will partly come into effect in the school year 2011/2012. The revised NCG are based on the school legislations of 2008.

The revision of the curricula for the three school levels is based on national development of the eight key competences recommended by the European Union. The National Qualification Framework is under development and encompasses all education offered in the country, be it academic studies, VET, arts studies, special education or adult education.

The Structure of Schooling

The Icelandic Parliament is legally and politically responsible for the school system. The Parliament determines the basic objectives and administrative framework of the educational system. All education comes under the jurisdiction of the Ministry of Education, Science and Culture. Education in Iceland has traditionally been organized within the public sector, and there are relatively few private institutions in the school system. Almost all private schools receive public funding.

The municipalities are responsible for the operation of pre-primary and compulsory education. Upper secondary schools and higher education institutions are run by the State. The Ministry of Education, Science and Culture monitors the implementation of the all educational laws and regulations.

The Ministry of Education, Science and Culture issues National Curriculum Guides for pre-primary, compulsory and upper secondary education. The National Curriculum Guides stipulate the schools' pedagogical role, objectives and organisation of school activities and general policy in teaching and instructional organisation. The professional operation of pre-primary and compulsory schools is to be supervised by relevant municipality and the Ministry of Education, Science and Culture. The upper secondary schools are supervised by the Ministry of Education, Science and Culture.

The construction and the running of pre-primary schools (including all salaries and operation cost) are by law at the expense and the responsibility of municipalities. Funds are allocated to the municipalities from the national income taxation to fund among other things the construction and operation of pre-primary schools. Parents contribute a substantial amount towards operating costs at the pre-primary level. The share that parents contribute varies from one municipality to another and in some cases depends on the circumstances of the parents.

The cost of education at the compulsory level (primary and lower-secondary) is entirely borne by local municipalities, except for educational materials and the nationally coordinated examinations. All decisions regarding the construction and maintenance of school buildings and facilities are made by the local municipalities in question.

Costs for new construction and initial capital investment for equipment at the upper secondary level are met in such a way that the state pays 60% and the local municipalities, one or more, that are formally parties to the construction of the school, pay 40%. All other costs at the upper secondary level are allocated in the State budget. Agreements between the Minister of Education, Science and Culture and individual upper secondary schools, made for a period of 3-5 years at a time, specify main emphases in school activities, school curricula, study offer, organisation of instruction, quality control and evaluation, as well as other matters which the parties to the agreement consider feasible. The implementation of these agreements are to be reviewed annually and valid agreements revised if the parties to the agreements consider that necessary.

The Legal Framework

Laws governing the three first levels of the educational system in Iceland are: The Pre-Primary School Act from 2008, the Compulsory School Act from 2008, the Upper Secondary School Act from 2008. The National Curriculum Guides provides the details of how the laws are to be implemented and define more clearly the educational role of schools and the main objectives of instruction in individual subjects in accordance with that role. More detailed provisions regarding the implementation of the laws are to be found in numerous regulations at each school level, which the Ministry of Education, Science and Culture issues on the basis of law that is in effect.

The pre-primary school level is governed by the Pre-primary School Act from 2008. The Act defines pre-primary schools as the first level of the educational system and according to the Act, pre-primary schools are to provide education and care for children below the age at which compulsory education begins. Children's interests and welfare is the primary mission of all pre-primary school activities and learning through play shall be encouraged in a creative environment.

According to the Pre-primary School Act, the local municipalities are responsible for the operation of pre-primary schools. They are to establish and operate good pre-primary schools for children and manage the schools in accordance with the law. Furthermore their obligation is to organise specialist services for pre-primary schools. They take care of monitoring pre-primary school operations and encourage cooperation between pre-primary schools as well as between other school levels.

A Compulsory School Act was passed in June 2008. The Act introduces a set of changes that are mostly a continuation of previous legislative developments. The administration of the schools that are run by the municipalities is clarified and decentralised, and the role, rights and duties of parents and children outlined. A great emphasis is placed on the general welfare of pupils and the inclusion of all children in the school irrespective of origin or handicap. More weight is put on quality assurance and that the schools and municipalities assert their accountability towards pupils, parents and society, develop internal quality processes and provide information about their activivties and results. Nationally coordinated examinations are set in grades 4, 7 and 10, with the focus on their role as a guide for pupils, parents, and schools.

Education at the upper secondary level is governed by the Upper Secondary School Act from 2008. The Upper Secondary School Act primarily defines the framework for education at that level, its objectives, the role and responsibility of the State and local municipalities as well as other parties that are involved in providing education at this level.

Freedom to establish non-state schools

The same law and regulations apply to privately run schools as to schools operated by the municipalities and the State.

Local municipalities have the power to allow parents or any private parties to operate a pre-primary school. All the private pre-primary schools get financial support from their local municipality, and therefore the private sector of the pre-primary level could be described as grant-aided private sector. In 2010 approximately 13% of all children in pre-primary schools attended privately run schools. It varies in which form private pre-primary schools are operated.

The Minister of Education, Science and Culture may provide accreditation to compulsory schools or parts thereof which are run by other parties than the municipalities, such as non-profit organisations or other recognised legal forms, given the consent of the municipality regarding the establishment of the school. The consent of the municipality may be subject to a certain maximum number of pupils. The Ministry of Education, Science and Culture may also authorise accreditation of compulsory schools or study programmes within general compulsory schools which are operated according to recognised foreign or international curriculum guide and study organisations. All private schools receive considerable financial assistance from the municipalities and in addition their pupils pay school fees. Teaching in private schools follows the National Curriculum Guide which is in effect for compulsory schools and pupils take the same nationally coordinated examinations in the grades 4,7 and 10. In 2010 approx. 2% of children at compulsory school age attend privately run schools.

The Minister of Education, Science and Culture can provide schools, other than public upper secondary schools, with accreditation to carry out instruction at upper secondary level subject to certain conditions. Accreditation of an upper secondary school provides confirmation that at the time in which accreditation was granted, the activities of the school complied with general conditions of the Upper Secondary School Act and other law and regulations issued under the Act.

Home schooling

Home schooling is allowed at the compulsory school level. Parents who wish to teach their children at home, in part or totally, must apply for such exemption from their municipality. A head teacher may provide an exemption in consultation with the School Board and specialist services. Children that receive instruction at home are exempt from compulsory schooling but must comply with regular evaluation and monitoring and undergo the nationally coordinated examinations according to the Compulsory School Act. If the parents´ are granted permission to teach their children at home, the municipality has to make a contract with a compulsory school in the municipality concerning advice, supervision and various services.

School choice not limites by family income

Compulsory school education in Iceland is free of charge for the pupil. Compulsory education shall generally be of ten years in duration. All children, in general between the ages of 6 and 16, are required to attend compulsory school. Praents who choose to send their child to a privately run school must pay tution fees.

School distinctiveness protected by law and policy

There are no differences in the provision of private education or in the legislative framework compared to the public sector. Privately run schools must also work according to regulations and the National Gurriculum Guides.

Non public schools accredited by a municipality or the Ministry of Education, Science and Culture, are free to work according to some philosophy as long as they meet meet certain standards. There are for example parent-operated pre-primary schools where a special association is formed to carry out the operation of the school, and there are organizations that manage and directing pre-primary schools that work in accordance with a particular ideology such as Montessori, Waldorf, and health or environmental oriented.

The Hjalli School Model uses sex-segregated strands for boys and girls in the pre-primary and compulsory school. Children are divided into separate divisions on the basis of their gender most of the time but brought together in mixed groups at certain times during the day so that segregation and integration on the basis of the child's sex is used in a revolving fashion to obtain the best possible results for each individual. According to the Hjalli School Model, boys and girls need different types of exercise and different reactions. The Hjalli School Model stresses clear rules of behaviour, care for other human beings and the environment. These schools are without traditional toys and the aim is to stimulate the children's own creative and imaginative powers.

There is one international school at the compulsory school level in Iceland. The school offers a dynamic learning environment for elementary school children in grades K-7 (aged 5-13). The emphasis is on international-mindedness and positive discipline in a bilingual environment. The school is located within a public compulsory school.

Decisions about admitting pupils

At the pre-primary level, parents can often choose between pre-primary schools within their own municipality, if there is more than one pre-primary school to choose from. Pre-primary schools are for all children who have not reached the age at which compulsory school begins, i.e. usually the year in which the child turns 6. However, few pre-primary schools accept children less than a year old, and usually the youngest children are at the age of 2. In municipalities where there are waiting lists for places at pre-schools children of single parents and students are often given a priority. All handicapped children have the same right as other children to attend pre-primary schools, and in many cases are given a priority status in regard to admission. The programme for the handicapped children is the same as for other children, but adapted to their ability.

The Compulsory School Act of 2008 stipulates that all children and adolescents between the ages of six and sixteen are required to attend school, and consequently there are no admission requirements for Icelandic compulsory schools. It is the duty of the local municipalities to see to it that all children from the age of six to sixteen have the opportunity to attend school. Under the law, compulsory education begins in the calendar year that the child turns six and ends at the close of the spring term the year in which the child reaches the age of 16. Parents can apply for their child to begin schooling earlier or later than its peers or they may be asked to give their consent that the child begins its schooling earlier or later than its peers. According to the Compulsory School Act, head teachers of compulsory schools have the authority to grant such exemptions after having referred the case to the local education office and received their assessment.

A child attends the school closest to its home. In local municipalities where there is more than one compulsory school, parents may request that their children be allowed to attend a school that is not in the school district where they live. Pupils, who are thought not able to attain the goals of the compulsory schooling due to learning disabilities are provided education in accordance with their abilities. Deaf, blind and otherwise disabled pupils are generally accommodated within a compulsory school or in in special divisions within a school. Here more information on education for children with learning disabilities can be found.
There are schools all over the country for children of compulsory school age. It varies in different areas how long the children remain at school on a daily basis. It is customary for children living in rural areas to be bussed to and from school every day, free of charge.
All pupils who have completed compulsory education have equivalent education

or have reached the age of 16 have the legal right to upper secondary education, regardless of their results in the 10th and last grade of compulsory school. Those that have the right to enroll in upper secondary school, also have the right to study until the age of 18.

Each upper secondary school is responsible for admission of pupils. The obligations of each upper secondary school regarding pupil enrolment and the requirements for admission made by the school are prescribed in an agreement between the upper secondary school and the Ministry of Education, Science and Culture. The upper secondary school may place specific demands for enrolment in individual branches of study in the upper secondary school regarding preparation and study results.
Pupils may appeal to the Minister of Education against decisions made by the school as regards admission to a school and possible exclusion from a school.

Decisions about staff

In recruitment of head teachers and school personnel at pre-primary and compulsory level, provisions of the Local Government Act apply as well as further provisions of the local government board agreement as applicable. To be recruited as pre-primary school head teacher, an applicant shall hold the title of pre-primary school teacher and have acquired additional education in management or have experience as teacher at the pre-school level. To be recruited as Pre-primary school teacher, an applicant shall have acquired the right to use the title of Pre-primary school teacher

The requirements for recruitment of head teacher or compulsory school teachers are stipulated in the Act on Education and Recruitment of Teachers and Head Teachers in Pre-School, Compulsory School and Upper Secondary School. Individuals who have been convicted for violating provisions of the Criminal Act may not be hired for this purpose. Upon recruitment, the person's criminal record is available or the head teacher is authorised to obtain information from the official charge sheet.
To be recruited as a compulsory school teacher, an applicant shall have acquired the right to use the title of compulsory school teacher. To be recruited as compulsory school head teacher or compulsory school assistant head teacher, an applicant shall hold the title of compulsory school teacher and have acquired additional education in management or have experience as teacher at compulsory school level. Schools which teach accordin to the Waldorf policy, can hire teachers specially educated in the field, but tehy must also have education according to the provision of the above mentioned Act.
To be recruited as an upper secondary school teacher, an applicant shall have acquired the right to use the title of upper secondary school teacher. The aim is that upper secondary school teachers carry out teaching in subjects or within study fields covered by their education. When recruiting people for head positions

in upper secondary school, the applicant shall hold the title of upper secondary school teacher and have acquired additional education in management or have experience as teacher at upper secondary school level.

Accountability for school quality

The Ministry of Education, Science and Culture is responsible for the evaluation and monitoring of educational institutions, both public and private, and of the entire educational system in Iceland.
External evaluations are organised by the Ministry of Education, Science and Culture and include evaluation of schools/institutions as a whole, internal evaluation methods or other defined parts of school activities. At pre-primary and compulsory school levels, the municipalities can conduct their own external evaluation of schools and school activities.
The objectives of evaluation and quality control in pre-primary, compulsory and upper secondary schools are:

a. To provide information about school activities, school achievements and development to educational authorities, school personnel, receiving schools, parents and pupils.
b. To ensure that school activities are according to law, regulations and the national curriculum guides for pre-primary, compulsory and upper secondary schools.
c. To increase the quality of education and school activities and encourage developmental work.
d. To ensure that pupils' rights are respected and that they get the service they are entitled to according to law.

Schools and specific aspects of school activities at all educational levels may be subject to an external evaluation organised by the Ministry of Education, Science and Culture. External evaluations are conducted by independent evaluators whom the Ministry hires for each task. The purpose of evaluating schools externally is to obtain an overall picture of each school's activities or of specific aspects there at any given time. Attention is directed towards various features of the school's internal activities, such as administration, teaching, development work, co-operation and communications within the school study achievements and the connection between the school and society. Internal evaluation methods at all school levels may be subject to external evaluation.
Legislations on pre-primary, compulsory and upper secondary education place strong emphasis on regular internal evaluation by schools/institutions. Each school is to systematically evaluate the achievements and quality of school activities with active participation from school personnel, pupils and parents as relevant.

Every school is expected to implement methods to evaluate its work, including its teaching and administrative methods, internal communications, and contacts with parties outside the school. Schools are free to choose among systems that each develops for its own use or more common quality-management procedures, but should in any case include significant elements of internal monitoring. Internal evaluation is a way of working systematically on quality and improvements in school operations. Internal evaluation is also a way of disseminating knowledge and information on school operations. An internal evaluation is to include the school's policy and objectives, a definition of the ways in which these are to be achieved, an analysis of the strengths and weaknesses of the school's operations and a plan for improvements. Its main objective is to make it easier for school personnel to work towards the school's objectives, assess whether they have been achieved, review them and encourage improvements. This applies to objectives and emphases provided for in legislations, regulations and the national curriculum guides, as well as to local objectives which the school includes in its school curriculum guide.

Teaching of values

The new National Curriculum Guides manifest a new educational policy whose principal objective is systematically to nurture knowledge, skills and attitudes which enhance the strengths of the individual in the future, to be a critical, active and competent participant in an egalitarian and democratic society. The core of the education policy comprises six Fundamentals: literacy, sustainability, democracy, equality, health and welfare, and creativity.
The Curriculum Guides will take effect at the beginning of the 2012-2013 academic year, and will be implemented over the next three years.
In the preparation of the new Curriculum Guides, the Minister of Education, Science and Culture made a decision that special attention should be paid to the role of the school system in the development and reconstruction of society which is now taking place. She thus established certain focusses in the process of preparing the Curriculum Guides, whereby individual and social values in public education at the three school levels are defined as Fundamentals of education. This applies to both public and private schools.

The Fundamentals are embodied in the Curriculum Guides at every school level:

- Choice of subjects and content of teaching, play and study are to be informed by the Fundamentals.
- Work procedures and methods learned by children and youngsters are influenced by ideas which emerge in discussion of the Fundamentals.
- Working methods of teachers and other school staff should be defined by the Fundamentals, in such as way as to promote autonomy, initiative and development in the work of the school.
- When the work of the school is evaluated, an assessment must be made of whether, and how, the Fundamentals have made their mark on teaching, play and study, and on the work of the school as a whole.

The Fundamentals are:

- Literacy: the principal objective of literacy is that pupils be active participants in recreating and rewriting the world, by creating their own meanings and responding in a personal, creative manner to what they read, via the media and technology available to them. As in the past, it is of great importance that children should master certain reading and writing skills; but attention is now also paid to all technologies which pupils can use in communication, study and signification – in their own interests and those of society.
- Sustainability: Sustainability is concerned with taking account of the interaction of environment, the economy, society and welfare. Definitions of *sustainability* and *sustainable development* generally entail the idea that the environment should be passed on to future generations in no worse a condition than we have received it; and that we should seek to meet the needs of the present day without impairing the possibilities of future generations to meet their needs in their turn. The economy of each society plays a vital role with respect to rational use of resources, and a fair division of them. Thus it is important that economic growth should neither be based on, nor lead to, excessive encroachment on nature. Production and consumption are constants in society, and within the economic life of the individual. An understanding of our own environmental footprint, and that of communities and societies, is conducive to sustainable development and moderation.
- Democracy: In a democracy, individuals take a stance on moral issues, and are active participants in the shaping of society. In a democratic society, citizens must enjoy human rights, and share decision-making in all major fields of their lives. Democracy is premissed on the citizens' shared responsibility and consciousness and activity, which makes them capable of shaping their society, and having an influence at a local and national level. Democracy is important within the school. In the first place, schools must take account of the fact that children and youngsters will become participants in a democratic society, and hence it is vital for them to learn about such societies. Secondly, schools must ensure that respect for the human values of every individual is upheld in all its work. The principle is that children and youngsters learn to practise democracy, by learning about democracy, within a democracy.
- Equality: Education on equality entails a critical examination of received ideas in society and its institutions, with the aim of teaching children and youngsters to identify the factors which lead to discrimination against some groups, and privilege for others. Equality is used as an umbrella term, covering a number of factors; a selection of these follow, in alphabetical order: Age, class, colour, culture, disability, gender, kinship, language, nationality, philosophy, religion, residence, sexuality. At all school levels, education on equality should take place, with discussion of how the above-mentioned factors can lead to discrimination or privilege in people's lives. Emphasis must be placed upon boys and girls being offered the most equal and widest possibilities. Nowhere within the school system, neither in content nor in procedures, should there be any impediments in the way of either sex.

- Health and Welfare: Health is grounded in mental, physical and social wellbeing, regardless of social status. It is a product of a complex interplay of the individual, his/her circumstances, and the environment. All the work of the school must nurture health, and systematically promote welfare and wellbeing, as children and youngsters spend much of their day in school. Education must be provided on physical exercise, motor skills must be enhanced, and a safe environment must be provided which encourages everyone to be physically active. Account must be taken of this in physical education teaching and all other school activity. By the same token, within the school environment healthy eating must be promoted, through education along with availability of a varied range of foods. The principal aspects of health on which emphasis must be placed are a positive self-image, exercise, nutrition, rest, mental wellbeing, good communication, safety, hygiene, sexual health, and understanding of one's own and others' feelings.
- Creativity: Creativity entails the shaping and presentation of objects, the making of something, doing something new or different from what the individual knows, or has done before. Creativity is to discover, enjoy, stimulate curiosity and interest, activate the imagination, and play with possibilities. Creativity breaks up conventional patterns, rules and systems, and provides a new vision of phenomena and of received ideas. Creativity is built upon critical thinking, and on methods which constantly open up new possibilities; and hence the creative process is no less important than the outcome. Creativity also entails the practical application of ideas. Methods in creative arts and scholarly disciplines are often characterised by creativity, initiative and originality. It is desirable to see such methods in all study and in the work of the school.

References

Law on the Educational Testing Institute, no. 168/2000
Local Government Act, no. 45/1998
The Compulsory School Act 2008, no. 91/2008
The Constitution of the Republic of Iceland (Constitution) no. 33/1944
The Pre-Primary School Act, no.90/2008
The Upper Secondary School Act, no. 92/2008

Act on Education and Recruitment of Teachers and Head Teachers in Pre-School, Compulsory School and Upper Secondary School

National Curriculum Guide for Compulsory Schools (status of a regulation): 2004
National Curriculum Guide for Pre-primary Schools (status of a regulation): 1999
National Curriculum Guide for Upper Secondary Education (status of a regulation): 1999
National Curriculum Guide for Compulsory Schools. General Section (status of a regulation): 2011

Eurydice; Information on Education Systems and Policies in Europa. Eurypedia 2011. http://eacea.ec.europa.eu/education/eurydice/index_en.php: Eurypedia 2011, Iceland.

Israel

by Moshe Cohen-Eliya[1] and Amos Zehavi[2]

Overview

Overall, the Israeli system, as formulated by law, reflects an attempt to accommodate religious as well as language diversity within the Israeli educational system, on the one hand, and to ensure that each pupil acquires some basic skills and internalizes a core of democratic values, on the other hand.

In recent years, however, there has been a controversy in Israel regarding the role of ultra-orthodox (Haredi) Jewish private schools. A dramatic increase was reported in the number of pupils attending these schools, rising from 7.6 percent of all Jewish pupils attending primary school in the 1989/1990 school year to 28.9 percent of all such pupils in 2010/2011. This increase can partly be attributed to a sharp increase in the funding of such schools, which in some cases is even greater than the funding granted to public schools (secular and religious). However, the substantial funding of Haredi schools was not accompanied by effective supervision of the curriculum taught in these schools.[3] In practice, most of these institutions do not teach the required core curriculum, nor do they teach subjects such as citizenship, which are aimed at the cultivation of democratic values.[4]

Private education in Israel, and more specifically Haredi education, fails to inculcate in its students the social and political norms that constitute the bedrock of democracy. Moreover, in contemporary 'knowledge society' it is also imperative that students acquire a broad set of academic skills that would enable them to contribute to the economy as adults. At least in so far as the Haredi education system is concerned, the State of Israel has failed to guarantee such an education. The central reason for this failure is the political power of the ultra-orthodox community which is employed to jealously protect ultra-orthodox schools from almost any form of state oversight despite generous state funding. As a result, the private school system in Israel (including to a lesser extent non-religious schools)

---

1 Author of the 2004 version
2 Author of the revised 2012 version
3 Shiffer, 1998; Zehavi, 2011
4 Shiffer, 1998; Zehavi, 2011

is characterized by a unique combination of high public subsidies juxtaposed with exceptionally weak state accountability and control.

The Structure of Schooling

Schools in Israel are organized on the basis of the language in which teaching is conducted and on the basis of the distinction between public - including both secular and religious - and private schools. In school year 2009/2010, approximately 73 percent of all students in the State attended schools which teach in Hebrew, while approximately 27 percent attended schools which teach in Arabic.

59 percent of all Jewish students attend non-religious public schools and 18.4 percent of all Jewish students attend public religious schools (for 2010/2011). 99 percent of all Arab students attend public schools which teach in Arabic. Public schools are established and funded by the State or by local authorities and are subject to the curricula created by the State. Private schools are divided into "recognized" and "unrecognized" schools. A "recognized" private school is a school which meets certain standards set by the Minister of Education and receives public funding. "Recognized" Hebrew schools include the majority of the schools which serve the Israeli Haredi community, as well as ideological schools, such as those promoting humanist and anthroposophist education. The "recognized" Arab schools include a small number of Church schools, considered elite educational institutes, which are attended by Christian and Muslim students comprising less than one percent of all Arab students in Israel. The "unrecognized" private schools are exempt from any state curricular supervision and receive more limited state funding than recognized schools (55 percent of per pupil public funding). The unrecognized category is comprised of independent Haredi schools which in school year 2006/2007 were attended by some 7.4 percent of all Jewish students at the primary school level.[5]

As part of a reform in the education system, decided upon in 1968, most institutes of education have been divided into three levels: primary schools (grades 1-6); lower secondary schools (grades 7-9); and upper secondary schools (grades 10-12). The central object of the reform in education was to promote integration and allow students from lower socio-economic backgrounds to attend lower secondary schools together with students from more affluent backgrounds.

In Israel, control of public schools and supervision over "recognized" private schools is conducted by the central government in collaboration with local authorities. In recent years, central government control has been reduced while local authorities have become increasingly involved in regulating the field of

5 Israel Central Bureau of Statistics, 2011; Vurgan, 2007a

education. The bulk of funding for public schools is provided by state funds. Local authorities allocate plots for the construction of schools while the State finances the bulk of building expenses. In addition to this, some schools independently raise funds by means of non-profit organizations. The pedagogic arena is supposed to be the purview of the central government alone; however local authorities are gnawing at the central government's authority in this area too. Nowadays, local authorities engage in a variety of affairs including the design of new modes of schooling, curriculum planning and development, research, supervision and educative evaluation. The area of teacher employment is jointly controlled. Most teachers in primary schools are employed by the central government, while most teachers in secondary schools are employed by the local authorities.

The Legal Framework

The right to education received explicit recognition in the Declaration of the establishment of the State of Israel, 1948. However, this declaration is not a constitution. The Basic Law: Human Dignity and Liberty, Israel's new partial constitutional bill of rights, does not explicitly protect the right to education. Recently the Supreme Court rejected attempts to interpret the constitutional right for Human Dignity in a broad manner so as to include protection of every person's right to education.

The statutory arrangements in the field of education in Israel are complicated, and there appears to be a need to codify the State's laws of education. The four principal statutory arrangements are the following:

The State Education Law, 1953 canceled partisan control of public education and established two central streams: secular public education (Jewish and Arab) and Jewish religious public education. Public education is education provided by the State on the basis of a curriculum approved by the Minister of Education. The law details the objectives and values which Israeli public education is to realize, these include: teaching respect and patriotism, the realization of Jewish and Democratic values, ensuring human rights, respecting cultural differences, developing the student's personality, affording students with basic skills, developing critical and independent thought and enabling every student to enjoy equal opportunity.

The Compulsory Education Law, 1949 establishes that children between the ages of 3 to18 (grade 12 inclusive) must attend an education institution. The law further states that students between the ages of 5-18 (grade 12 inclusive) are entitled to education free of charge. The State is responsible for the realization of the right to free education; however, the maintenance of schools is the joint responsibility of both the State and the local education authority.

The Schools Supervision Law, 1969 established conditions for the licensing and opening of schools in Israel. This Law enacted a supervisory regime which applies to the vast majority of schools in Israel. Its objective is to ensure that all schools, private ones included, provide an education that meets certain minimum standards set by the Ministry of Education.

The Education Ordinance, which was originally enacted during the British mandate, grants certain schools, which are not subject to the School Supervision Law, with somewhat more autonomy. Thus, for example, section 6 of the Ordinance determines that "the representatives of the Ministry of Education may at any reasonable time enter any school, with the exception of those which are not supported by the State and which were established or are operated by religious associations". In addition, it has been established that the Director-General of the Ministry of Education "may not require changes in the curriculum or in [these] school's internal management".

Freedom to Establish Non-State Schools

The State Education Law grants parents an explicit right to determine which type of public school their child will attend. Moreover, in recent years courts have also emphasized parents' right to choose the school they find most appropriate for their children.

In Israel there is extensive liberty to establish non-government schools. The School Supervision Law conditions the opening of a school on receipt of a license from the Director-General of the Ministry of Education. In order for such a license to be issued, the Director-General must be persuaded that an adequate level of teaching will be maintained in accordance with curricular standards. To determine this, inspectors must conduct an examination of the following: The class schedule and timetable, the quality of the teaching staff, the school structure and the school's financial viability. The law does not prohibit the establishment of a school for the purpose of financial profit.

The law does not place limits on the opening of schools by different religious, national or social groups and it maintains neutrality in its demands. This notwithstanding, the Minister is granted wide discretion with regards to the funding of schools and this has been the cause of discriminatory funding of schools associated with certain social groups. As demonstrated in research conducted by Shiffer (1998), the Haredi (private "recognized") education system in the State of Israel receives even more funding than public education. According to Shiffer, "the diverse branches of the Haredi education system are doubly advantaged: both because of the relatively low number of pupils in their classrooms, which allows for more personal attention to the needs of each student, and because they have more hours of teaching (both absolutely and relative to the number of students).

This state of affairs, which is a direct result of the increasing political power of Haredi parties in Israel, stands in contrast with the spirit of the statutes on education. In 2002, following petitions submitted to the Israeli Supreme Court in which petitioners argued that State funding was dispensed in a manner which discriminated against secular private schools vis-a-vis Haredi private schools, the Ministry of Education set up a committee chaired by Dr. Shoshani to examine the various methods of financing. The committee recommended that "recognized" private schools which teach the core curriculum and meet standards set by the Ministry of Education be allowed no more than 85 percent of the funding allocated to public schools, while "unrecognized" institutions which teach the core curriculum may receive no more than 60 percent of the funding allocated to public schools. The Minster of Education endorsed the committee's recommendations in full. A later blue ribbon commission – the *Dovrat* commission (2005) – recommended capping funding for recognized private schools at even a lower rate: 65 percent. Nonetheless, funding formulas did not fundamentally change and circa 2012 most recognized private schools receive 75 to 100 percent of public funding for public schools.

Home Schooling

The Compulsory Education Law grants the Minister of Education authority to exempt children and parents from compulsory schooling for special reasons and in accordance with an instruction to be published in official records. According to the Director General of the Ministry of Education's 2002 directive, "the position of the Israeli education system is that the place of students of the compulsory education age is within the institutional educational framework. Educational authorities ought to do everything possible to allocate a suitable learning environment for each student. Consequently, requests for home education will be approved only in most exceptional cases, where it can be proven beyond any doubt that the request for home education derives from a formulated outlook which rejects institutional education of any form, or where it can be so proven that there are extraordinary circumstances, unique and most exceptional, because of which a child is unable to attend a recognized educational institute".

The authority to approve or deny home education is in the hands of the Director General. The permit is granted every year for one school year only. A child for whom home education was approved must meet the standards set by the educational system. Despite the stringent formal stand taken by the Director General, the Ministry of Education, in fact, approves the vast majority of requests. For example, in 2006/2007 the Ministry approved 155 requests and denied only 8. Moreover, according to some reports, the actual number of children in home schooling is significantly higher than the official figure.[6]

6 Vurgan, 2007b

School Choice not Limited by Family Income

The 1968 reform in the Israeli education system was designed to integrate members of different social groups in lower secondary schools (grades 7-9). The initiators of the reform hoped to reduce social divisions, to lessen the alienation between members of different social and ethnic groups by means of the education system, and to weaken the correlation between students' socio-economic background and their educational achievements. This reform allowed poor families to have access to better public schools for their children, albeit not ones close to their homes.

In addition, the reform enabled children from poor families to attend a number of elite private schools (grades 7-9) without having to pay school fees (though the Ministry of Education itself does not pay for the extra school fee in private schools). However, the right to enter such schools is not dependent upon the free choice of the parents with low income but rather on a decision made by the Ministry of Education. Despite the fact that nearly 45 years have passed since the decision to integrate schools was made, researchers have contradictory opinions as to the contribution of integration to the reduction of rifts among different social groups. In any event, it was only applied to a relatively brief part (3 years) of the student's total years of schooling thus limiting its effectiveness.

Distinctive Character

Consideration for the distinct cultural characteristics of the various religious and national communities in Israel does not end with the possibility of operating private schools: it is also expressed in the existence of diverse frameworks within public education itself.

As we pointed out before, public education itself gives expression to the distinct characteristics of two important minority groups in Israel. The State Education Law establishes Jewish-religious education as one of the forms of education founded and funded by the State. The law and the regulations enacted under it stipulate that the curricula for educational institutes of this form will be determined by the Minister of Education in agreement with the council of religious-state education: a council established by law. Thus the legislator guarantees the unique character of religious public schools.

The State Education Law also recognizes the distinct character of the Arab Israeli minority, which represents a fifth of the State's population. This law stipulates that "within non-Jewish educational institutes, curricula will be adapted to the conditions particular to such institutions". Regulations enacted in accordance with the law in 1996 establish an advisory council for Arab education, whose members are educators from the Arab sector. This council is charged with recommending to the Minister, inter alia, on the "formation of an educational policy...which will ensure the equal status of Arab Israeli citizens while giving due consideration to their linguistic and cultural distinction and their heritage". In this matter one should note that the State Education Law, as amended in 2000, asserts that one of the goals of public education is to "recognize the language, culture, history, heritage and unique tradition of the Arab population and other population groups in the State of Israel, and to recognize the equal rights of all Israeli citizens".

It appears therefore that insofar as public schools are concerned, consideration for the distinct character of Jewish-religious and Arab schools in Israel is manifested in three ways: First, the establishment of distinct educational institutions for each of the communities; Second, the formation of advisory councils including representatives of the minority groups. These councils are appointed to advise the Minister of Education in determining the educational policy and appropriate curriculum for these groups' schools. Third, the statutory assertion that curricula must be adapted to suit the distinctive characteristics of each of the communities.

Insofar as private schools are concerned, it appears that the Israeli legislator seeks to balance between the desire to maintain the private schools' unique characteristics and the need to ensure that such schools provide their students with a worthy education. The degree to which the Ministry of Education interferes with the autonomy of private schools is a derivative of the aforementioned distinction established in the law between "recognized" and between "unrecognized" private schools.

In compliance with the State Education Regulations (Recognized Institutions) 1953, an educational institute will not be declared as a recognized institute of education unless "the institution implements the core curriculum". The core curriculum consists of a set of subjects which each educational institute is required to teach a set number of hours. The regulations stipulate that "the core curriculum in a recognized institute will be 75 percent of the total school hours in an official institute of education; however the Minister may authorize proportions other than these". The regulations also establish a supervisory mechanism to ensure that this requirement is met.

However, in the "recognized" educational institutes serving the Haredi community there is a very large gap between what is required by law and that which occurs in practice. The Ministry of Education's inspectors charged with supervising Haredi education are themselves Haredi and seek to reduce supervision over Haredi institutes as much as possible. The problem is most acute in boys' classes in the Haredi community's secondary schools. While primary Haredi education includes arithmetic and Hebrew studies, Haredi secondary schools for boys only teach religious studies.[7] As Shelhav and Friedman clarify, one of the central

7 Schwartz, 2000; Shiffer 1998; Zehavi, 2011

goals of Haredi education is to prevent children's exposure to other lifestyles and simultaneously to present the modern secular lifestyle as the essence of evil. The Haredi population feels threatened by the modern world around it and is haunted by fear that its younger members might elect to cross the lines and join secular society. This constant sense of threat is the main reason for the almost complete absence of general studies from the curriculum of Haredi boys' secondary schools.

The political system's lackadaisical attitude to enforcing "recognized" schools' legal obligation to teach at least 75 percent of the curriculum taught in public schools stems, for the most part, from the political clout of Haredi parties in Israel. Instead of balancing between the preservation of the distinctive character of the Haredi community and the requirement that "recognized" schools provide their students with an education sufficient to afford them equal opportunity, the State opted to give the first interest decisive preference over the latter. The Israeli High Court of Justice, nevertheless, took a very different position from that of the government. In one decision for recognized private primary schools[8] and a different ruling applied to secondary schools,[9] the Court decreed that the introduction and implementation of a state approved core curriculum constitutes a prerequisite for public funding. These controversial rulings spurred the Haredi political parties into action. Haredi parties tend to be kingmakers in Israeli politics something that affords them considerable political clout. In 2008, the Haredi parties managed to pass legislation that explicitly enabled the continuation of public funding, albeit at a reduced 60 percent level, for secondary level ultra-orthodox schools that taught only religious subjects and failed to adopt a state approved core curriculum.[10]

Although the majority of ultra-orthodox children study in recognized private schools, a sizable minority of primary school children (over 50,000) study in "unrecognized" educational institutions that enjoy an even greater degree of autonomy than the recognized schools. These institutions are sometimes called "exempt" institutions because the Minister of Education has exempted the parents of children attending such schools from the obligation to send their children to a public or "recognized" private schools. "Unrecognized" schools receive proportionately less financial support than "recognized" institutes (55 percent of public school funding compared to 75-100 percent), and their curricula are in practice exempt from the supervision of the Ministry of Education.

From the above one can deduce that Israeli law tends to relate the degree of supervision over private schools to the extent to which the State funds education in such schools. As the proportion of financing which a school receives from public funds increases so too does the Ministry of Education's authority to intervene

8 HCJ 2751/99 2000
9 10296/02 2004; 4805/07
10 Zehavi, 2011

in setting the school's curriculum. However, as described above, insofar as the Israeli Haredi community's private schools are concerned, this principle is not put into practice. These schools receive funding, in some instances greater than private education institutes; however their curricula are not subject to effective supervision.

Decisions about Admitting Pupils

Registration for public schools is generally done in accordance with registration areas and not on the basis of academic achievements. Consequently, such schools cannot select their pupils. Private schools, quite differently, including those receiving varying degrees of state support, enjoy more autonomy in selecting their pupils. Such schools are permitted to pick candidates on the basis of academic achievements and/or their compatibility with the school's religious or ideological outlook. It is interesting, however, to note that a few private religious schools are willing to accept students of other religions. Thus, for example, church schools, considered the most elite educational institutions in the Israeli Arab sector, accept many Muslim pupils.

Private schools' wide discretion with regards to admissions is limited by the Pupils Rights' Law, 2000.This law prohibits educational institutions from exercising discrimination in student admittance or in class makeup on the basis of ethnic-group, socio-economic background or for reason of political outlook. The law defines the prohibition on discrimination as a criminal offense. Moreover, in accordance with the Schools Supervision Law, the Director General of the Ministry of Education is authorized to issue a closing order against a school which acts in breach of this prohibition.

According to the letter of the law, this stipulation applies to public schools, and to private "recognized" schools, but not to "unrecognized" schools. However, it would seem that these latter institutions are subject to the Prohibition on Discrimination in Products and Services Law, 2000, which includes a prohibition on discrimination in the provision of educational services. It should be noted that under Israeli law the principle of anti-discrimination does not only apply to the State. This principle also applies indirectly to private entities providing a service to the public.

In practice, discrimination in pupil admissions is an issue for numerous Haredi private schools. Most notably, in 2009, the High Court of Justice ruled that a Haredi girls' school in the town of Immanuel actively segregated *Ashkenazi* (Jews of European descent) from *Sephardic* (Eastern descent) pupils and that segregation violated the principle of equality. The Court ordered the school to desegregate. However, *Ashkenazi* parents were unwilling to send their children to the integrated school. The Court determined that the parents' refusal constituted contempt of court and ordered to incarcerate the parents for a period of two weeks. The Haredi leadership viewed the Court ruling as a direct attack on the Haredi education system's autonomy and staged a massive protest. Ultimately, the Court agreed to a compromise that enabled the opening of a new "exempt" private school that would admit the children of those parents that objected to desegregation.[11]

Decisions about Staff

The Israeli Equal Employment Opportunities Law, 1988 prohibits discrimination in admission to work on the basis of sex, race, nationality, ethnicity, sexual preference, religion and other reasons. The applicability of the principle of equality is qualified by a provision which permits discrimination "if it is necessitated by the nature and essence of the task or position". Israeli courts have not yet been called upon to rule whether an educational institution may select staff on the basis of religious or philosophical concordance with the goals and outlook the school seeks to promote.

However, the State Education Law, 1953 specifically stipulates that the "council for public-religious education may, for religious reasons alone, cancel the appointment or continued service of a principal, inspector or teacher in a public-religious institution." In other words, to the extent that Jewish religious public education is concerned, concordance with the religious outlook of the school may be a prerequisite for staff employment. In practice, religious Jewish public schools require teachers and administrative staff members to attend the school in modest attire and require male staff to wear a yarmulke (traditional skullcap).

Accountability for School Quality

In Israel a two-fold method is used to hold schools accountable for academic and other outcomes. First, the State operates a system of supervision over educational establishments in accordance with the School Supervision Law, 1969 and the Education Ordinance. Under this system, Ministry of Education inspectors' are authorized to enter any school and inspect it and to demand and receive any information from the school principal which may be required for the purpose of supervising the school. According to the provisions of the Education Ordinance, a school principal must, inter alia, "supply the inspector appointed to supervise the institution with any information he requests"; and the principal of the school and its teachers "must co-operate with the inspector supervising the institute, heed to his advice and follow his instructions". The School Supervision Law also stipulates that "Curriculum, school books, supplementary literature, teaching-aids and the school's educational achievements will be subject to the Ministry of Education's supervision and adapted to the general provisions practiced in

11 Almog and Perry-Hazan, 2012

schools of such type". This supervisory system focuses upon the 'the input' of schooling (staff qualifications and resources).

Second, the State administers standard tests which examine the output of every educational institution. These tests include the matriculation exams: success in these exams is also a condition of admission in to higher education. Additionally, the State conducts various exams (including international exams) to assess the achievements of school students well before graduation. In the early 2000s, the Ministry of Education established general standardized tests (*Meitzav*) for three grade levels. These tests are administered in all schools apart from Haredi schools for boys.[12] In 2011, however, one group of ultra-orthodox schools agreed to administer 'culturally sensitive' standardized testing. Still, circa 2012, most Haredi schools do not administer these obligatory tests. International exams (e.g., PISA) are conducted on a regular basis in Israeli schools.[13] Private schools appear to have a high refusal rate (for participation) making comparisons of exam results across sectors methodologically problematic.

It should be noted that the State does not examine (and is not capable of assessing) the degree to which students in private schools, both recognized and unrecognized, internalize democratic values. Consequently, the degree to which private schools are held accountable for the teaching of democratic values is very limited to the point of non-existence.

Teaching of Values

The 2000 amendment to the State Education Law details the goals of public education, and, inter alia, lists the following values:

- To bestow the principles stated in the Declaration of the Establishment of the State of Israel and the values of the State of Israel as a Jewish Democratic State and to develop an attitude of respect for human rights, basic liberties, democratic values, obedience to the law, the culture and outlook of others, and to educate to strive for peace and tolerance in relations between peoples and between nations;
- To educate a person to love humanity, to love his people and his country, to be a loyal citizen of the State of Israel, who honors his parents and family, his heritage, his cultural identity and his language;
- To encourage involvement in Israeli social life, a will to accept tasks and to fulfill them with dedication and responsibility, a desire for mutual aid, contribution to the community, voluntarism and to strive for social justice in the State of Israel;
- To develop an attitude of respect and responsibility for the natural environment

[12] Zehavi, 2011

[13] Velmer, 2011

and a connection to the land, its views and animal and plant life;
- To recognize the unique language, culture, history, heritage and tradition of the Arab population and other population groups in the State of Israel, and to recognize the equal rights of all citizens of the State of Israel.

Section 28 of the School Supervision Law, 1969 states that the supervision of schools, including private schools subject to the law, is intended to ensure that education in those institutions is based on the above principles detailed in the State Education law. The law further states that schools' curriculum, school books, supplementary literature, teaching aids and educational achievements will be subject to the supervision of the Minister of Education and will be adapted to the general provisions practiced in schools of such type. These provisions in effect place a legal obligation upon private schools to teach the same values as taught in public education establishments. Additionally, section 32 of the Supervision Law grants the Director General of the Ministry of Education authority to close down a school if "incitement against the State is practiced or tolerated within the school".

The State Education (Recognized Institutions) Regulations, 1953 determine that one of the conditions for the recognition of an educational institute is that the institute implements the Core Curriculum".

Following petitions to the Israeli Supreme Court, the Ministry of Education established a core curriculum for primary education. As mentioned before, the implementation of the core curriculum is a precondition for obtaining high levels of state funding. It should be noted, however, that the core curriculum for primary education, as established in 2003, focuses on traditional educational content and does not obligate "recognized" private educational institutions and "unrecognized" institutions to teach subjects of a more value orientated nature, such as civics. The core curriculum defines the teaching of democratic values in primary education as "recommended" and not as an obligation or a condition for recognition or funding.

From a legal perspective there is therefore tension between the provisions of the School Supervision Law, which obligates all schools subject to the Ministry of Education's supervision to act in accordance with the values stated in the State Education Law, and between the practical reality as exemplified in the core curriculum of the Ministry of Education which, for the time being, does not in fact obligate schools supported by the State to teach such values.

References

Abu-Saad, Ismael and Vernon Hendrix "Organizational climate and teachers job satisfaction in multi-cultural milieu: The case of Bedouin Arab schools in Israel" 15(2) *International Journal of Educational Development* 141 (1995).

Almog, Shulamit and Lotem Perry-Hazan "Contesting Religious Authoriality: The Immanuel "Beis-Yaakov" School Segregation Case" *International Journal for the Semiotics of Law* (online 2012).

Cohen-Eliya, Moshe and Yoav Hammer "An argument from Democracy against school choice: A critique of Zelman v. Simmons-Harris" 49 *Loyola Law Review* 859 (2003).
Facts and Figures: http://www.education.gov.il/minhal_calcala/netunim.htm#B

Gibton, Dan et al., "How principals of autonomous schools in Israel view implementation of decentralization and restructuring policy: Risks, rights and wrongs" 22(2) *Educational Evaluation and Policy Analysis* 193 (2000).

Gibton, Dan et al, "The role of legislation in educational decentralization: The case of Israel and The United Kingdom" 76(3) *Peabody journal of Education* 81 (2002).

Goldring, Ellen B., "System-wide diversity in Israel: Principals as transformational and environmental leaders" 30(3) *Journal of Educational Administration* 49 (1992).

Goldstein, Stephen, "Multiculturalism, parental choice and traditional values: A comment on religious education in Israel" in *Children's Rights and Traditional Values* 118 (G. Douglas and L. Sebba eds.,1996).

Ilan, Shachar, *Utra-Orthodox Jews Inc.* 316-318 (2000) (Heb.).

Israel Central Bureau of Statistics, *Statistical Abstract of Israel* (2009, 2010, 2011).

Mari, Sami, *Arab Education in Israel* (1978).

National Task Force for the Advancement of Education in Israel [Dovrat Commission],

"National Programme for Education [Dovrat Report] ," (2005) (Heb.).

[The] Ministry of Education, Culture and Sport of Israel, The Report of the Committee for the Examination of the Funding System (2002) (Heb.).

Sabba, Leslie and Varda Shiffer "Tradition and the right to education: The case of the ultra-orthodox community in Israel" in *Children's Rights and Traditional Values* 160 (G. Douglas and L. Sebba eds., 1996).

Schwartz, Robert, "School Accountability – An Elusive Policy Solution: The Israeli Experience in Comparative Perspective," 20 *Journal of Public Policy* 195 (2000)

Shelhav, Yossef and Menachem Friedman, *Spreading Through Seclusion: The Haredi Community in Jerusalem* (1989) (Heb.).

Shiffer, Varda, The Haredi Education System in Israel: Allocation, Regulation and Control (1998) (Heb.)

Svirski, Shlomo et al, "Governmental Funding to the Haredi Jews Sector," (1998) (Heb.)

Velmer, Tomer, "Shas School Students to Take Standardized Tests," Ynet.

Vurgan, Yuval "The Education System in the Ultra-Orthodox Sector," Knesset Research and Information Center, Jerusalem (2007a) (Heb.).

Vurgan, Yuval, "Home Schooling," Knesset Research and Information Center, Jerusalem (2007b) (Heb.).

Zehavi, Amos, "Regulating non-government schools: Explaining success and failure," 5 *Regulation & Governance* 446 (2011).

Jordan

by Mahasen M. Aljaghoub[1]

Overview

Jordan was established in 1921 with the dissolution of the Ottoman Empire under the rule of Prince Abdullah I, who established what was then called the Emirate of Transjordan. It is bounded to the north by Syria, to the east by Iraq, to the southeast and south by Saudi Arabia, and to the west by Palestine. Jordan is a crossroads connecting Asia, Africa, and Europe. Jordan's constitution stipulates that the country is a hereditary monarchy with a parliamentary system, and specifically guarantees the rights of Jordanian citizens, including the freedoms of speech and press, association, academic freedom, political parties and freedom of religion.

Due to the lack of natural resources, Jordan relies to a great extent on its human resources. The population of Jordan is largely young as people under the age of fifteen constitute the largest component of the population. The growth of population constitutes a major challenge to the educational system, and the government has a great concern about the pressure of refugees on the country's limited resources and in particular on its educational systems.[2] Jordan has an excellent reputation in the region for education, boasting an adult literacy rate above 92 percent and a 95.7 percent gross enrolment rate. [3]

The general objectives of education stem from the philosophy of education which is (in accordance with Article 3 of the 1994 Education Law) based upon the Jordanian Constitution, the Islamic Arab civilization, the principles of the Great Arab Revolt and the national experience of the country. The basic philosophy of education is to develop responsible citizens who believe in the basic principles of the constitution; the rights and the responsibilities of citizens; honesty and dedication to work; responsible behavior; and fruitful cooperation with others based on democratic relationship and to develop an understanding of the natural, social, and cultural environment starting with the home and ending with the world as a whole and to develop pupils physically, socially, mentally, and emotionally, taking individual differences into consideration.

---

1 Associate Professor of International Law, The University of Jordan

2 Gavlak, 2007.

3 Health and education, Published in The Report: Jordan 2011.

According to its National Agenda, Jordan aims to boost its educational reform and gender equality. One of the impressive reforms with regards to education is the national strategy which known as "Education Reform for a Knowledge Economy," aiming at creating an educational system where the students are producers of knowledge and leave the educational system with the skills necessary to be a productive part of a knowledge economy. The other national project is the Jordan Education Initiative (JEI), which aims at equipping students with skills and knowledge to participate effectively in the new era.

Legal framework

The 1952 Jordanian constitution provides for freedom of religion, provided that religious practices are consistent with "public order and morality;" According to the Constitution, Islam is the state's religion. Since Jordan believes in the right of education for all, the Constitution has guaranteed this right.

Article (2/6) stipulates that "The government shall ensure work and education within the limits of its possibilities and it shall ensure a state of tranquility and equal opportunities to all Jordanians."

Article (19) provides that "Congregations shall have the right to establish and maintain their own schools for the education of their own members provided that they comply with the general provisions of the law and be subject to the control of the of Government in matters relating to their curricula and orientation".

Moreover, Article 20 guarantees the right of education by stating that primary education was to be compulsory for Jordanians and free of charge in government schools and to this end the government shall ensure work and education within the limits of its possibilities and shall ensure equal opportunities to all Jordanians.

It is important to note that before the independence of Jordan, in 1946, education was only available to people who were able to afford it, however, after independence, Act No.20 made education compulsory for all children up to grade six. In 1964 the Jordanian Parliament passed the Education Act No.16, which made education compulsory up to grade nine. (six years of primary and three years of secondary education) . A 1994 Education Act expanded basic compulsory education to ten years and introduced comprehensive and applied secondary education streams lasting two years to be provided free of charge.

To sum up, the most important laws and regulations which regulate education in Jordan are:

The Education Law of 1994 which regulates kindergarten, basic and secondary education. This Act enunciates the philosophy and objectives of education, the educational policy, the functions of the Ministry of Education, and the tasks of the Boards of Education. It contains also some elements regulating curricula and textbooks, general examinations, the structure of the Ministry, as well as the functioning of private and foreign educational institutions.

Regulation No. 1 of 1995 on the organization of the Ministry of Education whichdefines the administrative structure of the Ministry and its basic units and committees at all levels (central level, governorates and districts), as well as their main tasks.

Regulation No. 41 of 1997 on scientific research for the development of the educational process establishes the objectives of educational research at the Ministry, and it defines the tasks of the Research Committee for developing the educational process.

Regulation No. 59 of 1993 on educational certification and training concerns the establishment of the Educational Certification and Training Committee at the Ministry of Education. And lastly Regulation No. 42 of 1992 on the equivalence of certificates concerns the establishment of the Committee on the equivalence of certificates and its main tasks and functions.

The structure of Schooling

Jordan has traditionally placed great emphasis on education and relied heavily on its human resources for its economic and social development. According to Article 7 of the 1994 Law, the education system consists of a two-year cycle of pre-school education, ten years of compulsory basic education, and two years of secondary academic or vocational education, after which students sit for a General Certificate of Secondary Education Exam (*Tawjihi*).

Education is free and obligatory from grades one to ten, and thereafter is free for another two years. The Ministry of Education is now making it mandatory for students to be computer literate and to be able to apply their computer studies to their regular studies, especially in scientific and mathematical courses.

The educational system is centralized with the Ministry of Education being represented by regional directorates of education who have the role of disseminating policy statements and initiatives from the upper levels of the educational system to individual schools and overseeing the performance and practices of schools.

In accordance with the Regulation No.1 of 1995, the MOE is constituted of the central administration, which is responsible for designing educational policies and plans for the implementation of polices, and then from the General Directorates of Education in the twelve governorates (or provinces) who supervise educational policy and lastly from the District Directorates of Education in the governorates who are responsible for supervising educational policy at the directorate level in the governorate or district. Each District Directorate is headed by the director of education assisted by directors for technical and administrative affairs.

Pre-school education

According to Article 8 of the 1994 law, children at the age of 4 years (or at least 3 years and 8 months) are allowed to enter kindergartens, which are institutions offering non-compulsory preschool education. Kindergartens are mainly operated by private and non-governmental organizations.

In accordance with the above mentioned provision, Preschool education, aims at providing an adequate educational environment and care for well-balanced growth on a non-compulsory basis. The Ministry of Education (MOE) supervises all preschool institutions according to its policy and legislation, along with the Ministry of Health which is a strong partner in empowering families in caring for their children during these early stages.

Performance of children at this level is evaluated through the follow-up of their participation in the diversified activities and parents are continuously informed on the progress and growth of their children. The school year at the preschool level consists of 28 weeks and kindergartens run 28 hours per week; most public kindergartens start at 8:00 and finish at 12:30.[4] The Ministry of Education reports that in 2007/08 there were 1,262 kindergartens, of which two under MOE, 103 under other governmental authorities and 1,157 in the private sector. The total enrolment was 90,613 children (48,266 boys and 42,347 girls).[5]

Primary Education

According to Article 10 of the 1994 Law, Primary education comprises ten years of compulsory schooling starting at the age of 5 years and 8 months. According to this law primary education offers a well-balanced education in the social, emotional, intellectual, physical and spiritual aspects of the student's personality growth for lifelong learning. According to Article 9 of the mentioned Law, primary education aims at preparing the learners to:

- be consciously acquainted with the history, principles, rules and values of Islam, incorporating them into their character and behaviour;
- master the basic skills of Arabic language to be able to use it easily;
- know the basic facts and events related to the history of the Islamic and Arab nation and of the Jordanian people in its Arab and Islamic profundity, in particular, and its humanity in general;
- follow social behaviour rules and take into account commendable social traditions, habits and values;
- love, be proud of, and shoulder responsibilities towards their homeland;

---

4 UNICEF, 2009.

5 MOE, 2008.

- love their family and society and shoulder responsibilities towards them;
- master the basic skills of at least one foreign language; deal with numerical systems, basic mathematical processes and geometrical figures, and use them in everyday life;
- absorb basic scientific facts and generalizations and their experimental bases, and use them to explain natural phenomena;
- think scientifically, using the process of observation, data collection, organization, analysis, deduction and making decisions and judgments based on them;
- comprehend the scientific basis of the forms of technology and use them properly;
- be keen on the safety, cleanliness, beauty and wealth of their environment;
- be aware of the importance of their physical fitness and health, and practise suitable sport and health activities;
- have aesthetic taste in the various arts, and express their own artistic interests;
- be able to perform handicraft skills matching their abilities and interests, make an effort to develop them, and have respect for manual work owing to its basic function in social life;
- assimilate diligence, work, persistence and self-dependence values in achievement, realization of self-capability, earning a living and self- sufficiency;
- express their talents, special abilities and creative aspects;
- accept themselves, respect others, consider their feelings and appreciate their merits and achievements;
- appreciate the value of time and made good use of their leisure time;
- strive for self-instruction and the development of their competencies.

The Ministry of Education reports that in 2007/08 there were 3,053 basic education schools, of which 2,137 were under MOE, 16 under other governmental authorities (such as the Ministry of Defense), 176 run by UNRWA and 724 in the private sector. A total of 1,904 schools were co-educational, 782 were schools for boys and 367 were girls' schools. The total enrolment was 1,297,905 students (664,174 boys and 633,731 girls), of whom 914,937 students were in schools administered by MOE, 246,545 in the private sector, 122,068 under UNRWA, and 14,355 students in schools run by other governmental authorities.[6] In 2008/09, the net enrolment ratio at the basic education level (age group 6-15 years) was estimated at 97.6 percent (97.5 percent for boys and 97.7 percent for girls).
The survival rate to grade 5 was 99 percent (98.8 percent for boys and 99.2 percent for girls) in 2007/08. Basic education drop-out rates are minimal (an average of about 0.4 percent).[7] According to the World Bank, the transition rate to secondary education was 79 percent in 2005/06.

6 MOE, 2008.

7 Ministry of Planning, 2010.

Secondary education

Secondary education is free but not compulsory and consists of two years of study for students who completed the basic education cycle. It is designed to prepare students for higher education or for entry into the labour market. Secondary education comprises two streams: comprehensive secondary (academic and vocational) and applied secondary (Article 12 of the 1994 Law). The two-year comprehensive secondary education programme concludes with the General Secondary Education Certificate examination in the following specializations: academic (scientific, literary and Shari'a or Islamic law) and vocational (industrial, commercial, agricultural, nursing, hotel and home economics). The certificate qualifies students to enroll in universities. In accordance with Article 11 of the 1994 Law, Secondary education, aims at preparing students to be able to:

- use the Arabic language to increase their ability to communicate, develop their scientific and literary culture, consider the fundamentals of correct language structure, and relish its arts;
- adapt to environmental changes in their country in its natural, demographic, social and cultural dimensions, to exploit and maintain them well, and improve their potentials;
- derive their culture from their nation's past and present heritage, and be aware of the necessity of conscious openness to world civilization and contributions to it;
- interact with the cultural environment of their society and try to develop it;
- be aware of the importance of family, its coherence and role in social life;
- consolidate their self-confidence, appreciation of other human beings, and respect for the dignity and freedom of others;
- exemplify the principles, rules and values of Islamic ideology, adopt them in their behaviour, and understand the values and convictions in other heavenly religions;
- seek the progress, prestige and pride of their country, and be keen to participate in solving its problems and achieving security and stability;
- know the conditions and issues of their nation, be proud of belonging to it and seek its unity and progress;
- work in a team, know the rules and forms of democracy and practise them in dealing with others, and believe in principles of social justice;
- be aware of international issues and problems and of the importance of international understanding and peace built on justice and rightness;
- perform their duties and adhere to their rights;
- master one foreign language at least;
- absorb mathematical and logical concepts and relationships and use them in solving problems;
- look for data sources carefully and have command of collecting, storing, processing and means of benefiting from data;
- absorb new scientific facts and their applications, be able to verify them experimentally, and know their role in human progress;

- protect the environment, keep it clean, and develop its potential and wealth;
- absorb health information and rules pertaining to balanced physical and psychological growth, and practise them;
- relish artistic work and express their artistic interests in works according to their capabilities;
- seek professional qualifications, economic independence and self- sufficiency;
- use their free time for practising useful hobbies and recreation activities and for developing them;
- reflect Arab, Islamic and humanistic values and perfection in their behaviour;
- use common sense in dialogue, tolerance in dealing with others, and courtesy in listening;
- develop themselves through self-learning and lifelong education.

At the end of the secondary cycle, students passing the national examination receive the secondary school certificate. The Ministry of Education reports that in 2007/08 there were 1,230 academic secondary schools (of which 1,038 under MOE and 167 privately owned), 16 vocational secondary schools (all run by MOE), 76 academic and vocational secondary schools (of which 73 administered by MOE), and two applied secondary schools (one under UNRWA and the other run by MOE). The total enrolment in academic secondary education was 153,326 students (70,618 boys and 82,708 girls); 20,816 students (12,123 boys and 8,693 girls) were enrolled in vocational secondary education, and 724 boys (of whom 569 under UNRWA) in applied secondary education.[8] According to the World Bank the overall completion rate of secondary education is about 70 percent, with almost 30 percent of students dropping out after grade 10.

Freedom to establish non-state schools

According to Act No. 3 of 1994 one of the responsibilities of the Ministry of Education is to establish and administer public schools at all levels and to supervise private ones. Public, or government, schools are under the Ministry of Education or other ministries such as Health, Defense, or Social Welfare. Private schools might be either national or "foreign." National schools were those established and run by individual citizens or agencies. Foreign schools were those established and administered by non-Jordanians, either individuals or agencies with no clear affiliation to any congregation. There are 4 types of schools in Jordan:

1. Governmental Ministry of Education Schools
2. UNRWA schools
3. Military Schools
4. Private Schools

[8] MOE, 2008.

The Ministry of Education encourages the private sector to invest in education through the establishment of educational institutions at the different educational levels. School plans in private education institutions are established in accordance with MOE regulations, and under its supervision.

Schools at the basic and secondary education levels are usually established by individuals, companies and charitable societies and they apply curricula approved by the Board of Education and abide by admission rules and holiday instructions.

Several institutions other than the MOE but under its supervision participate in the delivery of education services. For instance, the Ministry of Social Development educates students with special needs and those with learning difficulties. The Directorate of Education and Culture of the Armed Forces administers nineteen specialized schools. The United Nations Relief and Works Agency for Palestinian refugees in the Near East (UNRWA) is responsible for the administration of schools for Palestinian refugees. In addition, there are some other non-governmental organizations (such as the Queen Alia Fund for Social and Voluntary Work and the General Union of Charity Societies) assisting educational institutions at the kindergarten level, and those for pupils with special needs. The Noor Al-Hussein Foundation (NHF) administers the Jubilee School, established in 1989, which caters to gifted students beyond the ninth grade of basic education
All type of schools have to use the national curriculum and follow the regulations of the Ministry of Education. It is important to note that there are many Christian schools in Jordan which educate students from both Christian and Muslim families such as the Rosary Sister's School run by the Catholic Church, the National Orthodox School run by the Orthodox Church in Jordan, Ahliyyah School for Girls, the Bishop's School for Boys, and the Schneller School are run by the Anglican Church in Amman. There are also a school for the blind, a school for the deaf, and a school for physically handicapped students run by the Anglican church.

Decisions about admitting pupils

The basic criterion for admission to public schools is the proximity of one's home to the school, and therefore, priority goes to those closest to the school. This criterion was set by the Ministry and schools cannot come up with different criteria or give priority to students based on academic or non-academic reasons. Private schools, by contrast, may adopt their own admission policies. For instance, most private schools require admission interview exam. Moreover, some of the elite schools might interview the parents as well.

Teaching staff

Teachers in public schools are appointed by the Ministry of Education. The Education Act No. 3 of 1994 stipulates that every teacher in any stage, from kindergarten to secondary cycle, must have a university degree (at least a bachelor's degree), whereas the supervisor hold a postgraduate degree. Basic education teachers must hold a bachelor's degree and secondary school teachers must hold a bachelor's degree and a one-year postgraduate diploma.

The need for teachers is identified at the school level and sent to the central Ministry to appoint teachers as needed from the Civil Service Bureau. Movement of teachers from school to school within the Field Directorates at that level. Public school principals have no hiring or firing authority. Teachers are appointed through competitive measures and on the basis of existing needs, specialization experience and educational qualification. A preference is given to some categories, such as orphans of fathers who served in the Jordanian army, poor families and the handicapped who hold an academic qualification, provided that their percentage does not exceed 5 percent.
Teacher promotion takes place after passing five years in a class or category. It is possible to be promoted earlier if the teacher gets a higher academic degree, or if his/her performance is outstanding.

Salaries and allowances are classified according to academic qualifications, category, grade and nature of work. The Civil Service Regulation applies to all employees, including teachers.

It has been claimed that teachers have become one of the lesser-regarded professions in Jordan in recent years. While the preparation for the teaching profession used to attract the best students, it is now ranked at fifth place in a list of six preferences. It is said that the best students become medical doctors, the second tier becomes engineers, the third tier will enter business, the fourth the law profession and only the fifth aims at becoming teachers, and the sixth tier move on to become English language and literature graduates. It is also said that the treatment of teachers, e.g. low salaries, low social regard, etc., leads to de-motivated teachers and as there is no continuous training for teachers once they leave university, they are often not up to par with the latest developments in both methods and contents of their profession.[9]

In addition to the above mentioned qualifications, the better private schools will require multilingual teachers with outstanding communication and other skills. As in public schools, teacher selection is not based on religion, belief or political affiliations. Generally speaking hiring and firing teachers are in the hands of school principals.

Evaluation of pupils is one of the responsibilities of the teachers. The school gives students certificates at the end of each academic year, from grade 1 to first year of

9 Baseline report – RCE Jordan at http://www.ias.unu.edu/resource_centre/RCE percent20Jordan_1.pdf

secondary education.[10]

School Choice Limited by Family Income

There are two main categories of schools in Jordan, public and private. Over 70 percent of Jordanians attend public schools.[11] Private schools fees relatively high, However, it should be noted that Jordanians as a community are highly committed to giving their children a decent education, which places a high burden on family budgets.

Even if public education is free in Jordan, families encounter expenses related to uniforms, transportation, and materials. Choice of school depends on various issues, such as place of residence, household economy, and educational aspirations, among others. Choice of private school probably is to a large extent dependent on family income. Families can register their children whereever they want but no transportation is provided if the school is not within walking distance and priority of admitting students goes to those living closer to the school.
For private schools, tuition fees vary greatly depending on the infrastructure, the type of educational programme they adopt, and their affiliation with external accreditation agencies. Some of the programmes that are adopted at private schools are international Baccalaureate IB; IG; SAT, GCSE and others. Those schools are more suitable for high income families. More reasonably priced private schools usually teach the national curriculum without structured extra curricula activities.
As mentioned previously, UNRWA schools are essentially open for Palestinian refugees, but the choice also depends on where the student lives. Closeness to a school is important for most people. To conclude, in families with higher income, parents tend to have higher education than poorer parents, and they are thus in a much better position to help and support their children through school.

School Autonomy

The school is considered the central unit of the educational process and it is managed by the principal, assisted by adequate staff to provide the necessary services. Public Schools receive a budget every year from the Field Directorate but they are unable to conduct any revenue generating activities and keep the money to spend on their schools. The school budget line items are set by the Ministry and there is little flexibility or leeway in that regard.[12]
Each Directorate has a mentoring department which is responsible for evaluating the performance of schools and teachers. Subject mentors are assigned to oversee

10 MOE, 2008.
11 UNESCO Institute of Statistics, 2006.
12 WorldData on Education VII Ed 2010/11.

and evaluate a number of teachers in several schools and to provide them with assistance, support and follow-up. The visits could be evaluative or supportive for teachers, as each mentor is required to write a report about each teacher's performance by the end of the schooling year, and this report forms part of the overall assessment of teachers' professional performance which has implications for their ranking. In addition, mentors may conduct workshops for teachers when needed, as they are required to support teachers to improve their performance.[13]
Curriculum is considered to be the most centralized element of the Ministry. All schools (including private schools) have to use the national curriculum that is developed by Jordanian experts (most of whom are Ministry employees). Books outside the curriculum (supplementary or just resource books to be placed in the library) have to be vetted by the central Ministry of Education. Private schools have to go by the vetting process for any books outside the national curriculum. The curriculum for each subject is detailed by grade level in a formal document issued by the Ministry of Education; it is then translated into curriculum materials which teachers use for planning their instruction.

Teaching of values

The Ministry of Education realizes that education must be responsive to the current and future needs of the learners and reflect the development of the country. A high-quality education system maintains high ethical values. According to Article 3 of the 1994 Law of Education, the aims of Education are: (i) building up citizens who believe in Allah, understand Islamic doctrine, and are committed to Islamic and Arab supreme values, loyal to their country, principles and nation, fully aware of their rights, performing their duties in a way which creates a balanced personality in all aspects and leads to an aware openness on others while maintaining their identity; (ii) preparing citizens who are well-equipped with skills and knowledge required for the knowledge-based economy (knowledge, communication and intercommunication, teamwork, scientific thinking, personal, technology, future career, and scientific research skills) in order to contribute in building up their community; (iii) providing learning opportunities for all, and achieving equality and equity in educational services on the qualitative and quantitative aspects, focusing on quality development of education in line with students` learning levels.[14]

References

An Analysis of ICT Integration within the_Jordanian Education System by Atef Abuhmaid, A thesis submitted to the University of Technology, Sydney In fulfillment of the requirements for the degree of Doctor of Philosophy, 2008

---

13 Ministry of Education, 2005.

14 MOE, 2008.

Ministry of Education. Directorate of Educational Research and Development. *The development of education. National report of the Hashemite Kingdom of Jordan.* Presented at the 48th session, of the International Conference on Education, Geneva, 2008.

Ministry of Planning and International Cooperation. United Nations in Jordan. *Keeping the promise and achieving aspirations. Second National Millennium Development Goals Report. Jordan 2010.* Amman, 2010.

UNESCO Amman Office and UNESCO Regional Bureau for Education in the Arab States. *UNESCO National Education Support Strategy (UNESS): The Hashemite Kingdom of Jordan.* Beirut, July 2008.

UNICEF. *Jordan's Early Childhood Development Initiative: Making Jordan fit for children.* UNICEF Regional Office for Middle East and North Africa, 2009.

Woman and Man in Jordan in figures 2010

World Data on Education, Données mondiales de l'éducation, Datos Mundiales de Educación VII Ed , 2010/11

Web resources

Ministry of Education: http://www.moe.gov.jo/ [

National Center for Human Resources Development: http://www.nchrd.gov.jo/ [In Arabic and English. Last checked: October 2007.]

México

by Rosa Elena Terán Morales[1] and Jorge Alberto Mahecha Rodríguez

Overview

According to the Mexican "Education Sector Program 2007-2012,"[2] while progress has been made in expanding coverage in basic education and in reducing gender and regional inequalities in educational services, there are still serious lags. Over 30 million people did not complete or never attended primary or secondary school. This means that one third of the Mexican population has not had access to basic education or could not finish it. Despite increases in coverage, the Mexican education system still presents serious deficiencies: high failure and dropout rates of pupils, particularly in early teenage to teenage population, and low levels of learning. The prevailing school education system, as demonstrated by national and international tests still fails to fully develop in pupils the skills to solve problems creatively and effectively, and to be better prepared for the challenges they will find later in life or when integrating into the labor market.

Counterbalancing this panorama, innovations proposed by the Integral Reform of Basic Education (RIEB by its Spanish acronym), which involve a competency-based approach and a classroom project methodology, may be Mexico's entry into a new level of education quality. This could be possible to the extent that principals and teachers are able to make these guidelines real in their schools and classrooms. This would also require continuous monitoring and evaluation to ensure appropriate implementation throughout the country. In the RIEB, plans and programs emphasize the development of life skills required to be successful in the globalized world of the twenty-first century, and the use of higher order, problem-solving skills.

Mexico has achieved clear educational progress in the last two decades, mostly in terms of coverage; however, social demand exceeds state educational offer, especially in upper secondary education. This lack of coverage is particularly severe in indigenous regions, adding grievance to their poverty and social exclusion. The demand for quality education must be more radical and urgent in schools where students are from the most disadvantaged and vulnerable backgrounds. For them, school is often the only opportunity to prepare for a better future and break the bond that links poverty to the marginalization and ignorance.

---

1 Program Director, *Enseña por Mexico*

2 SEP, 2007.

As a whole, the Mexican education system has shown considerable growth over the years. This is a consequence of state efforts to guarantee the right of education for all Mexicans and demonstrates the vocation of the Mexican state to promote education at all levels. The gradual integration of the Mexican education system and the number of services offered, are evidence to this growth, but financial and accountability challenges remain.

The magnitude of these efforts is due in large part to the desire to keep increasing the GDP share of resources devoted to education. Although this growing trend suffered a decline after 1981, in the "lost decade" for Latin America, in 1988 it began to recover, rising by 5 percent of GDP with the explicit aim of keeping it tied to the stabilization and growth of the national economy, rather than determining it from other social factors or financial restrictions. According to OECD, in 2008 Mexico spent in education 5.8 percent of its GDP (including public and private). This places Mexico at the OECD average in terms of education spending.

An important achievement for the country is the increased access to higher education. According to the 2010 census, the average schooling of the population over 15 years rose to 8.6 years.[3] However, problems such as illiteracy linger on, particularly in the rural areas.

The Structure of Schooling

The highest educational authority in Mexico is the National Secretariat of Education (SEP from its Spanish acronym). The SEP designed a national curriculum and textbooks which must be followed by all schools in the country, whether public or private. In this sense, the Mexican education system is highly centralized. With a population of over 112 million, Mexico is the tenth most populated country in the world and third in the Americas. A country of such size has an equally massive schooling system: 34.4 million pupils who account for almost a third of the total population attend 226,374 schools.[4]

Education in Mexico is made up of three main levels: basic, middle higher, and higher. Basic education is compulsory, and comprises two levels, primary and secondary (note that latter corresponds to intermediate rather than secondary education in the United States). Vocational education can be accessed just by completing basic primary education.
Middle higher education (known as "preparatoria") is equivalent to secondary schooling in Europe and the United States. It can have a technical strand or an academic (aimed at higher education) strand which is known as "Bachillerato". This last strand leads to undergraduate and postgraduate education. The education system also offers adult education (literacy, primary and secondary education,

3 INEGI, 2010.
4 SEP 2011.

formal training for work) and indigenous education or bilingual and bi-cultural services (preschool, primary and secondary).

Article 10 of the General Law of Education describes the structure of the Mexican school system, made up of: a) pupils and teachers; b) educational authorities; c) plans, programs, methods and teaching materials; d) the educational institutions of the State and of its decentralized bodies; e) the individuals' institutions with authorization or with recognition of official validity of education; and f) the higher education institutions to which the law grants autonomy.

The system offers educational services through two main channels: schooling and open education. Schooling provides education to groups of pupils who daily go to an educational institution according to the official educational schedule, while open education serves pupils who cannot attend a school to continue or finish their education. Open education is conveyed to pupils by means of pedagogical advising without the need for going to school every day; pupils subject themselves to a series of exams in order to certify their progress in the fulfillment of the program. Open education is provided with resources such as study guides and texts published specifically for this type of schooling.

The process of expansion of the Mexican educational system modified the old elitist patterns of access to the most exclusive institutions, but inequality of schooling opportunities in the different social sectors has tended to transfer to the post-basic educational levels, particularly the mid-higher and higher levels to private institutions. There are still educational disparities among the states and regions of the country.

The Legal Framework

The legal framework for education in Mexico begins with the Constitution (1917). Particularly, article 3 recognizes education as the right of every citizen. This article also defines broad nation-wide goals for education in a sociological perspective: it defines the role of education in Mexican society, and the corresponding characteristics it should have in order to make its social contribution: it should be free, secular, and should aim for the advance of science, technology and human development of Mexican citizens.

Articles 3 and 31 of the constitution were modified in March 1993. In July of the same year the General Law of Education (LGE) was adopted. This law replaced the old Federal Education Law. LGE (1993) further elaborates the sociological goals of education in Mexican society, and defines responsibilities for each government level (state, federal) in education. The Federal government is in charge of the definition of a national curriculum, which is accompanied by national, free textbooks. State governments do make a minor contribution to the definition of contents of those educational materials. LGE also defines educational levels and types of education in Mexico (i.e basic, adult, work education), and states rules regarding the financing of education, the promotion of educational equality in the Mexican nation, and the rules by which non-state educational institutions should adhere.

The LGE also defines mechanisms by which families and society can participate in the school life. The role of these two actors is mainly observational, though they are encouraged to monitor proper school operation. According to article 69 of the General Law of Education, a Social Participation School Council, with broad educational and social representation, should function at every school. Among its duties are to be familiar with the school calendar, the educational goals, and the progress of school activities in order to help the teacher to implement them better; to take note of the evaluations that educational authorities carry out; to foster teachers' and parents' collaboration; to propose rewards and recognition for pupils, teachers, school executives, and employees; to promote out-of-school activities which reinforce pupils' education; to carry out participation, coordination and spreading actions for civil defense and school emergencies; to encourage family and community interest for pupil performance; to give opinions on pedagogical matters; to help to reduce the bad social conditions which have an influence on education; to carry out specific works of improvement of school facilities; to support the school daily tasks and to carry out different activities for the benefit of the school.

The LGE gave rise to the Education Sector Plan 2007-2012 (SEP, 2007) and the "Alliance for Education" (2008) between the federal government, state governments and the National Union of Education Workers (SNTE). Education Sector Plan 2007 – 2012 defined six strategic goals for Mexican education. The first is to increase educational quality. Goals two and five are related to broaden educational opportunities, increase equality in education and to create educational institutions able to provide such quality education. Goal number three is aimed at fostering the use and application of Information Technologies in education. Goal four is about offering education for human development which strengthens civil society and finally goal six is about the improvement in the management of educational institutions, and the further participation of communities in school affairs. The alliance for education, although not of legal character, is an important political commitment of several social sectors (government both state and federal, education workers). The alliance states the intention of several state agencies and the SNTE to take action in favor of the improvement of education quality.

Schooling is regulated by the SEP. This is recognized in the Organic Law of Federal Civil Service (1976). This law was amended in February and May 1992. Article 38 establishes the role of the SEP. The Internal Regulations of the SEP were issued in March 1994, describing the specific functions of the Minister of State Education, of the Undersecretaries, of the State offices, and of the decentralized Administrative Organs of the SEP.

Regarding curricular issues in schooling, Agreement 592 (2011) was an important legal advance in order to further integrate curriculum of the different levels of Mexican education. The agreement describes in detail pedagogical foundations, general guidelines for the common Mexican school curriculum. It also details competences, achievement indicators and specific contents for all areas of the curriculum. It also includes guidelines for ethnic and indigenous education. It is the main official curricular document in Mexico.

Freedom to establish non-state schools

The right of private sector individuals or organizations to provide educational services is fully recognized in the legal framework, starting with the federal constitution and the general law of education. Education provided by non government actors is subject to the same regulations as government education. Every private school in Mexico should be properly licensed by the Secretariat of Public Education (SEP). As a consequence, certifications provided by private schools are valid nationwide.

Every kind of individual or organization is eligible to open a school, in as much as is compliant with SEP regulations. No organization has a particular advantage regarding the process of starting a school.

There are no privately-operated state schools in Mexico, as is the case with the charter schools in the US or similar schemes in other Latin American countries. Non-profit institutions, however, can open schools aimed at low income families.

Home schooling

The Mexican constitution in its article 31 states that it is an obligation of every Mexican citizen to have their children to attend either public or private institutions in order to receive proper education. The obligation of parent to have preschool, primary and secondary education is further stated in article 4 of the General Law of Education.

However, there is a loophole which seems to have been used by some home schooling families. The National Institute for Adult Education (INEA by its Spanish acronym) is able to test pupils older than 15 years who for one or another reason have been out of the school system. INEA test results and educational processes can be recognized by higher education institutions, allowing the entrance of pupils not coming from the school system to higher education. Such cases are however, rare.

School choice not limited by family income

Low income families in Mexico can only choose to send their children to state schools in the geographical area where they live. The Secretariat of Public Education, however, asks private schools to provide scholarships depending on the number of pupils they have. These are assigned mostly to pupils of the same institution. Conversely, high SES families are the only ones who can afford the cost of elite, private schools. There are middle class private institutions as well, which tuition is suited to the economic capacity of its corresponding target families.

Private schools must conform to the SEP requirements, and they are frequently evaluated. Private schools are generally expensive, so parents have to choose the most feasible option according to their budgets. In some cases schools offer scholarship programs for those pupils who cannot afford their charges. Such scholarships are awarded mainly on the basis of merit and pupils receiving them must maintain academic performance standards.

In public schools parents have some range of school choice, as to the geographical area in which they live. Admission is conditional on the available places in each school.

School distinctiveness protected by law and policy

Distinctive character

Public schools have an official national curriculum which is used nationwide. There is only one subject matter which is freely decided by each Mexican state; typically the study of Geography and History of the corresponding state. This is the only conspicuous difference between the national curriculum and that of the states.

Private schools are located primarily in the capital cities of the states. It is only after 1940, with the end of the period of conflict over Catholic schooling and the call for "national unity," which included the promise of respect for private initiative, that private schools emerged and began a period of significant growth: in 1934 there were 2,872, by 1940 this had declined to 1,555, but by 1970 the number almost doubled to reach 3,280. For these schools, the reform bill that allowed the teaching of religion was not an actual allowance: under the cover of extracurricular activities as "values", "human development", etc.., religious instruction was a common practice in private schools, despite education supposed to be secular. [5]
The private school sector is diverse and complex: many important schools remain Catholic in orientation, whether served by lay teachers or religious congregations. Along with Catholic schools are international schools such as the Franco-Mexican school, the Japanese lyceum, the German School or the American College. There

[5] García Alcaraz, 2002.

are also schools that boast innovative pedagogical models. During this century private schools have also expanded to education levels government has been unable to fully cover: early childhood education (especially child care), preschool, primary, secondary and now education secondary and higher. It is undeniable that in all cases, private schools offer education to social sectors with which certain parents identify culturally and socially. Parents who attend these institutions pay for a service than they expect to be of superior quality to that of public schools and which is aimed at adding value to the education of their children.

Decisions about admitting pupils

Only pupils who meet admission requirements may enter state schools. Tests correspond to ages for each school grade, and are not meant to exclude pupils from the system: if pupils do not achieve the expected results, they enter re-enforcement programs to be promoted to the next school year at the same level as their peers.

In private schools, either religious or international, there are admission requirements of academic and financial nature. The religious schools prefer parents which share their faith, without this being explicit. There is flexibility on the part of the government for religious schools: freedom to practice their rites inside its premises is guaranteed, for example in Catholic and Jewish schools. Public schools are secular (Article 3 of the Constitution)

When a pupil must switch from school to another, this is done in accordance with the number of students in the receiving institution.

Decisions about staff

In the public education sector, the Federal government in conjunction with State governments is in charge of appointing teachers to their corresponding teaching places. Teachers for preschool or primary schools study in "Basic Normal Schools" (Escuelas normales), institutions devoted specifically to teacher training. This training typically lasts 4 years. There are also "Higher Normal Schools" (Escuelas Normales Superiores) which can train secondary teachers. Usually only graduates from Basic Normal schools do access such training programs. Non-pedagogical higher education undergraduates are also eligible to become secondary teachers.

Both private and public Normal Schools share the same curriculum, and once students graduate from such schools they are entitled to a teaching position. In order to be formally appointed, teachers must take a National Test for Entering the Teaching Service. Usually teachers are appointed to schools in the area they have been trained. To be appointed as teacher in the public sector in Mexico is reliant only on academic qualifications and state exams. Whichever their formal training is, in order to be appointed as teachers in the public school system, potential teachers should belong to the National Union of Education Workers (SNTE).

Once teachers are in the teaching career ("Carrera Magisterial"), their tenure is regulated by a ranking system called *escalafón* which may grant them economic stimulus. The participation in this tenure ranking system is voluntary and is aimed at three main goals: Stimulating the quality of education by recognizing teaching labor, Reinforce the interest of teachers for continuous professional development, and to improve the life conditions and social living standards of Basic Education Teachers. The tenure ranking system has five levels, A, B, C, D and E. In order to advance along these levels factors such as years of service, academic qualifications, professional development activities and in-school performance are taken into account. The General Direction of Higher Education for School Professionals regulates normal schools and follows up teacher performance. [6]

Teachers in private schools at preschool and primary levels should have authorization from the Secretariat of Public Education. In order to become secondary teachers, potential teachers should take a test at the National Center for the Evaluation of Higher Education. Private institutions can select teachers in accordance with their mission.

Accountability for school quality

Federal and state governments, through multiple agencies and school officials, coordinate the administrative and technical control of teaching in primary and secondary schools.

The principal or headmaster, at the school level, carries out planning, guidance and accountability functions, and has responsibility for staff, material resources and financial administration. In secondary schools, assistants help headmasters with their duties; the teaching staff plans, guides and evaluates education in the group they are responsible for. The Technical-consultative council defines aspects of the organization and integration of the service and carries out the necessary consultations for the improvement of implementation of the plan and of the syllabuses. In secondary schools the educational assistance staff provides the following services: educational guidance, school medicine, social work and prefecture.

Each school develops a School Transformation Strategic Plan that includes four dimensions: curriculum educational dimension, a dimension of social participation, organizational and administrative dimension, turning all is relative to standards for Basic Education. The TEAP / PAT as a planning tool makes it possible to coordinate the content and the support that the different programs

[6] SEP, 2009.

and projects offer in order to make more efficient their implementation and the human and material resources used for enhancement and for compliance.

In a school district, supervisors and general inspectors (for secondary education) carry out general technical-pedagogical functions, provide administrative supervision, and link between the national/regional authorities and the school authorities. Supervisors must know the educational needs of the community; they must organize and promote school work in all its aspects and link the national educational policy features to the specific achievements of each school. The yearly plan of the school is sent to the area supervisor and to the general inspectors (for secondary education) by the headmaster, so that they can include it in the work plan of the corresponding area.

Once the yearly operative program of the primary education system is elaborated, the supervisor has a specific program for his/her area or sector, which he will have to supervise so that schools carry it out. As this makes apparent, the supervisor of the school area does the technical supervision of school functioning, according to the rules and the requirements that the educational authorities prescribe. However, the internal control of the provision of education is completely up to the school headmaster and the supervision of the educational task in each class is the responsibility of the appointed teacher.

The school headmaster, by means of the supervisor, assembles and sends to the superior educational authorities the requested additional information, such as the list of staff members, statistical data on pupil situations at the beginning and at the end of the course, the different methods of pupil control, the need for teaching materials, equipment, maintenance, school census, technical information, etc. The educational authorities responsible for the operation of the primary and secondary education levels send the staff and the material resources to schools, in accordance with the budget that has been approved.

The evaluations – as an objective mechanism of accountability – which teachers do every day, though based on the required syllabus, are carried out with informal, non standardized instruments and the results are interpreted according to each teacher's specific experience, so they are not comparable in practice. Since the requirements are adapted by each teacher to his or her specific conditions, which is not incorrect, this does not provide a national measurement with a single parameter, the official program of education). This means that, in order to establish a national evaluation system, it is necessary to have measurements done by external technicians. External measurement allows uniform measurement instruments and standards, guaranteeing administration on an equal basis and interpretation of results with the same criteria.

For this purpose, since 2006 there has been a National Assessment of Educational Achievement in Schools, ENALCE. The purpose of ENALCE is to generate a single national measure to provide comparable information from the knowledge and skills with pupils in the subjects evaluated. This would allow:

1. Encouraging the participation of parents and youth in the educational process.
2. Providing elements to facilitate the planning of teaching in the classroom.
3. Meeting specific requirements for training teachers and administrators.
4. Processes underpinning effective and relevant educational planning and policy.
5. Meeting criteria of transparency and accountability.

There is a recent scheme of incentives for scores on the ENLACES test in basic primary education. Schools which obtain high scores can be given economic incentives. There are no sanctions for lower scores. Apart from this recent initiative, accountability for school quality in Mexico is mostly based in inputs than in outcomes.

Teaching of values

The Federal Constitution defines public education as secular; hence, it does not favor any religion or ideology to be thought in public schools. However, in order to promote the cultural diversity of the nation, along with the peaceful coexistence of its citizens, National agreement 592 of 2008 recognizes the importance of education in diversity and inclusion of marginalized social groups. One of the four main pillars on which Mexican curriculum is structured is called "Personal development and education for pacific coexistence", which is aimed at promoting a certain set of values: democracy, peace, freedom and respect for the law and the community. This field of study encompasses human rights, civics and moral education.

The SEP also has the Operative Program for Transparency and Battle against Corruption in the field of the educational sector. It is developing a quality and transparency culture in the public service by improving the work systems, methods and processes and the appropriate information of the most relevant aspects of the Ministry of Public Education. This initiative is framed in the National Program of Transparency and Battle against Corruption in the field of the Federal Civil Service issued by the SECODAM, which is now the Ministry of the Civil Service.

References

SEP 2007. Programa sectorial de Educación 2007 – 2012. Retrieved at: http://www.sep.gob.mx/es/sep1/programa_sectorial

SEP 2011. Principales cifras del censo escolar 2010 – 2011. Retrieved at: http://www.sep.gob.mx/work/models/sep1/Resource/1899/2/images/principales_cifras_2010_2011.pdf

Mexican Constitution, 1917, Article 3. Retrieved at: http://www.diputados.gob.mx/LeyesBiblio/pdf/1.pdf

Mexican General Education Law, 1993. Retrieved at: http://www.diputados.gob.mx/LeyesBiblio/pdf/137.pdf

Alliance for Education, 2012. Retrieved at: http://alianza.sep.gob.mx/pdf/Alianza_por_la_Calidad_de_la_Educacion.pdf

Organic Law of Federal Civil Service, 1976. Retrieved at: http://www.diputados.gob.mx/LeyesBiblio/pdf/153.pdf

Agreement 592, 2011. Retrieved at: http://basica.sep.gob.mx/reformasecundaria/doc/sustento/Acuerdo_592_completo.pdf

García Alcaraz M.G. (2002). La distinción entre educación pública y privada. Revista Educación y Cultura, SNTE, México. Disponible en: http://www.latarea.com.mx/articu/articu16/garcia16.htm

OECD (2011). Education at Glance. OECD indicators, Country note –México. Available at: http://www.oecd.org/dataoecd/32/9/48667287.pdf

INEGI (2010). Mexico un Vistazo. Available at: http://www.inegi.gob.mx/prod_serv/contenidos/espanol/bvinegi/productos/integracion/pais/mexvista/2010/mex_2010.pdf

SEP, 2009. Manual de Carrera Magisterial. Available at: http://www.sep.gob.mx/work/models/sep1/Resource/2241/1/images/LINEAMIENTOS_GENERALES_2011.pdf

New Zealand

by Carol Mutch[1]

Overview

New Zealand's adoption of market-led principles to radically restructure its education system in the 1980s has attracted world-wide attention. Langley summarises the intentions behind the reforms as: "greater simplicity, more accountability, greater transparency, more responsiveness to national and local needs, more flexibility and less bureaucracy." He continues:

> The implied philosophy of the reforms was that stand-alone institutions, governed primarily by parents, and competing for students, would inevitably lead to better teaching and learning, and hence a better quality public education.[2]

A recent OECD report describes New Zealand education as "one of the most devolved school systems in the world,"[3] although Alcorn suggests that the Australian state of Victoria is a more extreme example of the self-managing school ethos.[4] Twenty years on from the reforms of *Tomorrow's Schools*, the report card is mixed. Commentators in a recent publication (*Tomorrow's Schools – 20 years on*, Langley, 2009) outlined some of the successes as: providing an "important foundation for a modern and more responsive school system"[5]; "increased independence and flexibility [enabling] New Zealand principals to put new ideas into practice quickly" [6];"excellent gains in the professionalism of principals

---

1 Associate Professor, Faculty of Education, University of Auckland, New Zealand

2 Langley, J. (Ed.). (2009). *Tomorrow's Schools: 20 years on*. Auckland, New Zealand: Cognition Institute, p. 10.

3 OECD (2012), *Review of Evaluation and Assessment in Education: New Zealand*, Paris: Author, p.13

4 Alcorn, N. (2011). Meat in the Sandwich: The Impact of Changing Policy Contexts and Local Management of Schools on Principals' Work in New Zealand 1989-2009. *New Zealand Journal of Teachers' Work, Volume 8, Issue 2, 122-140.*

5 Fancy, H. (2009), Re-engineering shifts in the system. In J. Langley (Ed.), *Tomorrow's Schools: 20 years on*. Auckland, New Zealand: Cognition Institute, p. 41.

6 Bendall, M. (2009), A leadership perspective. In J. Langley (Ed.), *Tomorrow's Schools: 20 years on*. Auckland, New Zealand: Cognition Institute, p. 107.

and teachers"[7] ;"principals more mindful of their parent communities and [who] relished their decision-making powers"[8]; and smooth running boards of trustees.[9]

Each of the commentators also maintained that a self-managing school system had not provided all the answers. While they suggest that no one would wish to return to the system prior to *Tomorrow's Schools*, it is timely to reconsider the areas that were unsuccessful and to find a way forward that meets the needs of an increasingly diverse school population and ever-changing global context. Langley (2009) summarised the issues raised by the commentators in this 20th anniversary publication. One is the *fragmentation of the system* with so many decision making points as each Board of Trustees sets up their own policies and protocols and so many agencies each oversee their own parts of the system. Allied to this is the *lack of policy coordination* with no mechanism for linking the agencies together. Another issue is the *dominance of managerialism* and increasing levels of compliance and this, in turn, impacts on *industrial issues* such as teacher workloads. *Variation in capacity* at the local level has seen some schools and some boards of trustees more successful than others and the intention to have schools compete rather than collaborate has had *unintended consequences* for the most vulnerable populations. Overall, the most striking outcome is that there is no comprehensive evidence that standards of teaching or levels of student achievement have risen as a consequence of the reforms. Langley concludes with his prediction for the future, which he sees as passing through three stages:

> The first is the realisation that improvement in the achievement of children, and especially those children who are missing out, does not necessarily occur simply because administrative reforms occur. It occurs largely as the result of the quality of teaching. The second is a gradual move away from the relentless external accountability created by a doctrine of managerialism, and towards an accountability through the development of professional standards, ethical standards, and focusing on evidence-based best practice. The third is the process of collecting and examining evidence about what works and what does not work in teaching and learning, and using this as a basis for policy and practice. This stage is, in most respects, the most difficult but also the most important.[10]

Regardless of where people stand on the success or otherwise of the education reforms, they would agree the most pressing problem in New Zealand schools is

7 Hattie, J. (2009), Tomorrow's schools – yesterday's news: The quest for a new metaphor. In J. Langley (Ed.), *Tomorrow's Schools: 20 years on*. Auckland, New Zealand: Cognition Institute, p. 121.

8 Wylie, C. (2009), Getting more from school self-management. In J. Langley (Ed.), *Tomorrow's Schools: 20 years on*. Auckland, New Zealand: Cognition Institute p. 135.

9 McQueen (2009), Towards a covenant. In J. Langley (Ed.), *Tomorrow's Schools: 20 years on*. Auckland, New Zealand: Cognition Institute p. 21.

10 Langley (2009), p.15.

characterised by uneven student achievement. While international comparative studies (such as Progress in International Reading Literacy Study [PIRLS], which assesses the readiness of fifteen-year olds to apply to real the world what they have learned in school), place New Zealand students up with the best in the world, there is a "long tail of underachievement" which falls along ethnic and socio-economic lines.

It is the problem to which everyone refers – but the suggested solutions vary markedly and the debates often fall along ideological lines. Those leaning to the left (teachers, their unions and left-leaning politicians) suggest less compliance and more professional development on how to engage diverse and disaffected students; conservative members of the public and politicians want more compliance and accountability through mechanisms such as National Standards; and neo-liberal politicians and free-market business leaders want to free up the system even more and introduce new 'charter schools' which will be government-funded but free of government constraints.

New Zealand is a small, sparsely populated country in the South Pacific. Its location, history and size have led to a unique set of education policy developments over the past twenty years as it has been influenced by international trends but adapted these to local conditions. These developments have faced a contested trajectory, with proponents and detractors often settling along ideological lines. This chapter outlines the current situation, including a discussion of New Zealand's educational context providing commentary on why developments around freedom, autonomy and accountability have happened in the way that they have. It is followed by discussion of the structure of the schooling system and its legislative framework before outlining the variety of options within the system. It closes by returning to the theme of accountability before putting current issues and debates into their present and future context.

In 2010, a team from the OECD visited New Zealand as part of the *Review of Evaluation and Assessment Frameworks for Improving School Outcomes* series. In preparation for the visit, a team of writers from the four education agencies (the Ministry of Education, the Education Review Office, the New Zealand Qualifications Authority and the New Zealand Teachers Council) prepared a country background report (Ministry of Education, 2010). This background report, plus the OECD's final review report (OECD, 2012) provide a detailed account of the aims, structure, problems and proposed solutions for the New Zealand schooling sector – and much of the material in this report will be drawn from these sources. Both documents highlight the strengths of the system and the current concerns – and the fact that, sometimes, a particular policy, such as devolution, can have both positive and negative consequences.

The executive summary of the Ministry's country background report summarises important matters this way:

> New Zealand's education system is characterised by a high level of devolution. Responsibility for the governance, administration and management of individual schools rests with an elected Board of Trustees. The Board of Trustees employs all school staff, manages property, controls school finances, and sets the policies that govern the school.... The self-managing school model supports flexibility, responsiveness to local communities and innovative practice but this also places significant expectations on principals and school leaders.[11]

The OECD report on assessment and evaluation describes the New Zealand situation as follows:

> New Zealand's approach to evaluation and assessment combines central control over policy development and standard setting with a large measure of devolved responsibility for the implementation of evaluation and assessment. Schools benefit from considerable autonomy in the organisation of the various components of evaluation and assessment at student, teacher and school level. At the same time, schools have multiple accountabilities – to their communities, the Ministry of Education, the Education Review Office (ERO), the New Zealand Teaching Council and the New Zealand Qualifications Authority.[12]

Overall, student achievement in New Zealand schools, as measured by international comparative studies such as the Trends in International Mathematics and Science Study (TIMSS), Progress in International Reading Literacy Study (PIRLS) or Programme for International Student Assessment (PISA), is high. New Zealand students score significantly and consistently above the OECD average, with a high number of New Zealand students in the top five per cent. What these studies show, however, is that among the high-achieving countries, New Zealand has the widest dispersion of scores from highest to lowest and that while *Māori*, Pacific and students from low socio-economic settings do appear in the high range, they are over-represented in the lower range. Another interesting factor revealed by these studies is that there are more pronounced differences *within* schools than *between* schools – leading commentators to highlight the difference that individual teachers make to student achievement.

Over the past ten years, considerable resources have been put into collating and analysing international and national research, such as the Ministry of Education's *Best Evidence Synthesis Programme*, in order to determine the factors that will impact most on reducing these disparities and lifting school performance. These have informed the Ministry's *Statement of Intent*, which has as its overall

---

11 Ministry of Education (2010), *OECD Review on Evaluation and Assessment Frameworks for Improving School Outcomes: New Zealand Country background report*, Wellington: Author, p. 1.

12 OECD (2012), p. 24.

vision: "A world-leading education system that equips all New Zealanders with the knowledge, skills and values to be successful citizens in the 21st century." The goals include increased participation in early childhood education, improved literacy and numeracy, relevant skills and qualifications, integrated tertiary education and labour market needs, and "Māori achieving success as Māori", through a "capable, efficient and responsive" Ministry.

The context in which the system has evolved has led to structures similar to other countries but with particular local variations. Factors leading to such variations include location, history, size and politics.

New Zealand's location in the South Pacific means that it was initially inhabited by Polynesian travellers, who settled in the islands about 800AD and became known as Māori. They lived virtually undisturbed until the arrival of European sealers, whalers, missionaries and settlers in the late 1700s/early 1800s, leading to the signing of the Treaty of Waitangi in 1840 between Māori chiefs and the British Crown. The Treaty gave Māori the rights of British citizens but they were to retain sovereignty over their lands – issues that have been largely unresolved until recent moves to provide land reparation and compensation. New Zealand is a mainly bi-cultural society (in 2009, European New Zealanders making up 68 percent of the population and Māori 15 percent) with a growing multicultural population (9 percent Asian and 7 percent Pacific Island origin). This diversity is predicted to increase within the next five years when over half the school-age population will be from mixed or non-European heritage.[13] This will change the face of schooling and impact on future educational policy making.

New Zealand's educational history has been strongly influenced by the structures and traditions of the early settlers from the British Isles but adapted to a less class-based division of society. The 1877 Education Act set up primary years schooling that was to leave some of the excesses of class privilege and religious disharmony behind with a system that was "free, compulsory and secular". By the early 20th century, more comprehensive secondary, rural and correspondence schooling options were also available. In the 1930s, the following statement by the Prime Minister, Peter Fraser, became the cornerstone of New Zealand's educational philosophy for the next forty years:

> The Government's objective, broadly expressed, is that every person whatever his level of academic ability, whether he be rich or poor, whether he live in town or country, has a right as a citizen, to a free education of the kind for which he is best fitted, and to the fullest extent of his powers. So far is this from being a mere pious platitude that the full acceptance of the principle will involve the reorientation of the education system.[14]

---

13 Statistics New Zealand (2010) retrieved from www.stats.govt.nz/

14 Cited in Alcorn, N. (1999), *To the fullest extent of his powers: C.E. Beeby's life in education.*

The social upheaval of the 1960s and the economic downturn of the 1970s led to a re-evaluation of the education system as it appeared not to be delivering its promise. This coincided with similar calls to review education worldwide, for example, Callaghan's Ruskin College speech (1976) in the UK, and *A Nation at Risk* (1983) in the US. In 1984 and 1987, the New Zealand Treasury briefing papers stressed the necessity for reforming education. Policy papers *Administering for Excellence* (1988) and *Tomorrow's Schools* (1988) set these recommendations in motion and the 1989 Education Act completely overhauled the administration of education – a decision that has been well-documented.[15]

Another factor in New Zealand's context section is size. The current population is 4.4 million (Statistics New Zealand, 2012) distributed over two main islands with less than 15 people per km^2. The small size means that it has been easier to enact policy changes more swiftly than in a federalised system such as Australia or the United States, or a highly bureaucratic system such as Japan or Korea. The low density means that seeking local solutions by devolving responsibility to individual schools, many with school populations less than 300 students, means that there are fewer barriers encountered in implementing rapid change.

A final factor is the impact of politics. New Zealand has a uni-cameral parliament which is democratically elected every three years. The leader of the party with the most seats (or most able to create a coalition government) becomes Prime Minister. Lack of a second house of parliament and no formal constitution are seen by some commentators as not providing the necessary checks and balances in government decision making, but this also allows for governments to act quickly and responsively, especially if they only have a three year term in which to do so. One of the negative aspects of the short governmental term in office is a lack of coherent long-term educational planning. Recently, for example, a Labour (centre-left) government conducted a comprehensive ten-year consultation and revision of the curriculum and streamlined the Ministry's oversight, delegating even more curriculum decision making to schools. When the National party (centre-right) came to power, they quickly implemented National Standards (curriculum benchmarks), bringing more control back to the centre, which contradicted the curriculum autonomy that schools had just been granted. The balance between giving schools freedom and autonomy but ensuring quality and accountability is a tension that the system has not yet fully resolved.

Wellington, New Zealand: Victoria University Press, p. 99.

15 See, for example, Butterworth, G., & Butterworth, S. (1998). *Reforming education: The New Zealand experience 1984-1996*. Palmerston North, New Zealand: Dunmore Press; Fiske, E. & Ladd, H. (2000), *When schools compete. A cautionary tale*, Washington: Brookings; Langley (2009); Thrupp, M. (1999). *Schools Making a Difference: Let's be Realistic! School Mix, School Effectiveness and the Social Limits of Reform*. Buckingham, Philadelphia: Open University Press.

In summary, the New Zealand system is characterised by centralised control over education policy, including funding provision, curriculum, assessment and evaluation with delegated responsibility to schools and their Boards of Trustees for school budgets, staffing, resources, teaching and learning. This provides high levels of local autonomy and decision making but increased responsibility, complexity and workloads, with New Zealand principals having higher workloads than those in other OECD countries. Maintaining consistency within and across schools to provide equitable outcomes for all students has been also highlighted as a concern and has led to increased compliance and accountability.

The structure of schooling

The 1989 New Zealand Education Act dissolved the Department of Education and it is regional boards and replaced them with a stream-lined policy-focused Ministry of Education. Governance and management of individual schools was devolved to Boards of Trustees elected by the school's parent community. There is no intermediate layer between the Ministry and individual schools.

It is compulsory for children between the ages of six and 16 to attend school but most children begin on their fifth birthday and students can remain at school until age 19. Schooling in New Zealand is provided free through state (national government) owned and operated schools. 85 percent of schools fit this category. A further 11 percent are 'state-integrated' schools which receive government funding, teach the national curriculum, and whose students participate in national assessments and qualifications. These schools have a defined 'special character' which they can retain in their approach to teaching and learning. Private (fee-paying) schooling is an option which is taken up by schools with a particular religious or philosophical stance who wish to retain their independence but only 4 percent of schools fit this category. Within the special character provision are over 20,000 students in Maori-medium schools. More detail on these options is provided later.

The schooling system is divided into three levels: early childhood, primary and secondary (although there are overlaps in rural areas, some school types or special character settings, which are explained in more detail later). Early childhood education goes from birth to five. Current government policy aims for 20 hours per week of subsidised early childhood education in approved centres. About 95 percent of children have some form of early childhood education before attending school. Options include kindergartens, play centres, *Kohanga reo* (*M□ori* language settings), Pacific language centres, Montessori, home-based and a range of commercial enterprises. This sector has its own curriculum and set of regulations.

Primary education is available from ages 5-12 (year levels 1-8). In 2009, there were approximately 2000 primary schools with about half a million students.

Secondary education goes from ages 13-18 (year levels 9-15). In 2009, there were over 300 secondary schools with about 300,000 students.

The legal framework

The education reforms of the 1980s set up the key pieces of legislation relating to education – the State Sector Act (1988) and the Education Act (1989). The State Sector Act is the overarching legislation that defines the agencies that constitute the State Sector, their roles, responsibilities and accountabilities. It gave the State Services Commissioner the responsibility for appointing chief executives to government agencies, such as the Secretary for Education (the Chief Executive of the Ministry of Education) or the Chief Review Officer (the Chief Executive of the Education Review Office). These chief executives are accountable to the State Services Commissioner who conducts their performance review against government priorities. The Act also made provision for school Boards of Trustees to become 'Crown Entities' ultimately responsible to the government of the day. The Education Act more specifically covers the responsibilities of the education agencies and their staff. The Act replaced the Department of Education and its regional offices with the Ministry of Education; formed 'self-managing schools ' by giving governance to Boards of Trustees; established the Education Review Office to evaluate and report on the quality of education provision within state-funded pre-tertiary education institutions and services; and created the New Zealand Qualifications Authority to oversee the development and monitoring of a credible secondary assessment and qualifications system.

Currently, the government of the day sets the direction for policy in all areas of the State Sector. The State Services Commission oversees the implementation of these directions and priorities through its Managing for Outcomes accountability framework. The government of the day also appoints a Minister of Education (and the legislation allows for a Minister of Tertiary Education separate from the Minister responsible for schooling and another Minister for the Education Review Office). Currently one Minister holds both the Education and Education Review Office portfolios. The Minister of Education, together with the Ministry of Education, set a work plan for the next five years. This is updated each year in the Ministry's Statement of Intent. The Ministry reports annually against its *Statement of Intent* to Parliament.

The Ministry and other agencies meet these priorities by focusing on particular functions. The Ministry's key functions are oversight of education policy, curriculum, assessment and schools or students at risk. They also provide schools with their buildings, operational budgets and teachers' salaries. Schools receive their operational budgets based on student numbers, year levels of students, the socio-economic status of the school's community (called decile ratings) and location (whereby isolated schools receive an adjusted allowance to cover their distinct needs).

State schools and state-integrated schools are governed by individual Boards of Trustees, the members of which are elected every three years from, and by, the school's parent community. The Board also includes the principal (who is employed by the Board), a teacher representative and, in secondary schools, a student representative. The Board oversees the school's charter (the document that sets out the characteristics of the school, its vision and the goals and targets it sets for student achievement). From that overarching document, it prepares annual and longer term plans, sets school policy (within the framework of the national guidelines), and reports annually to the school community and the Ministry of Education. Boards of Trustees employ all school staff, manage school property, control the school's finances and set policy priorities, in conjunction with the school principal, as the school's chief executive. The work of Boards is audited each year by the Office of the Auditor General for financial probity and reviewed on average every three years by the Education Review Office for adequate governance.

Freedom to establish non-state schools

Despite the small size of the country's student population, which is less than would be found in many cities in the rest of the world, there are a wide variety of schooling options. Only 4 percent of schools are fully fee-paying private schools as it is possible to meet the needs of different religions, philosophies and communities through the state or state-integrated system. Private schools (or independent schools, as they prefer to be called) are often high status religiously-based schools. They are governed by independent boards, own their property and set their own fees. About 25 percent of their income is subsidised by the state. They can teach to the *New Zealand Curriculum* or other programmes such as International Baccalaureate. Recent reports indicate that independent schools are struggling in the current economic climate despite government subsidies and that some will either need to close or to integrate into the state system. Independent schools are seeking more government support. If their schools do close, the government will have to take responsibility for their students on a full-time basis and therefore, they say, supporting independent schools would be a more cost-effective option.

The Private Schools Conditional Integration Act (1975) was set up to allow for schools to maintain the best of both worlds – they could receive state funding and yet maintain their particular special character. Eleven per cent of schools now take up this option. They are subject to the same requirements as state schools, for example, to teach the *New Zealand Curriculum* and be reviewed by the Education Review Office, but can maintain their own religious or philosophical basis. State-integrated schools receive the same funding per student as state schools and the government meets the cost of teachers' salaries. The school's buildings and land are privately owned and schools can charge attendance fees to meet their property maintenance and development costs. A designated proprietor, for example, a church or trust, who owns the school, is responsible for setting and maintaining the school's special character. Some features of the Act are that: (a) a private school can become part of the state education system while retaining its special character as reflected through its teaching and practices; (b) the school receives state funding when it integrates into the state sector but can continue to teach religious education or a particular philosophy; (c) the school can limit entry to the school to pupils whose parents subscribe to the school's special character; (d) key teaching positions can be 'tagged' which means that a key factor in the process of appointing someone to this position is their suitability in terms of the special character of the school. The later 1989 Education Act allowed for schools to be set up with a special character provision without having to be a private school first. The largest group of state-integrated schools are from the Catholic Education System but there are also other Christian denominations, Jewish, Muslim, Montessori, Steiner and alternative schools.

Home schooling

Students living more than 5 kilometres walking distance from the nearest school (or public transport to school) may be exempted from attending school but will be required to enrol in *Te Kura*, the Correspondence School, or they can be home schooled. Many schools contract public transport operators to provide school buses that deliver students to the school gate in the morning and home again at the end of the school day. This became especially necessary after many small rural schools were amalgamated in the 1990s.

For students in isolated locations, or at home recovering from illness, travelling overseas or temporarily unable to attend their local school, *Te Kura*, the Correspondence School, provides teaching in both English and *te reo M□ori* from early childhood to Year 13. The curriculum is provided through various electronic means and, where possible, face-to-face opportunities for students to get to know their learning advisors and liaison teachers. *Te Kura* also accepts dual enrolments, where a student enrolled in another school can take an option not available at their local school. Originally set up in 1922 to cater for the most isolated students, by 2009, it had about 4000 full-time students and 11,000 dual enrolments. These also included teen parents, students excluded from school, students attending regional health schools and students with special education needs. *Te Kura* is a state-funded school and is reviewed by the Education Review Office.

As it is compulsory for students between the ages of 6 and 16 to be enrolled in a school, it requires an exemption from the Ministry of Education to school students at home. In 2009, approximately 3500 families took up this option, educating nearly 7,000 students from home. The reasons included dissatisfaction with the formal schooling system, religious or philosophical beliefs, or concern for children's safety, for example, from bullying. The requirement for exemption is quite open although the forms require detail about the proposed curriculum, timetable and teaching space. Parents must satisfy the Secretary of Education that their child will be taught 'as regularly and as well as in a registered school'. The Ministry of Education issues exemption certificates and advises the Education Review Office that these students are being home schooled. ERO undertakes occasional reviews to ensure that students are receiving an education appropriate to their needs and that they are not being disadvantaged by being educated at home. Parents are required to update their home schooling intentions every six months. A small supervisory allowance is available to supplement teaching materials and activities. Some parents use this to purchase teaching support or materials from *Te Kura*, the Correspondence School, or to buy other ready-made curricula.

School choice not limited by family income

Most New Zealand schools are run by the State (85 percent fully state schools and a further 11 percent state-integrated). While there is no legal requirement for students to pay fees, parents pay for stationery and other course-related costs, school trips and outdoor education activities. Schools often request a school donation which can be tax deductible for parents. Many schools choose to have distinctive uniforms but these are not compulsory. International students holding valid student visas can also be enrolled in state-funded schools, provided they pay the appropriate international student tuition fees. A number of schools use international student fees to supplement their state funding.

Within the state-funded system there are a range of school types. At primary school level, a student could attend a full primary (Years 1-8); a contributing primary (Years 1-6), an intermediate (specialising in Years 7 & 8 – most common in larger centres), a middle school or junior high (Years 7-10), or a composite or area school (Years 1-13 – most common in rural areas). At secondary level, a student could attend a secondary school (Years 9-13), an extended secondary school (Years 7-13) or a senior high school (Years 11-13) as well as the options that span both primary and secondary years. These options have developed over many years depending on the size of the community and are adapted as local populations increase or decrease or in response to particular community preferences.

State schools are co-educational at the primary level, and may be either single sex or co-educational at the secondary level. State-integrated schools usually follow this pattern but private schools are more often single-sex. With recent concerns about boy's education falling behind, some schools are choosing to have single-sex class options.

The medium of instruction for most state-funded, state-integrated schools and private schools is English. There is an English-medium curriculum (*The New Zealand Curriculum*) for state and state-integrated schools. These schools can also provide full immersion *te reo Māori* units or classes or bi-lingual English/*te reo Māori* classes, in which case they will follow the *Māori* language curriculum (*Te Maurautanga o Aotearoa*) or a mixture of the two. The 1989 Education Act allows for the establishment of full immersion schools which teach in *te reo Māori* and have a distinctive cultural approach. *Kura Kaupapa Māori* are state special character schools where teaching is in *te reo Māori* and the school's aims, purposes and objectives reflect the *Te Aho Matua* philosophy or that of the local *iwi* (tribe). *Kura Kaupapa Māori* can either be primary, composite or secondary schools. Approximately three percent of students participate in *Māori*-medium schooling.

The flexibility in the system allows for a range of pedagogical approaches. Montessori, Steiner and *Kura Kaupapa Māori* have already been mentioned. Other schools within the state system, such as Discovery One (a primary school) and Unlimited (a secondary school), in Christchurch, are more experimental in approach. They do not have traditional classrooms or teachers but flexible spaces and learning advisors who negotiate learning tasks with students and their families. Until the Christchurch earthquakes, these two particular schools were located in the heart of the city and used the public facilities such as libraries, parks and businesses as integral parts of their curriculum and students learned through an inquiry approach.

The policy for students with special education needs is that they can enrol in the school of their choice (in as much as children with regular needs can). Students are assessed as having mild, moderate or high needs. For students with high needs, particularly severe disabilities, there are special schools available but parents can still choose to have them in a regular school situation, either in a special unit attached to a school or in a regular classroom. Funding is available to support schools to provide adaptations to buildings and specialist support. Most students with special education needs receive the support and services from the school they attend, although parents of special education students report they do not feel welcome at all schools and that the quality of support varies. Schools can arrange for specialist teachers to provide services, or make a referral to the Ministry of Education's Special Education unit who can assess the child's learning needs, to determine if additional services and resourcing are required, such as special equipment to help them learn or move around. Assessment is done by the class teacher and school staff with specialists from appropriate agencies. This information forms the basis for the student's Individual Education Programme (IEP). A range of specialists work with children with special education needs, including specialist teachers, speech-language therapists, special education advisors, occupational therapists, physiotherapists, psychologists and advisors on deaf children. Students with special educational needs or disabilities can stay in schooling until they turn 21.

Gifted and talented students are also catered for within regular classes and schools. Schools choose various ways to respond to the needs and interests of these students. Schools have largely discarded the practice of streaming (placing students in streams according to ability) but organise students in a range of flexible groupings within and across classes. Gifted and talented students may be scattered across classes but brought together for enrichment programmes, clustered into particular classes for specialist teaching, or placed in an accelerated class or programme.

State and state integrated primary schools do not normally have boarding (live-in) options although schools often arrange home-stay opportunities for international students. Secondary schools can have boarding facilities, many of which were set up for students from rural areas who wished to come into a larger school or population centre. Private schools might have boarding facilities at both primary and secondary levels.

While outsiders studying the New Zealand might already consider New Zealand as a system of charter schools, the term has quite specific meaning here. An educational commentator outlines his understanding of the international meaning:

> Charter schools receive public money but are not subject to some of the rules, regulations, and statutes that apply to other public schools in exchange for some type of accountability for producing certain results, which are set forth in each school's charter. Charter schools are opened and attended by choice. Where enrolment in a charter school is oversubscribed, admission is frequently allocated by lottery-based admissions systems. Some charter schools provide a curriculum that specializes in a certain field — e.g., arts, mathematics, or vocational training. Others attempt to provide a better and more efficient general education than nearby public schools. Some charter schools are founded by teachers, parents, or activists who feel restricted by traditional public schools – others are established by non-profit groups, universities, and some government entities or companies.[16]

In March, 2012, the leader of the ACT party, one of the government's coalition partners announced that 'charter schools' would be set up in Auckland and Christchurch to lift student achievement. What was meant in this case was not what was already available through the current options but a new variation – government-funded but privately-run schools. A government advisory committee has been set up and a business consortium has already shown interest in setting up a primary and secondary school under this scheme. Opponents have raised concerns that this has been done without consultation, is targeting vulnerable populations, especially given the Christchurch earthquakes, and has not been proven to be successful elsewhere. How this policy will play out will be watched with interest from both sides of the debate.

---

16 Guerin, D. (2011). The NZ Charter Schools Debate #1[a weblog]. Posted December 6th 2011 on Ed Blog: Tertiary education news and views.

Decisions about admitting pupils

Most school students attend the appropriate school closest to their home but they can enrol at any state school which does not have an enrolment scheme. An enrolment scheme (The Education Amendment Act 2000) is designed to avoid the overcrowding of popular schools. Under the scheme, students have the right to enrol if they live within the home zone determined by the school. If they live outside the zone, the school may set criteria in order to select students before opening up places to ballot. Students who live outside the school's home zone can be admitted, if there are places available, in the following order of priority: special programmes; siblings of currently enrolled students; siblings of past students; children of past students; children of board employees and staff; all other students. If there are more applications than available places then selection must be through a randomly-drawn ballot.

State-integrated schools can expect parents of students wishing to attend that school to support their faith or philosophy. It is not unknown for parents wishing to enrol their child in a popular school out of their zone for them to move to a rental property within zone to gain enrolment. For highly popular schools, properties for sale or rent will be described as being in the school zone, and will often be more expensive than nearby properties that are outside the school zone.

Aspire Scholarships are provided by the government for up to 50 students from low income families who would like to attend a New Zealand private secondary school. The scholarship can only be used at fully registered private secondary schools (that is, independent schools). It cannot be used at state or state-integrated schools. The scholarship contributes up to $15,000 per year for school fees and up to $1,500 per year for course related costs.

Decisions about staff

Staff who teach in state-funded schools must be registered by the New Zealand Teachers Council (NZTC). They must be of good character and fit to be a teacher; a satisfactory teacher or likely to be a satisfactory teacher; proficient in English or *te reo Māori*; and committed to the *Code of Ethics for Registered Teachers.* In order to gain registration they must have trained in a pre-service teacher education institution registered by NZTC and meet the Graduating Teacher Standards or, if they received their training overseas, have their qualifications recognized by the New Zealand Qualifications Authority (NZQA). A newly-qualified teacher then has a two-year supervised induction programme in the school before being fully registered. Once fully registered, a teacher must meet the Registered Teacher Criteria in order to maintain a practising certificate, issued by NZTC. The school attests, through the teacher appraisal system, that each teacher they employ meets the 12 criteria under the headings of 'professional relationships and professional values' and 'professional knowledge in practice'. Staff in schools (teaching and non-teaching) must also undergo a police check to ensure that they are safe to be around children and to work in a school environment. Teachers arriving from overseas who had not reached full registration or staff without qualifications but with particular skills (such as teaching *te reo Māori*) can apply to NZTC for a Limited Authority to Teach certificate.

The Ministry of Education determines staffing numbers appropriate for the size and needs of a school but schools can use money from their operational grant to employ further staff if they see the need. Teaching staff have their salaries paid by central government and set by a collective contract between the appropriate union and the Ministry.

Independent (private) schools are not bound by the requirements of NZTC or the teacher union collective agreements but use these as a guide to make their own staffing decisions. If charter schools are introduced, they will also be free to make their own staffing and salary decisions. Schools of special character can 'tag' positions to ensure that successful candidates support the particular religion or philosophy of that school.

Accountability for school quality

While schools have high levels of autonomy and freedom, they are also subject to high levels of accountability and compliance. The *Managing for Outcomes* framework sets the high level goals by which the State Services Commission reviews the education agencies. The four education agencies (the Ministry, ERO, NZQA and NZTC) all have accountability and improvement functions. Each agency deals directly with schools and their Boards of Trustees in relation to the matters within their purview.

The Education Review Office (ERO) evaluates the quality of early childhood and school education, including *Māori*-medium, home schooling and other alternative options. Private schools, which are covered by different provisions, are evaluated but not to the same level of detail as state-funded schools. The Education Review Office also evaluates the quality of leadership and governance provided by each school.

The New Zealand Qualifications Authority (NZQA) manages the New Zealand Qualifications Framework which is the register of all secondary and non-university tertiary qualifications. These include Unit Standards (modular vocational assessments) and the two external assessments for secondary students – the National Certificate of Educational Achievement (NCEA) and the New Zealand Scholarships. NCEA is available at three levels and is gained by passing enough credits through achievement-based internal (but externally moderated) and external assessments.

The New Zealand Teachers Council (NZTC) establishes and maintains the standards for teacher performance by monitoring teacher education programmes, registering teachers and promoting the code of ethics for the teaching profession. They also deregister teachers who have been found guilty of misconduct or incompetence.

At the individual school level, the regulatory framework for schools is set by two sets of guidelines – the *National Education Guidelines* and the *National Administration Guidelines*. The *National Education Guidelines* include national education goals, curriculum policy, curriculum statements and, most recently, a set of National Standards for reading writing and mathematics. The *National Administrative Guidelines* outline the requirements related to (a) the provision of teaching and learning programmes; (b) school-wide planning, self review and reporting; (c) employment and personnel management; (d) financial and property management; (e) the provision of a safe physical and emotional environment; and (f) other legislative requirements such as student attendance.

The functions and roles are as follows: *system accountability* is managed by the Ministry through the collection, collation and analysis of aggregated data, and supplemented by ERO who conduct focused cross-sector evaluations of particular areas of interest. *School accountability* is maintained by charters, planning and reporting requirements, roll returns, targets and analyses of variance, all of which are forwarded to the Ministry of Education by individual schools; schools conduct their own self review and are externally reviewed and publicly reported upon by ERO; the Auditor-General carries out financial audits; schools are required to report to their local communities; and NZQA gathers and reports on matters related to assessment and qualifications in secondary schools. *Teacher performance* is overseen by individual schools through their attestation and appraisal schemes; teachers are police-vetted and registered by NZTC; and teachers are observed and interviewed as part of ERO school reviews (but not individually assessed). *Student achievement* is monitored and assessed by teachers who feed achievement data to senior management and Boards of Trustees to inform school-wide decision making; the processes by which students are taught and assessed are reviewed by ERO; students' achievement data is recorded by the school, the Ministry, NZQA (if relevant), and shared with students and their parents through written, oral and/or electronic means.

State-integrated schools and independent (private) schools can have further accountabilities relating to their proprietors, international affiliations, religious order or local *iwi*. Catholic schools, for example, are reviewed every three years by their diocese to assess the way in which the Catholic faith is upheld and fostered.

To date, New Zealand has resisted high-stakes national testing. Up to Year 11, there are no nationally administered common assessments. At primary school level, the focus is on formative assessment (assessment *for* learning) rather than summative assessment (assessment *of* learning). Teachers use a wide-range of data-gathering tools from learning conversations, student work samples and portfolios to nationally-normed tests to come to an 'overall teacher judgement'.

Several external measures are used to gain a system-wide understanding of well New Zealand students are achieving. One is the comparative data available from international comparative studies such as Trends in International Mathematics and Science Study (TIMSS), Progress in International Reading Literacy Study (PIRLS) or Programme for International Student Assessment (PISA). Such international comparisons have had a major impact on government policies and Ministry strategies. The Minister of Education states in the Foreword to the *2010-2015 Statement of Intent*:

> New Zealanders are rightly proud of our education system. We are home to some of the best schools, the best teachers and the best students in the world. But the gap between our high performing and our low performing students is one of the widest in the Organisation for Economic Co-operation and Development (OECD), and this government is determined to address underachievement in our schools, and to drive improved educational performance right across the system to improve education outcomes for all New Zealanders. [17]

Another external measure is through a programme called the National Education Monitoring Project (NEMP) which subjects a randomly chosen but representative sample of school students at Years 4 and 8 to a series of assessments including individual pen and paper tasks, one-to-one demonstrations and group activities. The tasks aim to measure achievement, skills and attitudes. Each curriculum area is assessed on a four-yearly cycle. To support the improvement of assessment practices, some of the NEMP assessment tasks are released to schools for their own use or to support the design of school and classroom-based assessment (others are kept back for longitudinal comparison). Teachers involved in the administration and marking of these tasks also receive valuable professional development in assessment.[18]

With a change to a centre-right government in 2008, a third measure, National Standards, has been introduced into primary schools. There are several reasons for this new policy. The first is to give parents understandable assessment information that gave them a clearer idea of how their children compared to other children of a similar age. The second is to provide benchmarks for what standards

---

17 Ministry of Education (2010), p. 2.

18 Gilmore, A. (2008, July). *The NEMP: More than just a role in accountability and monitoring change over time: a powerful resource for building teacher assessment capability and providing assessment resources.* Paper presented at the 6th Conference of the International Test Commission, Liverpool, United Kingdom.

students should achieve at each level of their primary schooling. The other is to make teachers and schools more accountable for how well their students are achieving. National Standards have been introduced in reading, writing and mathematics for English-medium schools and the equivalent in *te reo* for *Māori*-medium schools with the addition of oral language, given its central place in *Māori* culture.

At secondary school, up to Year 11, schools use a similar range of assessments while also introducing students to formal examination-style assessments. From Year 11, students enrol in NCEA to gain credits in the achievement standards nearly 100 subjects or in unit standards which are vocationally-related (or both). Level 1 is usually achieved at Year 11 (age 15), Level 2 at Year 12 (and meeting a particular set of achievement standards grants entry to university) and Level 3 at Year 13. Particularly able students can also sit the New Zealand Scholarship examinations in Year 13. These recognise excellence in each subject area and reward high-achieving students with financial assistance towards their university studies. There are 33 subjects available at Scholarship level. School results in NCEA and Scholarship are made publicly available. Although the Ministry does not rank schools, newspapers often publish lists of school rankings based on these results. Other publications use student achievement as only one measure and use more complex criteria to publish 'value-added' rankings.

ERO reports are also made publicly available and provide a measure of school quality. ERO reviews schools using evaluation indicators based on 'six dimensions of effective practice': student learning, engagement, achievement and progress; effective teaching; leading and managing the school; governing the school; a safe and inclusive school culture; and engaging parents, *whānau* (extended families) and communities. While ERO do not rate, rank or label schools, (for example, as 'failing') and reports are expressed in developmental terms, the return schedule for a school is often taken as a *de facto* rating. Where schools are struggling, ERO might return in 1-2 years. Where schools are meeting the review criteria and conducting their own self review well, ERO might return in three years. Where a school has an on-going record of high quality self and external review, ERO might return in 4-5 years.

With a change of government in 2008 from centre-left to centre-right, a range of educational concerns were raised. One policy was able to combine several solutions. Introducing national benchmarks as part of the drive to improve numeracy and literacy achievement and combining this with easy-to-understand reporting to parents and gaining large-scale data on student achievement to identify poor performing schools and teachers could all be achieved through the National Standards policy. This initiative was met with hostility from schools, including teacher unions, principals associations and individual Boards of Trustees – concerned that the standards were untested, unnecessary and had not been successful in other countries in lifting achievement. They argued that comprehensive information was already available through a range of assessment tools and parents were well-informed on children's progress. A further concern was that the results could be used to produce school 'league tables' or be tied to teacher performance pay. The legislation tied National Standards to school's charters and the planning and reporting requirements. The standards themselves, along with exemplars, were provided to schools. Some schools refused to implement the standards and resistance was met with including a school's compliance as part of their ERO review.

Teaching of values

Although state schools are secular, the legislation covering the New Zealand education system allows for other philosophies and beliefs to be taught in state-integrated and private schools. Some state schools also have optional religious teaching from which parents can withdraw their children. The *New Zealand Curriculum* outlines the vision, principles and values that underpin the curriculum. The vision is for young people who will be: "confident, connected, actively involved, and lifelong learners." The principles, "put students at the centre of teaching and learning, asserting that they should experience a curriculum that engages and challenges them, is forward-looking and inclusive, and affirms New Zealand's unique identity." The section outlining values also discusses developing understanding of one's own values and tolerance for the values of others. It states, "Values are deeply held beliefs about what is important or desirable. They are expressed through the ways in which people think and act." [19] The curriculum goes on to list the values that "enjoy widespread support" as: excellence; innovation, inquiry, and curiosity; diversity; equity; community and participation; ecological sustainability; integrity; and respect for themselves, others and human rights. It is expected that these will be integrated throughout curriculum content and pedagogy.

Conclusion

New Zealand's education system has attracted considerable interest over the last 20 years as the results of the education reforms of the 1980s have been observed and evaluated. The New Zealand 'experiment' has had successes in involving parents in school governance, giving school leaders more decision making power and opening up a series of schooling options for a wide range of communities. It has made little difference to the achievement of New Zealand students overall, who still perform in the top quartile of international comparative studies, nor to the 'long tail' of underachievement. One of the side-effects of the reforms has been increasing compliance as governments seek ways to address the underachievement issue but find that many initiatives they implement are

19 Ministry of Education (2007), *The New Zealand Curriculum.* Wellington: Author pp. 8-10.

not necessarily welcomed by the education or academic communities. How to resolve the philosophical and ideological differences and bring together diverse education stakeholders to build on the evidence about 'what works' in education and put coherent and cohesive long term planning and resourcing in place is the issue that needs most attention if New Zealand is to continue to be a country followed with admiration for its commitment to education.

Philippines
[reprinted from the 2004 edition, reviewed 2012 by Vivien M. Talisayon]

by Vivien M. Talisayon and others[1]

Overview

The basic educational system in the Philippines consists of six years of elementary education (primary- Grades 1-4, and intermediate - Grades 5-6) and four years of secondary education (first year to fourth year high school). The entry age at Grade 1 is 6 years old. The country has about 13 million students (NSCB, 2002) in elementary schools (93 percent in public schools, 7 percent in private schools) and about six million high school students (78 percent in public schools, 22 percent in private schools).

Major current issues in the Philippine educational system stem largely from inadequate resources nationwide. One issue is quality schooling and student achievement in large classes (40-100 students per class) due to lack of teacher items and classrooms, and shortage of instructional materials like textbooks. Another issue is the upgrading of the great mass of poorly qualified teachers, for example, non-majors teaching subjects like science and mathematics, leading to low (about 50 percent) student achievement.

Structure of Schooling

The Department of Education is the government agency tasked to supervise and regulate the elementary and high school system, both public and private. The Central Office which formulates educational policies has three bureaus: Bureau of Elementary Education, Bureau of Secondary Education, and Bureau of Non-Formal Education. The bureaus are headed by directors. The highest official in the Department is the Secretary assisted by Undersecretaries and Assistant Secretaries.

The Department has 17 regional offices headed by regional directors. Each region has divisions under the leadership of superintendents. Under each division are the schools headed by principals or school heads. The regional directors,

---

1 Contributors to this chapter: Vivien M. Talisayon (coordinator), and Eulalia N. Bentillo, Elena C. Cutiongco, Nenalyn P. Defensor, Crescencia C. Joaquin, Anunciacion V. Lara, Editha M. Marcelo, Aniceta M. Ortinero, Marietta R. Otero, Felicitas E. Pado.

superintendents and school heads are tasked to implement the policies of the Department. Each Regional Office is given a budget by the national government for salaries, maintenance and operating expenses, and for capital outlay.

The Division Superintendent is assisted by a Local School Board headed by the Governor of a province to plan education programs in the division and allocate local resources to implement such programs. The Division Office makes decisions on hiring teachers based on recommendations from the school principal and education supervisors.

The principal is the administrative and academic head of an elementary school or high school. In the primary grades (Grades 1-4), a teacher handles all subjects in one school day for one class at a grade level. At the intermediate grades (Grades 5-6), schools may adopt a departmental system, with teachers assigned to teach up to five classes in the same subject at the same grade level daily.[2]

Free tuition is provided in public schools for Grades 1-6. Private schools charge varying tuition rates. Some private elementary schools offer optional additional year after Grade 6 before the secondary level.

Tuition is free in public high schools, but attendance is not compulsory by law (PIER 2001). High schools are structured departmentally by subject areas. Teachers per subject area teach up to five classes daily. Standard class period is 40 minutes.
The Department of Education prescribes a national curriculum for elementary and high schools. Elementary education aims for functional literacy of students in communication arts in English and Filipino, Mathematics, Social Studies, and Science. The objectives of secondary education are to continue to promote the objectives of elementary education and to develop in students the skills for productive endeavor and work, and to prepare them for formal higher education. Regional and Division Offices are encouraged to have modifications and initiatives to make the curriculum more appropriate to regional or local conditions.

Legal Framework

The 1987 Philippine Constitution provides that the state shall allocate the highest budgetary allocation to education, protect and promote the right of all citizens to quality education at all levels and shall take appropriate steps to make such education accessible to all. Among the specific provisions in the Constitution (Article XIV) regarding education are:

---

2 Contributors to this chapter: Vivien M. Talisayon (coordinator), and Eulalia N. Bentillo, Elena C. Cutiongco, Nenalyn P. Defensor, Crescencia C. Joaquin, Anunciacion V. Lara, Editha M. Marcelo, Aniceta M. Ortinero, Marietta R. Otero, Felicitas E. Pado.

1. Free public education at elementary and high school levels
2. Compulsory elementary education (Grades 1-6) for all children of school age (Age 6 and above)
3. State power over educational institutions
4. Relevance of educational system to the needs of people and society
5. Optional religious instruction in public elementary and high schools
6. English and Filipino as official languages in communication and instruction with regional languages as auxiliary media of instruction

The Education Act of 1982 provided for the establishment of an integrated system of education. The Act stipulated that the establishment of new schools or conversion of existing schools from elementary to national secondary schools or from secondary school to national secondary school shall be done through legislation. Private schools, except pre-schools are allowed to operate only if they convert into stock or non-stock corporations which include religious institutions.

Establishing a private school also requires the approval of the government through the Department of Education. The Act also established the Ministry of Education, Culture and Sports (renamed Department of Education in 2000), the government agency tasked to formulate general education objectives and policies, promulgate rules and regulations necessary for the administration, supervision and regulation of the education system, and provide for the establishment and maintenance of a complete, adequate, and integrated system of education relevant to national development goals.

The Act also encouraged the creation of public schools at the barangay level, or by municipal, city, province or regional governments. It also established the creation of local private school board in every municipality or city, whose main function was to manage and disburse the special private education fund to finance various school programs and projects.

Republic Act No. 6655 of 1988 established and provided for a free public secondary education. This law converts and integrates the administration, supervision and control of all public secondary schools, including the payment of teacher and school personnel salaries in the Department of Education.

Republic Act 7722 and Republic Act 7796, passed in 1994, transferred the supervision of higher education and trade schools from the Department of Education to the Commission on Higher Education and Technical Education and Skills Development Authority, respectively.

Freedom to Establish Non-State Schools

The authority to grant a permit or recognition to open and operate private schools is the exclusive prerogative of the government as provided for in Section 4(1) of Article XIV of the 1987 Constitution. Republic Act 3075 empowered the Department of Education to supervise, inspect and regulate all elementary and secondary schools and prescribe the necessary rules governing their operations.

By requiring prospective schools to secure a permit before operating, the State ensures their compliance with at least the minimum standards set by the Manual of Regulations for Private Schools.[3]

Republic Act 7798 also provides that any private school to be established must incorporate as a non-stock or stock educational corporation in accordance with the provisions of the Corporation Code of the Philippines. Private schools established after September 1982 shall be owned solely by Filipino citizens, corporations, or associations at least sixty percent of the capital of which is owned by such citizens, except those allowed to be established by religious groups and mission boards, pursuant to the Constitution and special laws. [4]

Home Schooling

Home Study Program

Home Study Programs are implemented by interested divisions of the Department of Education in consonance with the 1987 Constitution (Article XV) which provides that quality education at all levels be made accessible to all Filipinos, and that non-formal and indigenous learning systems, as well as self-learning and out-of-school study programs, particularly those that respond to community needs be developed.

The Divisions of Quezon City and Rizal in the National Capital Region have home study programs. The objectives of the home study program in Quezon City are to:

provide an affordable secondary education for all, and bring about an opportunity to enhance the quality of life of the citizenry;.

give opportunity for sickly and working students to finish their secondary schooling; and

help solve the school problem of shortage of teachers and classrooms.

Students in the program are issued the same textbooks in all subjects for the school year. They are given topics to study every week and required to answer

[3] Sarmiento, 1995.

[4] CBSI, 1996.

questions given by teachers at the end of each topic. Contact sessions of students and teachers are on Saturdays. These sessions are for clarification of difficult topics encountered by students during the week.

The program in Quezon City addresses educational needs of working students such as factory workers, baby sitters, vendors, canteen helpers, janitors, laborers, salesladies, sickly and street children who are willing to finish secondary education.

Admission requirements include at least 80 percent average rating in English, Mathematics, Science and Filipino at the elementary level, employment certificate if employed, and medical certificate if sickly.

The Local Government Code provides that local government units financially support home study programs. The officials participate in the operation of the program through the Local School Board.

The Home Study Program as implemented in some public schools is not in the organizational structure of the Department of Education. The public authority regulating the program is the Division superintendent through the school principal. Regulation is in the form of management of resources appropriated for the program by the local government.

Parents of children admitted to the program understand that full authority on instruction, guidance and supervision is given to the teachers. Some educated parents may help in the preparation of homework. Majority of the parents are busy earning a living that education is really left to the teachers.

Accreditation and Equivalency Program

This program was instituted in 1981 (Presidential Executive Order No. 733) to broaden opportunities of deprived, disadvantaged, under-served, deserving members of society, specifically out-of-school youth, and give due recognition and importance to learning acquired outside of the formal school system.

Target participants of the program are dropouts from elementary and secondary schools for at least one year, youth who never attended a formal school, and those presently employed and need to upgrade their academic level for re-entry into formal school, job entry or promotion, and self-fulfillment.

The principal instrument used is the Philippine Placement Test, a battery of tests for assessing basic learning skills and competencies covering the subject areas of communication arts (English and Filipino), mathematics, science, and social studies. Effectivity of the grade/year placement of the successful examinee is at the opening of the next school year.

School Choice Not Limited by Family Income

Parents' choice of the school, especially elementary school, is often influenced by its accessibility. A school may be selected because of its proximity to the family residence, or it may be along the way or near a parent's place of work. To illustrate, faculty and staff of a state university prefer to send their children to the laboratory grade school and high school of their university for proximity, as well as discounted fees and perceived quality of instruction.

School proximity is sometimes preferred by parents over quality of education. For instance, parents in rural areas opt to send their children to nearby multigrade schools with two grade levels per classroom than to far mono-grade central schools.[5]

Other factors influencing parents' choice of a school are perceived quality of school instruction and the school where parents are alumni. A factor that may override school proximity is parents' preference for religious instruction in a private school. Parents' religion may be the deciding factor to send a child to a Catholic, Christian (Protestant) or Islam (madrasah) school. Madrasah schools are located in southern Philippines, in the island of Mindanao.

Parents' ethnicity is another factor, particularly for Chinese Filipinos. A few private schools have mostly Chinese Filipino students. Expatriates like the Japanese have put up private schools exclusively for their children.

Another consideration in parents' choice of schools at the secondary level is the child's inclination or talent. For the science-inclined, the country has science high schools, including the Philippine Science High School System and sixteen regional science high schools. The Philippine High School for the Arts is another special public school. Additional reasons for the choice of these schools are financial and non-financial benefits. The Philippine Science High School System offers full scholarship to its students, including dormitory expenses. Moreover, prestige is associated with the scholarship, and the quality of education results in a higher probability of acquiring a tertiary level scholarship and admission to a quality university.

Parents may decide on a vocational/technical school for their children for earlier livelihood prospects, in addition to the students' vocational/technical interests. Finally, parents whose children have learning disabilities usually have no choice but to send their children to special education schools or centers.

---

5 TEEP, 2002a.

School Distinctiveness Protected by Law

The right to school distinctiveness is expressed in Section 2 of Article XIV of the 1987 Philippine Constitution. Section 2 encourages " non-formal, informal, and indigenous learning systems, as well as self-learning, independent, and out-of-school youth study programs, particularly those that respond to community needs".

In the same article, Section 5 affirms, too, the right to school distinctiveness, to wit: "The State shall take into account regional and sectoral needs and conditions and shall encourage local planning in the development of educational policies and programs.

Section 5 also provides "adult citizens, the disabled, and out-of-school youth with training in civics, vocational efficiency and other skills".

Section 10 (Science and Technology) and Section 14 (Arts and Culture) are implemented in the establishment of regional and national science high schools, and a national high school for the arts, respectively.

Distinctive Character of Schools

The distinctive character of a school depends on a number of conditions, such as: purpose for which it was established, entity or institution managing/operating the school, location of the school, kind of pupils and teachers, quality of its facilities, school curriculum, and admission policy. The distinctiveness of a school is expressed in its vision-mission and, in the case of public high schools, in the law or Republic Act that established the school.

Regular public schools, elementary or secondary schools, have the same free admission policy and the intended curriculum provided by the Department of Education.. However, their distinctiveness lies in the quality of implemented curriculum (what is taught) and achieved curriculum (what is learned), depending on their location and access to educational resources, quality of teachers and educational administration, and community support. These schools are under the supervision of the Department.

Other public schools like laboratory schools of state universities and colleges, and some vocational/technical schools differ from regular schools in terms of purpose and institution managing them. The laboratory school, run by a state college/university, tries out educational innovations of the institution, has its own curriculum, and serves as a school mainly for the faculty and staff. The state colleges and universities are under the supervision of the Commission on Higher Education.

Public vocational schools are administered by the Department of Education (DepEd). Some technical schools are privately-administered. Their curriculum is the prescribed Basic Education Curriculum with some vocational/technical applications.

Public science high schools have a science-oriented curriculum, distinct from the curriculum of regular public high schools. Furthermore, the Philippine Science High School System is under the Department of Science and Technology and not governed by DepEd polices. The regional science high schools, other public science high schools, and the Philippine High School for the Arts (for the gifted in the arts), are all supervised by DepEd..

Private elementary and high schools are required to have as a minimum/core curriculum the Basic Education Curriculum prescribed by DepEd. Various kinds of entities/institutions establish and operate private schools, resulting in different vision-mission, curriculum orientation (e.g., religious or secular), and admission policies (e.g., exclusively for girls or boys). The quality of teachers and facilities often reflects the thrusts and financial capability of the schools.

Decisions about Admitting Students

Article XIV, Section 6 of the 1987 Philippine Constitution states that admission to any private school is open to all students who meet its specific standards, requirements and regulations as indicated in printed materials. Similarly, the public school system is open to all students who meet set standards.

Although elementary education is compulsory, children seeking admission to a public school have to meet its standards (e.g., minimum entry age of 6 years old for an elementary school). Private schools can have additional admission criteria like passing an entrance examination. Regular public schools have no entrance examination. Moreover, private schools have fees determined by their board of trustees or management.[6]

A student's failure to satisfy academic standards of a school is a legal ground for the school refusing re-admission of the student. Violation of school rules is another ground for denying a student's re-admission.

Decisions about Staff

Hiring, deployment, development and promotion of public school teachers are covered by guidelines of the Department of Education. Regional Offices of the Department oversee the recruitment, selection and appointment of public school

6 Sarmiento, 1995.

teachers to ensure that the most qualified applicants are hired, pursuant to the guidelines. The Division offices in each region and the school heads implement the guidelines.

Applicants without teaching experience are ranked according to: Licensure Examination for Teachers (30 percent), interview (30 percent), education (30 percent), and work experience (10 percent). For applicants with teaching experience: Licensure Examination for Teachers (30 percent), teaching experience (30 percent), interview (30 percent), and education (10 percent).

In giving teacher assignments in public elementary or secondary schools, priority is given to bona fide residents of a community where the school is located, provided the teacher meets the minimum qualification for the position (Republic Act No. 8190). Promotion of teaching and non-teaching staff in public schools is governed by rules and guidelines of the Civil Service Commission. Conditions of employment of non-teaching staff are also in accord with labor laws and regulations.

Private schools need to observe labor laws and regulations for the employment conditions of their teachers and non-teaching staff. However, school management, in consultation with its board of trustees, has greater flexibility in hiring, deployment, promotion and development of teachers and other staff.

In selecting teachers, public schools require formal qualifications, a Bachelor's Degree in Education for high school teaching and a Bachelor's Degree in Elementary Education for elementary school teaching. Applicants should have passed the Licensure Examination for Teachers.

In addition to these qualifications, private faith-based schools require applicants to sign a contract which states that they will abide by the philosophy and religious practices of the school. Applicants of a similar religious affiliation/persuasion are given preference.

A study of the Department of Education on Teacher Effectiveness (TEEP, 2002b) proposed a teacher appraisal system that is guided by meritocracy, integrity, and transparency. The appraisal system for teacher selection, promotion, deployment and development includes objective criteria, tried out instruments, systematic procedures, and committees (instead of only one education official) involved in appraisal and decision-making. The appraisal system covers four stages of professional development that emerged from the data, namely: beginning teacher stage, experienced teacher stage, expert teacher stage, and near-retirement stage.

Accountability for School Quality

Compliance with the law, continuous assessment of quality of education provided, and working towards improvement of teaching practice are among the measures implemented by the Department of Education to ensure school quality.

The curriculum for elementary and secondary levels is formulated by the Bureau of Elementary Education and Bureau of Secondary Education through a consultative process with stakeholders and experts. Teachers use the curriculum guide in planning and implementing daily lesson plans. The Regional Supervisor for each discipline and the Division Supervisor oversee the proper implementation of the intended curriculum. School principals or heads check lesson plans of teachers.

Private schools may modify or enrich the national curriculum based on their school's philosophy and vision-mission. A well-articulated curricular program is one requirement of the Department of Education in granting permits to private schools to operate.

The Department likewise regulates use of instructional materials, especially textbooks. A textbook committee examines the textbooks for general readability, accuracy and relevance of content, and appropriateness of strategies. The Department approves textbooks and other materials used in public schools and oversees distribution of selected textbooks for nationwide use. Private schools, on the other hand, are given the option to choose their textbooks and other instructional materials.
The Department has a training arm, the National Educators Academy of the Philippines, that conducts or supervises national in-service training for elementary and secondary school teachers. In addition, each region, division or school, at the initiative of its head, conducts training programs for teachers based on training needs assessment.

Evaluation of students is done periodically to determine if students meet the requirements for the grade or year level. Students who pass 75 percent of the requirements, as indicated by formal and informal measures, are promoted to the next grade or year level. Those who fall short of the passing level are retained. Students who complete the requirements of the 6-year elementary education receive a certificate and move on to the secondary level. Similarly, students who meet the requirements of the four-year secondary education receive a certificate and can move on to tertiary level.

National achievement tests had been administered for several years to Grade 6 and Grade 10 students. Recently, achievement tests were given to Grades 4 and 7, partly due to international tests in science and mathematics given at those grade levels in the country.

An overall school quality process is school accreditation. Private elementary and high schools apply for accreditation by the Philippine Association for the Accreditation of Schools, Colleges and Universities. The Department of Education has piloted a similar process for the public elementary and secondary schools.

An incentive system tested for high-performing public elementary and secondary public schools (TEEP, 2002c) has the following basic components: (1) vision-mission/school culture, (2) supervision and administration, (3) curriculum and instruction, (4) school facilities, (5) school and community partnership, (6) teacher performance, and (7) learner outcomes. As in the private school accreditation process, the piloted system has three levels, with Level 3 as the highest level that is valid for five years. One recommendation is the implementation of the incentive system by an independent body composed of education officials from public and private sectors.

Teaching of Values

The teaching of values in the public school system had been for decades mainly in the subject, Good Manners and Right Conduct, now generally called Values Education. In private schools, the subject is Christian Living, which integrates religious beliefs for sectarian schools.

The values education curriculum for public high schools (Grades 7-10) in the nineties focused on the self, others, country and God. Student performance, using a multiple-choice values self-inventory based on real-life dilemma situations, increased significantly from Grade 7 to Grade 10.[7] Average performance of high school students in the inventory was significantly higher than that of a college sample, with the college student mean scores declining from lower to upper years.

In the current school curriculum, the teaching of values is embedded in the subject, *Makabayan*, where values are integrated in areas such as social studies, art education, music and physical education. Values integration is also encouraged in other subjects, namely, Science, Mathematics, English and Filipino, wherever appropriate.

References

CBSI Editorial Staff, *New Corporation Code of the Philippines and the Revised Securities Act*, Manila: Central Book Supply, 1996.

Constitutional Commission, *ThConstitution of the Republic of the Philippines*, Quezon City: Constitutional Commission, 1986.

7 UNESCO Philippines, 1997.

Department of Education, *Makabayan* Curriculum Integrating Values Education. Metro Manila: Department of Education, 2002.

Department of Education Orders
No. 2, s. 2002. Guidelines on the Hiring of Public School Teachers.
No. 29, s. 2002. Merit Selection Plan of the Department of Education.

Project for International Education Research, *Workshop Report: A Study of the Educational System of the Philippines*, Washington, D.C.: PIER, 2001.

National Statistical Coordination Board, *2002 Philippine StatisticalYearbook*. Manila: NSCB, 2002.

Sarmiento, Ulpiano III, *Manual of Regulations for Private Schools*. Quezon City: Risen Publishing, 1995.

Third Elementary Education Project, *Cluster 4.2 Study, Final Report on Cost-Effectiveness and Institutionalization of the Multi-grade Program in Public Elementary Schools*, Study conducted by the University of the Philippines College of Education for the Department of Education, 2002a..
--------, *Cluster 7.1 Study, Final Report on Teacher Effectiveness*, Study conducted by the University of the Philippines National Institute for Science and Mathematics Education for the Department of Education, 2002b.
--------, Cluster *7.2 Study, Final Report on the Incentive System for High Performing Public Elementary Schools*, Study conducted by the University of the Philippines National Institute for Science and Mathematics Education for the Department of Education, 2002c.

UNESCO Philippines Project, *Final Report on the Evaluation of the Implementation of the DECS Secondary Values Education Program in the National Capital Region*, Study conducted by the University of the Philippines College of Education for UNESCO Philippines, 1997.

Qatar

by Louay Constant, Charles A. Goldman, and Gail L. Zellman[1]

Overview

The government education system in Qatar has undergone significant change since 2002, when a comprehensive reform of the education system began. The reform, referred to as *Education for a New Era*, completely overhauled a centralized education system run by a Ministry of Education. Currently, the government system is made up of semi-autonomous Independent schools that run their own day-to-day operations subject to conditions specified in a time-limited contract. There is also a limited voucher-based program that enables eligible students to attend private schools. A Supreme Education Council (SEC), the education policymaking entity of the state, oversees the K-12 system; responsibilities are divided between two institutes, the Education Institute and the Evaluation Institute. The Education Institute is responsible for selecting school leaders for the Independent schools, negotiating the contract and monitoring adherence to it, and providing curricular and instructional support to the Independent schools. The Evaluation Institute is responsible for overseeing the design, development, and administration of the assessment system and reporting data from that system. The Evaluation Institute issues school report cards to help schools make improvements and parents make informed education decisions. The SEC also oversees the Higher Education Institute which provides counseling, manages scholarships, and oversees quality assurance for higher education.

About 80 percent of Qatar's population is comprised of non-citizens who come to the country from many other countries seeking employment. In general, laborers

1 RAND Corporation. The authors' research has been supported by the Supreme Education Council of Qatar. Much of the material in this paper is . derived from two sources: Constant, L., Goldman, C.A., Zellman, G.L., Augustine, C.H., Galama, T, Gonzalez, G, Guarino, C.A., Karam, R, Ryan, G.W., and Salem, H. "Promoting Quality and Variety Through Public Financing of Privately Operated Schools in Qatar. *Journal of School Choice*, Routledge, London, U.K., 2010, and Brewer, D., Augustine, C., Zellman, G.L., Ryan, G., Goldman, C.A., Stasz, C., Constant, L., *Education for a New Era: Design and Implementation of K-12 Education Reform in Qatar*. Santa Monica, CA: RAND-Qatar Policy Institute, 2007. As a result, these sources are not cited explicitly in most places. Address all correspondence to Louay Constant, RAND Corporation, 1776 Main Street, Santa Monica, CA 90407, USA. E-mail: constant@rand.org

do not bring their families, while professional workers do. The government provides free schooling in government schools for all nationals as well as non-nationals who have at least one parent employed by Qatar's government or a government-owned company. For children of other non-nationals, private companies often provide tuition assistance for private school attendance. Qatar requires education up to grade 9 or until a student reaches 18 years of age, whichever comes first (Emiri Decree, 2001). Students generally enter grade 1 (primary school) at age six and remain in primary school through grade 6, when they move to preparatory school (7-9) and then secondary school (10-12). A number of Independent schools and most private schools offer up to two years of Kindergarten beginning at age four. Government schools are gender separated. Boys up to grade 4 and girls in all grades are taught by a mix of Qatari and expatriate female teachers. Boys after grade 4 are taught by male teachers, almost all expatriates, since few Qatari men are teachers.

As shown in Table 1, as of the 2010-2011 Academic Year, total student enrollment in the entire education system (government and private) was just over 180,000. Approximately half (47 percent) of the total student population at that time was enrolled in the government's Independent schools; the rest was enrolled in various private schools: international schools (37 percent), community schools (12 percent), and private Arabic schools (4 percent). The Independent schools are required to implement the national curriculum standards. Arabic is the primary language of instruction, but math and science are taught in English. The private international and community schools administer curricula that originate from their home country or an accredited international body; the private Arabic schools rely on a curriculum similar to that used in the government schools, and teach largely in Arabic.

Table 1. Student Enrollment by School Type (Academic Year 2010-20

School type	Students		Schools	
	Number	%	Number	%
Government				
Independent	85,863	47	170	58
Private				
Arabic	7,916	4	24	8
International	67,193	37	75	26
Community	21,056	12	24	8
Other	190	0.1	1	0.3
Total	**182,218**	**100**	**294**	**100**

Source: Evaluation Institute - Supreme Education Council (2011a), Schools and Schooling in Qatar, 2010-2011.

The Structure of Schooling

Prior to 2002, the Ministry of Education controlled every aspect of school operations. The Ministry developed the curriculum, hired and assigned staff, dictated and enforced standardized instructional approaches, and carried out limited student assessments. Under the new system, Independent schools run their day-to-day operations with Education Institute oversight. The Education Institute approves a school education plan; the operator implements the plan and is held accountable for implementation of the curriculum and for student outcomes.

The new system is built around a framework intended to include the following four elements:

- *Autonomy.* The new, Independent schools operate autonomously, subject to the conditions specified in a time-limited contract granted by the state of Qatar.

- *Accountability.* Independent schools are held accountable to the government through regular audits and reporting mechanisms, as well as through national student assessments, parent feedback, and other measures.

- *Variety.* Interested parties may apply to operate schools, and diverse schooling options are to be offered. Each Independent school is free to specify its educational philosophy and operational plan.

- *Choice.* In the reform design, parents are allowed to select the school that best fits their child's needs. The extent of choice would be very minimal at first because only a small number of Independent schools would open each year. But ultimately, this competition for students and resources is intended to make government-funded schools more responsive to parents' demands.

The Supreme Education Council is headed by a President and a Vice President and no less than seven members with renewable four-year terms. The reform decree specified that the SEC would meet at least four times a year. An Executive Committee made up of a Chairperson, Vice Chairperson, and three other members chosen by the SEC President meets once a month to carry out more direct oversight of the institutes, as well as review strategic plans, ensure implementation of those plans, and preside over any issues that require more immediate decisions.

The Education Institute selects Independent school operators, negotiates and monitors their contracts, and supports Independent schools on an ongoing basis. It also specifies the policies (e.g., regarding admissions, finance, and reporting requirements) that Independent school operators are expected to use as guidelines as they draw up their educational plans, which are required for attaining Independent school status. The Education Institute (through the Private

Schools Office) is also responsible for licensing private schools, a responsibility previously carried out by the Ministry of Education. The Education Institute has the authority to issue vouchers to attend private schools.

The Evaluation Institute is responsible for overseeing the design, development, and administration of the assessment system and reporting data from that system. The Evaluation Institute publicly issues school report cards that describe key aspects of schools, such as school performance, activities offered, and parent satisfaction. These report cards provide information to help parents make more-informed school choices and to assist schools in focusing their attention on areas most in need of improvement.

In general, Independent schools have autonomy to run their day-to-day operations, but they are subject to guidelines in their use of funds, staffing, and implementation of the curriculum as specified in their education plan and Independent School Operating Agreement (ISOA). Each Independent school signs a three-year agreement with the SEC which is renewable at the end of the three-year term.

Initially, the Independent Schools operated in parallel to the Ministry schools, but under a separate governance structure (Figure 1). Each year a certain number of Ministry schools were selected by the Education Institute to become Independent schools, and some newly constructed schools were started as Independent schools. As the number of Independent schools grew and the number of Ministry schools declined, the Ministry of Education was phased out and its functions incorporated into the Education Institute and the Evaluation Institute respectively. The last of the Ministry-run schools (approximately 70 schools) were converted in 2010.

Figure 1. Qatar's Education System Immediately After the Reform (2002-2009)

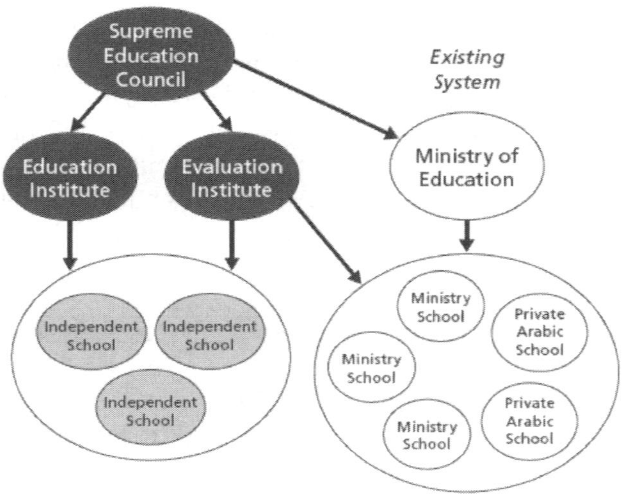

Source: Brewer et al. (2007)

At the outset of the reform, in 2003, the Supreme Education Council commissioned an expert organization to lead the development of new internationally-benchmarked curriculum standards, working closely with Qatari institutions and professionals. Schools were expected to implement the standards using teaching resources from an approved list developed by the Education Institute, but they were given flexibility to use additional resources. The curriculum standards developed for Arabic, English, mathematics and science did not prescribe particular teaching approaches. The reform design emphasized student-centered pedagogy, which put student needs at the center of instructional practice and typically included varied instructional groupings, including small groups and one-on-one instruction (in contrast to the centrally prescribed and teacher-focused lesson plans of the Ministry). To promote opportunities for such student-centered pedagogy, the reform placed a strict limit on class size of 25 students, later expanded to 30 to try to meet the large demand for places (in contrast to the larger Ministry classrooms, which sometimes exceeded 40 students). Schools were also encouraged to expand the pedagogical options available to teachers and to help teachers acquire the skills needed to display them by establishing a school culture marked by flexibility, experimentation, and sensitivity to students' progress and needs.
The Education Institute recognized early on that the new Independent schools would require substantial support in implementing the new curriculum standards and in fundamentally shifting their approach to teaching and learning. To provide this support during the first few years of the reform, the Education Institute contracted with a number of international expert organizations to provide direct support to each new generation of Independent schools. A School Support Organization (SSO) assigned to work daily in each new school advised the school leadership on the design of the school's education plan, worked closely with teaching staff on classroom instruction and group planning, and helped develop and implement in-school teacher training.[2]

In addition to school-based support and training, the Education Institute provides training to Independent school instructional staff. Some of these training programs are full-time for a year. Others are shorter and less intense and often focus on specific subjects. Professional development today is based on the National Professional Standards for Teachers and Leaders (NPSTL), which are internationally benchmarked performance standards for teachers and school leaders. Professional development programs are intended to be aligned with those standards; those organizations that deliver these programs are

[2] In the U.S., these types of organizations are also referred to as Education Management Organizations (EMOs), and are sometimes hired by states or school districts to take over the entire management of poor performing schools. In the Qatar case, the SSOs were contracted to provide support to the existing leadership and instructional staff of the Independent schools. The SSOs were hired by the Education Institute based on their experience working with autonomous schools in their home countries.

expected to be accredited through an articulation agreement with a university or an international accreditation body. The SEC will also be commissioning the development of a national professional qualifications framework that may also be a benchmark for future training programs.[3]

Unlike the Ministry schools where virtually every aspect of school finances was handled centrally, Independent schools develop their own budget, are given operational funds from the Education Institute on a per pupil basis, and are permitted to spend these funds as schools see fit subject to general financial regulations. Schools receive per-pupil funding, disbursed quarterly, for operational expenses based on enrollment levels. The amount given to each school depends on the school's level (primary, preparatory, or secondary), with students with special needs qualifying for 20 percent augmentation of the per-pupil allotment. As of 2007–2008, per-pupil allotments were QAR 18,000 ($4,860) for primary, QAR 19,400 ($5,238) for preparatory, and QAR 21,800 ($5,886) for secondary schools.[4] Schools originally hired and paid teachers; later, teacher payroll was moved from the individual schools to a central system. Now, schools receive a more limited per-pupil allotment to cover non-staff expenses. New schools are given an advance against their first-year operating funds for start-up expenses, such as special equipment or facilities not included in the operating budget.[5]

The Legal Framework

In Qatar, laws are promulgated by Emiri Decree. In November of 2002, the Emir of Qatar, Sheikh Hamad bin Khalifa Al-Thani issued Decree No. 37 that established the Supreme Education Council (SEC) as the overarching education policymaking body with the Education and Evaluation Institutes as the oversight entities. In 2009, Emiri Decree No. 14 was issued as part of a broader government reorganization to bring all government entities in line with Qatar's newly released National Vision 2030. The decree formalized the roles, responsibilities, and authorities of the SEC and its associated institutions, the Education Institute, the Evaluation Institute, and the Higher Education Institute.

In the early years of the *Education for a New Era* reform, policymakers were faced with significant new information and a number of perceived concerns about the reform. In response to these concerns they made several significant policy changes that addressed these concerns while, it was argued, maintaining or enhancing the provision of a high quality education.[6]

3 SEC, 2007a.
4 Guarino et al., 2009.
5 Education Institute, 2004, p. 15.
6 Supreme Education Council, 2006.

Two key changes concerned who could operate Independent schools and their profit status. To promote a variety of schooling options for students, the original reform design allowed any individuals or groups from the community to apply for the position of school operator as part of their proposal to run a school. The first generation of Independent schools included two operator teams from private schools, one from higher education, and the remaining nine were at some time officials or school leaders employed by the Ministry of Education.

The first Independent schools were privately incorporated for-profit companies. Under Qatari law, these companies had to be overseen by a minimum of two owners, one of whom had to be Qatari. Therefore, teams of operators formed, frequently combining a business person with an educator. Policymakers, however, became concerned about the public perception that private enterprise would earn profits educating children (or might have incentives to cut expenses and lower quality) and that non-specialists were in charge of schools. In March 2006, a new policy required that Independent schools be organized as nonprofits with a single operator who is a Qatari national and also the school's principal.[7]

These policy changes have quieted public fears about profit-taking but have reduced the involvement of those from outside the education establishment (i.e., business, industry). Some larger community influence does remain, however, since each Independent school is required to have a Board of Trustees that includes members of the school community who represent business, community, and parent interests.

Freedom to establish non-state schools

Qatar's large foreign expatriate population has driven the establishment of a wide range of private schooling options. As mentioned previously, there are internationally accredited private schools; community schools established by expatriate communities residing in Qatar that implement a home country curriculum; and private Arabic schools that implement a regional or local curriculum in Arabic. Under the Ministry of Education, these schools were required to obtain a license and were subject to site inspections to ensure minimal compliance with safety regulations. The Ministry of Education did not monitor other aspects of operations, but over time Qatari policymakers became concerned about the quality of some of these schools.

Since the *Education for a New* Era reform began 10 years ago, the Supreme Education Council has led various efforts to raise the quality of existing private schools as well as to promote establishment of additional private schooling

7 Supreme Education Council, 2006.

options. The Private Schools Office in the Education Institute issues licenses to private schools, a function previously assigned to the Ministry of Education. To receive a license, private schools must adhere to several conditions: They are required to implement the Qatari curriculum standards, or accredited international curriculum standards, and they must have an assessment system to track student progress.[8]

Private schools generally have considerable discretion to recruit staff as long as candidates meet minimum requirements to carry out their job responsibilities. The Education Institute also inspects private schools facilities, and expects private schools to generally align their schedules with Qatari holidays and the SEC academic year calendar. Private schools also have to get approval for tuition and fees from the SEC.

The SEC requires that Qatari students constitute no less than 25 percent of the student body of the international private schools (not the community schools). Similar to the Independent schools, private schools are required to establish a Board of Trustees. Qatari students in private schools are required to participate in the nationally administered student assessments and surveys overseen by the Evaluation Institute (and schools may extend this participation to all students). Additionally, to enhance, assess, and objectively report on the quality of private education, the Evaluation Institute launched the Qatar National School Accreditation (QNSA) system in 2011.[9] The system provides a quality assurance mechanism for private schools unlikely to be able to gain international accreditation, as is the case with many private Arabic schools.[10] This mechanism permits such schools to become voucher eligible.

To expand high quality private schooling options, the SEC invited internationally reputable schools to establish branch campuses in Qatar through its "Outstanding Schools Program". From 2008 to 2009, three such schools were opened in Qatar with plans for more over the ensuing years.[11]

Home schooling

Home schooling falls under the umbrella "parallel" or "alternative" schooling. Another form of parallel schooling includes "evening" schools, primarily for adult learners who did not complete school during their school-age years. In general, parents and caregivers may home school children if one of two conditions

8 Supreme Education Council, 2012a. Existing private schools were required to establish proof that they implemented the Qatari curriculum standards or internationally accredited curriculum standards by the 2009-2010 academic year.

9 Evaluation Institute - Supreme Education Council, 2011b.

10 Bikson, Moini and Stasz, 2010.

11 Supreme Education Council, 2012b.

stated in the regulations are met: (1) child has extenuating circumstances such as health or medical reasons (including cognitive disabilities) whose special needs cannot be met in a regular classroom/school setting; and (2) child has reached an age for which compulsory schooling no longer applies (over the age covered by compulsory schooling law).[12]

The SEC regulates home schooling in a number of ways. Home schooling curricula are still expected to follow the SEC curriculum standards, and similar to Independent schools, home schools can choose the resources they wish to use as long as they cover the content in the standards. The SEC expects all parallel schooling (evening schools and home schools) to transition to full implementation of the curriculum standards by 2014-2015. Parents or care givers are expected to register each home schooled child at a designated school, and homeschoolers have access to resources and other supports provided by the Education Institute through those schools. According to the SEC, there are just over 3,000 registered homeschooled children. Homeschooled children may participate in the end of year exams administered at the registered school, typically after normal school hours.[13]

School choice not limited by family income

The SEC has had a limited education voucher program in place since 2008. It began as a pilot program that subsidized tuition for Qataris enrolled in a small number of private schools, then expanded to include more schools in 2009-2010, and scaled-up further in the 2012-2013 academic year to include all Qataris enrolled in those eligible private schools. Qatari nationals will be eligible for a QAR 28,000 ($7,560) tuition voucher that they can use to defer private school tuition costs. Currently, this policy is a tuition subsidy for Qatari nationals already enrolled in eligible private schools, but conceivably could be expanded to spur demand for private schooling for families whose children are currently enrolled in the government system. Ultimately, the SEC envisions the education vouchers program to be the overarching framework for providing government education in Qatar.[14]

[12] Education Institute, 2011; SEC, 2011; SEC, 2012c.
[13] Education Institute, 2011; SEC, 2011; SEC, 2012c.
[14] SEC, 2012d.

School distinctiveness protected by law and policy

Distinctive character

Each Independent school is required to submit an education plan that specifies the key elements of school operations (e.g., curriculum, pedagogy, use of technology, professional development plan, assessments plan, etc.). The Education Institute provides a detailed education plan template that Independent school operators are expected to complete and get approved prior to the beginning of the first school year of operations.[15]

Each Independent school, in developing its education plan, is asked to specify the school's vision, mission, and goals, and these are made available on the SEC website.[16] Schools may develop their own unique vision and mission and specify goals, as long as they are aligned with general SEC goals. In the education plan, Independent schools articulate how they expect to reach these goals. The education plan template provides schools with examples of how the school day should be organized, but Independent schools may develop their own daily schedule as long as it meets the minimum time allotments for each subject required by the SEC. The Education Institute reviews all of the Independent school plans to verify that minimum requirements have been met. For example, the Curriculum Standards Office reviews the curriculum plans of all Independent schools and verifies that they meet the requirements for achieving the national curriculum standards. All Independent schools must obtain approval on their curriculum plan prior to start of operations.
Compared to the previous system under the Ministry of Education, Independent schools have more room to develop their own distinctive character. Some schools have developed a distinctive character because of strong leadership and a supportive staff, while other Independent schools do not demonstrate a unique curricular or pedagogical approach. The rapid conversion of all Ministry schools to Independent status has made it challenging to provide enough encouragement to newly Independent schools to support their departure from Ministry approaches; some newly Independent schools did not wish to change anything at all. More time is needed to develop a cadre of school leaders and teachers who are willing to do things differently.[17]

Decisions about admitting pupils

The Education Institute has established criteria for student admissions to Independent schools; school operators must agree to comply with specific

---

[15] Supreme Education Council, 2010a.
[16] Supreme Education Council, 2012e.
[17] Zellman et al., 2009; Guarino et al., 2009.

enrollment priorities. Eligibility for government schooling in Qatar is limited to Qatari nationals, Gulf Cooperation Council (GCC) nationals, children of government employees (including government-owned companies), children of employees of certain non-governmental organizations, and children with disabilities.[18] Families who are not eligible under these conditions can apply for enrollment in a government school, but must pay certain fees.[19] Otherwise, government schooling is free for all eligible students. First preference for admission is given to students already enrolled in the Ministry school before its conversion to an Independent school. If spaces remain, Qatari nationals, regardless of where they live, can gain admission. Non-Qatari nationals who live within the school catchment area, siblings of already enrolled students, and children of school employees are given next admissions consideration. Independent schools are not permitted to use the results of assessments in their admissions procedures.[20] Independent schools enrolling students with disabilities are required to make provisions for those students based on a Supreme Education Council policy framework on additional educational support needs.[21] The Supreme Education Council is also expanding Technical and Vocational Education and Training (TVET) options for students by opening two new schools.

In terms of admissions to private schools, as mentioned previously, enrollment in private schools must be at least 25 percent Qatari. This does not apply to community schools which follow the curriculum of their home country. Otherwise, private schools are free to develop their own admissions criteria.

Decisions about staff

The Education Institute issues staffing guidelines that the Independent schools must abide by. Independent schools may recruit their own staff, but the Education Institute ultimately approves all hires. The staffing guidelines are specified in the education plan template that the Education Institute provides to operators as well as in the personnel bylaws.[22] In the education plan template, minimum staffing requirements are set based on school size, number of buildings, and grade levels. Independent schools must specify staffing roles and responsibilities, and develop a staffing plan that is consistent with both Education Institute guidelines and Qatari labor law that specifies working hours, holidays, and both employer and employee rights and responsibilities.[23]

---

18 For detailed requirements see Supreme Education Council 2012f.
19 SEC, 2012f.
20 SEC, 2010a.
21 Supreme Education Council, 2009.
22 SEC, 2010a; SEC, 2012g.
23 SEC, 2010a.

The personnel bylaws specify compensation requirements for Qatari nationals, as well as general guidelines that employers must follow in managing their personnel. Qatari nationals have additional rights and benefits with which Independent schools must comply. For example, Independent schools must adhere to a minimum salary and benefits scale for Qatari nationals; these rules do not apply to non-Qatari individuals who schools hire locally or from abroad.[24]

These personnel policies have evolved over time. Initially, first generation operators had the freedom to recruit teachers from any country to fulfill teaching and staffing needs. For example, five of the 12 first generation schools hired native English speakers because English is the language of instruction in mathematics and science. It was expected that these teachers would be more expensive; operators had to budget accordingly. By the second generation, however, the government's Qatarization policy, which aims to promote employment of Qataris in local firms, set target levels for Qatari staff in Independent schools. As mentioned above, targets differ by level and type of school in recognition of the different balances of Qatari and expatriate teachers available to teach boys and girls at different ages; targets ranged from 20 percent in boys' secondary schools to 70 percent in girls' secondary schools.[25] Independent schools are expected to make best efforts to meet Qatarization targets in their recruitment and retention of Qatari teachers.

In addition to Qatarization goals, a 40 percent increase in the base salary of Qatari nationals in the Civil Service was instituted in September 2007 in response to nationwide increases in the cost of living, driven largely by increases in the price of real estate. To fund the mandated salary increases, the SEC increased per-pupil allotments by QAR 2,000 for all primary schools and by QAR 1,000 for preparatory girls' and secondary girls' schools, beginning in 2007–2008. These increases are meant to "encourage more Qatari involvement in the reform initiative" and "ensure that Qatari staff in independent schools enjoy the same living standards as their partners in other official sectors."[26] Later, all teacher employment and pay was moved to a central administration and removed from the per-pupil allocation, although schools continue to exercise substantial choice in the initial selection of their new teachers.

Accountability for school quality

In principle, the Reform is designed to depend on market forces to foster schools' accountability for performance. To provide the information required to inform the market, policy makers, and the schools themselves, the Evaluation Institute utilizes the Qatar National Education Data System (QNEDS), which

---

24 SEC, 2012g.

25 Supreme Education Council, 2005.

26 Supreme Education Council, 2007b.

incorporates national tests in Arabic, English, mathematics, and science for grades 3 through 12 as well as a comprehensive set of surveys administered annually to all principals, teachers, students (above grade 3), and parents. Qatar has also participated in a number of international student assessments. Since 2006, Qatar has participated in the Programme for International Student Assessment (PISA) and the Progress in International Reading Literacy (PIRLS). Since 2007, Qatar has also participated in the Trends in International Mathematics and Science Study (TIMSS). All schools that teach in Arabic or English (whether government or private) are required to participate in these international assessments.
In the country's initial participation in the international assessments, overall performance was low. Qatar ranked near the bottom of country rankings in TIMSS 2007 math and science and 2006 PIRLS, and Qatar's first participation in PISA 2006 showed similarly low performance in reading, math, and science.[27] Qatar's scores improved in the 2009 PISA administration with overall average scale scores increasing in all three subjects: science (30 points), math (50 points), and reading (60 points).[28] Nonetheless, Qatar's overall performance remains well below the OECD average, and increased efforts are required to bring performance on par with other wealthy nations.[29] Qatar participated in the 2011 TIMSS and PIRLS administrations, but those results have not been released yet; Qatar is currently participating in the 2012 administration of PISA.

In addition to results from the international assessments, the Evaluation Institute publishes annual school report cards that provide information on average grade-level national and international test scores, parent and student satisfaction, and school program and facility offerings. These report cards were at first issued for Ministry, private Arabic, and Independent schools, allowing parents to make an informed choice as to the best school for each child. More recently, the report cards also include other private schools. Funding follows the student: if operators cannot attract students, in theory, their budgets should be reduced and they may be forced to close or turn over operation of the school to another operator.

In addition, the Evaluation Institute carries out a Triennial School Review (TSR) – an in-depth review of each Independent school conducted once every three years. A team from the Evaluation Institute carries out a site visit and selects five to seven areas (out of 20) to focus on in the assessment. The Evaluation Institute team speaks to staff, students, and parents, observes classrooms, and studies learning materials. Areas looked at include "school leadership and management, teaching and learning, standards and achievements, curriculum and learning environment, staffing deployment and development, and the

27 Mullis et al., 2008; Martin et al., 2008; Mullis et al., 2007; OECD, 2007.
28 OECD, 2007; OECD, 2010.
29 SEC, 2010b.

relationship between parents, community, and the school."[30] The Evaluation Institute produces a public report of its findings on each school.

The Education Institute issues each operator a three-year renewable contract. As there was no information at first on which to calibrate appropriate performance goals, the SEC decided that for the first generations of Independent schools, they would not specify performance goals. The SEC has not introduced such goals into later contracts as a condition for renewal but does consider performance on the national tests in making renewal decisions. Additionally, schools deemed well-performing are granted greater autonomy, while schools that are not performing as well are more closely monitored.

In addition to tracking of outcomes-based information, school budgets are subject to some spending controls. The Education Institute holds schools fiscally accountable through a monitoring process that tracks school expenditures and operator's resource allocation decisions. Three methods apply: external audits, the establishment of an internal monitoring system at each school, and a set of guidelines and requirements to which schools must adhere. Internal monitoring systems must include a set of policies and procedures regarding financial matters, a budget development calendar, a computer-based accounting system, a system for payroll services, and banking arrangements. Mandatory budget guidelines include ways to use any surpluses, financial operations, and salary floors for Qatari staff. Schools submit reports throughout the year directly to the Education Institute so that it can assess compliance with these guidelines and work with schools to ensure that they are in compliance with the above reporting requirements.[31]

Teaching of values

According to the ISOA, Independent schools are expected to abide by certain conditions, including adopting the customs, traditions, and principles of Qatari society. All Independent schools are expected to include as part of their core curriculum Islamic Education, Arabic language, and Social Studies with a focus on Qatari history.[32]

Private school curricula may not contradict Qatari values and morals. Private school curricula must promote the national identity of Qatari students.[33] By 2010-2011, all private schools had to set aside a minimum number of hours to teach Arabic to Arabic-speaking students and Islamic Studies to Muslim students and Qatari history to all students.

[30] SEC, 2012h.
[31] Guarino et al., 2009, p. 49.
[32] SEC, 2010.
[33] Supreme Education Council, 2012a.

Conclusions

Qatari policymakers' pursuit of an ambitious reform of the government school system has significantly changed the country's education landscape. Once dominated by Ministry-run government schools and community schools for the significant expatriate communities residing in the country, Qatar's education system today includes Independent schools, internationally-accredited and well-respected private schools, and a tuition vouchers program that may spur further expansion of the private school system. Independent schools have benefited from an internationally-benchmarked curriculum that holds students to performance standards while encouraging well-trained teachers to meet the needs of individual students. A comprehensive data system enables parents and other stakeholders to assess their own child's progress and to evaluate which schools best align with their child's needs. However, parental choice is limited at this time since most Independent schools are oversubscribed. Other efforts to modernize the education system include plans to launch an e-learning initiative that allows teachers to place instructional content online for students and parents to access readily through the internet.[34]

The infrastructure that supports the reform has also been enhanced. Over the past five years, the country has developed and adopted a Qatar National Vision (QNV) 2030 based on four pillars: human development, social development, economic development, and environmental development. This vision provides the framework within which all sectors, including education, will operate. The Supreme Education Council has overseen the development of an Education and Training Sector Strategy (ETSS) linked to the National Vision that outlines desired outcomes, associated initiatives to achieve those outcomes, and indicators to track progress. The ETSS outlines major initiatives intended to expand compulsory schooling to grade 12, revise the K-12 curriculum to better address Qatar's social and economic needs, modernize adult basic education, and expand vocational options and pathways through the education system.

The challenge now, as the reform encompasses all government and many private schools, is to support the system's new strengths and resist a return to the old ways with which many are comfortable. Making the necessary improvements will require substantial effort driven by an informed understanding of the reform's progress. Fortunately for the children of Qatar, resources are available and mechanisms are in place to make this happen. The emphasis on quality and human capital development in the QNV 2030 and the accompanying ETSS lays out a plan that leads the way forward. The Evaluation Institute's data system and school report cards, coupled with

34 Supreme Education Council, 2012i.

the establishment of a monitoring process for the reform itself, will enable educators and policymakers to continue to shape and improve education and pursue the ambitious goals of the reform.

References

Bikson, T. K., C. Stasz, and J. S. Moini. "Raising Private School Quality Through Accreditation: The Case of Qatar," paper presented at the 2010 American Educational Research Association (AERA) Annual Meeting, Denver, 2010.Brewer, D. J., Augustine, C. H., Zellman, G. L., Ryan, G., Goldman, C. A., Stasz, C., & Constant, L. (2007). Education for a new era: Design and implementation of K–12 education reform in Qatar. Santa Monica, CA: RAND Corporation. Retrieved from http://www.rand.org/pubs/monographs/MG548

Constant, L., Goldman, C.A., Zellman, G.L., Augustine, C.H., Galama, T, Gonzalez, G, Guarino, C.A., Karam, R, Ryan, G.W., and Salem, H. (2010). "Promoting Quality and Variety Through Public Financing of Privately Operated Schools in Qatar. Journal of School Choice, Routledge, London, U.K.

Emiri Decree, Law No. 25 for Year 2001 Regarding Compulsory Education, Doha, Qatar.

Education Institute. (2004). Finance handbook. Doha, Qatar: Author.

Education Institute (2011). Memorandum on Law 2 for Year 2011: Parallel Education Policy.

Evaluation Institute - Supreme Education Council. (2011a) Schools and Schooling in Qatar 2010-2011: A Statistical Overview of Aspects of Schools and Schooling in Qatar, Doha, Qatar (Retrieved on July 8th, 2012 from http://www.education.gov.qa/EVI/SchoolingReport/English-10-11.pdf).
Evaluation Institute – Supreme Education Council. (2011b). "Qatar National School Accreditation (QNSA)," presentation given at the Launch Meeting for QNSA, Doha, 2011.

Guarino, C. M., Galama, T., Constant, L., Gonzalez, G., Tanner, J. C., & Goldman, C.A. (2009). Developing a school finance system for K–12 reform in Qatar. Santa Monica, CA: RAND Corporation. Retrieved from http://www.rand.org/pubs/monographs/MG839

Martin, M. O., Mullis, I. V. S., & Foy, P. (with Olson, J. F., Erberber, E., Preuschoff, C., & Galia, J.). (2008). TIMSS 2007 international science report: Findings from IEA's Trends in International Mathematics and

Science Study at the fourth and eighth grades. Chestnut Hill, MA: TIMSS & PIRLS International Study Center Boston College.

Mullis, I. V. S., Martin, M. O., Foy, P., (with Olson, J., Preuschoff, C., Erberber, E., Arora, A. & Galia, J.) (2008). TIMSS 2007 international mathematics report: Findings from IEA's Trends in International Mathematics and Science Study at the fourth and eighth grades. Chestnut Hill, MA: TIMSS & PIRLS International Study Center Boston College.

Mullis, I. V.S., Martin, M. O., Kennedy, A. M., and Foy P. (2007), Chestnut Hill, MA: TIMSS & PIRLS International Study Center, Boston College.

OECD. (2007). PISA 2006: Science Competencies for Tomorrow's World, Volume 1: Analysis. OECD. (Retrieved on July 31, 2012 from http://www.oecd.org/pisa/pisaproducts/pisa2006/pisa2006results.htm#Vol_1_and_2).

OECD. (2010). PISA 2009 at a Glance. Programme for International Student Assessment, OECD Publishing (Retrieved on July 31, 2012 from http://dx.doi.org/10.1787/9789264095298-en).

Supreme Education Council. (2005). Public concerns about independent schools clarified. (Retrieved on July 8th, 2012 from http://www.english.education.gov.qa/content/resources/detail/2195).

Supreme Education Council. (2006). New policies correct system's weaknesses and support reform. (Retrieved on July 8th, 2012 from http://www.english.education.gov.qa/content/resources/detail/3568).

Supreme Education Council (2007a). National Professional Standards for School Teachers and Leaders. (Retrieved on July 16, 2012 from http://www.english.education.gov.qa/content/resources/detail/4532).

Supreme Education Council. (2007b). Independent schools budget is increased. (Retrieved on July 8th, 2012 from http://www.english.education.gov.qa/content/resources/detail/4657).

Supreme Education Council. (2009). Additional Educational Support Needs: Learning Difficulties, Disabilities, and Behaviour Support. A Pack of Policies, Guidance Documents and Support Materials for Schools, June 2009.

Supreme Education Council (2010a), Al Khita Al Taaleemiya Al Istratijiya 2010-2011, Madrasat ______ Al Thanawiya Al Mustaqila Lil Banat, Strategic Education Plan 2010-2011, __________ Secondary Girls Independent School: School Operator, February 28th, 2010 [sample education plan].

Supreme Education Council (2010b). Qatar's PISA 2009 Results, A Positive Indicator. (Retrieved July 31, 2012 from http://www.english.education.gov.qa/content/resources/detail/12676).

Supreme Education Council (2011). Khitat Marhaliya Li Tatweer Al Taaleem Al Muwazi Tatamasha Maa Istratijiyat Al Tanmiya Al Wataniya, Phased Plans to Develop Parallel Education Consistent with National Development Plan.

Supreme Education Council (2012a). Conditions and Requirements for Obtaining a License for a Private School, Doha, Qatar. (Retrieved on July 8th, 2012 from http://www.english.education.gov.qa/section/sec/education_institute/pso).

Supreme Education Council (2012b), Qatar's Outstanding Schools Program. Retrieved July 8, 2012 from http://www.english.education.gov.qa/section/sec/education_institute/pso/_outstandingschools.

Supreme Education Council (2012c), Al Taaleem Al Muwazi, Parallel Education. Retrieved July 8, 2012 from http://www.education.gov.qa/section/sec/education_institute/_alternativeeducation.

Supreme Education Council (2012d), Al Siyasat Al Munathama Lil Qasaem Al Taalimiya, Organizing Policy for Education Vouchers. Retrieved July 8, 2012 from http://www.sec.gov.qa/vouchers/Polices.pdf.

Supreme Education Council (2012e), Independent Schools. Retrieved July 8, 2012 from http://www.english.education.gov.qa/schools/EISsearch.htm.

Supreme Education Council (2012f), Admissions Policy. Retrieved July 8, 2012 from http://www.english.education.gov.qa/section/sec/education_institute/admission.

Supreme Education Council (2012g), Guiding Articles for the Personnel Bylaws. Retrieved July 8, 2012 from http://www.english.education.gov.qa/section/sec/education_institute/newrules.

Supreme Education Council (2012h), Review of Independent Schools. Retrieved July 8, 2012 from http://www.english.education.gov.qa/section/sec/evaluation_institute/seo/_is_review.

Supreme Education Council (2012i). Thirty Independent Schools Apply for E-Learning Portal LMS Project. Retrieved July 16, 2012 from http://www.english.education.gov.qa/content/resources/detail/16510.

Zellman, G. L., Ryan, G. W., Karam, R., Constant, L., Salem, H., Gonzalez, G., Goldman, C.A., Al-Thani, H., Al-Obaidii, K. (2009). Implementation of the K–12 education reform in Qatar's schools. Santa Monica, CA: RAND Corporation. Retrieved from http://www.rand.org/pubs/monographs/MG880.

South Africa

by Rika Joubert[1] and Willem van Vollenhoven[2]
with Johan Beckmann and Justus Prinsloo

Overview

It is common knowledge that South Africa went through a profound transformation in 1994. The transformation and events following in its wake were guided by a new constitution and a new legal framework for every sector of public life, including education. The system is still "far from equilibrium", which makes describing it very challenging.

The Postscript (under the heading National Unity and Reconciliation) to the Constitution of the Republic of South Africa, Act 200 of 1993 (the so-called "Interim Constitution") (since repealed by the Constitution of 1996 (Act 108 of 1996) probably articulates the expectations, hopes and fears that South Africans carried into the post 1994 era best:

This Constitution provides a historic bridge between the past of a deeply divided society characterised by strife, conflict, untold suffering and injustice, and a future founded on the recognition of human rights, democracy and peaceful co-existence and development opportunities for all South Africans, irrespective of colour, race, class, belief or sex. The pursuit of national unity, the well-being of all South African citizens and peace require reconciliation between the people of South Africa and the reconstruction of society.

The adoption of this Constitution lays the secure foundation for the people of South Africa to transcend the divisions and strife of the past, which generated gross violations of human rights, the transgression of humanitarian principles in violent conflicts and a legacy of hatred, fear, guilt and revenge.

These can now be addressed on the basis that there is a need for understanding but not for vengeance, a need for reparation but not for retaliation, a need for ubuntu [*ED: humanity or humanness*] but not for victimisation.

---

1 Director of the Interuniversity Centre for Education Law and Policy and Associate Professor at the University of Pretoria

2 Associate Professor at the University of North-West

The education sector is also shaped by the subsequent constitution of 1996, education and other relevant legislation, common law and case law as well as by policy. Due to the fact that the Constitution and the suite of laws that accompanied it were to a degree the result of a political compromise and, due to the very nature of compromises, all the laws relevant to education have undergone regular amendments since 1994. They now look significantly different from their original forms. Since 1996 and up to 2009 the Constitution has gone through 19 amendments while the South African Schools Act 84 of 1996 has been amended 8 times since 1996 (and a new set of amendments was approved by Parliament early in 2011).

Prior to 1994, the administrative structures responsible for education in the country were a direct function of the political system which had applied up to that time. Separate education administrations and schools for "Black, Coloureds, Indians and Whites" existed in those areas of the country which had not been cut up into smaller homeland areas, and that separate administrations for education existed in the territories at that time described as Bophuthatswana, Ciskei, Gazankulu, KaNgwane, KwaNdebele, KwaZulu, Lebowa, QwaQwa, Transkei, and Venda. There were therefore fourteen education administrations, some of which had been further subdivided on a provincial basis, giving as many as eighteen education administrations in addition to the administration at national level, which had to be parceled out between the nine provinces which were established after the 1994 elections.

Since 1994, the government has worked to transform all facets of the education system. The fragmented and racially duplicated institutions of the *Apartheid* era have been replaced by a single national system including nine provincial sub-systems. Consistent and persistent efforts are being made to make education structurally accessible to all who were previously denied, or had limited access to it, and thus to realise the ideal of nine years of compulsory schooling. Marginalised or vulnerable groups have received particular attention in the form of inclusive education programmes. Most recently, "no fee" schools have assisted indigent learners[3] into schools.

Moreover, education financing has been redirected specifically towards considerations of equity, redress, accessibility and affordability. School governance has been decentralised, with greater autonomy devolved onto school governing bodies (including the right to charge fees). Educators' qualifications have been improved. A new curriculum high on knowledge and skills and based on the values of the *Constitution* has been introduced and streamlined and procedures set in place to monitor educational quality.

The higher education system has been reformed and rationalised, and a new

3 In South Africa the term 'learners' is used for pupils and students

further education and training system is being established. In the space of seventeen years, a far more equitable, efficient and better quality system of education has been created.

Each of the nine provinces has a provincial legislature, which is created in terms of section 104 of the *Constitution the Republic of South Africa*[4]. The provincial legislature is empowered to pass laws on those matters over which the province exercises either complete or concurrent jurisdiction. It is therefore possible for a provincial legislature to adopt a provincial Act or Acts regulating policy information for, and the provision of, education within the province in question. A highly important function of a provincial education department is that it is responsible for the provision of education in provincial education institutions, as well as for the regulation of those institutions which are not public institutions, excluding institutions for higher education.

South Africa's political philosophy and goals are reflected in its schools. The enormous political changes which have occurred and equally fundamental social changes which are occurring in the country have faced the schools with daunting challenges, complicated by budgetary limitations.
The Structure of Schooling

In terms of section 104(1) of the *Constitution* education is a concurrent competence in South Africa, but what is interesting is that only certain aspects of education are described as "concurrent" competences. The provision of schooling is a provincial matter, subject to any norms and standards for the provision of schooling as laid down by the Minister of Basic Education in the national sphere.

The White Paper on Education and Training (Government Notice 196 of 1995) remains the most comprehensive and authoritative articulation of the government's education policy. White Paper presents the values and principles that should, in the view of the then Ministry of Education, drive national policy and these include:

1. The necessity to reconstruct and develop education and training due to the legacy of apartheid. This implies the need for redress of educational inequalities among the sections of the people who have suffered particular disadvantages, or who are especially vulnerable.
2. Education and training are basic human rights. The state has an obligation to protect and advance these rights, so that all citizens irrespective of race, class, gender, creed or age, have the opportunity to develop their capacities and potential, and make their full contribution to the society.
3. Parents or guardians have the primary responsibility for the education of their children, and have the right to be consulted by the state authorities with respect to the form that education should take and to take part in its governance.

4 Act 108 of 1996

Parents have an inalienable right to choose the form of education which is best for their children, particularly in the early years of schooling, whether provided by the state or not, subject to reasonable safeguards which may be required by law. The parents' right to choose includes choice of the language, cultural or religious basis of the child's education, with due regard for the rights of others and the rights of choice of the growing child.

4. The state has an obligation to provide advice and counseling on education services by all practicable means.
5. The system must increasingly open access to education and training opportunities of good quality, to all children, youth and adults, and provide the means for learners to move easily from one learning context to another, so that the possibilities for lifelong learning are enhanced.
6. The state's resources must be deployed according to the principle of equity, so that they are used to provide essentially the same quality of learning opportunities for all citizens.
7. The principle of democratic governance should increasingly be reflected in every level of the system, by the involvement in consultation and appropriate forms of decision-making of elected representatives of the main stakeholders, interest groups and role players.
8. The creation of a culture of accountability.
9. The active encouragement of mutual respect for people's diverse religious, cultural and language traditions, their right to enjoy and practice these in peace and without hindrance, and the recognition that these are a source of strength for their own communities and the unity of the nation.
10. The education system must counter the legacy of violence
11. The curriculum, teaching methods and textbooks at all levels and in all programmes of education and training, should encourage independent and critical thought.

General education and training is regulated in the first instance in the national sphere by the *South African Schools Act 84 of 1996*. This Act seeks to provide a uniform basis for the provision of schooling in all the public schools of the nation. Provincial education departments may, if they wish, pass additional legislation regulating the operation of schools within their provinces, but in terms of the principle of concurrence these must be consistent with the law in the national sphere.

Education in South Africa can be broken down into the following sectors/bands[5]:

- early childhood development (ECD);
- general education and training (GET), consisting of:
- grade R to grades one to three (the Foundation Phase)
- grades four to six (the Intermediate Phase)

5 OECD, p. 47

- grades seven to nine (the Senior Phase)
- further education and training (FET), including grades 10 to 12;
- adult basic education and training (ABET);
- special needs education (SNE);
- higher education (HE).

Schooling is compulsory for all children from the year in which they turn seven to the end of the year in which they turn fifteen (or the end of grade nine, whichever comes first)[6]. A National Qualifications Framework (NQF) integrates education and training at all levels.

In South Africa in 2010, there were 30,586 established public and registered independent education institutions. Of these, 25,850 were ordinary schools and 4,736 were other education institutions – namely, ECD centres and special schools. In 2010, there were 12,644,208 learners and students in the basic education system, who attended 30,586 education institutions and were served by 439,394 educators.[7]

South Africa's annual education budget is already 22 percent of the total state expenditure which is high compared to other countries where the norm is in the order of 16 percent. Nevertheless, in terms of the population growth and other related educational factors (for example, the state of serious disrepair of physical resources in disadvantaged schools and the uneven teacher qualifications), the potential for increased demands for education is very real and South Africa will most likely not escape the harsh realities of providing mass education with ever diminishing financial resources[8].

Government's aim has been to restructure the entire education system and overcome its racial, gender and anti-poor bias. But while constitutional imperatives directed the trajectory of change, the chosen policy mechanisms were often the result of intense political contestation between various educational and other interest groups, especially big business and organised labour. Debates on the effectiveness of education policy since 1994 have revolved around whether policy is insufficiently ambitious, given what is seen as an inconsequential emphasis on redress, or insufficiently practical, given historical and economic limitations and incapacities.

Curriculum reform in South Africa has been of a scale arguably unparalleled in the history of curriculum change[9]. Overturning the curriculum of the *Apartheid* government and replacing it with one that supported a human rights-

6 S. 5 of South African Schools Act, 1996
7 Department of Basic Education, 2012
8 OECD, p. 37
9 OECD, p. 169

based education was an immediate systemic challenge for the *post-Apartheid* government.

The Legal Framework

Neither of these *standard* models has been followed by the drafters of the *Constitution.*
Rather they adopted for South Africa a governmental structure that is based on the principle of “co-operative government” under which each *sphere* (not *level*) of government (national, provincial and local) retains its own unique character but cannot function totally independently of the other spheres; all spheres must participate and co-operate in mutual and reciprocal relationships. No sphere is subordinate to another; it is a federal state without a distinct hierarchy of governmental entities. As stated in the *Constitution* (s 41(1)(h)), all spheres of government must “co-operate with one another in mutual trust and good faith by [among other things] ... (iii) informing one another of and consulting one another on, matters of common interest; [and] (iv) co-coordinating their actions and legislation with one another ....” Education (except higher education) is one of the functional areas enumerated in Schedule 4 of the *Constitution* wherein the national and provincial governments exercise concurrent jurisdiction[10]

According to Article 29 of the Bill of Rights contained in the *Constitution*, everyone has the right to a basic education, including adult basic education and further education, which the State, through reasonable measures, must make progressively available and accessible. Specifically:

1. Everyone has the right
    a. to a basic education, including adult basic education; and
    b. to further education, which the state, through reasonable measures, must make progressively available and accessible.
2. Everyone has the right to receive education in the official language or languages of their choice in public educational institutions where that education is reasonably practicable. In order to ensure the effective access to, and implementation of, this right, the state must consider all reasonable educational alternatives, including single medium institutions, taking into account:
    a. equity;
    b. practicability; and
    c. the need to redress the results of past racially discriminatory laws and practices.
3. Everyone has the right to establish and maintain, at their own expense, independent educational institutions that:
    a. do not discriminate on the basis of race;

[10] Malherbe, 2005

b. are registered with the state; and
c. maintain standards that are not inferior to standards at comparable public educational institutions.

4. Subsection (3) does not preclude state subsidies for independent educational institutions.

Legislation Governing Education

In the functional area of education, both the national and provincial governments have concurrent jurisdiction. As a result, the national government has adopted a number of statutes, notably the National Education Policy Act (NEPA)(1996) and the South African Schools Act (SASA) (1996).

The National Education Policy Act, Act 27 of 1996 (NEPA)

The National Education Policy Act (NEPA) (1996) was designed to inscribe in law the policies, as well as the legislative and monitoring responsibilities of the Minister of Basic Education, and to formalise the relations between national and provincial authorities. It laid the foundation for the establishment of the Council of Education Ministers (CEM), as well as for the Heads of Education Departments Committee (HEDCOM) as inter-governmental forums to collaborate in developing a new education system. As such, it provides for the formulation of national policies in general and further education and training for, *inter alia*, curriculum, assessment and language policy, as well as quality assurance[11].

The Act was promulgated to "provide for the determination of national policy for education; to provide afresh for the determination of policy on salaries and conditions of employment of educators; and to provide for matters connected therewith".

Section 3(3) provides that, subject to the Constitution, national policy shall prevail over the whole or a part of any provincial policy on education if there is a conflict between the national and provincial policies. It is an attempt to regulate conflict that might possibly arise from the concurrent legislative authority of the national and provincial spheres of government.

Section 3(4) provides that, subject to the provisions of subsections (1) to (3), the [appropriate] Minister shall determine national policy for the planning, provision, financing, co-ordination, management, governance, programmes, monitoring, evaluation and well-being of the education system. The Minister may determine national policy for among others -

---

11 OECD, 38

(a) education management information systems,
(b) the organisation, management and governance of the national education system;
(c) facilities, finance and development plans for education,
...
(e) the ratio between educators and students / learners;
(f) the professional education and accreditation of educators;
(g) the organisation, management, governance, funding, establishment and registration of educational institutions;
(h) compulsory school education;
(i) the admission of students to education institutions, which shall include the determination of the age of admission to schools;
...
(l) curriculum frameworks, core syllabuses and education programmes, learning standards, examinations and the certification of qualifications, subject to the provisions of any law establishing a national qualifications framework or a certifying or accrediting body;
(m)language in education;
(n) control and discipline of students at education institutions: Provided that no person shall administer corporal punishment, or subject a student to psychological or physical abuse at any education institution;
(o) education support services, including health, welfare, career and vocational development, counselling and guidance for education institutions, within the functional responsibility of a department of education;
(p) co-operation between the Departments and -
  (i) other state departments;
  (ii) provincial education departments;
  (iii) local government; and
  (iv) non-government organisations;
...
(r) executive functions required to implement national education policy determined in terms of this Act, including the implementation of measures to address past discriminatory practices.

Section 4 contains directive principles of national education policy echoing in many respects the White Paper 1 of 1995, including:
(a) the advancement and protection of the fundamental rights of every person guaranteed in terms of Chapter 2 of the Constitution, and in terms of international conventions ratified by Parliament (viii) of every person to use the language and participate in the cultural life of his or her choice within an education institution;
(b) enabling the education system to contribute to the full personal development of each student, and to the moral, social, cultural, political and economic development of the nation at large, including the advancement of democracy, human rights and the peaceful resolution of disputes;

Section 5 provides for consultation on national education policy and provides as follows:

(1) Policy contemplated in section 3 shall be determined by the Minister after consultation with such appropriate consultative bodies as have been established for that purpose in terms of section 11 or any other applicable law, and with the Council.
(2) The policy contemplated in section 3 shall be determined by the Minister with the concurrence of the Minister of Finance in so far as it involves expenditure from the State Revenue Fund.
(3) Nothing in this section shall limit the discretion of the Minister to consult whomsoever he or she wishes for advice on the determination of national education policy.

The above-mentioned section 11(1) refers to consultative bodies and provides that the Minister may by regulation establish a body to be known as the National Education and Training Council (NETC) and other bodies to advise him or her on any matter contemplated in section 3 or any matter identified by the Minister. The NETC has not been established, and its non-establishment seems to militate against the principle of democratic governance.

Section 6 contains provisions regarding consultation on legislation. It provides that:

Legislation on a matter referred to in section 3 shall be introduced in Parliament or, in the case of regulations, be published in the *Gazette* only after consultation between the Minister and -

(a) the Council, in respect of education at education institutions; and
(b) all the parties in the Education Labour Relations Council established by section 40 of the Labour Relations Act, 1995 (Act No. 66 of 1995), in respect of any matter falling within the objectives of that Act.

The fact that legislation shall be introduced only after such consultation is problematic in the sense that the Council with which the minister must consult has not yet been established. There is no compulsion on the minister to establish it. It could also give rise to questions regarding the legality of legislation enacted since the promulgation of this section.

The South African Schools Act, Act 84 of 1996 (SASA)

The South African Schools Act (SASA) (1996) promotes access, quality and democratic governance in the schooling system. It ensures that all learners have right of access to quality education without discrimination, and makes schooling compulsory for children aged 7 to 14. It provides for two types of schools – independent schools and public schools. The provision in the Act for democratic school governance, via school governing bodies, is in place in public schools country-wide. The school funding norms, outlined in SASA, prioritise redress and target poverty with regard to the allocation of funds for the public schooling system. SASA has been amended by *the Education Laws Amendment Act 24 of 2005*, so as to authorise the declaration of schools in poverty stricken areas as "no-fee schools" .No-fee schools are fully subsidized and parents are not required to pay school fees. In 40% of the more affluent public schools parents are still legally obliged to pay school fees.

In brief, as noted in the Preamble, the general purpose of SASA is to establish a new legislative system which sets "uniform norms and standards for the education of *learners* at *schools* and the organisation, governance and funding of *schools* throughout the Republic of South Africa".

In terms of the *South African Schools Act,* a "school" is a public (or independent) school which enrolls learners in one or more grades between Grade zero and twelve. There are two categories of public school: an ordinary public school or a public school for learners with special education needs. In term of section 15 of this act, a public school is a "juristic person" with the legal capacity to perform its functions in terms of the Act. In terms of its legal personality (a juristic person) the school is a legal subject (like a natural person) and has the capacity to be a bearer of rights and obligations. The public school may enter into a contract with another legal subject (e.g. a company) to purchase textbooks; but it also carries all the responsibilities and liabilities attached to its status (e.g. it is liable in the case of breach of contract).

The *South African Schools Act* distinguishes between *governance* and *professional management,* assigning the former to the governing body and the latter to the principal of the school[12]

The *South African Schools Act* adopted a model of school governance that devolved significant powers to School Governing Bodies (SGBs)[13]. Governing bodies are composed of the school principal and elected representatives of parents, educators, non-teaching staff and (in secondary schools) learners and they may also co-opt non-voting members. Parents have a majority stake in order to ensure that previously marginalized constituencies have a greater voice. Governing bodies are juristic persons with the power to enter into contracts, to sue and be sued.

A basic set of functions is stipulated for SGBs[14].
They are required to:
- develop and adopt a constitution and mission statement for the school;
- determine the admissions policy of the school, subject to certain restrictions;

---

12 S 16(1)
13 S 16
14 S 20

- administer and control the school's property, buildings and grounds, including the right to rent them out for fundraising purposes;
- recommend to the Department of Basic Education the appointment of teaching and non-teaching staff;
- develop a budget for the school, which could include schools fees, for approval at a meeting of the parents.

The Further Education and Training Act (1998), Education White Paper 4 on Further Education and Training (1998) and the National Strategy for Further Education and Training (1999-2001). The latter provides the basis for the development of a nationally coordinated further education and training system, comprising the senior secondary component of schooling and further education and training (FET) colleges. It requires these FET institutions, established in terms of the new legislation, to develop institutional plans, while making provision for programme-based funding, as well as a national curriculum for learning and teaching[15].

The Higher Education Act (1997) provides for a unified and nationally planned system of higher education. It furthermore gave the green light for a statutory Council on Higher Education (CHE), which advises the Minister while being responsible for quality assurance and promotion.

A whole spectrum of legislation, including the Employment of Educators Act (1998), to regulate the professional, moral and ethical responsibilities of educators, as well as the competency requirements for teachers. The historically divided teaching force is now governed by one Act of Parliament and one professional council – the South African Council of Educators (SACE).

The South African Qualifications Authority (SAQA) Act (1995) provides for the establishment of the National Qualifications Framework (NQF), which constitutes the scaffolding for a national learning system that integrates education and training at all levels. The joint launch of the Human Resources Development Strategy by the Minister of Labour and the Minister of Education on 23 April 2001 reinforces the resolve to establish an integrated education, training and development strategy that will harness the potential of our adult learners.

In 2012 the new framework, The Curriculum Assessment Policy Statement (CAPS) is introduced in schools. The National Curriculum (Grades R to 12) embodies the vision for general education to move away from a racist, apartheid, rote model of learning and teaching, to a liberating, nation-building and learner-centred outcomes-based initiative. In line with training strategies, the reformulation is intended to allow greater mobility between different levels and between institutional sites, as well as to promote the integration of knowledge

15 OECD, 40

and skills via learning pathways. Its assessment, qualifications, competency and skills-based framework encourage the development of curriculum models that are aligned to the NQF in theory and practice.

The Education White Paper on Early Childhood Development (2000) provides for the expansion of, and full participation by 5-year-olds in pre-school reception grade education by 2010, as well as for an improvement in the quality of programmes, curricula and teacher development for 0-to-4-year-olds and 6-to-9-year-olds.

Education White Paper 6 on Inclusive Education (2001) explains the intention of the Department of Education to implement inclusive education at all levels in the system by 2020. Such an inclusive system will allow for the inclusion of vulnerable learners and reduce the barriers to learning by means of targeted support structures and mechanisms. This, in turn, will improve the participation and retention levels of learners in the education system, particularly with regard to those learners who are prone to dropping out.
Freedom to establish independent schools

"Independent" schools consist of the private schools established in the previous school system, and of the independent schools that have emerged since the democratic changes. In terms of section 53 of the *South African Schools Act*, former private schools registered under a law regulating school education in South Africa and which existed immediately prior to the commencement of the Schools Act, are deemed to be independent schools.

There are various categories of independent schools, including educational (charitable) trusts, close corporations and companies. The legal status of an independent school will therefore depend on its legal position in terms of the law that regulates its existence: for example, in the case of a company or close corporation, the Companies Act, 1973, or the Close Corporations Act, 1984, respectively, will determine the nature of the school, its rights, obligations and liability in terms of the law. However, over and above these prescriptions, independent schools also function as a category of school within the legal framework of the South African education system and are compelled to adhere to public law provisions (legislation) which regulate overall (national) education norms and standards, as mentioned above. Other forms of state control exist in regard to registration and funding, the registration of educators, educators' labour relations and regulation by means of provincial legislation.[16]

The 'dual' role (legal status) of independent schools in the private and public sector, and the extent of state control where issues such as national education norms and standards, registration and subsidisation, educators' employment, and the status of the school as an institution or functionary 'exercising a public

16 SQUELCH, 84-100, 133-156.

power or performing a public function in terms of any legislation' are at stake, have not yet been resolved and will remain under discussion for some time.[17]

As in most other democratic regimes, 'independent" and therefore non-public schools are subject to direct and indirect means of state control, - chiefly through registration and funding. The question inevitably arises, "how private (independent) are private (independent) schools? Although they have a free choice of the type of education they provide (for example special, religious – or culture – based) they have to meet certain conditions for registration and without registration they cannot (legally) survive."[18]

Everyone has the right to establish and maintain, at his own expense, independent educational institutions that

- do not discriminate on the basis of race;
- are registered with the state; and
- maintain standards that are not inferior to standards at comparable public educational institutions.

Private educational institutions cannot be used in ways that are inconsistent with the Bill of Rights as enclaves of apartheid and the perpetuation of past privilege.[19]

Subsection 4 confirms that the fact that in terms of subsection 3 these private or independent institutions must be established and maintained at one's own expense does not preclude the state from subsidising such institutions.

Although the general principle of school choice is not constitutionally recognised, the right to choose between private and public schools is provided for, as well as the right to be educated in a preferred language. Parents' freedom of choice regarding religious matters has been covered to an extent by providing voluntary religious observances in public institutions.[20]

Home schooling

No explicit constitutional provision is made for the right to freedom of choice regarding home education, nor the right of parents to have their children educated according to their own religious and philosophical convictions. More and more White Christian parents choose homeschooling, many of them because they believe that the prescribed National Curriculum aims to transform the education system through:

---

17 S 239(1)(b)(ii) of the *Constitution.*
18 See also BRAY (1997) 101.
19 MALHERBE, 53.
20 MALHERBE, 53.

- Interfaith studies: Children are not only compelled to study religious practices of other faiths. They are forced (in the Learning Area Arts and Culture) to take part in spiritual practices from other cultures. These include song, dance, and rituals of spiritual and erotic nature. One outcome requires creating designs reflecting "nature gods" from various cultures.
- Multiculturalism: Children are compelled to spend much more effort on cultures other than their own and are assessed accordingly. Research on cultural transmission (and the curriculum itself) claims that children will, therefore, adopt little of their own cultures and that a combined "Fusion"-culture will develop.
- Ideological coercion: Throughout the curriculum almost all creative expressions of science and culture must pay homage to the ideologically selected set of prescribed values. Children are forced to interpret almost all projects, analyses, investigations and other work in such a way that it pays homage to the prescribed value system of the current government.[21]

Although the South African School Act[22] provides for the registration of a learner for education at home, there does not appear to be an express right in this regard. A child may also be exempted from compulsory school attendance for reasons such as long-term illness, severe disability or distance from schools cannot reasonably be expected to attend a school. Such a child must receive an education that meets the minimum requirements of the curriculum and the standard of education in state schools. The parents must also comply with such other reasonable conditions as the education department may set.
School choice not limited by family income

When the South African Schools Act, 1996 came into effect on 1 January 1997, the principal objective of the Act was "to provide for a uniform system for the organisation, governance and funding of schools". The Act imposes other important responsibilities on the state with respect to the funding of public schools. The basic principles of state funding of public schools derive from the constitutional guarantee of equality and recognition of the right of redress. The Act provides that:

> The State must fund public schools from public revenue on an equitable basis in order to ensure the proper exercise of the rights of learners to education and the redress of past inequalities in educational provision.[23]

These principles therefore underlie the national norms and minimum standards for public school funding which the Minister of Basic Education is required to

---

21 www.pestalozzi.org
22 S 51
23 S.34(1).

determine[24]. The SASA follows the Constitution[25] in establishing the right of any person to establish and maintain an independent school at his or her own cost, and sets out the grounds on which a Provincial Department of Education must register an independent school. The *Constitution* does not preclude state subsidies for independent education institutions.

An important assumption underlying these national norms and standards for school funding is that the national and provincial levels of government will honour the state's duty, in terms of the Constitution and the SASA, to progressively provide resources to safeguard the right to education of all South Africans. However, educational needs are always greater than the budgetary provision for education. To affect redress and improve equity, therefore, public spending on schools must be specifically targeted to the needs of the poorest. This will apply to both the General Education (grades 1-9) and the Further Education and Training (grades ten to twelve) phases.

New National Norms and Standards for School Funding[26] became national policy in April 1999 and apply uniformly in all provinces. They are aimed at achieving equity in the distribution of resources by progressively redistributing nonpersonnel expenditure to schools. Schools are divided into five categories, based on the country's poverty index. Every year the Minister of Education publishes the National Norms and Standards for School Funding with the updated National Targets Table[27] to include the indicative target amounts allocated to every child in the five poverty quintiles. All learners in quintiles one to three (60 percent of the public school learners nationally) do not have to pay school fees for 2012. Parents of learners attending a quintile four or quintile five schools may apply for exemption of payment of school fees.

The SASA imposes a responsibility on all public school governing bodies to do their utmost to improve the quality of education in their schools by raising additional resources to supplement those which the state provides from public funds[28]. All parents, but particularly those who are less poor or who have good incomes, are thereby encouraged to increase their own direct financial and other contributions to the quality of their children's education in public schools. The Act does not interfere unreasonably with parents' discretion under the law as to how to spend their own resources on their children's education.

According to section 36, the SGB must take all reasonable measures to supplement the funds provided by the state to improve the quality of education,

---

24 S 35
25 S 29(3)
26 Norms and Standards for School Funding, 1998
27 Par. 109 of NNSSF
28 S 36

and such measure is to raise school fees which will enable SGB's to supplement the insufficient resources supplied by the State. It is already often noticed that this stipulation causes problems for about 60 percent of the parents of the poorer schools (and approximately 60 percent of South African schools are underprivileged)[29]

One of the roles of the governing body of each school, under section 39 of the law, is to set the level school fees, together with provisions for those parents unable to pay, since "no learner may be refused admission to a public school on the grounds that his or her parent is unable to pay or has not paid the school fees determined by the governing body"[30]. On the other hand, section 40 provides that "a parent is liable to pay the school fees determined in terms of section 39 unless or to the extent that he or she has been exempted from payment in terms of this Act."

The SASA requires the Minister of Education to make regulations about the equitable criteria and procedures for exemption of parents who are unable to pay school fees[31] .The regulations reflect the national norms in this document, and apply uniformly in all provinces.

The submission that every person can demand from the state the right to have established schools based on a common culture, language or religion is not supported by the language of section 32 (c). This section does not say that every person has the right to have established, by the State, educational institutions based on such a common culture, language or religion. What is provided is that every person shall have the right to establish such educational institutions. Linguistically and grammatically it provides a defensive right to a person who seeks to establish such educational institutions and it protects that right from invasion by the State, without conferring on the State an obligation to establish such educational institutions.[32]

Thus the government may fund independent schools, but it is not required to do so.
The *South African Schools Act*, section 48, carries this logic forward by providing that

(1) The Minister may, by notice in the Government Gazette, determine norms and minimum standards for the granting of subsidies to independent schools after consultation with the Council of Education Ministers and the Financial and Fiscal Commission and with the concurrence of the Minister of Finance.

---

29 CONRADIE, 87ff.

30 S 5.3

31 S 39 (4)

32 *In the Matter of the Gauteng Provincial Legislature*, Constitutional Court of South Africa, Judgment no. CCT 3W95, dated 4th April 1996.

(2) The Member of the Executive Council may, out of funds appropriated by the provincial legislature for that purpose, grant a subsidy to an independent school.

Under the *National Norms and Standards for School Funding,* for funding independent schools promulgated by General Notice 2362 of 12 October 1998, an independent school could be considered for subsidy if it is registered by the provincial education authorities;

Certain conditions must be complied with before the Head of Department will register an independent school:

- The standards of the school should not be inferior to those of a comparable public school.
- The admission policy of the school may not discriminate on the grounds of race;
- The school complies with the grounds for registration contemplated in subsection (2);
- The Member of the Executive Council may determine other conditions for registration by notice in the Provincial Gazette;
- The Member of the Executive Council may also by notice in the Provincial Gazette determine requirements for criteria of eligibility for subsidies, conditions of subsidies and the democratic governance of registered independent schools (article 50 c).

Specific requirements could also touch on the admission of learners at independent schools to examinations conducted by the education departments, the keeping of registers and other documents by the schools. According to this section 50, different requirements may be made in respect of different schools, and affected parties must be allowed a reasonable time to comment on any requirements the Member of the Executive Council of the province intends to determine.

Requirements for public funding include that the school:

- has made an application for funding in the prescribed manner;
- has been operational for one school year;
- is not operated for profit;
- is managed successfully according to a management checklist (see below),
- agrees to unannounced inspection visits by provincial officials; and
- has not been established in direct competition with a nearby uncrowded public school of equivalent quality.

In addition to these conditions, the following conditions applied to independent secondary schools. A secondary school may be considered for subsidy if:

- its grade 12 pass rate is 50% or more of fulltime candidates writing the examination in the prior year;
- the repetition rate in grades 11 or 12 is not more than 20 %;
- it does not engage in practices that are calculated to artificially increase the grade 12 pass rate [such, presumably, as encouraging weaker learners to drop out].

Another form of public subsidy for the choices made by parents has occurred through the provision of the South African Schools Act[33] that an independent school may become a public school, through approval of the provincial education authorities.
School distinctiveness protected by law and policy

Management at school level is undertaken jointly by the school governing body (SGB) and the School Management Team (SMT), consisting of the principal and senior members of staff. Schools are partially funded by the State and cannot claim unlimited freedom of decision-making in all areas of institutional management, even if they fund that area or a specific service themselves.

As in other countries, it is the provisions of law which define the responsibilities to be exercised at the school level which provide the most scope for educational distinctiveness. The South African Schools Act requires that each individual school have a governing body representing parents, teachers, and community members and (as appropriate) learners, with broad responsibilities:

(1) Subject to this Act[34], the governing body of a public school must

(a) promote the best interests of the school and strive to ensure its development through the provision of quality education for all learners at the school;
(b) adopt a [school] constitution;
(c) develop the mission statement of the school;
(d) adopt a code of conduct for learners at the school;
(e) support the principal, educators and other staff of the school in the performance of their professional functions;
(f) determine times of the school day consistent with any applicable conditions of employment of staff at the school;
(g) administer and control the school's property, and buildings and grounds occupied by the school, including school hostels, if applicable;
(h) encourage parents, learners, educators and other staff at the school to render voluntary services to the school;
(i) recommend to the Head of Department the appointment of educators at the

33 S 49
34 S 20

school, subject to the Educators Employment Act, 1994 . . .;
(j) recommend to the Head of Department the appointment of noneducator staff at the school, subject to the Public Service Act, 1994 . . .;
(k) at the request of the Head of Department, allow the reasonable use under fair conditions of the facilities of the school for educational programmes not conducted by the school . . .

These functions could be summarised as policy making functions: section (1) (a) to (d), motivational functions: section 20 (1) (e) and (h) and organisational tasks: section 20 (1) (f), (g), (i), (j) and (k).

Section 21 of SASA provides also for allocated functions, which SGB's may apply for, - besides the general functions assigned to SGB's. These are chiefly financial management responsibilities[35], not taken in charge by the state, especially vis-à-vis the previous model C schools which had been self-managing under the apartheid government; they maintained their self-governing status regarding the allocated functions and did not have the choice to apply for the status of ordinary public schools funded in full by the state.

Some observers are concerned that the responsibilities vested in governing boards go well beyond the capability of the parents and staff available in many schools. "Governing a school involves day-to-day management and administration and provincial education departments (and their district agencies) will have a mammoth task in governing and/or monitoring the governance of these schools. The lack of capacity of a governing body to assume responsibility for the governing of the school may also have the potential to exacerbate existing cleavages between privileged and disadvantaged communities."[36]

In recognition of this reality, the South African Schools Act requires that[37]

Out of funds appropriated for this purpose by the provincial legislature, the Head of Department must establish a programme to

(a) provide introductory training for newly elected governing bodies to enable them to perform their functions; and

(b) provide continuing training to governing bodies to promote the effective performance of their functions or to enable them to assume additional functions.

35 eg: maintenance and the improvement of the school's property, the purchase of textbooks and other educational material, to pay municipal charges, ¼

36 BRAY, 47.

37 S 19

Distinctive character

The most difficult aspect of school distinctiveness at present has to do with the language of instruction. The Constitution stipulates that learners have a right to be taught in the (official) language of their choice if practicable[38]. They must inform the school which language they wish to be taught in when applying for admission. Schools, in turn, are expected to take their requests into account and to be seen to be working towards multilingualism.

Nevertheless, it seems that the perspective towards cultural diversity and language rights was sometimes overlooked in the heated atmosphere generated by the dispute over single-medium institutions. There is still an obligation on the state to provide such education where reasonably practicable.[39] In order to ensure the effective access to, and implementation of this right, the state must consider all reasonable educational alternatives, including single medium institutions, taking into account equity, practicability and the need to redress the results of part racially discriminatory law and practice.[40]"

The South African Schools Act, in turn, provides that "the governing body of a public school may determine the language policy of the school subject to the Constitution, this Act and any applicable provincial law"[41]

This is by no means a simple matter, or one that has only practical implications. There are strongly emotional arguments for recognizing the nine official African languages as in every respect equal to English and Afrikaans, and for urging White parents to ensure that their children learn at least one African language, as does the Working Group on Values in Education in its recent report. On the other hand, many parents who themselves received a "Bantu education" using an African language believe that this was the result of a deliberate policy to deny them access to opportunities that depend upon strong proficiency in English, and want to ensure that their children are not similarly denied. There are also strong views, among Afrikaners, about the need to ensure that their language does not take second place to English as a common national language[42].

According to the Language in Education Policy[43]

- only official languages may be used for instruction
- from Grade Three onwards, all learners have to study the language they are

---

[38] S 29(2)
[39] MALHERBE (1997), 65.
[40] S 29(2)
[41] S 6(2) of the South African Schools Act
[42] Department of Education, 1997,
[43] Department of Education, June 1997

taught in and at least one other approved language
- language may not be used as a barrier to admission
- governing bodies must stipulate how their schools are promoting multilingualism
- failing a language will result in failing a grade.[44]

Decisions about admitting learners

Government policy on school admissions and school fees is guided by three basic principles:
- Equity: to ensure that government gives the same basic resources to all government schools
- Redress: to give more government resources to learners in historically disadvantaged communities so that they have more money for textbooks and stationery, and it is possible to build schools in areas where none exist and upgrade existing schools
- Access: to make sure no one is excluded from attending school on the basis of race or religion or because they cannot afford to pay school fees.

The South African Schools Act[45] stipulates that "(1) A public school must admit learners and serve their educational requirements without unfairly discriminating in any way. (2) The governing body of a public school may not administer any test related to the admission of a learner to a public school, or direct or authorise the principal of the school or any other person to administer such test."

In terms of sec 9(3) of the Constitution, the admissions policy cannot unfairly discriminate against learners in any way. Therefore an admission policy cannot exclude a learner on the following grounds[46]:
Nonpayment of school fees or registration fees in previous or current school year
His or her parents do not subscribe to the mission statement of the school
His or her parents have refused to enter into a contract in terms of which the parent waives any claim for damages arising out of the education of a learner
The learner has registered late.
His or her parents cannot afford a uniform or school books
S/he is not a South African citizen.
Language
Disability
Overcrowding in the school
Race, culture, or religion
HIV status
Pregnancy

44 www.gov.za/yearbook/education.htm
45 S 5
46 South African Schools Act, s. 5

Only when the provincial offices of the Department of Basic Education determine a school as being full, learners can be refused admission.

The court held in the *Mikro* case that learners' right to language of tuition is not unqualified (Western Cape Minister of Education and Others v Governing Body of Mikro Primary School and Another, 2005) and that it can only be enforced if a certain number of learners have the need for tuition in a specific language and also if no adequate alternative school exist[47] .In another court case on a similar issue the court held that learners should be admitted as the school was operating on half capacity (Hoërskool Ermelo, 2009). This is in line with the principles of equity, practicality and redress which justify the transformation of the school from a single-medium public school to a parallel-medium public school.

Independent schools cannot be registered (and thus cannot operate legally) if they discriminate in admission on the basis of race.[48]

While public schools may have a distinctive character, and even a religious one, the law stipulates that applicants may not be denied admission "on the grounds that his or her parent does not subscribe to the mission statement of the school"[49] This prohibition "reflects seriously on the ability of the governing body to manage the school according to the needs of the democratically/traditionally accepted ethos of the school."[50]

Decisions about staff

An amendment to the South African Schools Act, adopted in 1997 expanded the powers of school governing boards by allowing them to employ professional and nonprofessional staff, rather than simply recommending appointments to provincial authorities, but with significant conditions.

An ongoing problem regarding policy on teachers, which is well recognised by the South African authorities, is the lack of a satisfactory database on all aspects of the teaching force. Significant information lacunae exist on demand and supply, retention patterns, mobility, subject shortages and so on. Plans are afoot for a comprehensive electronic database that, when in place, should greatly assist informed policy and planning. The appointment procedures for teachers have been a cause of some concern. Teacher selection is done by the school governing bodies (SGBs), and it has been suggested that sometimes the SGBs (including parent representatives) may not be well equipped for this role. There have also been complaints of local interests and relationships unduly influencing teacher

47 Fleisch & Woolman, 78

48 S 46 (2) of the Constitution

49 S 5 (3) of the South African Schools Act

50 BRAY, 45.

selection. Proposed appointments are subject to the confirmation of the provincial departments of education, which are the teachers' employer.[51]

The staff .must be employed in compliance with the basic values and principles referred to in section 195 of the *Constitution*, and the factors to be taken into account when making appointments include, but are not limited to

a) the ability of the candidate;
b) the principle of equity;
c) the need to redress past injustices; and
d) the need for representivity.

In 2006, the Department of Education issued The National Policy Framework for Teacher Education and Development in South Africa. The Framework posits as a starting point the strategic importance of the teacher's role and accepts that teachers "work in extremely complex conditions, largely due to the pervasive legacies of Apartheid, but also as a result of the new policies needed to bring about change in education" (p. 6). The document expresses concern about teacher shortages and the poor image of teaching and commits itself to "an appropriately-pitched recruitment campaign promoting the visibility, attraction and challenge of teaching as a career" (p. 12).
Accountability for school quality

The South African Qualifications Authority (SAQA)[52] was established to oversee the development of the National Qualifications Framework (NQF), covering standard setting and quality assurance. The objectives of the NQF include creating an integrated national framework for learning. Access, mobility and progression are other key objectives, as is the need to enhance quality in education and training. The speedy redress of past discrimination in education, training and employment is another main objective. The NQF will attempt to move the measurement of achievement in education and training away from input towards outcomes.[53]

A new national curriculum framework for schools (Curriculum 2005), based on the concept of "outcome-based education" (OBE), was introduced in Grade One in 1998. Fourteen years later, in 2010 it became clear that learners produced by this system were not ready to fulfill their place in society and lack basic skills of

---

51 OECD, 302

52 Section 16A (1) (b) (i) and (ii) of SASA is clear that the principal of a school is accountable for –(i) the academic performance of that school in relation to minimum outcomes and standards and procedures for assessment determined by the Minister in terms of section 6A; and (ii) the effective use of available resources
The principal must also prepare and submit to the appropriate Head of Department an annual report in respect of the above two provisions.

53 www.gov.za/yearbook/education.htm

reading, writing and arithmetic. South Africa was ranked last in the International Mathematics and Science Study (TIMSS) since 1995[54].

In 2012 the new framework, The Curriculum Assessment Policy Statement (CAPS) is introduced in schools. CAPS is a single, comprehensive, and concise policy document, which will replace the current Subject and Learning Area Statements, Learning Programme Guidelines and Subject Assessment Guidelines for all the subjects listed in the National Curriculum Statement Grades R - 12 (Education, 2012). CAPS for the Intermediate Phase (grades 4 to 6) and Grade 11 will be introduced in all schools in 2013, and already the system is being prepared for this important change to the curriculum The Department of Basic Education (DBE) is currently orientating hundreds of provincial and district subject advisors, for all subjects, on the changes that will be introduced so that implementation of CAPS in schools is strengthened.

Learners in independent schools are entitled to academic standards not inferior to those in comparable public schools.

Teaching of values

Section 1 of the Constitution sets out the basic values on which the *Constitution* (and consequently the entire South African dispensation) is based. Many experts regard these values as the most significant part of the Constitution which names the following values: human dignity, the achievement of equality, the advancement of human rights and freedoms, non-racialism and non-sexism, supremacy of the constitution and the rule of law, universal adult suffrage, a national common voters roll, regular elections and a multi-party system of democratic government to ensure accountability, responsiveness and openness. The new human rights culture is based on the founding values in Section 1 which include human dignity, equality, non-racialism and non-sexism, the supreme authority of the Constitution, and the rule of law in South Africa. The South African Schools Act aims at providing one national department enhancing the culture of human rights.

As the first major curriculum statement of a democratic government, it signaled a dramatic break from the past. Despite these noble goals for social and educational change, there is a perception that schools are not assisting in either creating new social values or the skilled population that the country requires in order to compete globally. In part, it must be recognised that education (or even a curriculum) cannot change society or on its own produce national development. Vesting such hopes in education is bound to lead to disillusionment. Education, and getting it right, are however important because more and better education to a higher level

54 Reddy, 91

for all is both a good in itself and can create the conditions for enhanced social and personal development.

Another recent report, Values, Education and Democracy, issued by the Ministry of Education on behalf of a distinguished working group, assigns to the schools a major role in building societal consensus around a set of goals intended to promote civic peace and cooperation. The recommendations are, as so often, rather unspecific.[55]

There are at least three key elements to an educational philosophy. The first is to develop the intellectual abilities and critical faculties among all of the children and young adults in our schools. Secondly, the educational philosophy of democracy should emphasise inclusiveness. It is equally important to develop a culture and ethos in schools that actively include all learners no matter their background in the formal and informal aspects of a school's life. This requires an enhanced degree of linguistic and cultural dexterity, tolerance and appreciation of difference on the part of teachers and administrators. Thirdly, educational philosophy should provide learners with the tools to solve the many problems that come with being human throughout the life cycle.

The report makes the following recommendations:

- The adoption of a social contract between educators, administrators, parents, trade unions and professional associations based on the values defined in the document.
- Preservice and inservice training of teachers in, educational inequality and the need for equity, an African language, the performing arts.
- The appointment of a panel of historians, archaeologists and human biologists, who would make recommendations regarding, the strengthening of history teaching at schools, the quality of teacher training in history and human biology.
- The introduction of a school based artistinresidence programme as a first step towards introducing performing arts programmes at schools.
- The adoption of a tougher policy against illegitimate and harmful discrimination in schools.
- The introduction of schoolsbased debating societies.
- The introduction of a national grid of adult learning opportunities.
- The promotion of social honour and an embrace of South African national symbols.
- Research on the nature and scale of the diversity of our schools' learners and educators[56] .

55 education.pwv.gov.za/Policies_Reports/Reports_2000/Values_Edu_Demo.pdf

56 http://education.pwv.gov.za/Policies_Reports/reports_2000/Values.htm

References

BRAY Elmene, "Education in Transition: The Impact of the Draft South African Schools Bill of 1996," in *Education under the new Constitution in South-Africa,* edited by DE GROOF Jan and BRAY Elmene, Leuven (Belgium): Acco, 1996.

BRAY Elmene, "The legal status of schools," in *Human rights in South African Education,* edited by DE GROOF Jan and MALHERBE RASSIE, 1997

CONRADIE J., "Norms and standards for the funding of public schools: the second step towards self-managing schools," in DE GROOF Jan, HEYSTEK J. et alii, *Governance of educational institutions in South Africa. Into the new millennium,* 2000.

CURRIE I., "Minority rights: education, culture and language," in CHASKALSON M et alii, *Constitutional Law of South Africa,* 1996.

DEPARTMENT OF EDUCATION. National Norms and Standards for School Funding, 1998

DEPARTMENT OF BASIC EDUCATION. Education Statistics in South Africa. 2010. Published in February 2012, p. 3.

DEPARTMENT OF BASIC EDUCATION Annual Report 2009/10

DEPARTMENT OF BASIC EDUCATION. Curriculum Assessment Policy Statements (CAPS). [Online]. Available from: http://www.education.gov.za/Curriculum/CurriculumAssessmentPolicyStatements/tabid/419/Default.aspx. Accessed: 6 April 2012.

DLAMINI C., "The relationship between Human Rights and Education," in *Human rights in South African Education,* edited by DE GROOF J.and MALHERBE R., 1997, p. 39–52.

FISKE, E.B., AND H.F. LADD Elusive Equity: Education Reform in Post-Apartheid South Africa, (2004), Brookings Institution Press, Washington.

FLEISCH, B. & WOOLMAN, S. 2007. On the constitutionality of single-medium public schools. *South African Journal of Human Rights,* 9(22): 78.

GRIMOND John, "Africa's Great Black Hope," *The Economist,* February 24, 2001, 3-16.

MALHERBE E. F. J., "Die onderwijsbepalings van die 1993 grondwet," *TSAR,*

1995.
MALHERBE. E.F.J. "Conflicts of competence in education: the South African example", read at the third international conference on federalism, 2-5 March 2005, Brussels, Belgium.

MALHERBE R., "A fresh start I: Education rights in South Africa", in *European Journal for Education Law and Policy* 4, Kluwer Law International, 2000, p. 4955

OECD. Reviews of National Policies for Education: South Africa. 2008, p.47-49

SQUELCH Joan, *Private Education in South Africa: The Legal Status and Management of Private Schools* (DEd thesis Unisa 1997).

VISSER P. J., "The Rights and Duties of Learners: Some Basic South African Principles, in *The Legal Status of Learners in Europe,* edited by DE GROOF Jan and PENNEMAN Hilde, Kluwer Law international, The Hague, 1998, 439455.

Working Group on Values in Education, *Values, Education and Democracy,* Department of Education, South Africa, 2000.

Head of Department: Mpumalanga Department of Education and Another v Hoërskool Ermelo and others 2009 (ZACC)

Western Cape Minister of Education and Others v Governing Body of Mikro Primary school and another 2005 BCLR 973 (SAC)

United States

by Charles L. Glenn and Charles J. Russo[1]

Overview

The public educational system of the United States, which is loosely coupled at best, is marked by a strong tradition of local (but not necessarily schoollevel) decisionmaking that traces its origins to seventeenth century New England. Local school officials, through their governing bodies, operate within a framework of laws and regulations enacted at the state level but often applied unevenly by local school systems in the absence of strong state administrative controls. One result is that.

> this kind of legal structure creates lots of wiggle room for educational innovators. One can fight local battles to change the rules or move someplace else where the regulatory climate better suits one's pedagogical imagination. And since the question of just who ultimately is responsible for the education of children (parents? the state?) has never been squarely resolved in America, the country has accommodated many alternatives to public schools.[2]

'Public education' – that is, schooling provided by local school boards in the United States – is frequently criticized for a variety of real as well as imagined failings and yet enjoys an almost mythical status as the institution which is believed to knit together this highly diverse and constantly changing society.[3]

> What [Americans] have, in effect, is a normative attachment to the public schools and an affective inclination to see the public schools in a sympathetic light, whatever the latter's actual performance might be. . . . two-thirds of Americans say the public schools deserve support even when they are performing poorly . . . many private school parents share this same attachment to the public school system. . . . Fortythree percent of public parents say they wouldn't feel right putting their kids in private schoolsa profoundly important fact, given that so many of these same parents think that private schools are actually *better* than public schools.[4]

---

1 Panzer Chair in Education and Adjunct Professor of Law, University if Dayton.

2 Stevens, 6.

3 Glenn 1988.

4 Moe 2000, 87-88.

In the service of the integrative mission attributed to the common public school, any references to Christianity (though not necessarily to other religions) have been banished from public schools as potentially divisive, even when that has required the suppression of aspects of history, literature, and social studies. The insistence upon the 'neutrality' of the public school has been so insistent that many teachers even hesitate to discuss traditional virtues in teaching about sexual and other behavioral issues.[5] The United States Supreme Court has decreed, however, that its judgments forbidding government support of religion do "not foreclose teaching about the Holy Scriptures or about the differences between religious sects in classes in literature or history . . . (*School District of Abington Township v. Schempp and Murray v. Curlett*, 374 U.S. 203, 300 (1963)). This is a fine line, indeed, that prohibits teaching of religion but permits instruction about religion in public schools.

Nonstate schools have suffered under two contradictory perceptions. In the nineteenth century and for much of the twentieth, Catholic, Lutheran, and other schools – many of which instructed in languages other than English – were established primarily by the churches of immigrants, and were accused of teaching 'unAmerican' values and retarding the assimilation of their pupils.[6] Another smaller but highly prestigious group of 'independent' schools were considered elite refuges for families unwilling to mix with the common people in the common public school.

Fear of immigrant separatism led to provisions in many state constitutions forbidding the granting of public funds for schools not operated by government even as other jurisdictions sought to prevent such schools altogether or to subject them to harassing oversight. It was after the Civil War and the post-war focus on reconstruction – both of the devastated South and also of disrupted lives and families in the North – that what has usually been called 'Church and State' controversies became virulent in the United States. The Protestant majority, so recently at war over slavery and secession, united to insulate from the ordinary democratic process any efforts to obtain public funds for Catholic schools.

The courts have struck down barriers to operating nonpublic schools with a religious character but have, until recently, concurred in denying them direct public funding, instead preferring to provide aid such as reimbursement for transportation (*Everson v. Board of Education*, 330 U.S. 1 (1947) and eventually free transportation to and from schools, textbooks for secular instruction (*Board of Education of Central School District 1 v. Allen*, 392 U.S. 236 (1968)), instructional services for poor students (*Agostini v. Felton* (521 U.S. 203 (1997)), and, to a limited degree, vouchers (*Zelman v. Simmons-Harris*, 536 U.S.639 (2002)) under the legal construct known as the Child Benefit Theory pursuant to which the aid goes to

5 Moran.
6 Glenn 2012.

students and/ or their parents rather than their religiously affiliated non-public schools.

Uniquely among the nations included in this study, then, in the United States public support for the nongovernment schools chosen by some parents has been generally defined as a legal rather than a policy question. In other words, legislators have frequently enacted laws providing public support for nonpublic schools only to have them struck down by the courts on state or federal constitutional grounds. Only within the last decade has a series of court decisions opened the way to vouchers or other forms of public funding for these schools, whether religious or secular.

Arguably an even more significant recent development has been the adoption, by two-thirds of the states, of laws under which groups of parents, teachers and others can obtain approval and full public funding to operate 'charter schools' (independent public schools) and–in all the states–of laws under which parents can choose to educate their children at home.

The Structure of Schooling

There is no single educational system in the United States. Instead, there are fifty separate state systems (along with those in the District of Columbia, Puerto Rico, and a handful of other jurisdictions such as Guam) which share much in common, though without the sort of formal coordination which exists in other federal systems like Germany or Switzerland. All states provide twelve years of elementary and secondary schooling (the dividing line between elementary, intermediate, and secondary schooling varies among local school systems). State governments set requirements for schools operated by approximately 14,000 local school systems, each of which has an elected or appointed board that sets policies and appoints a superintendent to manage the schools.

Of the more than 50 million school children in America, about 6 million are educated in private schools, either attending nonpublic elementary and secondary schools or being homeschooled. Private schools include about onefourth of the elementary and secondary schools and approximately 11 percent of the elementary and secondary enrollment in the U.S.

The most recent major development, charter schools, are public schools operated by private, civilsociety groups, and thus neither fully public nor fully private in the conventional sense. A charter school is run by a board of directors, the composition of which is regulated by the charter proposed by the organizers and approved by the state (or, in some cases, another public agency). The board of directors is responsible for hiring and dismissing staff, budgeting, curriculum development, and the general operation of the school. The charter school is fully funded by the state and may not charge tuition to parents.

> Traditionally, Americans have defined a public school as any school run by the government, managed by a superintendent and school board, staffed by public employees, and operated within a public sector bureaucracy. . . . Now consider a different definition: a public school is any school that is open to the public, paid for by the public, and accountable to the public for its results.[7]

Since the enactment of charter school legislation in Minnesota in 1991, 42 states and the District of Columbia have adopted charter laws with bipartisan political support. The longstanding dichotomy of public and private schooling has thus been transcended by a new organizational form with a new and still-developing legal status. The fact that some charter school boards have contracted with for-profit school management firms to operate their schools adds a further – and controversial – element to the situation.

There are a number of recentlyfounded school management firms, of which the best-known is Edison, which currently manage hundreds of district and charter public schools. Low performing urban school districts are increasingly turning to external management to manage schools under contracts in an effort to improve efficiency, though this is strongly opposed by the teacher unions, which have more influence with politically-elected boards.

One of the most interesting developments in the organization of American schooling is the concept of school districts "managing portfolios" of semi-autonomous schools, perhaps including charter schools, with the central office supporting rather than administering the educational activities. The Center for Reinventing Public Education at the University of Washington manages a "portfolio district network" which includes New York City, Los Angeles, Washington, DC, Baltimore, and the Recovery School District established in Louisiana after Hurricane Katrina. "New York, with 1 million students and 1,700 schools, manages its diverse portfolio of schools by setting up networks of schools linked by similar educational philosophies but not necessarily geography. The networks provide some central-management activities and are compared yearly for performance and principal satisfaction. Schools are free to switch networks yearly as they choose."[8]

The Legal Framework

The federal Constitution, adopted in 1789, makes no mention of education. Further, the Tenth Amendment, enacted in 1791 as part of the Bill of Rights, specifies that all powers not explicitly granted to the national government are reserved to the states. Of course, by its absence, education is key among the rights reserved to the states. In fact, in its only case on school finance, *San Antonio*

7 Finn, Manno and Vanourek, 16.

8 *Education Week*, July 18, 2012.

Independent School District v. Rodriguez, 411 U.S. 1, 35 (1973)) the United States Supreme Court declared that "[e]ducation, of course, is not among the rights afforded explicit protection under our Federal Constitution. Nor do we find any basis for saying it is implicitly so protected." Accordingly, public education is financed and controlled primarily by state and local governments acting in concert.

The Bill of Rights and later amendments to the federal Constitution, while not mentioning education, have had the effect in recent decades of giving the national government, and especially the federal courts, a major role in state and local policy and practices as long as a party can demonstrate that governmental action, whether on the federal or state level impacts a constitutionally protected right such as equal protection under the law. In fact, it was equal protection that afforded the Supreme Court the opportunity to act in *Brown v. Board of Education, Topeka* (347 U.S. 483 (1954)), the most important case involving education law in its history, which also served as a harbinger for major changes in American society well beyond schooling.

The First Amendment defines what has sometimes been referred to as the "first freedom" under the American system. Its first words are "Congress shall make no law respecting an establishment of religion, or prohibiting the free exercise thereof." The United States Supreme Court has held repeatedly that this language forbidding a state 'establishment of religion' consequently forbids public funding by any level of government for nonpublic schools with a religious character. Various exceptions will be noted below. The First Amendment also protects freedom of speech and of the press, rights which the courts have protected with respect to students and teachers in public schools.

The Fourteenth Amendment, adopted after the Civil War and the emancipation of slaves, has affected schools in highly consequential ways. The requirement of "equal protection of the laws" has placed the major part of the national burden of overcoming the effects of racial injustice on public schools not only through equal treatment of AfricanAmerican (and, subsequently, Hispanic) pupils, but also through various affirmative efforts to remedy the effects of raciallybased injustices that in some cases occurred generations ago. Thus, for example, if it can be shown that government policies in any community at some time in the past had the effect of causing residential segregation on the basis of race, a federal court might order that school attendance areas be redrawn in such a way as to overcome the segregatory effects of continuing residential patterns. Independent schools are not affected by such remedial requirements, though they are forbidden, by both federal and state (and, sometimes, local) law from discriminating against children or teachers, in admission, employment, or other respects, on the basis of race.

The Fourteenth Amendment has also been interpreted, by the United States

Supreme Court in 1925, to guarantee as a protected "liberty" the right to choose a private education. Confronted with an Oregon statute mandating that all children attend governmentoperated public schools, the Supreme Court ruled the statute unconstitutional, insisting that

> the fundamental theory of liberty upon which all governments in this Union repose excludes any general power of the state to standardize its children by forcing them to accept instruction from public teachers only. The child is not the mere creature of the state; those who nurture him and direct his destiny have the right, coupled with the high duty, to recognize and prepare him for additional obligations (*Pierce v. Society of Sisters of the Holy Names of Jesus and Mary*, 268 U.S. 510).

The Fourteenth Amendment also created a requirement of "due process" in the decisions made by government, including public schools. This requirement, often reinforced by state laws, affects how public schools handle pupil discipline and staff evaluation.

A considerable body of federal legislation affects public schools – and, to a lesser extent, private schools – which protect the educational interests of pupils with special needs as well as the right of pupils not to be discriminated against on the basis of race, sex, or national origin, including Title IV of the Civil Rights Act of 1964, Title IX of the Education Amendments of 1972, Section 504 of the Rehabilitation Act of 1973, the Equal Opportunities Act of 1974. For a recent summary of how these apply to charter schools, and the No Child left behind Act. Federal legislation and regulations also govern the provision of funding for specific purposes supported by the federal government, amounting to about 6 percent of the total expenditure of and for schools.

The fifty states (and the District of Columbia, Puerto Rico, and a handful of other jurisdictions such as Guam) bear the constitutional responsibility for education. Each state has a constitution which defines its responsibility for education. That of Massachusetts, the oldest (1780) written constitution still in effect, was drafted by John Adams, later the second president. It provides that

> Wisdom, and knowledge, as well as virtue, diffused generally among the body of the people, being necessary for the preservation of their rights and liberties; and as these depend on spreading the opportunities and advantages of education in the various parts of the country [that is, Massachusetts], and among the different orders of the people, it shall be the duty of legislatures and magistrates, in all future periods of this commonwealth, to cherish the interests of literature and the sciences, and all seminaries of them . . . to encourage private societies and public institutions . . . to countenance and inculcate the principles of humanity and general benevolence, public and private charity, industry and frugality, honesty and punctuality in their dealings, sincerity,

> good humor, and all social affections, and generous sentiments among the people (*Constitution of Massachusetts*, Part the Second, Chapter V, Section II, "The Encouragement of Literature, etc.").

It is the states that adopt detailed legislation and regulations and, in some cases, curriculum guidelines and outcome standards for schools. These vary considerably, and in some cases such as California are extremely detailed.

At present, forty-two states plus the District of Columbia and Puerto Rico have adopted laws permitting the creation of charter schools. Charter schools, which are public schools of choice, are typically operated as not-for-profit institutions by private groups either independently or occasionally in conjunction with public institutions such as universities, continue to survive challenges to their constitutionality. These laws vary considerably, but have in common that an approved charter school may not discriminate on racial or other proscribed grounds in the admission of pupils and must meet educational outcome standards that–characteristically–those proposing the school and the approving agency have negotiated during the approval process.

Freedom to establish nonstate schools

The right to establish nonstate schools is guaranteed by the national *Constitution*, as applied by the Supreme Court in *Pierce v Society of Sisters*. Even so, it is the duty of individual states to establish the conditions under which nonpublic schools may operate, and

> each state has its own approach to control of nonpublic schools; and in some, such as Nebraska, the private schools are very strictly regulated. In others, such as Florida, there is very little or no regulation of private schools; while some, such as Kansas, give the private schools the option of being regulated by the state or operating independent of state control.[9]

In most states, the primary oversight over nonstate schools is exercised by local public school authorities, which are responsible for ensuring that mandatory school attendance laws are complied with. This obligation can be met by attendance at a public school, a school generally equivalent to the local public schools, or by home schooling similarly equivalent to local public schools. This is a free-floating criterion, given the enormous range in quality and resources of public schools, and leads commonly to situations in which public school staff are sitting in judgment upon nonpublic schools which, at least in times of declining enrolments, are their competitors.

9 Furst and Russo, 2.

In most cases, it is important to add, approval of nonpublic schools occurs routinely and without difficulties on either side. The unproblematic character of much of this oversight has led some school choice advocates to propose it be adopted as the model of accountability for nonpublic schools that receive vouchers. States, they argue, should be prevented from "enlarging controls upon curriculum, facilities, and school employment policies beyond the modest regulations that have traditionally applied to private schools."[10]

Public charter schools are a new phenomenon – the first were approved, in Minnesota, in 1990 – that are not part of local public school systems but are sponsored and controlled by independent, self-selected boards and yet are part of the public education system; thus, these charter schools blur the distinction between 'public' and 'private' schools. In the states with "strong" charter school laws, the awarding of a charter to operate and be funded as part of the public education system is not dependent upon the approval of local authorities. Charters are awarded directly by the state and perhaps also by other entities such as public universities. In some states, depending on the enabling legislation, approval of the local authorities must be obtained, although sometimes there is a state-level appeals process from an unfavorable decision.

Private schools may become charter schools and consequently receive public funding in Arizona, for example, while in other states like Massachusetts only new startups and existing public schools may become charter schools. The process of obtaining a charter requires the proposers to spell out in detail the school's distinctive mission, how the school will operate, what standards will be used to judge its success.

> The establishment of multiple sponsoring authorities stands out as one of the most important factors in advancing charter schools. In 20002001, 57 percent of charter schools operating were approved by an entity other than the local school board. States with multiple sponsoring authorities or strong appeals process are home to 80.8 percent of the nation's charter schools.

By 2012 , there were 42 states with charter school laws. The National Center for Education Statistics reports that "[f]rom 1999–2000 to 2009–10, the number of students enrolled in public charter schools more than quadrupled from 0.3 million to 1.6 million students. During this period, the percentage of all public schools that were public charter schools increased from 2 to 5 percent, comprising 5,000 schools in 2009–10."[11]

---

[10] Coons and Sugarman 1992, 32.
[11] NCES 2012, Indicator 4.

Home schooling

In 1975, home schooling was illegal in most of the United States; at present, however, in all fifty states parents may educate their children at home without sending them to either a public or a nonpublic school; 36 of the states adopted such legislation between 1982 and 1993; Michigan was the last state to authorize home schooling, in 1995.[12]

Not that there is universal agreement in the United States that this practice should be permitted. The National Education Association (NEA), the larger of the two national teacher unions, "has voted to abolish home education every year since 1988 . . [stating that] 'home schooling programs cannot provide the student with a comprehensive education experience. . . . Instruction should be by persons who are licensed by the appropriate state education licensure agency, and a curriculum approved by the state department of education should be used.'"[13] In other words, parents educating their children should be required to be certified teachers.

The most recent study by the National Center for Education Statistics reports that

> In 2007, the number of homeschooled students was about 1.5 million, an increase from 850,000 in 1999 and 1.1 million in 2003. The percentage of the schoolage population that was homeschooled increased from 1.7 percent in 1999 to 2.9 percent in 2007. The increase in the percentage of homeschooled students from 1999 to 2007 represents a 74 percent relative increase over the 8year period and a 36 percent relative increase since 2003. In 2007, the majority of homeschooled students received all of their education at home (84 percent), but some attended school up to 25 hours per week. Eleven percent of homeschooled students were enrolled in school less than 9 hours per week, and 5 percent were enrolled between 9 and 25 hours per week.
>
> More White students were homeschooled than Black or Hispanic students or students from other racial/ethnic groups, and White students constituted the majority of homeschooled students (77 percent). White students (3.9 percent) had a higher homeschooling rate than Blacks (0.8 percent) and Hispanics (1.5 percent), but were not measurably different from students from other racial/ ethnic groups (3.4 percent). Students in twoparent households made up 89 percent of the homeschooled population, and those in twoparent households with one parent in the labor force made up 54 percent of the homeschooled population. The latter group of students had a higher homeschooling rate than their peers: 7 percent, compared with 1 to 2 percent of students in other family circumstances. In 2007, students in households earning between

---

12 Information is available from the Home Schooling Legal Defense Association at http://www.hslda.org/. For research results see http://www.nheri.org/.

13 quoted by Somerville, 3.

> $25,001 and $75,000 per year had higher rates of homeschooling than their peers from families earning $25,000 or less a year.
>
> Parents give many different reasons for homeschooling their children. In 2007, the most common reason parents gave as the most important was a desire to provide religious or moral instruction (36 percent of students). This reason was followed by a concern about the school environment (such as safety, drugs, or negative peer pressure) (21 percent), dissatisfaction with academic instruction (17 percent), and "other reasons" including family time, finances, travel, and distance (14 percent). Parents of about 7 percent of homeschooled students cited the desire to provide their child with a nontraditional approach to education as the most important reason for homeschooling, and the parents of another 6 percent of students cited a child's health problems or special needs.[14]

Opponents concede that, at least as assessed by standardized tests, the academic outcomes of homeschooled children are at least equivalent to those of the average of pupils in public schools. Concerns are expressed about social isolation, and anecdotal evidence suggests that many homeschooling parents share this concern and involve their children in a variety of activities outside the home. In many school districts, homeschooled children are allowed to participate in school activities such as sports, clubs, and laboratorybased classes, while in others they are not. The NEA's position is that "homeschooled children should not participate in any extracurricular activities in the public schools;" presumably the teachers' union is seeking to discourage homeschooling by marginalizing it.

A survey conducted by the federal government's National Center for Education Statistics in 1996 found that homeschooling families and families with children in private schools were more likely to be active in civic affairs than were public school parents. "Far from being privatized and isolated," an analysis concluded, "home schooling families are typically very well networked and quite civicly active."[15]

Each state regulates school attendance and home schooling as it chooses. A few examples follow. In Massachusetts, for example, approval by local public school officials is required. The expectation is that 900 hours a year of instruction will be provided at the elementary level and 990 hours at the secondary, in reading, writing, English language and grammar, geography, arithmetic, drawing, music, history, and *Constitution* of the United States, the duties of citizenship, health, physical education, and good behavior. The parent providing the schooling is not required to have any particular qualifications.

---

14 http://nces.ed.gov/programs/coe/indicator_hsc.asp

15 Smith and Sikkink (1999), quoted by Somerville, 9.

New York State requires that home schooling include, at appropriate grade levels, instruction in "patriotism and citizenship, substance abuse, traffic safety, fire safety; mathematics, reading, spelling, writing, English, geography, science, health, music, visual arts, and physical education; Grades 7-8:English, history and geography, science, physical education, health, practical arts, and library skills; United States and New York history and constitutions; participation in government, and economics." The instructing parent must be "competent," and must file, with local officials, quarterly reports listing the number of hours of instruction, description of material covered in each subject, and a grade or narrative evaluation in each subject, and also file an annual assessment based. In grades 4 and above, upon a standardized test or a written narrative evaluation prepared by a certified teacher, a home instruction peer review panel, or another person chosen by the parent with the consent of local officials.

California requires that the instructional program provided at home be the same as that of the public schools and in the English language. The parent must be "capable of teaching," and must provide instruction 175 days per year, 3 hours per day. No testing is required.

In South Carolina requires more home instruction, 180 days per year, 4 hours per day, in a range of subjects. The homeschooling parent must possess a secondary school diploma or the equivalent, and must maintain evidence of regular instruction including a record of subjects taught, activities in which the student and parent engage, a portfolio of the child's work, and record of academic evaluations, with a semiannual progress report. Homeschooled children must participate in the annual statewide testing program.[16]

Regulation is a sore point with home schoolers, and legal challenges are commonly brought against efforts by local school authorities to oversee home education which are perceived as intrusive.

The most recent development in this area is socalled "cyberschools," statefunded public schools that offer full-time instruction on-line, and now function in thirty states and serve about 250,000 pupils. As might be expected, these enterprises have proved highly controversial, being opposed by the teacher unions and also by local school distrists which, under state charter school laws, must pay for the participation of their pupils.[17] Thus, while districts have generally no financial obligations toward families who choose to homeschool, the situation changes if those families sign up for an on-line charter school.

These "virtual schools" also serve pupils who are attending regular schools, mostly at the secondary level, to offer courses that the local school does not provide or

16 .http://homeschool.crosswalk.com/laws.

17 Trotter, 21.

to do so in a different mode that suits the pupil's needs. It is estimated that in 2009-2010 there were 1,816,400 enrollments in such distance-education courses by pupils attending K-12 schools.[18]

Hundreds of books and websites offer guidance for homeschooling parents and it is possible to sign on with a variety of services (including the "cyber charter schools") which will provide curriculum, assessment, and eventual diplomas for the child educated at home. An entrant to what is becoming a crowded field of forprofit education providers, for example, announced that "Led by Dr. William J. Bennett the former U. S. Secretary of Education), we've developed a worldclass program providing everything you and your child need for a highquality education."[19]

School choice not limited by family income

The state control of schooling makes it difficult to generalize about parental choice of schools. As a pioneering effort to establish indicators comparing the states pointed out,

> In some states, parents have a wide selection of charter schools from which to choose, while in other states there are none. In some states, parents have access to private school options via vouchers or tax subsidies, while in other states they do not. In some states, parents can home school their children with relatively few restrictions, while in others this option is heavily regulated. In some states, school districts are small enough that parents can easily move from one to another, while in other states school districts are as large as counties or even the entire state, making choosing a different district very difficult. In some states, parents can transfer their children to other public school districts without having to move, while in other states that option is unavailable or restricted.[20]

It has been estimated that 36 percent of schoolchildren attend public schools chosen by their parents through residential choice, 11 percent attend public schools under school choice policies (such as magnet schools), 1 percent attend charter schools, 2 percent are schooled at home, 10 percent attend private and parochial schools, and 41 percent attend public schools that their parents have not chosen.[21]

Governmentoperated ('public') schools may not charge tuition, except in rare cases when a school system agrees to enroll a pupil who is not resident in the

---

18 http://www.inacol.org/press/docs/nacol_fast_facts.pdf
19 http://www.k12.com.
20 Greene.
21 Henig and Sugarman.

district; under some circumstances, the tuition is paid by the district of residence, in others by the family or, in the case of children who are 'wards of the state,' by a state agency.

The system of public funding of public schools is exceedingly complex and varied from state to state, the subject of perennial litigation, and unnecessary to discuss here. Even in the case of the recent phenomenon of 'charter schools,' legislators have generally not succeeded in rendering the financing arrangements clear and simple. In the words of a government report, "per-pupil base funding is only one component of an eclectic financing system involving numerous state and federal revenue sources, and, frequently, negotiations between charter schools and school districts."[22]

Programs to promote parental choice among public schools developed in the late 1960s to improve racial integration of schools. Magnet schools are public schools with a particular theme or program, operating under assignment or admission policies designed to attract and maintain a racially-integrated enrollment on a voluntary basis.

> The idea of a magnet school was to attract and enroll students based on their *interest*, not ability level, in either a particular subject or career, such as science, art, or business, or learning through a different instructional approach, such as an open school. By attracting students with common educational interests, and diverse abilities and socioeconomic backgrounds, a magnet school would enroll a racially heterogeneous student body and provide a unique educational experience. Thus, for a school district, a magnet school program could improve education quality through diversity and advance education equity.[23]

Most magnet schools have been established to satisfy the requirements of state-ordered or court-ordered desegregation, and several states (notably Massachusetts, New York, Missouri) and the federal government have provided substantial supplemental funding to enhance the attractiveness of magnet school programs as a "painless" way to achieve a measure of desegregation.

By contrast with alternative schools with a distinctive pedagogy (though the dividing line is by no means clear in particular cases), magnet schools could be said to reflect the renewed emphasis upon the content of the curriculum that has begun to characterize American education in recent years, and some are highly selective on academic or other grounds.

Going a step beyond magnet schools, a few school systems have abolished individual school attendance districts and all pupils are assigned to schools on

---

22 Nelson, Muir, and Drown

23 Blank, 78.

the basis of a process which requires parents to indicate preferences and seeks so far as possible to honor those choices. This method of assignment, often called "universal controlled choice," was developed in Cambridge, Massachusetts and has been emulated elsewhere as well.[24]

There are also a few desegregation-related programs under which transfers are permitted between local school districts, notably urban minority pupils transferring to suburban schools. The longest-established of these is the METCO program which began in Boston in 1968 and allows about 3,500 pupils to enroll, at state expense, in suburban schools; the largest is probably the St. Louis desegregation program.

Finally, state law may require that a pupil be permitted to enroll in an out-of-district public school at the expense of her district of residence when the latter does not offer some program to which she is entitled: for example, a particular vocational course, bilingual program, or service for pupils with a disability. Legislation has been enacted in Arkansas (1989), Idaho (1990), Iowa (1989, 1992), Massachusetts (1991), Minnesota (1987, 1988), Nebraska (1989), Utah (1990) and Washington State (1990) permitting pupils to enroll in districts where they do not live, with varying arrangements for state and residential district assumption of costs.

With a few exceptions, federal, state, and local governments do not fund the educational mission of nonpublic schools, regardless of whether these schools have a religious character. There is, in some states, funding support for support services such as transportation and textbooks, and for some supplemental educational services. These are provided on the basis of the "child benefit theory," that the services are provided to the children without benefitting the schools (and thus providing unconstitutional government support to religion).

The Supreme Court has struck down various state programs for funding of nonpublic schools on the basis of their religious character. Yet, this has not in practice led (with exceptions to be noted below) to public funding targeted to nonreligious nonpublic schools for which religious ones are ineligible. Obviously, if there were such programs it would place great pressure on faith-based nonpublic schools to abandon or compromise their religious character. While this was in fact the effect of some earlier programs for funding nonpublic higher education, it might be prevented by a recent decision by the Supreme Court which spoke of "the requirement of viewpoint neutrality in the Government's provision of financial benefits" (*Rosenberger v. University of Virginia*, 515 U.S. 819, 834 (1995)). In fact, a number of state constitutions prohibit public funding of any school not under direct government control, whether religious or not.

The exceptions include programs in Maine and Vermont that allow communities

---

24 Glenn 1991.

with no secondary schools to tuition resident youth into either public schools of other communities or nonpublic schools. In the past, students could use these public funds to attend religious schools, but Maine limited the program to nonreligious schools in 1981, and Vermont did so in 1995. The other example of treating religious and nonreligious nonpublic schools differently is the initial stage of the voucher program in Wisconsin, adopted in 1990, when low-income pupils could receive state funds to attend nonreligious schools. The state legislature amended this in 1993, and as of now the great majority of the participants are in religious schools.

Many state constitutions include explicit provisions (as the federal Constitution does not) forbidding such funding, and some, like that of Massachusetts, go further to forbid public funding of schools which are not "publicly owned and under the exclusive control" of public officials (Article CIII). Similarly, the Michigan Constitution prohibits public appropriations directly or indirectly to aid or maintain nonpublic pre-elementary, elementary or secondary schools. (Art. 8, Sec. 2). The Supreme Court of Michigan has interpreted this provision as prohibiting public payments to teachers in nonpublic schools

However, there are various exceptions in these provisions, as noted above. For example, many states provide bus transportation for pupils attending nonpublic schools, as a safety measure, and loan them textbooks. Publiclyfunded services are often provided to pupils with special educational needs attending nonpublic schools. The constitutional provision in Michigan, for example, has been held not to be a bar to nonpublic school student participation in federally subsidized programs designed to aid educationally deprived elementary and secondary school children, shared time programs, or special education services. State law, in fact, requires local school districts that provide transportation to their own pupils to also provide free transportation to nonpublic school students. Similar provisions are found in the laws of many states.

The large Federal program of aid to low-achieving pupils in schools with large proportions of low-income pupils includes a provision that those attending nonpublic schools must also be served. Two U. S. Supreme Court decisions in 1985 – *Aguilar v. Felton* and *Grand Rapids School District v. Ball* – were a devastating setback for the view that the state had a legitimate interest (as, for example, in France) in providing strictly secular services within the context of faithbased schooling. *Grand Rapids* struck down a program to provide supplementary courses such as arts and crafts, home economics, Spanish, gymnastics, chess, and model building during and after the regular school day in classrooms leased from nonpublic schools to pupils in those schools; the classrooms were leased by the school system, had to be free of religious symbols, and displayed a sign "public school classroom"! The Court decided that the teachers might be influenced by the "pervasively sectarian" atmosphere of the schools in which they worked (40 out of 41 participating nonpublic schools were faith-based) to indoctrinate the children in particular religious beliefs, that the program created the appearance of state endorsement of religion, and that the religious functions of the schools were subsidized indirectly through relieving them of other costs they might have borne.

Aguilar v. Felton struck down a federally-funded program under which employees of the New York City school system provided remedial instruction to poor children attending faithbased schools, on the basis that supervising those employees closely to ensure that they did not further the religious mission of the schools would necessarily create an "excessive entanglement" of public officials with religion (473 U.S. 373; 473 U.S. 402).

The Supreme Court appears to be returning to a more flexible stance in *Agostini v. Felton* (521 U.S. 203 (1997)). Obviating the earlier decision in *Aguilar* by dissolving the injunction that held the initial order in place, the *Agostini* majority declared "that the Court has abandoned [the] presumption that public employees placed on parochial school grounds will inevitably inculcate religion or that their presence constitutes a symbolic union between government and religion." The Justices were satisfied that there was no impermissible state incentive to promote religious practice since the "the aid is allocated on the basis of neutral, secular criteria that neither favor nor disfavor religion, and is made available to both religious and secular beneficiaries on a nondiscriminatory basis." There may, therefore, be a certain softening in the Court's assumption that everything which a faith-oriented school does involves indoctrination.

In the three pioneering 'public voucher' programs (Milwaukee, Cleveland, Florida), the parent with a child accepted to a participating nonpublic school is issued a voucher for an amount equal to or less than the per pupils cost in public schools. America's first publicly-funded school voucher program was enacted by the Wisconsin Legislature in April 1990, as the result of an initiative led by state Representative Annette "Polly" Williams, an AfricanAmerican Democrat representing Milwaukee. A similar voucher program was enacted by the Ohio state legislature for low-income pupils living in Cleveland, a city, like Milwaukee, with a heavily black enrolment in a notably unsuccessful public school system.

Use of public funds to support tuition at schools with a religious character had been forbidden by a succession of decisions by federal and state courts, based on the First Amendment to the federal Constitution and by 'anti-aid' language incorporated into state constitutions, mostly as a result of nineteenth-century suspicions about the immigrant-dominated Catholic Church.[25] The Cleveland voucher program was upheld by the Supreme Court, however, in *Zelman v. SimmonsHarris*, 536 U.S. 639, 652 (2002), ruling that, under a voucher program,

25 See Glenn 2012, which includes his expert testimony in a 2011 case challenging the anti-aid language of the 1876 Colorado *Constitution*.

government places the decision in the hands of parents; the Chief Justice, writing for the majority, reasoned that "[t]he incidental advancement of a religious mission, or the perceived endorsement of a religious message, is reasonably attributable to the individual aid recipients not the government, whose role ends with the disbursement of benefits."

Despite this green light at the federal level, the majority of states (which have the primary responsibility for schooling) continue to have constitutional provisions that are commonly interpreted to forbid even voucher programs. This is a rapidly-changing situation, and the reader is encouraged to consult the current information on vouchers and tuition tax credits available from the Education Commission of the States as well as from the Friedman Foundation for School Choice and other advocacy groups.[26] Moreover, insofar as *Zelman* is probably limited to the facts of Cleveland, a failing inner-city school that was operating under a desegregation order, vouchers may face an uphill battle in federal courts.[27]

School distinctiveness protected by law and policy

Few governments restrict the distinctiveness of independent schools. Even so, most states require local public school systems to ensure that the standard of education provided in local independent schools is generally comparable to that in the public schools. Insofar as this is obviously, a vague standard, its enforcement has in some cases been successfully resisted (see below).

Government oversight of nonpublic schools occurs in a variety of ways even in the absence of public funding.

> The state can "reasonably [ ] regulate all schools, to inspect, supervise, and examine them, their teachers and pupils." (*Pierce v. Society of Sisters of the Holy Names of Jesus and Mary*, 268 U.S. 510, 534 (1925)); mandate that the instructional language be English (*Meyer*); require private schools to provide an education that is "basic," "equivalent [to public education]" (*Yoder*. 406 U.S. at 213), or an "adequate education" (*Wolman v. Walter*, 433 U.S. 229, 240 (1977)) that meets "minimal educational standards" (*Yoder*, 406 U.S. at 239); regulate the "quality and nature" (*Board of Education v. Allen*. 392 U.S.236, 245 (1968)) of the curriculum consisting of "elemental skills" (*Wolman v. Essex*, 342 F.Supp. 399, 411, aff'd, 409 U.S. 808 (1972)) and "prescribed subjects of instruction" (*Allen*, 392 U.S. at 246 (1968)) "necessary for a productive and valuable life" (*Wolman* 342 F.Supp. at 411). The state may also set the standards requiring "minimum" hours of instruction (*Allen*, 392 U,S. at 246). Teachers may also be examined to ensure that they have received "specified training" (*Allen*, 392

---

[26] Education Commission of the States http://www.ecs.org/; Friedman Foundation http://www.edchoice.org/

[27] Russo & Mawdsley. 2002.

> U.S. at 246). The state may also inspect schools to ensure that they are in compliance with "fire inspections. Building and zoning regulations" (*Lemon v. Kurtzman*. 403 U.S. 602. 614 (1971)) and "safety standards" (*Wolman*).[28]

Despite this broad potential for interference, a state's excessive regulation may not eliminate the parent's right to direct the education of the child. In 1923, the Supreme Court struck down a statute from Nebraska that prohibited the teaching of German to elementary school age children. The Court determined that the law unreasonably interfered with the power of parents to control their children's education (*Meyer v. State of Nebraska*, 262 U.S. 390). Similarly, in 1927, the Supreme Court held that a statute from Hawaii unconstitutionally regulated the teachers, curricula, and textbooks of private language schools and placed control of the schools in public officers. "Enforcement," the Court said, "would deprive parents of fair opportunity to procure for their children instruction which they think important and we cannot say is harmful" (*Farrington v. Tokushige*, 273 U.S. 284, 298).

In 1976, the Supreme Court of Ohio resolved a constitutional challenge to the state's "minimum standards" governing nonpublic schools. The court determined that the standards were "so pervasive and all-encompassing that total compliance with each and every standard by a nonpublic school would effectively eradicate the distinction between public and nonpublic education, and thereby deprive these appellants of their traditional interest as parents to direct the upbringing and education of their children" (*Ohio v. Whisner*, 351 N.E.2d 750, at 768).

The challenge to state legislators in regulating private schools, then, is to draft legislation that 1) respects the fundamental right of parents to direct the education of their children, 2) protects the state's interest in an informed citizenry but avoids interference with religious beliefs unless compelling interests are at issue, and then only in the least restrictive manner, and 3) avoids comprehensive regulation of private education that would deprive parents of any choice in education. Different states have found different solutions to this challenge. Typically, responsibility is placed upon local public school systems (of which there are more than 14,000 in the United States) to ensure that pupils resident within their boundaries are attending schools (or receiving instruction at home) equivalent in scope and quality to that provided by the public system.[29]

Distinctive character

The largest system of private schools in the United States is operated by the Roman Catholic Church, though this sector has become less dominant than it was in 1970, when about 70 percent of private schools were Catholic. In 2009-

28 Randall, 75.
29 See Glenn 2000, 4261.

2010, 39.4 percent of private school pupils were in Catholic schools, and another 37.8 percent in other religious schools, with 22,8 percent in schools with no religious identity.[30] The number of pupils in evangelical Protestant grew rapidly in the 1970s and 1980s, though the growth has since leveled off, while Jewish and Muslim schools have also been growing.
Of the four million pupils attending private schools in 2009-2010, about 94,000 were in Jewish day schools, and 10,300 in Islamic schools.[31] More than 123,000 attended Montessori and 16,300 Waldorf schools. More than a million were in various flavors of Protestant schooling, mostly evangelical (that is, theologically conservative).

There are about 1,500 "independent schools," most of which belong to the National Association of Independent Schools (NAIS). This term has been appropriated by a subset of nonpublic schools that are in most cases selective and charge high tuitions.. Enrollment in NAIS schools, now more than 615,000, has been increasing . Median tuition in 2010-11 was $19,820 for day schools and $45,200 for boarding schools (including room and board). Most offer financial aid to some of their students: 26.7% on average with an average grant of $11,461, Of the total enrolment in NAIS schools, 26.7 percent are African-American, while 6.1 percent are Latino.[32]

Decisions about admitting pupils

Both federal and state law prohibit discrimination in admission to public schools (including magnet schools and charter schools) on the basis of race, sex (an exception is made for single-sex charter schools), national origin, and other protected categories, and require that school systems accommodate handicapped pupils in "the leastrestrictive environment" consistent with their needs.[33] Exceptions have been ordered by the courts in many situations over recent decades to permit race to be used as a basis for assignment of pupils in the remedial phase of a school desegregation case, though this is becoming less common.

Concerns have been raised about whether public magnet schools and (more recently) charter schools 'cream' the pupils who are easiest to educate, or perhaps increase racial isolation in urban districts. Magnet schools are specifically designed to achieve a desirable racial balance through admitting pupils in some predetermined racial proportions.

Charter schools, while forbidden to discriminate on the basis of race, are not generally required to achieve any particular racial proportions. Nationwide, a

30 http://nces.ed.gov/programs/coe/tables/tablepri3.asp
31 For an overview of Islamic schools in the United States, see Glenn 2010.
32 http://www.nais.org/
33 Office for Civil Rights, 5.

higher proportion of charter school pupils compared with percent of pupils in regular public schools are from low income families, but there is considerable variation among the states. Thirty percent of the pupils in charter schools in 2009-2010 were Black, and 26 percent Hispanic, reflecting the practice in many states of giving preference to charter applications proposing to serve pupils from low-income families. The most celebrated charter schools, such as the KIPP network of 125 schools in 20 states and the District of Columbia enrolling more than 39,000 students, has in fact been criticized by supporters of racial integration because the overall enrollment is 95 percent Black and Hispanic. Supporters counter that the same pupils would be attending heavily-minority district schools if it were not for KIPP, and would not be receiving such a challenging education.

Controversy has arisen over the failure of some to admit pupils with special educational needs and handicaps, on the grounds that they cannot provide appropriate services. Some charter school leaders insist that in fact they do serve such pupils, but resist labeling them as is the practice in district schools.

Some states allow charter schools to establish enrolment criteria which will enable them to pursue their distinctive educational mission

Controversy has also arisen over proposals to meet the needs of atrisk pupils through establishing, for example, a school serving only AfricanAmerican boys, with an allmale staff, or a school serving only adolescent girls considered at risk of pregnancy and premature school-leaving. In a few cases such initiatives have been able to withstand legal challenge.[34]

Nonpublic schools may establish their own criteria for admitting pupils, though an overt use of race as a criterion would be very likely to lead to a challenge from government regulators as well as loss of the school's tax-exempt status; such instances have grown extremely rare. Singlesex nonpublic schools are less and less common, though more to maintain enrolments than because of legal concerns. Schools with a distinctive religious character that do not receive public funding are free to use religious criteria in admissions decisions.[35]

Most Catholic schools, like other elementary schools in the private sector, do not have special requirements for admission other than proof of immunization, age, and residence. A third of non-public schools consider applicants' academic records during admission (table 2.3), but fewer of them use interviews (28 percent) or recommendations (9 percent) than do other private elementary schools. A significant proportion of the enrolment in Catholic education, and especially in urban schools, consists of nonCatholic pupils.

---

34 Glenn 1995.

35 see Glenn 2000, 193211.

Of "other religious" (neither Catholic nor conservative Protestant) schools, 28 percent used religious affiliation as an admission criterion. Conservative Protestant schools took religious affiliation into account somewhat more than other private schools: 34 percent of elementary schools and 25 percent of other schools used it in admissions decisions

Among students at conservative Protestant schools, teachers perceived moderate and serious problems somewhat less frequently than in other private schools: only 5 percent saw physical conflicts among students and weapons as problems, compared to 10 percent in private schools overall; only 7 percent saw racial tension and poverty as problems, compared to 13 percent; and only 20 percent saw student apathy and lack of preparation as a problem, compared to 26 percent.

Academic requirements for graduation were similar to those in other private schools, 51 percent of secondary conservative Protestant schools required a year or more of foreign language instruction for graduation.

Decisions about staff

Public schools are generally required to employ only teachers and administrators who hold the certification issued by their state, or by another state under an arrangement of mutual recognition of qualifications. State requirements for initial certification commonly include completion of a university-based program of teacher or administrator preparation, followed by successful completion of a probationary period before permanent certification is given.

State charter school laws in some cases (for example, Arizona, Florida, Massachusetts, Texas) exempt these schools from the requirement to employ only state-certified staff, and in other cases (Colorado) a waiver of the requirement is common. Charter schools usually have more freedom to replace underperforming teachers than do other public schools, and the evidence is that they make use of this freedom.

> Most teachers in traditional public schools work under multiyear contracts negotiated between a [local government] school board and a teacher union. Matters are rather different in charter schools . . .. In only 4 percent of the surveyed schools did teachers work under multiyear contracts. In most schools (63 percent), teachers had oneyear contracts. In a third of the schools, teachers had no contract at all.

As a result, "eighty percent [of the charter schools surveyed] indicated that they had terminated at least one teacher's employment for poor performance ."[36]

[36] Podgursky & Ballou, 9, 13, 15.

Some states require private schools to employ state-certified teachers (a constant demand of the teacher unions), but most do not. In general, the elite independent schools prefer to hire teachers with a degree in the humanities or sciences rather than in education, while other nonpublic schools are often not able to afford to pay the higher salaries that state-certified teachers are able to obtain in public schools.

Schools with an explicitly religious character may make decisions about staff based upon religious considerations, though such decisions may be challenged if the school has not been consistent and explicit about the implications of its religious character for teacher behavior.[37] Congress, in adopting the *Civil Rights Act*'s Title VII forbidding employment discrimination, stipulated in § 702 that it "shall not apply . . . to a religious corporation, association, educational institution, or society with respect to the employment of individuals of a particular religion to perform work connected with the carrying on . . . of its activities." Further on in the same statute Congress provided that (1) it was not unlawful to use religion, sex, or national origin as a criterion when it was "a bona fide occupational qualification reasonably necessary to the normal operation of that particular business or enterprise," and that (2) religion could be used as an employment criterion by an educational institution "owned, supported, controlled, or managed by a particular religion" or having a curriculum "directed toward the propagation of a particular religion." Obviously, Congress was concerned to make this "religious exemption" from nondiscrimination requirements broad and explicit; indeed, this exemption was strengthened in 1972 to ensure that it would cover all of the activities of a religious organization, and not just those activities religious in themselves.

The Supreme Court ruled in 1979 that laws regulating labormanagement relations could not be enforced upon religious schools; several recent decisions have been based upon this precedent. There have been few cases involving teachers in religious schools, but it seems clear that the burden is upon the school to show that enforcement of labor laws would require "inquiry into the religious function of the school" (*National Labor Relations Board v. Catholic Bishop*, 440 U.S. 490).[38]

Most recently, in *Hosanna-Tabor Evangelical Lutheran Church and School v. Equal Employment Opportunities Commission* (132 S. Ct. 964 (2012) a unanimous Supreme Court reaffirmed the principle that religious educational institutions have the right to apply their own hiring rules under the ministerial exception. In upholding the authority of officials at a Lutheran elementary school in Michigan to dismiss a contract teacher who was also a commissioned minister in the church, the Court struck a blow for religious autonomy in the operation of K-12 religiously affiliated non-public schools as well as their counterparts in higher

[37] see Furst and Russo, 306307.

[38] see Russo, 1990; *DeMarco v. Holy Cross High School*, 797 F.Supp. 1142 (1992).

education.[39]

American jurisprudence makes a simplifying but misleading distinction between schools that are under the direct control of a religious organization and schools that, although autonomous, are based upon a religious ethos; the former may take religion into account in personnel decisions, the latter must demonstrate that they are pervasively and not just residually religious in character. This distinction is a way for the courts to avoid difficult decisions about the extent to which a set of beliefs is "sincerely held" by a school which is not controlled by a church, but it is blind to the fact that such a school may well be more authentically distinctive – and more distinctively religious – because its ethos and character have been worked through rather than borrowed from an institutional connection.

The leading case addressing this question involved nonpublic schools in Hawaii whose founding document a century ago required that it hire Protestant teachers and teach morality. The Court of Appeals concluded that the Kamehameha Schools were not sufficiently religious to be entitled to use religion as a basis for making hiring decisions. In enacting Title VII, the court held, "Congress did not anticipate schools that disavow any effort to instill particular religious beliefs in their students would come within the exemption" and that

> the curriculum of the Schools has little to do with propagating Protestantism, especially in grades 712. Seventh and eighth grade students study the nature of religious belief and the tenets of major faiths, and high school students take a one quarter course exploring the interrelationship of western religions and Hawaiian culture, but efforts to propagate Protestantism are not evident in this or any other coursework or in required activities of the Schools. Courses about religion and a general effort to teach good values do not constitute a curriculum that propagates religion, especially in view of the Schools' express disclaimer of any effort to convert their nonProtestant students. The Schools' publications demonstrate religion is more a part of the general tradition of the Schools than a part of their mission, and serves primarily as a means for advancing moral values in the context of a general education (*Equal Employment Opportunity Commission v. Kamehameha Schools/Bishop Estate*, 990 F.2d 458 (9th Cir. 1993).[40]

A distinguished historian commented that this decision was of a piece with a general "assault on private institutions that want to preserve their religious traditions."

---

39 Russo & McGreal, 2012.

40 case discussed in Glenn (2000), 92, 206.

> The issue of hiring is crucial to a college's or university's existence as a religious institutioneven those that are relatively open. The University of Notre Dame, for instance, tries both to be open to wide diversity and to maintain a strong Catholic identity. As a Protestant at Notre Dame, I value that openness. But if the university had to drop all consideration of religion in its academic hiring, the overwhelming majority of professors and administrators would eventually have a profile of beliefs just like that of every other major university in the country. Notre Dame would cease to be a distinctly Catholic university, at least so far as its fundamental academic tasks were concerned. Religiously defined institutions are caught in a vise. For several decades, to qualify for Government aid, they have had to prove that their overall function and teaching are essentially secular. Now they have to prove that they are essentially religious if they are to maintain their religious identities in hiring. Those who value diversity and the rights of minorities should apply those principles in thinking about religiously based education. Diversity in American life should include room for diversity among institutions. If we are serious about multiculturalism, it does not make sense to deny a place for the institutions of religious subcultures. . . . Religious discrimination is so often mentioned in the same breath as racial and sexual discrimination that people come to think of them as equivalents. Yet the parallels take us only so far. Discrimination on the basis of religion can indeed be an immense evil. But if religion is central to the purpose of an institution, that organization cannot survive without the freedom to insure that at least some of its employees share its purposes. People who share a religious heritage should have the right to perpetuate that heritage through their educational institutions without penalty or prejudice. If they do not, then it is their values and practices – their religious freedoms – that are being trampled.[41]

The Ninth Circuit subsequently upheld the right of the Kamehameha Schools to exist. The court explained that insofar as the policy giving rise to the existence of the schools was designed to remedy the imbalance in educational achievement between native Hawaiians and other ethnic groups, and educational opportunities were available for non-native Hawaiians, it was constitutionally acceptable (*Doe v. Kamehameha Schools/Bernice Pauahi Bishop Estate*, 470 F.3d 827 (9th Cir. 2006), *cert. dismissed*, 550 U.S. 931 (2007)).

According to a National Center for Education Statistics study, teachers in conservative Protestant schools – the fastest-growing sector – had fewer formal qualifications, such as degrees, certification, and experience, than private school teachers in general. About 14 percent of conservative Protestant school teachers did not hold a bachelor's degree [a 4year postsecondary qualification], and 20 percent had fewer than 3 years of teaching experience. 44 percent of conservative Protestant school teachers did not hold a state teaching certificate. In line with

---

[41] Marsden, 23.

differences in qualifications, conservative Protestant school teachers also earned less, with over three-quarters receiving salaries of less than $20,000. Similarly, principals in conservative Protestant schools had lower education levels and fewer years of related experience than principals in private schools in general.

On the other hand, 54 percent of teachers in conservative Protestant schools were more satisfied with their salaries than were teachers in private schools overall (42 percent). Teachers in conservative Protestant schools also expressed greater levels of satisfaction in terms of class size, staff cooperation, and career choice, but they generally felt that they had less control over choice of textbooks and class content than private school teachers overall did.[42]

Accountability for school quality

Traditionally, it has been the responsibility of the boards for each of more than 14,000 local school districts – accountable to parents and other voters – to ensure that the education provided was of adequate quality. Competition among school districts was more often centered upon their sports teams than on academic achievement, though the latter was also a matter of interest for prospective residents of suburban communities and thus for real estate agents.

The primary means of comparison – and thus of accountability – was the scores obtained by graduating students on the college-entrance examinations known as the SAT and the ACT, each developed and administered by a private nonprofit organization rather than by government. Only New York State had its own examination at the end of secondary education, the socalled 'Regents Examination.'

Other commercially-available tests allowed school systems to assess the achievement of pupils in the lower grades. Typically these tests measure pupil achievement in relation to that of a sample of pupils nationwide, and not to fixed norms of knowledge and skill.

There is also an annual set of examinations, on a sampling basis, called the National Assessment of Educational Progress (NAEP), which is used to measure achievement in different states and school systems and changes over time. The NAEP is not designed to provide information about individual pupils.

It has only been over the last several decades that each state has developed a variety of forms of assessment of academic achievement, and in some cases examinations that must be passed in order to receive a secondary-school diploma from the local school system. These efforts have given rise to much controversy,

[42] nces.ed.gov/pubs/ps/97459ch3.

both as to the content of the examinations and also to the very idea of highstakes testing. Release of the results of state assessments have also increased demand for alternatives to underperforming public schools. Florida's voucher program allows pupils who attend such schools to transfer, at public expense, to private or other public schools, and the defenders of Cleveland's voucher program pointed out that the local public school system satisfied only three of the state's 27 performance criteria.

Apart from academic outcomes as measured by standardized tests, most states have few means of holding local school systems accountable for the quality of instruction provided. The idea of regular school inspection on behalf of state education authorities has never taken hold in the United States, though monitoring visits may be carried out in relation to particular program requirements or in response to complaints. The closest parallel to a system of inspection is the mutual accreditation of secondary schools by regional associations, based upon site visits every few years.

There are a variety of approaches to accountability for charter schools and voucher programs. In the Cleveland and Florida voucher programs and in the private voucher program supported by state tax deductions in Arizona, the 'market' of parental choice is the only form of outside accountability. Massachusetts, California, and other states set specific standards for charter schools, including test-score outcomes, graduation and attendance rates, and provision for pupils with special needs. Charter schools in Georgia are subject to a high-stakes accountability system.[43]

In general, accountability for results is of the essence of charter school programs.

> First, they empower state and/or local agencies . . . to enter into school-specific performance agreements with schools eligible to receive public funds and to withdraw the charters from schools that do not operate or perform as promised. Second, charter school laws allow parents and teachers to choose whether to be part of one school community or another.

More than a hundred charter schools nationwide have been closed by their authorizers for poor academic performance. Government agencies, however, "do not want to be forced to revoke a charter from a school in which absolute achievement levels are low but students are learning more than comparable students in conventional public schools."[44]

While the fundamental method of accountability for charter schools in most states is the results of standardized tests, several states also routinely monitor the

---

43 Gill, Timpane, Ross and Brewer, 41.

44 Hill & others, 3, 37, 49.

schools by onsite visits. “Team members are carefully trained to avoid imposing their own personal tastes about the ‘best’ methods of instruction. Their job is to search for ways to help schools become as effective as possible given their [that is, the school’s] goals and chosen methods.”[45]

Private schools are in general subject to much less government oversight than are local public schools, though the states have the power to regulate them. *Pierce,* while protecting the right to operate and to choose nongovernment schools, also noted

> the power of the state reasonably to regulate all schools, to inspect, supervise, and examine them, their teachers and pupils; to require that all children of proper age attend some school, that teachers shall be of good moral character and patriotic disposition, that certain studies plainly essential to good citizenship must be taught, and that nothing be taught which is manifestly inimical to the public welfare (*Pierce v. Society of Sisters of the Holy Names of Jesus and Mary,* 268 U.S. 510).

Based on the “high responsibility for education of its citizens, [a state] may impose reasonable regulations for the control and duration of basic education” (*Wisconsin v. Yoder,* 406 U.S. 205, 213). The state’s interest in an informed and selfsufficient citizenry capable of participating in a democratic society is generally cited to support the regulation of private schools.

The right to regulate is not without limitations, however. Nor may government, under the *Constitution,* seek to make nonpublic schools or social agencies its instruments in imposing particular viewpoints. While government has a general right to regulate in the public interest, there are limits, in any free society, upon how extensive this regulation may be; “the regulatory scheme [for schools] must not be so comprehensive, intrusive, and detailed as to eliminate the possibility of private schools offering a program of instruction that is distinguishable in important respects from the public school program.” As Van Geel points out, “the more the states attempt to regulate private schools the greater the likelihood they will stamp out the diversity these schools represent, and the promotion of diversity, the offering of alternative concepts and forms of education, is a central function served by private schools today.”[46]

An example of how the courts have placed limits upon state regulation of nonpublic schools is provided by an interesting case in Kentucky.

> The Kentucky State Board for Elementary and Secondary Education attempted to exercise control over nonpublic schools by requiring their teachers to be

45 Hill and others, 52.
46 Van Geel 1987, 23; 1976, 153.

> [state]certified and that textbooks used be from a stateapproved list. These requirements were developed based on a legislative enactment directing private schools to teach the several branches of study that were required of the public schools. The State Supreme Court held in *Rudasill* [589 S.W. 2d 877 (Ky.179)] that these requirements were in violation of the state constitution which states "... nor shall any man be compelled to send his child to any school to which he may be conscientiously opposed." The textbook requirements would result in nonpublic schools being very similar to public schools. Parents with conscientious opposition to the public schools would have no place to send their children to comply with the compulsoryeducation law.[47]

The principle of respecting the ways in which private schools differ from public schools is generally reflected in most, if not all, of the state education law codes. The various states take different approaches to regulating nonpublic schools, though none fund their core educational programs. Here are a few examples:

ALABAMA: State licensing is voluntary for schools operated by "a parochial, denominational, or religious organization, and/or as a ministry of a local church or group of churches on a nonprofit basis" or schools operated by "a community, educational organization, or group of parents, organized as a nonprofit educational corporation with the expectation of establishing a more favorable environment for those in attendance." Other private schools must hold a certificate issued by the state superintendent of education showing that the school conforms to the following requirements: (1) instruction is given by persons holding certificates issued by the state superintendent of education; (2) instruction is given in the several branches of study required to be taught in the public schools; (3) the English language is used in giving instruction; 4) a register of attendance is kept indicating every absence of each child from school for a half day or more. These requirements do not apply to church schools; for example, under the compulsory attendance law, children attending private schools, but not church schools, are required to attend "the entire length of the school term," and instruction at private schools, but not church schools, must be provided by persons holding certificates issued by the state superintendent of education.

CALIFORNIA: English is the basic language of instruction in all schools, public and private, in this state with a high proportion of immigrant children. The governing board of any private school may determine when and under what circumstances instruction may be given bilingually. Pupils proficient in English and fluent in a foreign language may be instructed in classes conducted in that foreign language. Students attending private schools are exempt from California's compulsory attendance law if the schools offer instruction in the several branches of study required in the public schools of the state.

---

47 Furst and Russo, 116.

MASSACHUSETTS: Attendance at a private school satisfies the compulsory attendance requirement if the school is approved by the school committee. It is the responsibility of the local school committee to approve a private school when satisfied that the instruction equals that in the local public schools in thoroughness and efficiency and in the progress made by the pupils. A school committee may not withhold approval based on the school's religious teaching. Since the quality of local school systems varies widely, there is no common standard applied to all private schools.

MICHIGAN: Unlike in Massachusetts, the state's Superintendent of Public Instruction has direct supervisory power over all private, denominational and parochial schools, and the state requirements are much more explicit. English must be the basic language of instruction in any nonpublic school. This mandate does not prohibit religious instruction in a foreign language, classes to become conversant in a foreign language, or bilingual instruction to assist limited English-speaking students. Private schools are prohibited from discriminating against an individual based on a handicap that is unrelated to the individual's ability to utilize and benefit from the school or the individual's use of adaptive devices. In addition, private schools are prohibited from utilizing textbooks and learning materials which promote or foster physical or mental stereotypes. Teachers in a private, denominational or parochial school giving instruction to children below the age of 16 (when compulsory attendance ends) must hold a teaching certificate that would qualify them to teach in like grades of the public schools, though the Michigan Supreme Court ruled in 1993 that this provision is unconstitutional when applied to families whose religious convictions prohibit the use of certified instructors. Attendance at a state approved nonpublic school satisfies the compulsory attendance statute if the school teaches subjects comparable to those taught in the local public schools to children of corresponding age and grade. Nonpublic schools must provide regular instruction in the constitutions of the United States and Michigan, and the history and present form of government of the United States, Michigan, and its political subdivisions. The State Board of Education is authorized to develop guidelines for expanding curriculum on the culture of ethnic, religious, and racial minority peoples, and the contributions of women. The guidelines must be made available to nonpublic schools, though these schools are not obligated to follow them. All of these provisions contrast with the general lack of regulation in states like Massachusetts.

TEXAS: In another state with a large Spanishspeaking population, the state requires English to be the basic language of instruction in all schools. Bilingual instruction may be offered when necessary to insure efficiency in English so as not to be educationally disadvantaged. Students attending a private or parochial school are exempt from compulsory attendance at a public school if the school includes in its course a study of good citizenship.

Obviously, states vary greatly in the degree to which they place specific requirements upon nonpublic schools.

Teaching of values

Teachers in public schools tend to be nervous about addressing questions of values and character, because of the persistent attacks from secularizing organizations upon anything that could be perceived as religious expression in schools. For example, the decision of a school system in New England to adopt the goals of the Massachusetts *Constitution* led to a challenge on the grounds that this was an illegal introduction of religious themes in the schools.

In recent years, however, there has been an increasing openness, on the part of policymakers and educators, to addressing issues of character in schools. There is, for example, new interest in a longstanding requirement in Massachusetts law that teachers "shall exert their best endeavors to impress on the minds of children and youth committed to their care and instruction the principles of piety and justice and a sacred regard for truth, love of their country, humanity and universal benevolence, sobriety, industry and frugality, chastity, moderation and temperance, and those other virtues which are the ornament of human society and the basis upon which a republican constitution is founded; and they shall endeavor to lead their pupils, as their ages and capacities will admit, into a clear understanding of the tendency of the above mentioned virtues to preserve and perfect a republican constitution and secure the blessings of liberty as well as to promote their future happiness, and also to point out to them the evil tendency of the opposite vices" (*Massachusetts General Laws*, Chapter 71: Section 30).

In a survey of state education officials conducted by the Center for the Advancement of Ethics and Character at Boston University, those from 36 states disagreed and only one agreed with the statement "Schools should *avoid* teaching values or influencing moral development. Character education is not a responsibility of the school." None disagreed and those from 36 states agreed that "There exists a set of *core* values/virtues upon which most Americans agree, regardless of race, religion, class, or culture, which can and should be taught in school." On the other hand, only 16 states have legislative requirements for character education, and in 14 states (which may include some of the same) it is included in curriculum standards or goals. In only four states is this included in requirements for teacher training. In short, the general support for the importance of teaching about values is not, in most cases, supported with concrete requirements.

References

Note that this country profile is adapted from the 2004 edition, and the reader is encouraged to consult the latest developments. Excellent sources of information on schooling in the United States include the Education Commission of the

States http://www.ecs.org/ for state laws and policies, which are too disparate and constantly-changing to be summarized adequately in this report, the National Center for Education Statistics http://nces.ed.gov/ for data and analyses on a wide range of topics, and *Education Week* http://www.edweek.org/ for reporting as well as links to many reports, both current and archival.

The discussion of state regulation of private schools draws heavily upon a report on all fifty states prepared by L. Patricia Williams, Special Assistant in the Office of Private Education, United States Department of Education. Links to many sources on the legal status of private schools can be found at http://sitemaker.umich.edu/kort.356/references.

Rolf Blank, "Education Effects of Magnet High Schools," in *Choice and Control in American Education, Volume 2: The Practice of Choice, Decentralization and School Restructuring,* London: Falmer Press, 1990.

John E. Coons and Stephen D. Sugarman, *Education by Choice: The Case for Family Control,* Berkeley: University of California Press, 1978.
--------, and , *Scholarships for Children,* Berkeley: Institute of Governmental Studies Press, 1992.

Chester E. Finn, Jr., Bruno V. Manno, and Gregg Vanourek, *Charter Schools in Action: Renewing Public Education,* Princeton University Press, 2000.

Lyndon G. Furst and Charles J. Russo, *The Legal Aspects of Nonpublic Schools,* Berrien Springs, MI: Andrews University, 1993.

Brian P. Gill, P. Michael Timpane, Karen E. Ross and Dominic J. Brewer, *Rhetoric versus Reality: What We Know and What We Need to Know About Vouchers and Charter Schools,* Santa Monica: Rand, 2001

Charles L. Glenn, *The Myth of the Common School,* Amherst: University of Massachusetts Press, 1988.
--------, "Controlled Choice in Massachusetts Public Schools," *The Public Interest* (103), April 1991.
--------, "Minority Schools on Purpose," in *Changing Populations, Changing Schools: 94th Yearbook of the National Society for the Study of Education,* Part II, edited by Erwin Flaxman and A. Harry Passow, Chicago: National Society for the Study of Education, 1995.
--------, *The Ambiguous Embrace: Government and Faithbased Schools and Social Agencies,* Princeton University Press, 2000.
--------, "Islamic Schools," in *Encyclopedia of Educational Reform and Dissent,* volume I, edited by Thomas Hunt, James Carper, Thomas Lasley, and C. Daniel Raisch, Sage Publications, 2010.

--------, *The American Model of State and School: An Historical Inquiry*, New York and London, Continuum, 2012.

Jay Greene, "The Education Freedom Index," <www.manhattaninstitute.org/html/cr_14.htm>

Jeffrey R. Henig and Stephen D. Sugarman, "The Nature and Extent of School Choice," in *School Choice and Social Controversy*, edited by Stephen D. Sugarman and Frank E. Kemerer, Washington, DC: Brookings Institution, 1999.

Paul Hill and others, *A Study of Charter School Accountability*, Washington, DC: U.S. Department of Education, 2001.

George Marsden,, "Church, State and Campus," *The New York Times*, April 26, 1994.

Terry M. Moe, editor, *Private Vouchers*, Stanford, CA: Hoover Institution, 1995.
--------, *Schools, Vouchers, and the American Public*, Washington, DC: Brookings Institution, 2000.

Jeffrey P. Moran, *Teaching Sex : The Shaping of Adolescence in the 20th Century*, Cambridge: Harvard University Press, 2000.

National Alliance for Public Charter Schools, *Measuring Up to the Model: A Ranking of State Charter School Laws*, Third Edition, January 2012.

National Center for Education Statistics, *Homeschooling in the United States: 1999* (NCES 2001033), Washington, DC: U.S. Department of Education, 2001a.
--------, *Private School Universe Survey: 19992000* (NCES 2001330), Washington, DC: U.S. Department of Education, 2001b.
--------, *The Condition of Education 2012* (NCES 2012–045), Washington, DC, US Department of Education, 2012.

J. Howard Nelson, Edward Muir and Rachel Drown, *Venturesome Capital: State Charter School Finance Systems*, Washington, DC: U.S. Department of Education, 2000.

Office for Civil Rights, *Applying Federal Civil Rights Laws to Public Charter Schools*, Washington, DC: U.S. Department of Education, 2000.

Paul E. Peterson and David E. Campbell, "An Evaluation of the Children's Scholarship Fund," PEPG/0103, Cambridge: Kennedy School of Government, Harvard University, 2001.

Michael Podgursky and Dale Ballou, *Personnel Policy in Charter Schools*, Washington, DC: Thomas B. Fordham Foundation, 2001.

E. Vance Randall, *Private Schools and Public Power : a Case for Pluralism*, New York: Teachers College Press., 1994.

Charles J. Russo. "*NLRB v. Catholic Bishop of Chicago:* Collective Bargaining in Roman Catholic Secondary Schools Ten Years Later." *Education Law Reporter, Vol. 57, No. 4,* 11131121 (1990).

Charles J. Russo & Ralph D. Mawdsley. "Equal Educational Opportunities and Parental Choice: The
Supreme Court Upholds the Cleveland Voucher Program." *Education Law Reporter, Vol. 169, No. 2,* 485-504, 2002.

Charles J. Russo & Paul E. McGreal, P.E. "Religious Freedom in American Catholic Higher Education." *Religion & Education, Vol. 39, No. 2,* 116-132 (2012).

Scott W. Somerville, "Legalizing Home Schooling in America," *Private School Monitor,* 21, 4 (Spring), 2001.

Mitchell L. Stevens, *Kingdom of Children: Culture and Controversy in the Homeschooling Movement,* Princeton University Press, 2001.

Andrew Trotter, "Cyber schools carving out charter niche," *Education Week,* October 24, 2001, 1, 21.

Tyll Van Geel, *Authority to Control the School Program,* Lexington, Massachusetts : D.C. Heath and Company, 1976.
--------, *The Courts and American Education Law,* Buffalo, NY: Prometheus Books, 1987.

Autonomy and Accountability in the New Era of American Education

by Cara Stillings Candal

When in 1965 the federal government passed the Elementary and Secondary Education Act (ESEA), the shape of American education was forever changed. The ESEA, which was conceived to target federal dollars to schools with high concentrations of socioeconomically disadvantaged youth, marked the first major federal financial involvement in K-12 education. Federal involvement in education, financial or otherwise, is significant, as the US federal government has no constitutional authority for education. Detractors of ESEA feared that the legislation would empower the federal government to drive policy in the 50 states. For good or ill, to a large extent, that fear has been realized.

The past decade of education reform in the United States has been marked by federal policies that tie accountability for outcomes and, to a lesser extent, the promotion of school choice to the money that states receive under ESEA. Though still a relatively small percentage (between 8 and 10 percent) of the funding that an average American public school receives, states and localities alike have become dependent upon the funding funneled to them by the federal government, and accepting that money means that states and localities must comply with certain federal requirements.

In 2001, the early days of the George W. Bush administration, Congress passed into law, with broad bi-partisan support, a new version of the ESEA titled "No Child Left Behind" (NCLB). For the first time in American education history, states that accepted federal ESEA funds, were compelled by the law to design curriculum standards and implement annual examinations at the K-8 level that would measure student progress toward those standards. The overarching goal of NCLB was that every child would be "proficient" (as defined by the state in which he or she lived) in reading and mathematics by the year 2014. Under the law, states were required to set benchmarks for their progress toward 100 percent proficiency—schools failing to meet annual benchmarks would be audited and supported but eventually closed or reconfigured if they failed to improve.

In hindsight, the success of NCLB is that it opened a nation's eyes to the diverse and unequal standards to which schools in different states and localities were held—if they were held to standards at all—before the law was passed. The reform brought to public attention a longstanding academic dialogue about the achievement gaps between rich and poor, minority and majority students in the United States. The ultimate failure of NCLB, however, was that it set unrealistic goals for student and school performance and that it caused schools, especially those that struggled to meet state standards, to focus too narrowly on only those aspects of curricula for which they are held accountable. Moreover, although the law required that all states *have* standards, it gave them too much autonomy in the creation of them; NCLB did not have an effective mechanism for ensuring that standards were similar or, more importantly, of similar quality from state to state.

In July 2009, when Barak Obama was elected president, the ESEA, the reauthorization of the ESEA was a task that had been languishing in Congress for two years—lawmakers could not agree on what a revised version of the law should look like. Obama, a dynamic new president, had strong ideas about what the content of any new education law should be, but it seemed doubtful that the new president would be able to convince many in his own party that some of the unpopular reforms he championed—such a greater accountability for teachers and an increase in the number of high-performing charter schools[1]—should be authorized and implemented.

Instead of rushing to redesign and reauthorize ESEA, the Obama administration instead moved quickly to authorize another federal education program as a part of the American Recovery and Reinvestment Act. The grant-based program, known as Race to the Top (RTT), in many ways picks up where NCLB leaves off, though it is unrelated to the law. Under the program, the federal government has been able to promote within states a new set of nationwide standards, known as the Common Core State Standards Initiative (CCSSI) and other reforms, some of which focus on providing greater school choice to families. As of August 2012, nineteen states have received RTTT funding to do things such as "adopt more rigorous standards and assessments," reform the recruitment and retention of highly effective teachers and principals, turn around low performing schools, and "build data systems that measure student success."[2]

1 Charter schools are privately-run, publicly funded schools that have been growing in popularity in the United States since their inception in the late 1980s. These schools are public and may not discriminate as to whom they accept, but in exchange for greater accountability for results, charter schools are more autonomous than their regular public counterparts. In most states that allow them (the majority of states), charter schools do not have to be unionized and charter school leaders have greater autonomy to hire and fire who they please, set operating budgets, and define their own missions, pedagogical approaches, and curriculum. Nationwide but particularly in some states, charter schools have performed very well and have become an attractive alternative for students and families not traditionally well served in the public system

2 Boser, Ulrich. March 26, 2012, "Race to the Top: What have we learned from the states so far? A state by state evaluation of Race to the Top Performance, The Center for American Progress. http://www.americanprogress.org/issues/2012/03/rtt_states.html.

If the turn of the century in US education was defined by the No Child left Behind Act and the curriculum standards and examinations that came with it, the Race to the Top era in American education is, in part, defined by a refinement of NCLB's vision: Supporters of Race to the Top believe that is emphasizes more equal access to more rigorous curricula and better teachers. Many believe that by focusing on charter schools as a mechanism for turning around low performing schools, it also emphasizes greater school autonomy and choice for parents.

But Race to the Top does not seek to refine or even advance all aspects of the NCLB agenda. It is of yet unclear what accountability for school and student performance will look like in the Race to the Top era. While "common assessments" are being crafted to align to the new Common Core State Standards Initiative (CCSSI), it is not clear how states and schools will be held accountable for performance on those examinations. It is also not clear what examinations will mean for students. States still have separate accountability systems in place from the NCLB era, many of which, according to experts, are weak at best, because they do little to hold students or failing schools accountable.[3] Moreover, because of its many unrealistic constraints, including the expectation that all students, even those recently immigrated to the United States, be proficient in reading and math by 2014, the Obama administration by June of 2012, had granted twenty-four states waivers from many of the accountability requirements they had agreed to under the law.[4]

Some important questions to ask about accountability measures in the Race to the Top era are:

1. Will accountability standards have no real connection to whether or not students pass on from one subject or grade to the next, or will the standards be used to signal to a student that he or she has skills to master before advancing to a new aspect of the curriculum?
2. What will student performance on examinations mean for teachers? Will teachers who fail to move students along be held accountable in some official manner? Will that accountability for teachers be consistent across localities? Across states?
3. What supports might be provided to teachers and students who fail to meet standard? To local districts? To states?

All of these questions have yet to be answered, and it is likely that it will be some time before stakeholders begin to understand what the answers should be. What is clear, however, is that these questions and the many others that have arisen in the Race to the Top era strike at the heart of what the balance between

---

3 Winkler, Amber M. "What should accountability look like in the Common Core era? "Common Core Watch," Thomas B. Fordham Institute, April 5, 2012, edexcellence.net.

4 Klein, Alyson. "Five more states get NCLB waivers," *Education Week*, June 29, 2012, edweek.org.

accountability for outcomes and a school's autonomy to help students achieve solid outcomes should look like.

The Race to the Top Era and Accountability

Stats that won RTT grant monies showed in their applications a willingness to "reform" their approach to education in a manner consistent with that deemed necessary by the authors of the program. In 2010, states were invited to submit proposals to the federal government, outlining their plans for reform. In competition with one another for federal money that was both unprecedented in amount and relatively scarce given the number of states vying for it, successful states learned early on that promising to do two key things (among many) would make them more likely to win the federal competition.

First, states that agreed to sign on to a national Common Core Curriculum were given preference in the first round of the competition. Second, states that agreed to reforms that would allow schools of choice, namely high performing charter schools, to expand their reach were also given preference.

The RTT competition is therefore geared toward simultaneously centralizing the content for which schools are accountable to teach children and providing schools and families with different options for configuring and selecting the *public* schools that children will attend top down accountability coupled with some autonomy for schools. The reality of the new accountability, however, is difficult to comprehend.

While the Common Core State standards, unlike No Child Left Behind, aim to bring all state standards up to a higher level of difficulty, there are concerns that they ultimately lower the high standards that some states had in place under No Child Left Behind. Perhaps more importantly however, it is as yet unclear how schools and states will be judged upon student performance. Perhaps more importantly, it is also unclear how states and schools that are judged to have inadequate student performance will be held accountable.

What is increasingly clear is that the proficiency goals to which schools and states were held accountable under NCLB will not survive in the RTT era, despite the fact that NCLB is still law while RTT remains only a federal grant scheme. Though the NCLB waivers granted by the Obama administration have been criticized in some circles, it is clear to most policy makers that most states NCLB accountability plans were not as effective as they could be and, because of these laws proficiency requirements, were unrealistic.

Importantly, support for releasing states from the requirements of NCLB has been coupled with general support for the Common Core Curriculum promoted under the RTTT program. The architects of the Common Core, which included state governors, school superintendents, education policy leaders, educators, and academics from across the country, claim that the curriculum better represents the kinds of skills that will help students to succeed in post-secondary education. They also note that the Core emphasizes depth of knowledge over breadth of content; it encourages schools and teachers to cover core content discursively—not only because of an emphasis on the importance of reading and writing across content areas but also because the Common Core expects that students be able to demonstrate knowledge and skill in multiple ways.

An emphasis on multiple ways of delivering, experiencing and assessing Common Core content is both a reaction to the multiple choice examinations that all states crafted under NCLB (which limited the ability of students to show what they knew and could do in relation to the standards) and recognition that different students require different approaches to teaching and learning to be successful. Problematically, however, it will be difficult to measure the value of each approach to delivering and assessing curricula, especially if meaningful measures of accountability are to be attached to the examinations that states and localities administer.

Whereas a standard multiple choice examination provides a common yardstick by which to measure what students know, allowing for multiple modes of assessment presents challenges. According to the two Consortia formed (with federal money) to create the assessments, in addition to a core of multiple choice items, the Common Assessments will include other measures of what students know and can do, including but not limited to: portfolios of student work, real time assessments of "performance" on a task (such as performing a laboratory experiment), and short answer and extended response writing tasks in multiple subject areas.[5]

Allowing different states, localities, and even teachers to choose and/or use these various assessment methods means that assessments will be more qualitative, subjective, difficult to deliver in valid ways, and difficult to score in reliable ways. Indeed, some states piloted the use portfolio and other performance based assessments under their No Child Left Behind accountability plans; on the whole results were very disappointing: "Separate studies by nationally respected researchers showed that as a school accountability tool, portfolio assessment was a huge flop in both states, yielding results that were wildly unreliable and very expensive to obtain.

Among the problems found:
- A failure to yield reliable comparative data.
- Large differences in the way teachers implemented portfolios.

---

5 "Coming together to raise achievement: new assessments for the Common Core Standards," (July 2011), Center for K-12 Assessments and Performance Management, Educational Testing Services.

- Major differences in the degree of difficulty of assignments, rendering "comparisons among students or groups of students highly misleading."[6]

Moreover, according to the two Consortia, which will pilot the assessments in 2012 and plan to first implement them in 2014, states and localities will need to rely upon technology to assess students.[7] Computer based testing has become widely used in many disciplines in recent years, especially for professional certification, but the availability and quality of technology varies widely from state to state, locality to locality, and even school to school; a lack of widely available or reliable technology could impact the ways in which students experience assessments and the ways in which educators receive and use assessment data.[8]
This important question about "how" accountability for outcomes will look in the Race to the Top era relates directly to whether or not accountability for outcomes (be it at the level of the student, the teacher, or the school) will be an idea that persists and prevails in the near future of American education policy. Will the US continue to emphasize the importance of measuring how well students are performing and how well individual schools are serving students and will they be able to do so in a valid and reliable way? Or, will an emphasis on accountability for outcomes fade in favor of a more flexible approach to delivering and assessing curricula? Can accountability that that provides incentives for good performance and doles out consequences for unsuccessful performance co-exist with an approach that could hold different students to different standards even when they are all learning from the same common curriculum?

The Race to the Top Era and Autonomy

Questions about accountability, while important, should not overwhelm discussion of the important autonomies that the RTTT era approach to curriculum and assessment provides to educators. For some, a more flexible approach to delivering and assessing curricula is a prerequisite for improving the quality of education in the United States overall.

Detractors of NCLB's one-size-fits all approach argue that the multiple choice assessment format that prevailed under NCLB prevents some students from demonstrating that they have mastered a skill. They also argue that too many states implemented standards under NCLB that favor breadth of knowledge (how many skills does a student possess within one subject area?) over depth of knowledge (how well can a student perform a specific skill and how deep is a student's understanding of a given concept?). There is a difference, detractors say,

---

6 Holland, Robert (2007), "Portfolios: A backward step in accountability," The Lexington Institute, Arlington, VA.

7 "Coming together to raise achievement," (July 2012).

8 "Computer adaptive testing poses challenges, expert warns," *Education Week*, May 25, 2011, edweek.org.

between being able to tick the right answer on a multiple choice math test and being able to explain how one arrived at the right answer or how the math concept under scrutiny applies to something in the wider world.

Importantly, as schools begin to focus on depth of knowledge over breadth of content and as schools and teachers are granted more flexibilities in how they assess student performance, the work of teaching, which has always been critical to student success, is likely to be highlighted in a way that it has not been before. Whereas under NCLB teachers were scrutinized for the data that their students produced (scores on multiple choice examinations), in the RTTT era it is likely that teachers will continue to be scrutinized for that data in addition to being scrutinized for the work or lack thereof that produced that data.

Qualitative measures of student work, such as portfolios, may be a more direct reflection on the work that a teacher demands of a student than it is of what students know and can do. Teacher evaluators who review such assessments may be more apt to question why a teacher made a certain curricular choice or opted to assess a student in a particular way. In this sense, the additional flexibilities that RTTT and the CCSSI provide to schools and families are an important components of a more general push to improve school quality across the states.

Also, under Race to the Top, states are strongly encouraged to foster innovative school options for parents, such as high performing charter or other schools that espouse a particular program or mission. Many charter schools, in particular, have produced strong outcomes for poor and minority students, and in many cases charter schools have allowed parents to choose a school well suited to the needs of their children. If, in the RTTT era, students and families have more school options, it stands to reason that the different ways in which schools can choose to deliver curricula and assess students could be better tailored to individual needs.

Coupled with this push for increased choice for families and students, RTTT also encourages states to provide localities with greater flexibility in how they hire, fire, and pay teachers. The grant scheme rewards states willing to experiment with differential pay for teachers—something that, in many states, has been difficult, if not impossible due to the strength of teachers unions. Moreover, encouraging states to authorize more charter schools means, (in states with policies that allow charters the right freedoms) that school leaders will be free from the constraints of teachers unions when it comes to hiring and firing teachers. Whereas in the traditional public school system it can take years and considerable amounts of paperwork to fire an incompetent or ineffective teacher, charter schools in many states have the autonomy to hire and fire teachers at will (though within legal reason).

These reforms do more than any other in American education history to address what is probably the biggest factor in the achievement gap that exists between poor and middle class, minority and majority students: a lack of quality teachers in the classrooms where they are needed most. As in many countries, research consistently find that effective teachers make the difference in student achievement that effective teachers are too scarce, especially in the nation's poorest communities.

RTTT even has a strong component that requires states receiving grants to design and implement strong teacher evaluation systems—systems that rely upon data generated by standardized tests, observations of teacher work, and other measures to determine whether or not a teacher is producing desired achievement results.[9] Most of these systems are still under development and will not be implemented for some time, and states are realizing the challenges inherent in creating a large scale teacher evaluation tool that yields meaningful information about teacher performance. Perhaps more problematic, unless other mechanisms are in place at the state level to ensure that objective and reliable student achievement data exists and to ensure that the teachers unions that dominate education politics in so many states are no longer able to protect low-performing teachers, the effectiveness of these teacher evaluation tools will be questioned.

Conclusions

The turn-of-the century in American education was characterized by a profound change in how policymakers, educators, parents, and students view the right to a quality education and how to determine whether or not quality education is being delivered. The *No Child Left Behind Act* put the US on a new path to emphasizing the importance of accountability for outcomes and ensured that the structure of education in the US began to look somewhat more similar to that in other countries, especially in Europe, where the importance of both centralized curricula and local autonomy are recognized. But the law itself was necessarily imperfect; it was only a first step in understanding how to balance central authority for the content of what students know and for student results with the autonomy to deliver education in a way specific to each community, each school, and each student.

The Race to the Top era in education builds off much of No Child Left Behind initiated while expanding the influence of the federal government, through incentive schemes, over the curricula that schools deliver and some of the mechanisms in place to deliver it, such as autonomous schools. It remains to be seen, however, if this era in education will be characterized by a kind of accountability backlash—an eschewing of accountability reforms based on objective and quantifiable measures of student results.

9 "Coming together to raise achievement," (July 2012).

A Snapshot of School Choice in the United States

by Paul DiPerna[1]

The United States has experienced unprecedented enactments and expansions of private school choice programs over the last two years. State legislatures and governors – highly influential policy actors in U.S. education – enacted thirteen new programs in this short time period.

Today there are 39 publicly-funded private school choice programs in 21 states and the District of Columbia, and it is estimated that these programs will collectively serve at least 245,000 school children in the 2012-2013 school year.[2] Most of these programs operate in the midwestern and southern parts of the country. The number of programs has more than doubled since 2006.[3]

The main focus of this chapter will be to highlight those public policies that advance parental choice of private schools in the United States, or private school choice. Currently there are four types of policy mechanisms that allow for private school choice: vouchers; education savings accounts; tax-credit scholarships; and individual tax credits and deductions.

Other mechanisms for school choice exist within public school systems, which will be briefly described near the end of this brief overview. These policies establish public charter schools and open enrollment programs. Virtual schools (sometimes called "cyber schools") emerged in the 1990s and may operate within either a private school choice or public school choice framework. We also briefly define and describe the current state of virtual schools.

Vouchers

Education vouchers (commonly referred to as "school vouchers" in the United

---

1 Friedman Foundation for Educational Choice.

2 For complete program profiles and descriptions, see Paul DiPerna and Jeff Reed, ed., *2013 ABCs of School Choice*, (Indianapolis, IN: Friedman Foundation for Educational Choice, 2013). Available onlilne: www.edchoice.org

3 In 2006, there were 18 private school choice programs. The 2012-2013 participation estimates provided by the Friedman Foundation for Educational Choice. Contact Paul DiPerna, paul@edchoice.org, for more information.

States) give parents the option of sending their children to the school of their choice, whether that school is public or private, including both religious and non-religious schools. Tax dollars typically expended by state government or a public school district are reallocated to parents in the form of a "school voucher" to pay partial or full tuition for their child's school. Milton Friedman, a Nobel Laureate economist, first proposed this original concept of "school choice" for U.S. education nearly 60 years ago.[4]

For the coming school year, 18 voucher programs will serve around 100,000 students. Most voucher programs have limits on student eligibility, based on household income, residential location, or if the child is disabled or has special needs. Over the last decade, the number of children using special-needs vouchers has grown by more than 400 percent (from roughly 5,000 students to 26,000 students). The number of students using vouchers based on other factors has grown by more than 250 percent since 2000 (from roughly 19,000 students to 67,000 students).[5]

Some new programs have the potential to become very large in scale. More than 500,000 students are eligible to qualify for a voucher in the state of Indiana. This program is entering its second year in 2012-2013 and projects to enroll about 10,000 students. More than 250,000 students are now eligible for school vouchers in Louisiana. These two voucher programs are the most expansive policies to date supporting school choice in the United States.

Education Savings Accounts (ESAs)

A close cousin to vouchers are education savings accounts ("ESAs", hereafter). ESAs allow parents to withdraw their child from a public district or charter school, and receive a payment into a government-authorized savings account with restricted, but multiple uses. Parents can then use these funds to pay for private school tuition, online education programs, private tutoring or saving for future college expenses. ESAs are a new school choice policy innovation.

Arizona, so far, is the only state to enact an ESA program. The ESA law bases eligibility on one of three considerations: the child has special needs; a child's parent is a member of the military; or the child attends a public school that is doing poorly within the state's accountability system.

---

4 Milton Friedman, "The Role of Government in Education," *Economics and the Public Interest* (1955).

5 Participation estimates provided by the Friedman Foundation for Educational Choice. Contact Paul DiPerna, paul@edchoice.org, for more information.

Tax-Credit Scholarships

Since the late 1990s, some U.S. states have been issuing tax credits to individuals and businesses if they contribute money to nonprofit organizations that distribute private school scholarships.[6] Such a public policy supports what are commonly referred to as "tax-credit scholarships." Anyone may start a nonprofit "scholarship granting organization" (SGO). Some states require that students meet certain income or other demographic criteria to be eligible for scholarships.

In the 2012-2013 school year, 14 tax-credit scholarships will serve an estimated 145,000 school children in 11 states. The largest (and oldest) programs operate in Arizona, Pennsylvania, and Florida. Louisiana, New Hampshire, and Virginia enacted tax-credits scholarship policies in 2012, and these states will be implementing the newest programs in the country.[7]

Individual Tax Credits and Deductions

Parents can receive a tax credit or tax deduction from government income taxes for approved educational expenses. This usually includes private school tuition as well as books, supplies, computers, tutors, and transportation. Even when tuition is not eligible for the credit or deduction, these programs still make school choice easier for parents because they relieve the burden of non-tuition expenses at private schools. Some programs restrict the income level of eligible recipients or the amount they can claim.

Currently, there are six individual tax credit/deduction programs in the United States. Iowa and Minnesota launched the earliest of these programs decades ago. At least a few hundred thousand U.S. taxpayers (in these six states) participate in any given year. In 2011, North Carolina enacted the most generous individual tax credit program that refunds up to $6,000 to families having children with disabilities or other special needs.

In the following section, we briefly describe other school choice options that exist within the traditional funding arrangements involving U.S. public schools.

Public Charter Schools

Charter schools are independent public schools that are exempt from many state and local rules and regulations in exchange for increased financial and academic

6 A "tax credit" allows an individual or business to reduce the final amount of a tax owed to government.

7 Participation estimates provided by the Friedman Foundation for Educational Choice. Contact Paul DiPerna, paul@edchoice.org, for more information.

accountability. These largely autonomous public schools are typically required to adhere to state-based standards and to administer state-approved assessments and testing programs.

The first public charter school opened in Minnesota in 1992, and thousands more have opened in the last twenty years. As of 2012, 41 states and the District of Columbia, have charter school laws. There are approximately 1.7 million students attending more than 5,400 charter schools in the United States. The regulations and funding of charter schools vary from state to state.[8]

Public Magnet Schools

The United States Department of Education (USDOE) defines "magnet schools" as a public school "that offers a special curriculum capable of attracting substantial numbers of students of different racial backgrounds."[9] According to USDOE, more than 2,700 magnet schools were operating during the 2010-2011 school year, serving about 2,000,000 students, nearly two-thirds of whom are African American, Latino, or other non-white race/ethnicity.[10] Magnet Schools of America, a nonprofit membership association, states there are more than 3,500 magnet schools in the United States.[11] These public schools of choice are typically found in large urban school districts such as Chicago, New York City, and Los Angeles.

Open Enrollment

Generally, open enrollment policies are implemented by state governments and public school districts, allowing a student to transfer from one public school to another public school within the same school district or nearby school district. The Education Commission of the States (ECS) defines and summarizes open enrollment in the United States:

> There are two basic types of open-enrollment policies in place in the states — intradistrict and interdistrict. Intradistrict open-enrollment policies allow a student to transfer to another school within his or her school district. Interdistrict open-enrollment policies allow a student to transfer to a school

8 We recommended the following sources for additional information about charter schools: National Alliance for Public Charter Schools, www.publiccharters.org
The Center for Education Reform (CER), www.edreform.com

9 United States Department of Education, *Magnet Schools Assistance Fund,* (Part C. SEC. 5302). Definition. Available online: www2.ed.gov/policy/elsec/leg/esea02/pg65.html

10 This is an low range estimate because the USDOE report does not include counts of magnet schools in four states: Arizona, Massachusetts, New Jersey, and New Mexico. See nces.ed.gov/pubs2012/pesschools10/tables/table_02.asp#r2

11 See www.magnet.edu

> outside his or her home district, but often require both the sending district and the receiving district to agree to participate.
>
> Open-enrollment policies are either mandatory or voluntary in nature, depending on the state. Mandatory policies require districts to participate in the program, often depending on the availability of space. Voluntary policies allow districts to choose whether to participate, again often depending on available space.[12]

According to ECS, 47 states have some form of open enrollment policy in place. Alabama, Maryland, North Carolina, and the District of Columbia do not allow intradistrict or interdistrict public school choice.

Virtual Schools and Digital Learning

Virtual schools (sometimes called "online schools" or "cyber schools") can be run publicly or privately, allowing students to work with their curriculum and teachers over the internet—in combination with, or in place of, traditional classroom learning. In some states, online schools must have a brick-and-mortar location where children go to receive online instruction. In other states, online instruction can be done from home. Over the last ten years, public policies have been established to allow for course enrollment ("course choice") as well as school choice.[13]

According to the International Association for K–12 Online Learning (iNACOL):

> There are now 30 states with full-time, multi-district schools that enrolled an estimated total of 250,000 students in 2010-2011, an annual increase of 25 percent. Maine, Indiana, and Tennessee are among the states that have, in the last two years, changed their laws to allow full-time online schools for the first time, or to allow significant growth in them.
>
> While 40 states have a state virtual school or similar state-led initiative, these programs are increasingly falling into two divergent categories: those that are sustainably funded at a level to have a real impact on their states, and those that do not have a level of reliable support. States in the former category include Florida, North Carolina, Michigan, Montana, Idaho, and Alabama. Other state programs are in decline, mostly due to funding cuts. These include programs

---

12 See www.ecs.org/html/issue.asp?issueid=22&subIssueID=326

13 We recommended the following sources for additional information about virtual schools and digital learning:
International Association for K–12 Online Learning, www.inacol.org
Connections Academy, www.connectionsacademy.com
K12, www.k12.com

in Maryland, Missouri, and California. Nonetheless, all state virtual schools together accounted for 536,000 course enrollments (one student taking one semester-long course) in 2010-2011, an annual increase of 19 percent.

In 2011, Florida, Utah, Idaho, Ohio, and Wisconsin were among the states passing new online learning laws that will change the education landscape in those states in coming years.[14]

Broad public support and positive school choice outcomes may provide motivation for new policy proposals.

U.S. public opinion appears to be solidly supportive of vouchers, tax-credit scholarships, ESAs, and charter schools.[15] Survey research can detect shifts in public opinion and levels of demand. The 2011 Education Next/Harvard survey reported a jump in support for education vouchers. In their article explaining the annual survey's findings, the authors conclude:

> On many questions of education policy, opinion has not changed materially over the past year... Only when external events require a rethinking of their position are they inclined to alter their views. For that reason, we find it to be of some significance that over the course of the past year the public has become much more supportive of school vouchers.[16]

Increasingly, school choice legislation is being supported by politicians, no matter their political party. Republicans are still more likely to sponsor legislation and push private school choice proposals, but Democrats are increasingly able to find political cover and reinforcement in the growing body of school choice research on student learning, competitive effects, and financial impacts. Ten out of eleven randomized field trial studies, the gold standard in the social sciences, have found statistically significant academic outcomes among some or all students who use school vouchers. Greg Forster, a colleague of mine, recently reviewed the empirical research on "competitive effects" and concluded that 19 of 20 studies have shown school voucher programs improving the academic performance at nearby regular public schools. Effects are small to moderate in most of these studies, which is reasonable since the programs are all currently small or thinly dispersed within a K-12 student population. No high-quality study has found a

---

14 For an overview of how states are implementing virtual schools and digital technologies, see John Watson, Amy Murin, Lauren Vashaw, Butch Gemin, and Chris Rapp, *Keeping Pace with K-12 Online Learning: An Annual Review of State-Level Policy and Practice*, (Evergreen Education Group, 2011), p. 5.

15 See Friedman Foundation for Educational Choice, K-12 & School Choice Survey Series (2010-2012).

16 William Howell, Paul E. Peterson, and Martin West, "The Public Weighs in on School Reform," *Education Next*, 11(4), (Fall 2011), pp. 10-22. The Education Next/PEPG archive is available online: www.educationnext.org/edfacts

negative impact on student learning among voucher participants or impacted public schools.

In light of the volatile economic conditions and increasing calls for government funding austerity, fiscal evaluations of existing school choice programs have become compelling support vehicles to advance private school choice policies. In a recent analysis of the Milwaukee Parental Choice Program, Robert Costrell estimates the overall annual fiscal benefit from the program reached $46.7 million in 2010.[17] The Florida Legislature's Office of Program Policy Analysis and Government Accountability reported that the Florida Tax Credit Scholarship Program saved taxpayers about $36.2 million in 2009 alone.[18] In the first year of its school voucher program, the State of Indiana returned $4 million to local school districts because of costs savings.

What can a policymaker do with these savings? These funds can be deposited into a state's rainy day fund, invested in infrastructure, applied to chronically stressed out programs (such as Medicaid, state unemployment insurance, unfunded public pensions), or returned to taxpayers as a rebate. There is evidence that private school choice programs offer fiscal flexibility for policymakers.

The public salience and research evidence appear to be reshaping politics and policy in state legislatures around the country. The Friedman Foundation for Educational Choice has estimated 130 school choice bills were introduced in state legislative sessions in 2011. That nearly doubled the legislative activity of 2010, and still represented a 34 percent increase in the number school choice proposals compared to 2009, the previous off-election year.[19]

---

17 Robert M. Costrell, "The Fiscal Impact of the Milwaukee Parental Choice Program: 2010-2011 Update and Policy Options," SCDP Milwaukee Evaluation: Report #22 (December 2010).

18 Gary R. VanLandingham, "Florida Tax Credit Scholarship Program Fiscal Year 2008-09 Fiscal Impact," Office of Program Policy Analysis and Government Accountability (March 1, 2010).

19 Friedman Foundation data collection using StateScape to compile school choice legislation (2008-2011).

Uruguay

by Pablo Landoni[1]

Overview

In 2008, Uruguay approved a new education law (Ley General de Educación, subsequently LGE),[2] as a result of a reform process begun by the new left-of-center government that took office in 2005.

The law adopted was a substitute for a law of deep significance, because it was the second law approved after the restoration of democracy in 1985, following a decade of military rule. This previous law[3] enjoyed the unanimous support of the political parties and social organization that made up the Comisión Nacional Programática (CONAPRO), a coordinating group for policies as the country returned to democracy.

The reform strategy adopted by the government that took office in 2005 has been defined as "bottom-up",[4] in the sense that it was intended that the law be the result of an extensive process of participation by educators and by society. The process began with the so-called "Debate Educativo" organized by a Commission of twenty-two individuals coming from the Ministry of Education, educational institutions, teacher and student organizations, and some civil-society organizations. Political participation was indirect, through the Ministry. The discussion was organized through regional assemblies in the entire country. This process culminated with the National Education Congress in 2006, with more than six hundred delegates from the most diverse civil-society organizations and public and private educational institutions. The opposition political parties stayed aloof from this process.[5]

In addition to emphasizing the participatory nature of the design of the new education law, there was an effort to distinguish it from earlier reforms. In particilar, it was a reaction against the so-called "Reforma Educativa" carried

1 Universidad Católica del Uruguay; translated by Charles L. Glenn.
2 Ley General de Educación No. 18.437
3 Ley No. 15.739, labeled 'Emergency'
4 Bentancur 2008
5 Bentancur y Mancebo 2010

out during 1995 – 2000. This reform, lead by the expert Germán Rama, had as objectives the improvement of educational quality and the increase of educational opportunities for the most needy groups. It was strongly criticized for its heavily centralized focus, with "top-down" decisions and a strategy of by-passing the traditional bureaucracy.[6] It was in short a statist and centralistic reform that, though contemporaneous with the processes of education reform in Latin America in the nineties, did not share with them the goals of institutional reorganization and decentralization of management, especially in providing greater autonomy to schools.[7]

The break with earlier educational policies is clear among the sponsors of the new Ley de educación, with one of its authors insisting that "the participation promoted [by this process] breaks with an authoritarian past that made the agents of education (above all teachers and students) the mere implementors of policies worked out in other settings".[8]

After the Congreso Nacional de Educación in 2006, the Administration drafted a bill which it sent to the Parliament. Since the bill did not include all of the resolutions of the Congreso, the teacher unions and the student organizations opposed it. The opposition political parties did not vote for the law, which was adopted with only the votes on the government side.

The new LGE seeks to create a new institutional architecture for the government of education in Uruguay. It creates a new "National System of Public Education" and several organisms of coordination of education policies. Nevertheless, it maintains the organizational structure of primary, intermediate, and technical education governed by an autonomous body called the "Administración Nacional de la Enseñanza Pública" (ANEP), upon which depend all public educational establishments.

Structure of Schooling

Preschool education serves children from three to five, and is obligatory for those four and five.

Elementary education usually involves six years of obligatory schooling, but there are variations: special education for children with different abilities, rural education with an additional three years of schooling similar to the lower stage of intermediate schooling, and basic education for adults.

The lower stage of intermediate education, for pupils who have completed

6 Mancebo 2002

7 Gajardo 1999 y Lanzaro 2004

8 Garibaldi 2007, p. 77

elementary education, involves three years of obligatory schooling. Article 26 of the LGE gives it the following objectives: "It will deepen the development of competencies and knowledge already acquired and will promote the theoretical and practical mastery of different disciplines, which may be artistic, humanistic, biological, scientific, and technological, among others."

The higher stage of intermediate education offers three modalities: general education, technical education, and vocational/technical education.

An innovation of the LGE is that it makes all of basic education, including higher intermediate education, obligatory, which implies 14 years of schooling. This goal is far from being achieved, given that the rate of graduation from higher secondary education in Uruguay was 31.77% in 2007, compared with Chile at 79.41% and Argentina at 68.37%.[9]

Organization of the Educational System

The agency responsible for education in Uruguay is the "Administración Nacional de Educación Pública" (ANEP). Under Uruguayan law, such an "autonomous entity" has its own juridical personality with competence in all parts of the country, and is not subject to the hierarchy of the Administration. Within the sphere of its exclusive authority defined by the law, no other branch of government may interfere with it.[10] The nature of its legal position limits the ability of the Parliament to exercise control over the actions of the education authorities.

Although education in Uruguay is a dual system with private institutions, their supervision is also a responsibility of the ANEP. That is to say, this state agency has the double function of providing orientation and direction to the whole national system of education (including regulation of the private subsystem, establishing norms and prucedures for its supervision and funding) while, simultaneously, acting as the administrative hierarchy of state instruction.

The Consejo Directivo Central (CODICEN) of ANEP has five members, three of whom are appointed by the President of the Republic with the consent of the Council of Ministers and prior approval of the Senate, and the other two are elected by the teachers. Among the required qualifications is at least ten years of activity in public education.

There are also subordinate councils with responsibility in different sectors of education: elementary, lower intermediate, upper intermediate, and vocational/ technical. These councils have three members each, two of them designated by the Central Council and the third elected by the teachers of that sector.

---

9 De Armas y Retamoso 2010

10 Aguirre Ramírez 1973

The main innovation introduced by the LGE is participation in the governance of education at the national and sectoral levels of representatives elected by the teachers themselves.[11]

At all levels, there are private schools which enrol 15% of the all students in the educational system.[12]

Description of the System

The educational system is strongly centralized in Montevideo, though there are administrative offices in the 19 regions of the country known as Departamentos, especially focused on elementary education; in reality, they function to pass communications from and to the center, where all the decisions are made. Very few decisions can be made at the school level.

The subordinate councils for the four sectors of education have the authority to appoint the teachers of public schools and to elaborate their programs of study. These powers are, however, limited by the fact that the Cebntral Council (CODICEN) has power over the budget, and thus determines the number of teaching positions and other resources, including the construction of schools.

The LGE entrusts to the subordinate councils the approval of plans of study for each of the sectors of education, but these must also have CODICEN's endorsement.

In summary, the Central Council (CODICEN) establishes the overall goals and coordinates the plans of study developed by the subordinate councils for the entire education system and, for state (public) institutions, approves the budget, spells out the status of staff, and removes those staff if necessary. With respect to non-state (private) institutions, CODICEN establishes the norms for supervisión.

The subordinate councils approve study plans and programs for their respective sectors of the entire education system and, for state institutions, appoint teachers and administrators and develop the budget. They authorize and supervise, but do not fund, non-state institutions.

As noted above, the ANEP enjoys an unusual degree of autonomy from the Ministry of Education and Culture and thus from political and popular control.[13]

The LGE established two coordinating bodies in which the Ministry participates. One is the Coordinating Commission of Public Education, together with

[11] Bentancur 2009
[12] Anuario Estadístico de Educación 2009
[13] Landoni 2008

ANEP and the University of the Republic, a public entity responsible for public higher education.[14] Its role is very limited because it can only coordinate and issue opinions on the educational policies of public education and make recommendations to the autonomous educational agencies. The second body is the National Commission of Education (COMINE), with 28 members, which is defined as a "national forum for deliberation on educational policies of the National System of Education, with a role of assessment and consultation".[15]

Another relevant factor is the small role of the private sector in the educational direction of the country. It participates in COMINE, with three delegates among 28 members. The coordination of private educational institutions with the rest of the educational system is not facilitated by the institutional architecture of the new law, in contrast with what has occurred in other countries of Latin America, in which there have been interesting transfers of successful experiences between the different sectors of education.[16]

Apart from its slight role in the articulation of policies, the non-state educational institutions tend to mimic the state sector of education. The existence of uniform plans and programs for the entire educational system, worked out centrally, limits the possibility for innovation in schools. The lack of public funding for private institutions also limits their development.

Legal Framework

The normative framework for education consists of the Constitution, the Ley General de Educación N° 18.437 of December 12, 2008, and in particular for the non-state sector, the Ordinance of CODICEN N° 14 of December 19, 1994.

The Constitution defines five principles related to education: educational freedom, exemption from taxes, mandatory attendance at certain levels of education, the social utility of free-of-charge public schooling, and the obligation to see to the moral and civil formation of those being educated.[17]

The first constitutional principle to note is educational freedom. Article 68, section 1 of the Constitution states that "Everyone is guaranteed freedom of education." This implies freedom to teach and freedom to learn, including the freedom to establish private educational institutions and to choose methods, programs, and instructional approach.[18] The same article recognizes the freedom of parents ajnd guardians to choose teachers or educational institutions that they consider

[14] *Ibid.*
[15] Article 43 of LGE
[16] Wolff 2005
[17] Risso 2005; Martins y Rotondo 2010
[18] Barbé Pérez 1981

most adequate for their children or wards.

The Constitution emphatically limits the intervention of the State to "maintaining hygene, morality, safety, and public order." The State may not impose methods of instruction nor prohibit education that is religious or of a particular philosophy or orientation, nor may it monopolize education.[19]

A second constitutional principle[20] exempts private educational and cultural institutions from national and municipal taxes as a subsidy for their services; there are no other forms of public subsidies, either to institutions or to students.

Article 70 deals with the obligatory nature of elementary and lower intermediate schooling, while subsequent legislation has extended this down to age four and up to higher intermediate schooling, thus from ten to fourteen years of obligatory schooling. In Uruguay, there is no freedom not to go to school.[21]

To put into effective practice the principle of obligatory schooling, article 71 stresses the social utility of free-of-charge public education at its various levels, including the university. In Uruguay, public education is free at all levels.

Article 71 section 2 makes it mandatory to pay attention, in all educational institutions, to the moral and civic formation of pupils. This principle reflects the thinking of the pioneer of public schooling in Uruguay, José Pedro Varela, who in 1875 said with respect to civic education that "...para establecer la República, lo primero es formar a los republicanos" (to make a Republic, first make republicans).[22]

The primary law in education is, as we have seen, the LGE adopted in 2008, reaffirming the constitutional principles and in some cases amplifying them.[23] It defines education as a fundamental human right, and calls upon the State to "guarantee and promote lifelong education of quality for all inhabitants, facilitating educational continuity".[24]

The LGE distinguishes between the principles of education in general and those of public education. The former is to be universal, mandatory, diverse and inclusive, participatory, and manifest educational freedom and freedom of teaching. Specific principles of public education provided by the State are that it be free, secular, and providing equal opportunities or equity.

---

19 Risso 2005
20 Article 69 of the Constitution
21 Martins y Rotondo 2010
22 Varela, 1964, p. 156
23 Martins y Rotondo 2010
24 Article 1 of the Constitution

Freedom to establish non-state schools

The educational freedom recognized by article 68 of the Constitution guarantees pluralism in curriculum and the freedom to establish non-state schools.[25] Article 57 section N of the LGE establishes the authority of the Consejo Directivo Central (CODICEN) to regulate the functioning of private education. The primary legal norm is Ordenanza N° 14 of December 19, 1994. Regulation occurs through a process called "habilitación" (accreditation) which confers official validity on studies carried out in private institutions by regulating the requirements that they must satisfy to be approved by the respective subordinate Councils for their level of schooling.

Private institutions that wish State recognition for their programs must follow this procedure, of which the principal conditions are the following:

a. Adequacy of facilities.

b. Acceptance of a routine of inspection covering both educational plans and programs and also administrative functioning.

c. Plans and programs equivalent to those required in public schools. Exceptions must receive express approval; in practice, private schools follow the official plans and programs and then supplement them with additional activities according to their educational orientations

d. Administrative requirements of very detailed information to be provided to the authorities.[26]

The legal framework does not limit the eligibility of those who seek to establish a school, but most private educational institutions take the form of non-profit civil associations or foundations. There is no legal preference for secular or religious organizations, and private schools may not be forbidden to provide religious instruction,[27] although this may not be included in the official plans and programs.

Although the requirements for the owner/sponsor of a school are broad, this is not the case for the selection of the Director,[28] who must be a Uruguayan citizen or resident for at least a year, and must have adequate professional training as defined for elementary or for intermediate-level schools. The position of the Director is crucial because he or she is responsible for the pedagogical orientation

25 Risso 2005
26 Martins y Rotondo 2010
27 Artícle 29 of the Constitution
28 Artícle 4 of the Ordenanza N° 14

of the school as well as serving as the interlocutor with government inspection and regulation.

There is no public funding for non-state educational institutions.

Home Schooling

Home schooling is not provided for in the Uruguayan educational system, but there are situations in which such arrangements could arise. One example would be the non-accredited institutions that prepare pupils for the examination given at the end of elementary school. Another example would be in intermediate education, which permits students to participate without attending classes on the basis of performance on examinations.[29] Both examples are exceptions to the system and there is not an arrangement under which families can assume responsibility for educating their children at home.

Article 7 section 2 of the LGE calls into question whether "home schooling" is possible in Uruguay, since it states that "Fathers, mothers, or legal guardians of boys, girls, and adolescents have the obligation to register them in a school and watch over their attendance and learning."

School choice not limited by family income

The Constitution ensures free choice of schools by stating in article 68 that "Every parent or guardian has the right to choose the teachers or schools desired for his/her children or wards." This constitution principle is only applicable in practice for those parents who can pay tuition in private schools.

Free choice is limited by the system of funding of education: state schools are subsidized in full, while non-state schools are exempted from taxes but receive no support for operating costs. This institutional arrangement has consequences in terms of efficiency, equity, and quality.[30] There is a captive market in public education that leads to overcrowding and to problems of quality. The differentiated dual system (public subsidized, private not subsidized) leads to social polarization that does not favor social integration and equity.[31]

In short, the State imposes obligatory education but only promoters without cost a single type of schooling, that of the State. "In our country, only those have effective educational freedom who have money and can pay the entire cost of

[29] Articles 99-102 of the Ordenanza N° 31

[30] Grindle 2001

[31] Da Silveira 2009

their choices".[32]

Freedom of choice is also limited in public education; families may not choose what public school their children will attend, since that is determined by where they live. At the elementary level, each school has a geographical attendance zone, and even if living near another school, a child can only attend the one for his or her zone. This is true also for intermediate schools outside Montevideo, but in that city, where half the population lives, there is an office that assigns students to schools on the basis of residence, transportation routes, and, to a limited extent, preference.

Because of the rigidity of this system, parents end up lying about their place of residence to get their children into better schools. It is clear that parents value choice of the school that their children will attend and look for ways to overcome the bureaucratic hurdles that prevent it.[33]

School Distinctiveness

As a result of the constitutional principal of educational freedom, the freedom of schools to choose their orientation and identity is recognized.[34] In practice, however, the study plans and programs that all schools – private as well as public – implement are those defined by the ANEP.

Private schools that seek accreditation thereby limit their distinctive character, especially with respect to establishing curriculum and educational management. The legal framework recognizes the power of private schools to adopt their own philosophical and pedagogical orientation,[35] limiting the State's action to protecting hygene, morality, safety, and public order. However, accredited private schools are circumscribed in differentiating their curriculum, since Ordenanza N° 14 article 5 states that "Accredited schools must adapt their courses to the plans and programs of public schools. They may develop a different plan of study if, in the judgment of the respective Council [that is, the subordinate council of ANEP with responsibility for the relevant sector of education], there is a reasonable equivalence with respect to goals, content, and evaluation guidelines." Thus, the board with direct responsibility for public schools is given authority over whether the competing private schools pursue the same goals in the same manner.

Application of the official plans of study imposes upon teachers in private schools the themes to be developed in the programs, the order in which they should be conveyed, and the time available to teach them. The role of the government

32 Da Silveira 1995, p.65
33 Da Silveira y Queirolo 1998
34 Barbé Pérez 1981
35 Artícle 68 of the Constitution

inspector is to evaluate if the teacher has followed this program adequately. The system functions in the same way in state and non-state schools.

In reality, practically all accredited private schools follow the official plans and programs, adding in supplemental time the contents and activities which give them their distinctive character.

With respect to educational management, accredited private schools find themselves subordinated to a series of administrative routines that limit their capacity to define distinctive institutional features: proposed schedule, attendance of teachers and pupils, evaluations and qualifications of pupils, medical certificates justifying absense of pupils, disciplinary cases involving pupils, teachers, or staff in accordance with criteria defined by the education authorities, and special obligations applicable to each level of education.

In the state system, given its centralized character, there are few opportunities to define a distinctive character for each school. It is true that the existence of Parent Commissions has allowed schools to acquire certain distinctive features. These are authorized to raise and administer funds and use them to hire extracurricular teaching and other staff, to buy educational materials, or to pay for minor repeirs and cleaning of schools. Studies have found that this occurs even in urban areas where families have limited incomes.[36]

The LGE introduced the creation in each school of a Participation Council made up of pupils, teachers, parents, and community representatives. So far these have not been developed to the point of evaluating their impact on the Parent Commissions.

In general terms, both educational sectors in Uruguay tend toward uniformity, with the exceptions described above.

Decisions about admitting pupils

The conditions for admitting pupils are entirely different in private and public schools. Private schools have a wide freedom this respect, with the State intervening only in cases that affect morality or public order. In general they use personal interviews to assess the fit of the applicant with the distinctive features of the school. There have been no legal cases involving discrimination in this regard.

There may be academic selection, especially between lower and upper intermediate schooling, and there are some schools that apply selectivity criteria even between their different levels.

---

36 da Silveira y Queirolo 1998

In public schools, the only criterion for admission is place of residence. At the elementary level and at the intermediate level outside of Montevideo, public schools may not admit applicants who live outside of their attendance zones. As noted above, there is an office in Montevideo that may, to a limited extent, take choice into account in making assignments to intermediate schools in the city.

Decisions about staff

The dual nature of the education system leads to different situations in the two sectors. In elementary schools in both sectors, it is not possible to be appointed as a teacher without professional training. Graduates of the four-year program in Institutos de Formación Docente orientación Magisterio, dependent on the ANEP, receive the title *maestro*. The LGE transforms these institutes into a new Instituto Universitario de Educación which is intended to raise teacher preparation to the level of university study, but this has not been implemented yet. All elementary teachers in Uruguay are qualified.

The situation is different in intermediate education. There are not enough licensed teachers (*profesores*) for all the programs. In lower intermediate schooling, only 8,075 teachers out of 14,887 (56%) are licenses, a proportion rising only to 64% in upper intermediate schooling.[37] Teachers without appropriate licenses are required to prove their suitability for the subject taught.

To respond to the problem of the low level of qualifications of intermediate-level teachers, the education reform of the period 1995-2000 gave priority to the creation of new institutes to train them.

Private schools have the freedom to select their staff on the basis of philosophical, religious, or pedagogical criteria. Ordenanza N° 14 specifies in article 21 (for elementary) and 33 (for intermediate education) that “the choice of teaching personnel is the exclusive competence and responsibility of the school.”

The accreditation system imposes certain limitations. In the case of elementary schools, teachers must have the qualification of *maestro*. Ordenanza N° 14 has detailed specifications for the various ways in which a teacher may be qualified for a position in a private intermediate school.

In the public system access to teaching positions is through a competition.[38] Teachers acquire the status of civil servants, which assures them of stability in their positions. The title of maestro is required for a job in elementary school and that of profesor for one in intermediate school. Given the insufficient number

37 Anuario Estadístico 2009

38 Article 26 of Estatuto del Personal Docente Resolución del CODICEN N° 9 Acta N° 86, December 20, 1993

of qualified intermediate teachers, there is a hierarchy of merit to select among those who are not licensed.[39]

Teachers are assigned to public schools by the appropriate subordinate Council of ANEP;[40] it is not the school that selects the teacher, but the teacher who selects the school.[41] Annually, teachers choose the schools in which they wish to exercise their functions and are assigned to those chosen in the basis of seniority. This system limits the capacity to form working teams, generates an intense instability of teachers in schools, and has the result that schools which are less attractive because of their physical location are served by teachers with less experience and qualifications.

The Director of a school has little chance to influence its performance, since the personnel system is insensitive to the particular needs of each establishment. An informal mechanism, the additional staff funded by Parent Commissions, offers a partial solution.

The pressure toward uniformity in the education system appears also in its human resources. The fact that teachers are trained in institutions dependent upon ANEP (and not in the universities) which teach according to official programs that are common to the entire system reinforces the logic of uniformity in the Uruguayan system.

Accountability for School Quality

Within the system, quality is evaluated basically in relation to the inputs of the system, of which the primary three are the qualifications of teachers, the curriculum, and schools' facilities. Evaluation of these requirements is similar for public and accredited private schools, and occurs in both cases through the inspectorate.

Uruguayan teachers are very critical of the system of inspection. In a survey in 2003, almost half contended that the inspection is an inadequate system of evaluation.[42]

The results of evaluation have different impacts in the public and private sectors. In the public sector, the evaluation of quality based on inputs follows a bureaucratic and centralized logic. The major impact of inspections is on the teaching careers of *maestros* and *profesores*. The possibility of promotion depends upon "qualified seniority," which has the effect that it is qualifications as judged by the inspectors

39 Article 13 of Estatuto del Personal Docente
40 Article 63, paragraph g of LGE
41 Da Silveira y Queirolo 1998
42 ANEP – UNESCO / IIPE 2003

that determines a teacher's.[43]

The limited impact of school Directors should be noted; not only do they have no power to select their teachers, but they have very little impact on the evaluation of promotion of the teachers in their schools. This makes it very difficult to create educational communities in schools.[44]

In private schools, the evaluations of the inspections function as a control mechanism. Ordenanza N° 14 specifies in article 19: "At the conclusion of the visit, the Inspector will provide advice and formulate the related observations in writing for the Director of the school and for the teacher in question." The evaluations of the inspectors have an impact on the maintenance of the school's accreditation and on the career of the teacher to the extent that they also teach in public schools.

In contrast with these "internal" evaluations based upon inputs, there is in Uruguay little accountability for the quality of educational processes. Because of the autonomous nature of the institution in charge of education, described above, there is little parliamentary or citizen control.[45] Of course, there have been some advances in the construction of systems of educational information and evaluation as a result of the policy directions of the education reforms of the nineties.[46]

In the process of education reform undertaken in the years 1995-2000, as part of the Program for Improvement of the Quality of Elementary Education ANEP created the Measurement Unit for Educational Outcomes (UMRE). UMRE carried out several evaluations using standardized tests to measure educational outcomes. By the end of that administration voices began to call for the institutionalization of a system of evaluation "with qualified personnel, making use of methods similar to those employed by UMRE with respect to technical standards and methods of discussion. In the immediate future the country will implement the application of international standardized tests that will allow comparison of the levels of quality in Uruguay with standards in other countries of the region and of the developed world".[47]

UMRE defined cautious strategies for the presentation and diffusion of the evaluations: "the educational authorities were very cautious in the management of national results, as well as in the comparison between the public and private systems, emphasizing the role of contextual factors in what is learned in school.

43 Article 13 of Estatuto del Personal Docente
44 Da Silveira y Queirolo 1998
45 Landoni 2008
46 Gajardo 1999
47 Mancebo y Torello 2000, p. 51

The information referring to individual schools was kept strictly confidential. Intended for three specific audiences: the government, the education authorities, and teachers and directors, information about the evaluation carried out reached the parents of pupils through the press".[48]

As a result, the evaluation of the quality of learning acquired distinctive characteristics in Uruguay. The education authorities decided to release only national aggregate data, with limited comparions between the public and private systems, and with information on each individual school espressly kept confidential.

This strategy responds to the idea which permeates education in Uruguay, that the State is an ardent defender of public education and of the conception of the State as educator.[49] The results of the evaluation are used as an instrument for learning within the education system, giving priority to passing down the results to each school in a confidential form and assuming that the information would be a means of professional development for educators.[50]

The outcome is that the standardized tests have little impact on schools. Each school, whether public or private, receives its own results and national aggregate results, but there no incentives have been set up connected with those results. The information generated a certain amount of debate about the quality problems of the education system in general, but has not stimulated schools to put in place procedures for improving quality.

Since 2003, Uruguay participates in PISA, provoking the use of the results in public debate.[51]

From an organizational perspective, the services of ANEP dedicated to evaluation have changed institutional location and roles, though the basic functions have remained the same.

The LGE introduced an important innovation in external accountability with the creation of the National Institute of Educational Evaluation (INEE). It is true that its creation has been the subject of intense and complicated debates, to the point that, a year and a half after the approval of the law, it still has not been possible to implement it.[52]

One of its charges is "to reveal the extent of accomplishment of the objectives and

48 *Ibid.*
49 Fernández y Bentancur 2008
50 Ravela et al 2001
51 ANEP 2007, Fernández 2010
52 Scrollini y Landoni 2011

means established for the different organisms, entities, and other educational institutions.".[53]

Article 116 of the LGE also requires it to carry out every two years a report on the Condition of Education in Uruguay that will take into account, among other aspects, the results of national or international evaluative testing in which the country participates, as well as access, coverage, and persistence at each level of schooling, the results of learning, the relevance and importance of the plans and the educational content, and the evolution and characteristics of educational expenditure.

However, the law establishes an important limitation on the diffusion of results in the final section of the article: "The policy of diffusion of this information will safeguard the identity of the students, the teachers, and the schools, in order to avoid any sort of stigmatization and discrimination." This provision was added in the final version of the article.

As a result, it seems likely that the process of accountability to parents and to citizens in general will be limited if information on results is provided only at a very general level. Perhaps this could be valid information for policy discussions at the macro level, but it will certainly inhib discussion at the intermediate level and that of individual schools, which is where the processes of citizen participation and, as a result, accountability are more evident.

As a result of the changes in education over the last decades it is possible to argue that the Uruguayan system of education now has more information available for those involved, but this has not been consolidated in a robust process of accountability.

Teaching of Values

The Constitution requires in article 71 that schools pay special attention to "the formation of the moral and civic character of the pupils." The LGE has a viewpoint more associated with education as a right and with education in human rights[54] than with formation of specific values.

> Article 3 (On the orientation of education). Education will be oriented toward the search for a harmonious and integrated life through work, culture, entertainment, care of health, and respect for the environment, and the responsible exercise of citizenship, as essential foctores in sustainable development, tolerance, the full enjoyment of human rights, peace, and understanding among peoples and nations.

---

[53] Article 115, paragraph c of LGE

[54] Bentancur 2009

> Article 4 (Human rights as a basis for the exercise of the right to education). Education shall be directed to those human rights stated in the Universal declaration of Human Rights and the Constitution of the Republic and in the set of international covenants ratified by our country, as essential elements incorportated at all times and as opportunity for proposals, programs, and educational activities, constituting a framework of fundamental references for education in general and in particular for educators in any of the aspects of their professional activity.

The LGE also calls for education in human rights:

> Article 40. Education in human rights shall have as a goal that those being educated, making use of a basic knowledge of the normative documents, will develop attitudes and internalize principles based on fundamental human rights. Education in human rights is to be considered a right in itself, an inseparable component of the right to education and a necessary condition for the exercise of all human rights.

In the Ordenanza that regulates private schools, the Administration of the institution is made responsible for the civic and moral formation of those being educated.

The concrete way in which the constitutional mandate has been implemented is through the programs of study of the different levels of education, as with the introduction in intermediate education of subjects entitled Social and civic Education and Citizenship Education.

Between 2001 and 2004, ANEP implemented an experiment in values education in public schools. Its basis consisted of "reaffirming the traditional direction of the country in public education, which has considered schools as privileged places for the rational and autonomous formation of personality and the construction of democratic citizenship, in partnership with the function of families".[55] Teachers were trained and some pilot workshops were implemented. The experiment was discontinued by the new education authorities who took over in 2005.

Various private schools have developed programs of education about values on the basis of the constitutional principal of educational freedom, apart from the official study plans.

55 Resolution of CODICEN N° 9 Acta Extraordinaria N° 21, December 21, 2001

References

AGUIRRE RAMÍREZ, Gonzalo (1973) *El Consejo Nacional de Educación.* En *MARTINS, Daniel H. y otros.. La Enseñanza Pública y Privada en el Uruguay: su Régimen Jurídico.* Montevideo: A. Fernández

ANEP - CODICEN (2000). Una visión integral del proceso de reforma educativa en Uruguay 1995 – 1999. Montevideo, ANEP

ANEP – CODICEN (2003). Documento de referencia para una experiencia en Educación en Valores (Anteproyecto para la discusión). Montevideo: ANEP

ANEP – UNESCO / IIPE (2003). Los Docentes Uruguayos y los Desafíos de la Profesionalización: Informe de difusión pública de resultados. Montevideo: ANEP

ANEP (2007) "Uruguay en PISA 2006: Primero Resultado de Ciencias, Matemática y Lectura del Programa Internacional de Evaluación de Estudiantes" Montevideo, ANEP.

BARBÉ PEREZ, Héctor (1981). Proceso Educativo del Uruguay: Régimen Jurídico, Caracterización y Prospectiva. Montevideo: Barreiro y Ramos.

BENTANCUR, Nicolás (2008) *"Las Reformas Educativas de los años noventa en Argentina, Chile y Uruguay Racionalidad política, impactos y legados para la agenda actual"* Montevideo, ICP

BENTANCUR, Nicolás (2008) La nueva legislación educativa en Uruguay: el derecho a la educación como compromiso de políticas Revista Propuesta Educativa No. 33. FLACSO Junio 2008. En http://www.propuestaeducativa.flacso.org.ar/dossier_articulo.php?id=41&num=33

BENTANCUR, Nicolás (2009) *"Ley General de Educación, derecho a la educación y políticas educativas. Estado de situación y desafíos futuros".* Ponencia presentada en las VIII Jornadas de Investigación Científica de la FCS- UDELAR. Montevideo.

BENTANCUR, Nicolás (2010) *Las políticas educativas tras el primer gobierno de izquierda en Uruguay: ¿transformación o reforma?* Ponencia presentada al III Congreso de Ciencia Política. Montevideo, AUCIP.

BENTANCUR, Nicolás y Ma. Ester Mancebo (2010) *El discreto encanto del gradualismo. Continuidad, restauración e innovación en las políticas educativas del primer gobierno de izquierda.* En Mancebo, Ma. Ester y Narbondo, Pedro (coord..) *Reforma del Estado y políticas públicas de la Administración Vázquez: Acumulaciones, conflictos y desafíos* Montevideo, ICP, CLACSO.

DA SILVEIRA, Pablo (1995). La Segunda Reforma: Por qué necesitamos una enseñanza post-vareliana y cómo podemos ponerla en marcha. Montevideo: CLAEH – Fundación Banco de Boston

DA SILVEIRA, Pablo (2009) *"Padres, maestros y políticos: El desafío de gobernar la educación"* Montevideo, Taurus.

DA SILVEIRA, Pablo y QUEIROLO, Rosario (1998). Análisis Organizacional: Cómo funciona la Educación Pública en Uruguay. En *Informe de Investigación Nª 10 CERES (Mimeo)* Montevideo: CERES

DE ARMAS, Gustavo y RETAMOSO, Alejandro (2010) *La universalización de la educación media en Uruguay: Tendencias, asignaturas pendientes y retos a futuro* Montevideo, UNICEF.

FERNÁNDEZ, Tabaré y BENTANCUR, Nicolás (2008): *"La enseñanza media en Uruguay: cuatro problemas estructurales y tres líneas de política para su rediseño institucional"*. REICE vol.6 num.4

FERNÁNDEZ, Tabaré (2010) Incertidumbres persistentes en la política de evaluación educativa en Uruguay Ponencia presentada al III Congreso de Ciencia Política. Montevideo, AUCIP.

GAJARDO, Marcela (1999). Reformas Educativas en América Latina: Balance de una década. En *Documentos del Programa de Promoción de la Reforma Educativa en América Latina y el Caribe Nª 15*. Santiago de Chile: PREAL

GRINDLE, Merilee (2001). La Paradoja de la Reforma Educacional: Pronosticar el Fracaso y Encontrar el Progreso. En *MARTINIC, Sergio y PARDO, Marcela (Ed.) Economía Política de las Reformas Educativas en América Latina* Santiago de Chile: CIDE – PREAL.

LANDONI, Pablo (2008) *"El Proyecto de Ley General de Educación y sus Desencuentros con los Paradigmas de los procesos de Reforma del Estado"*. Ponencia presentada al II Congreso de Ciencia Política. Montevideo, AUCIP.

LANDONI, Pablo (2010) *El debate sobre la creación de una Agencia de Acreditación en Uruguay: influencias externas y tensiones internas.* Revista Argentina de Educación Superior. En http://www.untref.edu.ar/raes/numeros.htm

LANZARO, Jorge (2004): *"La reforma educativa en Uruguay 1995-2000: virtudes y problemas de una iniciativa heterodoxa"*. CEPAL, Santiago de Chile.

MANCEBO, Ester (2002) *"La larga marcha de una reforma "exitosa": de la formulación a la implementación de políticas educativas"*. En Mancebo, Ester

9 789058 509116

Narbondo, P y Ramos, C. (Comp.) *Uruguay: la reforma del Estado y las políticas públicas en la democracia restaurada*. Montevideo: Banda Oriental-ICP.

MANCEBO, Ester y TORELLO, Mariella (2000). El Sistema Educativo Uruguayo: Estudio de Diagnóstico y Propuesta de Políticas Públicas para el Sector. Washington: BID, Departamento Regional de Operaciones 1.

MARTINS, Daniel H. y ROTONDO, Felipe (2010) *Régimen Legal de Educación – Ley No. 18.437 Normas Constitucionales e Internacionales* Montevideo, La Ley.

MINISTERIO DE EDUCACIÓN Y CULTURA (2010). Anuario Estadístico de Educación 2009. Montevideo: MEC

RAVELA, Pedro (Ed.) y otros (2001). Los Próximos Pasos: ¿Cómo Avanzar en la Evaluación de Aprendizajes en América Latina? En *Documentos del Programa de Promoción de la Reforma Educativa en América Latina y el Caribe Nª 20*. Santiago de Chile: PREAL

RISSO FERRAND, Martín (2005) *Derecho Constitucional* Montevideo, Fundación de Cultura Universitaria. Páginas 658 a 680.

SCROLLINI, Fabrizio y LANDONI, Pablo (2011) "Educación e Información Pública: Perspectivas para la Transparencia del sistema". En Revista Uruguaya de Ciencia Política - Vol. 19 – Montevideo, Instituto de Ciencia Política/ UDELAR.

VARELA. José Pedro (1964) Obras Pedagógicas: La Educación del Pueblo. Montevideo: Colección de Clásicos Uruguayos, Biblioteca Artigas Tomo I Vol. 49.

WOLFF, Laurence; NAVARRO, Juan C. y GONZÁLEZ, Pablo (eds.) (2005) *Private Education and Public Policy in Latin America*. Washington D.C., PREAL.